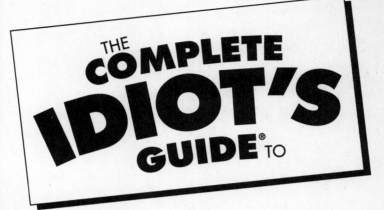

THE

# COMPLETE IDIOT'S GUIDE® TO

# Independent Filmmaking

## by Josef Steiff

### ALPHA

A member of Penguin Group (USA) Inc.

*For Victor*

# ALPHA BOOKS

Published by the Penguin Group

Penguin Group (USA) Inc., 375 Hudson Street, New York, New York 10014, U.S.A.

Penguin Group (Canada), 10 Alcorn Avenue, Toronto, Ontario, Canada M4V 3B2 (a division of Pearson Penguin Canada Inc.)

Penguin Books Ltd, 80 Strand, London WC2R 0RL, England

Penguin Ireland, 25 St Stephen's Green, Dublin 2, Ireland (a division of Penguin Books Ltd)

Penguin Group (Australia), 250 Camberwell Road, Camberwell, Victoria 3124, Australia (a division of Pearson Australia Group Pty Ltd)

Penguin Books India Pvt Ltd, 11 Community Centre, Panchsheel Park, New Delhi—110 017, India

Penguin Group (NZ), cnr Airborne and Rosedale Roads, Albany, Auckland 1310, New Zealand (a division of Pearson New Zealand Ltd)

Penguin Books (South Africa) (Pty) Ltd, 24 Sturdee Avenue, Rosebank, Johannesburg 2196, South Africa

Penguin Books Ltd, Registered Offices: 80 Strand, London WC2R 0RL, England

International Standard Book Number: 1-59257-390-8
Library of Congress Catalog Card Number: 2005925421

07   06   05      8   7   6   5   4   3   2   1

Interpretation of the printing code: The rightmost number of the first series of numbers is the year of the book's printing; the rightmost number of the second series of numbers is the number of the book's printing. For example, a printing code of 05-1 shows that the first printing occurred in 2005.

*Printed in the United States of America*

**Publisher:** *Marie Butler-Knight*
**Product Manager:** *Phil Kitchel*
**Senior Managing Editor:** *Jennifer Bowles*
**Senior Acquisitions Editor:** *Randy Ladenheim-Gil*
**Development Editor:** *Lynn Northrup*
**Production Editor:** *Janette Lynn*

**Copy Editor:** *Ross Patty*
**Cartoonist:** *Shannon Wheeler*
**Cover/Book Designer:** *Trina Wurst*
**Indexer:** *Brad Herriman*
**Layout:** *Angela Calvert*
**Proofreading:** *John Etchison*

# Contents at a Glance

**Part 1:**    **You Ought to Be in Pictures: Development**    **1**

1   *The Rookie:* You Too Can Be a Filmmaker    3
*Understand what it means to have a guiding vision and use your own experiences to make your movie unique.*

2   *Imitation of Life:* Moving Image Basics    11
*Engage your audience by finding the type of film that works best for your story.*

3   *The Poseidon Adventure:* Let's Make a Movie    21
*Learn the different ways to make movies and the steps most films go through.*

4   *The Elusive Idea:* Film Ideas    29
*Recognize an idea that has the potential to be a good film.*

5   *The Greatest Story Ever Told:* Story Elements    37
*Understand what makes a story dramatic and interesting for an audience.*

6   *Something to Talk About:* Communicating Your Story    49
*Make your film on paper first—by writing a script.*

7   *The Picture Writer:* Communicating Your Intentions    61
*Summarize your story so that you can tell others about it.*

**Part 2:**    **Buddy, Can You Spare a Dime? Pre-Production**    **77**

8   *Take the Money and Run:* Paying for Your Film    79
*Raise the money to make your film.*

9   *The Secret Garden:* Script Breakdown    89
*Analyze your script so that you're better prepared to direct your actors and shoot your film.*

10   *The Enchanted Drawing:* Pre-Visualization    99
*Plan each shot before you get to the set.*

11   *Strangers in Good Company:* Your Crew    115
*Hire the people you'll need behind the scenes to help you make your film.*

12   *Big Fish:* Your Cast    125
*Choose the actors who will bring your story to life on the big screen.*

13  *The Searchers:* Location Scouting                135
    *Find the perfect place to shoot your film.*

14  *Design for Living:* Production Design and Art Direction   145
    *Create an visual design for your film that reveals aspects of
    your characters and story.*

15  *Rushmore:* Scheduling Your Film                  153
    *Budget your time wisely so that you can get everything done
    when it needs to be.*

16  *Money Train:* Budgeting Your Film                165
    *Work within your means so that you won't run out of money.*

Part 3:    **Ready for My Close-Up: Production**         **177**

17  *The Miracle Worker:* Directing                   179
    *Run a smooth set so that you get the best work from your
    cast and crew*

18  *Through a Glass Darkly:* Camera and Lens          191
    *Know how the difference between film, video, and digital
    video (DV) will help you choose the right medium for your
    film.*

19  *Visions of Light:* Cinematography                205
    *Understand the ways you can affect the image through
    lighting, movement, and focus.*

20  *The Quiet Earth:* Location Sound                  221
    *Record dialogue and other sounds on the set to make your
    job in post-production easier.*

21  *Guess Who's Coming to Dinner:* Taking Care of the
    Cast and Crew                                     233
    *Keep your cast and crew happy; after all, you're depending
    on them!*

Part 4:    **Don't Worry, We'll Fix It in ... Post-Production**   **241**

22  *Edward Scissorhands:* Editing Your Picture       243
    *Choose and arrange your shots to create a film that your
    audience will understand and enjoy.*

23  *Sounder:* Sound Design                           257
    *Add sound effects to make your film a feast for the ears as
    well as for the eyes.*

24 *Strange Brew:* Special Effects    267
*Spice up your visuals with the fantastic and the unexpected (and sometimes, the gross).*

25 *Safe:* Titles and Credits    279
*Name your film and acknowledge all the people who helped you make it.*

26 *The Conformist:* Finishing Up    289
*Complete your film so that you have a copy you can show to an audience.*

**Part 5:    And the Winner Is ... Exhibition & Distribution    299**

27 *Living in Oblivion:* Press Kits and Publicity    301
*Market your film to the media by creating publicity materials.*

28 *The Conversation:* Interviews    311
*Talk about your film to the press.*

29 *The Last Picture Show:* Finding an Audience    317
*Exhibit your movie for everyone to see.*

30 *The Graduate:* You're a Filmmaker Now    327
*Reflect on what you've learned with an eye to the future.*

**Appendixes**

A Glossary    333

B Resources    339

Index    349

# Contents

**Part I:    You Ought to Be in Pictures: Development**    1

**1    *The Rookie:* You Too Can Be a Filmmaker**    3

Point and Shoot: What a Filmmaker Does .......................4
  *Product and Process* .......................5
  *Guiding Vision* .......................6
The "Eyes" Have It: Looking and Seeing .......................7
  *The Kitten Experiment* .......................8
  *Live a Little* .......................8
As You're Starting Out ... .......................9
The Film in Your Head Meets the Film You Can Make .......... 9

**2    *Imitation of Life:* Moving Image Basics**    11

Creating the Illusion of Motion .......................12
  *Photographic Medium* .......................12
  *Moving Images* .......................12
It's How You Say It: Modes of Filmmaking .......................13
  *Narrative* .......................14
  *Documentary* .......................14
  *Experimental* .......................15
Built to Last: Duration .......................15
It's What You Say: Telling Stories .......................16
  *Short Film Stories* .......................16
  *Feature Film Stories* .......................17
Audience Participation .......................18
  *Experience and Engagement* .......................18
  *Suspension of Disbelief* .......................19

**3    *The Poseidon Adventure:* Let's Make a Movie**    21

All Systems Go: Ways to Make Films .......................22
  *Institutional Filmmaking* .......................22
  *Independent Filmmaking* .......................24
How Most Films Get Made .......................26
  *Development* .......................26
  *Pre-Production* .......................26
  *Production* .......................27
  *Post-Production* .......................27
  *Exhibition & Distribution* .......................27

**4   *The Elusive Idea:* Film Ideas**                                                **29**

Write What You Know ...............................................................30
Finding Your Point of View ......................................................30
Choosing Ideas and Developing Themes ...............................31
Why This Film, Why Now? .......................................................33
That's Not the Way It Happened ............................................34
Writing Visually .........................................................................35
Being a "Good Thief" ...............................................................35

**5   *The Greatest Story Ever Told:* Story Elements**                    **37**

Smooth Sailing: The Seven "Cs" ..............................................38
  *Character* ................................................................................*38*
  *Conflict* ...................................................................................*39*
  *Conduct* ...................................................................................*40*
  *Conditions* ...............................................................................*41*
  *Context* ....................................................................................*42*
  *Crutch* .....................................................................................*43*
  *Configuration* ..........................................................................*43*
Making a Scene ..........................................................................47
Keeping in Step: Story Outlines ..............................................48

**6   *Something to Talk About:* Communicating Your Story**            **49**

Pen to Page: Script ...................................................................50
  *Master Scene Format* ..............................................................*51*
  *Split Script* ..............................................................................*55*
Thumbnail Sketch: Logline .......................................................57
Query Letters .............................................................................57
Pitching Your Idea ....................................................................58

**7   *The Picture Writer:* Communicating Your Intentions**             **61**

You Don't Need a Ring for This Proposal ...............................62
  *Theme: What's It All About?* ...................................................*65*
  *Goal: Why Say It Now?* ..........................................................*66*
  *Audience: Who's Listening (and Watching)?* ...........................*67*
The Doctor Is In: Synopsis and Treatment .............................68
  *Synopsis* ...................................................................................*69*
  *Treatments* ...............................................................................*71*

**Part 2:** **Buddy, Can You Spare a Dime? Pre-Production** **77**

**8** *Take the Money and Run:* **Paying for Your Film** **79**

Pocket Protectors: Investors ......................................80
*Sole Proprietorships* ..........................................*80*
*Corporations (C-Corps and S-Corps)* .........................*81*
*General Partnerships* ..........................................*81*
*Limited Partnerships* ..........................................*82*
*Limited Liability Companies (LLC)* ...........................*82*
Creative Fundraising 101 ........................................83
Credit Card and Loan Options ..................................84
Media and Arts Grants ..........................................85
In-Kind Services ..................................................86
What to Bring to the Table ......................................87

**9** *The Secret Garden:* **Script Breakdown** **89**

Reading the Blueprint: Text Analysis ...........................90
What You Know, What You Assume ...............................91
What I Meant to Say: Subtext and Themes ......................92
Breaking Down Scenes ...........................................94
Editing or Adding Scenes ........................................96

**10** *The Enchanted Drawing:* **Pre-Visualization** **99**

Subject Size and Shot Scale .....................................100
Divide and Conquer: Shooting the Scene in Parts ..............105
Outlines, Scripts, and Storyboards .............................110
A Little Goes a Long Way: Symbols and Metaphors ............113

**11** *Strangers in Good Company:* **Your Crew** **115**

Get a Grip: Crew Positions .....................................116
Finding Good Help ..............................................119
*Resumés and Reels* ...........................................*120*
*Interviews* ..................................................*121*
Paying the Piper: Union vs. Non-Union Crew ..................122
Letters of Agreement ............................................123
Skeleton Crew: The Bare Minimum .............................124

**12 *Big Fish:* Your Cast** **125**

Wanna Be in a Movie? ................................................126
Look for the Union Label: SAG and AFTRA .......................127
The Audition Process ................................................128
   *Getting the Word Out* ...........................................*128*
   *Using Your Audition Time Productively* .........................*130*
   *Inside the Audition* ............................................*131*
   *Callbacks* .....................................................*132*
   *Casting* .......................................................*133*
Getting Written Permission ..........................................133

**13 *The Searchers:* Location Scouting** **135**

The Look and Feel: Essence of Place ...............................136
Room to Move: Having Enough Space ...............................137
I Can't Hear You: Sound Considerations ............................137
Power Play: Electricity ..............................................138
Green Rooms, Restrooms, and Craft Services Areas ................139
Release Forms and Permits ..........................................139
Making It All Work ..................................................141

**14 *Design for Living:* Production Design and Art Direction** **145**

An Eye for the Details: Production Design ..........................145
Faking It: Sets .....................................................147
   *Flats* .........................................................*148*
   *Virtual Sets* ..................................................*149*
Power to the Props ..................................................149
Clothes Make the Character: Costumes .............................150

**15 *Rushmore:* Scheduling Your Film** **153**

Timing Your Script ..................................................154
Bits and Pieces: Breaking Down the Script for Production ....155
Juggling Where, When, Who, What ...............................156
All Work and No Play: A Reasonable Workday .....................159
Putting Together a Shooting Schedule ..............................161
Making Contingency Plans ..........................................163
Hear Ye, Hear Ye: Letting Everyone Know .........................164

**16  *Money Train:* Budgeting Your Film**                    **165**

Lining Up: Above and Below the Line Expenses ...................166

Putting Together Your Budget ................................169

Big-Ticket Items ................................170

Petty-Cash Expenses ................................172

Accountability: Keeping Records ................................172

Having Enough Money to Bring It Home ...........................174

Final Destination: Your Shooting Budget ........................175

**Part 3:  Ready for My Close-Up: Production**                **177**

**17  *The Miracle Worker:* Directing**                      **179**

Acting Up ................................180

Crewing Up ................................183

*Who's on First* ................................*184*

*ADing It All Up* ................................*185*

Productive Production Meetings ................................186

Calling the Shots ................................187

**18  *Through a Glass Darkly:* Camera and Lens**           **191**

Machine in a Box: Cameras ................................191

Latent Images: Film ................................192

*Perfs* ................................*193*

*Layers* ................................*193*

*Types of Filmstocks* ................................*194*

*Sensitivity to Light* ................................*195*

*Intermittent Motion* ................................*196*

Magnetic Fields: Analog Video ................................197

Ones and Ohs!: Digital Recording ................................199

Optic Nerve: Lenses ................................200

**19  *Visions of Light:* Cinematography**                  **205**

Light and Shadows ................................206

Qualities of Light ................................207

Three-Point Lighting ................................212

Qualifying Image ................................214

Directing the Eye ................................217

Look Like a Pro ................................218

**20** *The Quiet Earth:* **Gathering Sound** **221**

A World of Sound ....................................................................222
Read My Lips: Sync Sound ....................................................223
Rearranging Particles and Turning On or Off ....................225
   *Analog Recording* ...............................................................225
   *Digital Recording* ..............................................................226
Types and Placement of Microphones ................................227
Don't Be Afraid of the Wild ................................................230

**21** *Guess Who's Coming to Dinner:* **Taking Care of the Cast and Crew** **233**

The Filmmaker's Responsibilities ........................................234
The Way to a Crew's Heart: Craft Services ........................235
Expressing Your Appreciation ..............................................238
When You Have to Fire a Cast or Crew Member ................239

**Part 4:** **Don't Worry, We'll Fix It in ... Post-Production** **241**

**22** *Edward Scissorhands:* **Editing Your Picture** **243**

The Final Cut ........................................................................244
Linear vs. Non-Linear Editing ............................................244
Working with a Film Lab ......................................................246
Frame by Frame: The Editing Process ................................247
   *Syncing Rushes* ..................................................................247
   *Logging the Footage* ...........................................................247
   *Pulling Shots* ....................................................................248
   *Paper Edit* ........................................................................248
   *Assembly Edit* ..................................................................249
   *Rough Cut(s)* ....................................................................249
   *Get Feedback* ....................................................................250
   *Fine Cut* ...........................................................................250
Continuity Editing Makes the Story Clear ........................251
Temporal and Spatial Distortions: Aesthetics of Editing ........254

**23** *Sounder:* **Sound Design** **257**

Getting an Earful: The Art of Sound Mixing ....................258
Almost Never a Quiet Moment ............................................259
Mainly on the Plane: Sound Relationships ........................260
Make Your Own Kind of Music ..........................................263
Mix Master ............................................................................265

**24  *Strange Brew:* Special Effects** **267**

From Here to There: Transitions ....................................267

*Fade* ............................................................................268

*Dissolve* ......................................................................269

*Wipe* ...........................................................................269

*Freeze Frame* ...............................................................270

*Superimposition* ..........................................................270

It's Easy Being Green ...................................................271

Computer Animation and Modeling ...........................272

Creepy Special Effects on Set ......................................272

Other Special Effects ...................................................275

*Filtering the Image* .......................................................276

*Slowing Down and Speeding Up* ....................................277

*Throwing It in Reverse* ..................................................277

**25  *Safe:* Titles and Credits** **279**

Reading Lessons: Text That Can Appear in Films ................280

Setting the Mood: Choosing the Right Font and Size ...........282

Choosing the Right Placement .....................................284

Timing Is Everything: Titles on the Screen ........................286

**26  *The Conformist:* Finishing Up** **289**

Choosing a Release Format ..........................................290

Sounding Off ..............................................................292

Matching Picture: Conforming and On-Line Editing ...........293

*Negative Cutting* ...........................................................293

*On-Line Editing* ............................................................294

Dense Area: Optical and Digital Tracks ............................295

Please Release Me .......................................................297

Shelf Life: Archiving Your Film ....................................297

**Part 5:  And the Winner Is ... Exhibition & Distribution** **299**

**27  *Living in Oblivion:* Press Kits and Publicity** **301**

Spreading the Word: Press Kits ....................................302

Snapping It Up: Photos ................................................302

*Frame Enlargements* .....................................................303

*Production Stills* ...........................................................303

*Portraits* ......................................................................304

Say It with Words: Synopses and Names ...............................305

Most Wanted: Posters .............................................306

Are Giveaways Worth It? .........................................306

Just the Facts: Press Releases ...................................307

Getting to Know You .............................................307

Everyone's Talking: Reviews .....................................308

Preview Copies and Screeners ....................................309

**28  *The Conversation:* Interviews**                          **311**

Print, Radio, TV, and Chatroom Interviews .......................312

Never Too Proud to Beg: Soliciting Interviews ...................314

Turning Down Interviews .........................................315

Prepping for Interviews .........................................315

**29  *The Last Picture Show:* Finding an Audience**            **317**

Getting Your Film on the Screen .................................318

Let the Festivities Begin: Film Festivals .......................319

*Preparing Your Entry for Submission* ...........................*320*

*The Art of Negotiation* ........................................*322*

*Inside a Film Jury* ............................................*322*

Your New Best Friends: Distributors .............................324

Persistence Pays Off ............................................325

**30  *The Graduate:* You're a Filmmaker Now**                  **327**

That's a Wrap! ..................................................328

Brave New World of Independent Filmmaking .......................329

The World—or at Least Your Next Film—Awaits .....................330

Night Is Falling and the Time Is Now ............................331

**Appendixes**

**A  Glossary**                                                 **333**

**B  Resources**                                                **339**

**Index**                                                       **349**

# Foreword

A few years ago, at a small screening room in Santa Monica, Robert Altman was about to screen his new film for the first time, in front of friends and family. I was part of the editorial crew. Since we were only a few weeks into the director's cut, I hadn't yet spent much time with Bob, but I was in awe of him. He'd gathered a very Altmanesque group to view the film: Darryl Hannah was there; along with Embeth Davidtz, the film's co-star; and Nick Nolte, wearing pajamas and a robe.

Bob stood up, and my pulse rate quickened. Test screenings, even for friendly groups, are trying times for those in editorial. What if there's a sound glitch? What if the projectionist misses a changeover cue? What if (*gasp*) the film breaks?

Bob began to speak. He welcomed everyone to his "little picture." But I quickly realized that something strange was happening. As he spoke, he stammered a bit. He seemed unsure of his words. He was wringing his hands.

*Robert Altman was nervous about showing his movie.*

This maverick of independent film, who by this time had made over 20 motion pictures, including classics like *M\*A\*S\*H*, *McCabe & Mrs. Miller*, and *Nashville*, still got the jitters before showing his work!

Filmmaking can be terrifying. As a screenwriter, you face the terror of the empty page that you must fill with words and characters and ideas. As a director, you face countless obstacles and questions, both from your crew and from yourself—and from the people who are hoping your "little picture" will make them lots of money. As a freelancer, you face the frightening question at the end of every project: Will I find that next job?

And yet, the rewards are exhilarating. The charge you feel when you've written a great scene. The thrill of seeing, in front of your eyes, actors *becoming the characters you created*. And, as if that weren't enough, you get to share all of this with other people! To watch your movie with an audience and hear them sob or laugh or get angry or cheer … there's nothing like it.

Everyone has different reasons for making films. If you've purchased this book, you have your reasons as well. Lucky for you, Joe Steiff has done an incredible, exhaustive job of breaking down a seemingly daunting process into easily digestible morsels of information and advice. And he's done this in the same way he teaches his classes and directs his films: thoughtfully, in every sense of the word.

*The Complete Idiot's Guide to Independent Filmmaking* won't alleviate all your fears about becoming a filmmaker. Filmmakers face fear all the time; it goes with the territory. But how we arm ourselves against fear is through knowledge and the sharing of information and the joy of collaboration. Read this book. Soak up the information Joe has shared with you. And then get out there and find the collaborators you need to begin the thrilling ride of making your own movies.

—Phillip J. Bartell

**Phillip J. Bartell,** once a student of Josef Steiff's, is the writer-director-producer of two independent films, *Crush* and *L.T.R.* Over the years he has worked alongside numerous independent (or once-independent) directors, including Allison Anders, Roger Avary, Diane Keaton, Sean Penn, Robert Altman, Gus Van Sant, Spike Jonze, Rodrigo Garcia, and Curtis Hanson.

# Introduction

When I was in college, my best friend and I would daydream—usually during class—about running away from school and making movies in Hollywood. At the time, we thought that the only way to become filmmakers was to go to LA and work our way up through the system. For two rural college kids, filmmaking remained a fantasy, impossible because movie-making seemed too big, too expensive, too far away, and too scary.

A few years after graduation, I realized that I didn't need to go to Hollywood to make films. There were film schools that would train me and give me the chance to make movies. But film schools, while closer to my grasp, cost money. The trade-off was having access to equipment and services that were otherwise too expensive or difficult to obtain. An advantage to film schools is that they can provide a sense of camaraderie and a safe place to learn how filmmaking systems work.

But nowadays, with the development of digital technology and computer capabilities, we've seen the advent of desktop editing and a wider range of consumer cameras and formats. The modes of production have become less and less expensive, and you can have a virtually state-of-the-art production or post-production studio in your home. This means you can gain hands-on filmmaking experience on your own. And with the worldwide proliferation of film festivals, many of which encourage "amateur" filmmaking submissions, films made by people who have not been formally trained nor make their living in film can have their movies seen and appreciated.

Ultimately, in filmmaking, what's most important is your "reel"—what you've actually produced. No one asks to see your diploma; they ask to see what you've done.

Yes, you can still go to Hollywood and learn filmmaking by working your way up through the system. Yes, you can still go to a film school and learn filmmaking by taking classes. Or you can make your own movies right now. This book will help you get started.

## Who This Book Is For

As my friend Margie often reminds me, loving movies is not the same thing as loving filmmaking. Even if you've studied the extras on DVD releases or watched every movie released this past year, it's difficult to understand the process of making a film from watching one. That process is usually either kept invisible from the viewer or glamorized. There's no way a single book can be a comprehensive study of all aspects of filmmaking, but this book should give you a good overview.

This book is really for anyone who wants to better understand filmmaking. Maybe you're in junior high school and think you want to be a filmmaker. Or maybe you're a grandparent who has been making family home movies but now want to try your hand at filmic storytelling. Or maybe you're thinking about going to film school and want to get a head start.

Basically, this book is designed to give you an overview of how to make independent films. And to give you confidence in talking with other filmmakers and the people who work on films.

## How This Book Is Organized

People often think of filmmaking as simply holding a camera and shooting. But film-making covers everything that comes before and after that exhilarating moment of capturing images. Like the filmmaking process, this book is broken down into key stages of how a film comes to be, from conception to exhibition:

**Part 1, "You Ought to Be in Pictures: Development,"** takes you through the process of finding and developing an idea that has the potential to become a film. You'll see that idea get onto the page as a script, the first step in getting a film made.

**Part 2, "Buddy, Can You Spare a Dime? Pre-Production,"** looks at all the prepa-ration required to get your film ready to shoot, including the financing. Choosing a location, pre-visualizing your film, and finding your cast and crew are just a few of the things you'll be doing in pre-production.

**Part 3, "Ready for My Close-Up: Production,"** is the moment of truth for film-makers, when the cameras roll. Rehearsing actors, coordinating your crew, and all the technical aspects of getting your film "in the can" (or shot) come into play on your set during production.

**Part 4, "Don't Worry, We'll Fix It in … Post-Production,"** tracks the progress of your movie as you take the raw footage you've shot and turn it into a full-fledged movie by editing the picture and sound. At the end of post-production you'll have a finished copy of your film ready to show.

**Part 5, "And the Winner Is … Exhibition & Distribution,"** takes you the final few steps, when you let people know that you have a film for them to see.

In addition, there are two appendixes. Appendix A is a glossary of terms used in the book that you may find helpful to know. Appendix B is a list of films, books, websites, and software that will give you a starting point for taking the next step after reading this book.

If filmmaking is completely new to you, you may find it helpful to skim through the entire book to get a snapshot of the entire process and an understanding of what you're aiming for (showing a finished film to an audience) before you go out and start shooting. Keep in mind that any one of these chapters could be an entire book in its own right, so the goal is not to become an expert in every aspect of filmmaking but to know enough that you feel comfortable beginning the process of making your movie.

## Extras

You'll also find the following boxes interspersed throughout the book. They contain definitions of terms you may not be familiar with, helpful advice, things to watch out for, and interesting related information.

### Reel Trouble

These boxes warn you of situations that can waste your time or money, two things a filmmaker never has enough of.

### Staying in Focus

Here you'll find tips to help you make your film a reality.

### Defining Moments

Check these boxes for definitions of common filmmaking terms.

### Ditty Bag

Check out these boxes for miscellaneous information or ideas that you may find helpful.

## Acknowledgments

Filmmaking is all about collaboration. I only know what I know about film because I've had the privilege of working with some amazing people over the years. Here's the chance to thank some of them for that experience and for helping make this book a reality. A big thank you …

To my friends and colleagues who read portions of this book while it was being written, offering encouragement and critique, in particular Cari Callis, Mariano Di Marco, Francine Sanders, Sara Livingston, Dan Rybicky, Danny Kravitz, Lisa Ellis, Michael Caplan, Lyn Pusztai, Hal Shipman, and Dewaine Beard; and especially Sue Mroz and John Rangel, who enthusiastically read far more than their fair share. And to Lisa Formosa-Parmigiano, Ric Coken, Samantha Sanders, Gary Schultz, and Emily Reible, who are the best at what they do and gladly shared some of that expertise with me.

To the actors and friends who good-naturedly braved the cold and kindly consented to being photographed for the illustrations: James Bould, Christine Bunuan, Cora

Vander Broek, Todd Lillethun, Howard L. White, Clint Fletcher, Bill Whirity, and Robert Garabedian.

To Tim Troy (gaffer extraordinaire), Rebecca Gordon, Andrew Dowd, and my friend Gene at Warehouse Liquors—no, not for the reason you're thinking, but for giving me the drinking glass analogy for form and content that you'll be reading about a little later in this book.

To Tom Kesling, Margie Barrett, Charles Celander, Johnny Johnson, and Stasi Poulos, who each in their own way made things just a little bit easier during the hectic period of writing this book. And especially Eileen Coken, who saved my life (well, okay, I'm being a tad dramatic) on more than one occasion when it seemed that all technology had turned against me.

To Jacky Sach at BookEnds, and the editorial team at Alpha Books, including Randy Ladenheim-Gil, Janette Lynn, Ross Patty, and in particular Lynn Northrup, who made the hard work fun.

To my instructors at Ohio University, especially Don Kirihara, George Semsel, and Russ Johnson, who got me started on this path. And Ann Alter, Carol Beck, Wendey Stanzler, Wendy Weinberg, and Michael Moore, who gave me my first opportunities to work on films and to put what I had learned into practice. To J. D. Sharick for being the first person to invest financially in my films. And to Michael Rabiger, an outstanding filmmaker and mentor, whose example challenges me to be the best teacher and filmmaker I can be.

To JoAnne Steiff and my family for encouragement and support throughout my years of making films, teaching, and writing. And to Victor Cotic, who helped me better understand tax law and partnerships, but more importantly, read the book as a complete novice to filmmaking and made sure I was explaining what I meant as clearly as I could.

And finally to the students and faculty at Columbia College Chicago, who live the passion every day and continue to teach me. Each of these people has made the book in your hands better than it would have been if I had tried to do it all by myself.

## Trademarks

All terms mentioned in this book that are known to be or are suspected of being trademarks or service marks have been appropriately capitalized. Alpha Books and Penguin Group (USA) Inc. cannot attest to the accuracy of this information. Use of a term in this book should not be regarded as affecting the validity of any trademark or service mark.

# Part 1

# You Ought to Be in Pictures: Development

Like me, you want to make films. But what does that really mean? And where do you start?

The first part of the process is called development, which commonly refers to finding, dramatically shaping, and communicating a filmic or visual idea.

In Part 1, you'll see how to take your ideas and your unique view of the world to create a story that you can put on film. You'll learn some of the dramatic elements common to most films and some of the ways your story can be presented to others. And by doing this you'll begin your own development as a filmmaker.

# The Rookie: You Too Can Be a Filmmaker

## In This Chapter

- The basic responsibilities of a filmmaker
- The importance of observation and experience in filmmaking
- A few tips for the novice filmmaker
- Making the film you want to make

All good films start with two things: an idea, and a sense of what you want to accomplish. Being a filmmaker is a bit like being an artist, a business manager, a technician, a magician, a boss, a grunt, and a salesman—all rolled into one. Don't let that scare you, we have a whole book to get used to the idea.

You may be a rookie at this point, but in this chapter, we'll consider what it means to be an independent filmmaker, especially one just starting out. You may be surprised to learn that you already have many of the experiences, insights, and skills that you'll need. It's simply a matter of recognizing how you can apply them to this new adventure, making a film.

# Point and Shoot: What a Filmmaker Does

When you go to buy a new car, you are probably most aware of the sales associate—the person out front who *directs* your attention to the various models and guides your experience on the lot. But behind the scenes is an entire team of people—including the sales associate's boss—who *produce* opportunities to sell cars by making sure that inventory has been ordered, sold cars are washed and prepped for their new owners, bank application forms are available, ads have been placed to get buyers to come in, and the sales associates have everything they need in order to do their jobs. Trying to do all of this is a lot of work for one person.

Making films is similar. Large film productions often split this work into two primary roles: producing and directing. These roles are filled by two different people who each rely on a variety of others to help them. The producer keeps an eye on the entire production from start to finish, getting everything ready and making sure everything gets done. In the strictest sense, the director oversees the actual shooting of the film, the point where cameras roll and images are created. As a team, the producer and director share the responsibilities of making the film, and many people assume that this division is between the business side (producer) and the creative side (director).

*Independent filmmaking* is different. For a number of reasons we'll be exploring in this book, independent productions are usually more intimate, meaning that fewer people are involved. As a result, it's not uncommon for independent filmmakers to perform more than one role, and when we use the term *filmmaker* in this book, we mean the primary person who does both the producing and directing.

> **Ditty Bag**
>
> As you learn more about the roles of the producer and the director, you will realize that this distinction of who's all business and who's creative may not be entirely accurate. Producing requires a great deal of creativity, and directing requires good management skills.

**Defining Moments**

The definition for **independent filmmaking** will vary depending on who you're talking with, but for the purposes of this book, I am referring to the process of making films without the support of studios, production companies, or other institutions known for producing multiple films by a variety of different filmmakers. As a result, independent films are often extremely low budget in comparison to Hollywood movies, and as a result, are more likely to rely on strong character-driven stories rather than special effects.

As a combination of producer and director, you are responsible for the conception and/or development of an idea, and doing all the things necessary for that concept to come to life as a film screened before an audience.

Independent films are often a labor of love made by people whose passion for the idea or story is so strong that they will make the movie no matter what, even if they have to finance it themselves. And this is often the case. If you're interested in independent filmmaking because you want to get rich, trust me, there are easier ways to make money. Sure, you may have heard about an independent film that has garnered critical attention or been sold for a profit. But the vast majority do not bring riches to the people involved. Yet if they had it to do over again, those filmmakers would still make their films. They have an idea they believe in, something they want to say, something they want to show the rest of us. And that motivation is what drives an independent filmmaker.

Filmmaking is always a balancing act between resources and desire. The producing side of you needs to keep track of the finances and logistics. The directing side of you needs to keep track of the emotional heart of the film, what it is you want to communicate.

## Product and Process

As the filmmaker you are responsible for and create two different experiences: the experience of watching your film and the experience of making your film. In the first case, you're dealing with an audience; in the second, you're dealing with your cast and crew.

If you're anything like me, you probably first imagine sitting in a dark theater and watching your movie with an audience. You're thinking about the product—the tangible expression and result of all your hard work.

But that hard work is the process by which the film got made, and as the filmmaker, you are equally responsible for that experience. This means that you have to be able to do—or get other people to do—everything it takes to plan, prepare, shoot, and edit a finished film.

In the worst-case scenarios, too much emphasis on product can result in disregard for the people helping you, and they may rebel or even quit. With no one to help you, the film can't be done. On the other hand, too much emphasis on the process can result in the film never getting finished because you've lost sight of the goal or gotten behind schedule and gone over budget or you've simply lost momentum. You as the filmmaker have to keep an eye on both aspects, product and process, in order to assure that you are able to walk away with a completed film.

## Guiding Vision

Keeping your film on track requires a guiding vision. All I mean by this is that you have a sense of purpose, both creative and procedural.

Filmmakers who have strong guiding visions are often memorable because their films reflect a specific worldview through the filmmakers' interests, likes, and approaches. For lack of a better term, their films have personality. Alfred Hitchcock, Maya Deren, Martin Scorsese, Spike Lee, Mira Nair, Jane Campion, Atom Egoyan, Jean-Pierre Jeunet, David Cronenberg, Michael Moore, Quentin Tarantino, Todd Haynes—these are just a few filmmakers who provide a unifying vision that makes their films distinctly their own even when many other people have worked on them. (See Appendix B for more examples.)

Finding your own guiding vision may be a lifelong discovery, but the roots of it are already there inside you. Think about some of your favorite movies. There's a reason why you like them, and if you analyzed those movies carefully, you would find common elements among them. As you begin making your own movies, you'll notice ways in which they are similar to certain aspects of your favorite ones. These similarities reflect and resonate with the themes, stories, and styles you want to work with; they reveal facets and glimpses of your own guiding vision. And this guiding vision can help you keep your focus and make a film that is distinctly yours even as you have other people help you.

Filmmaking is hard work. As a result, most films are made by a group of people working together, requiring a certain degree of collaboration. The exact degree varies from film to film and filmmaker to filmmaker. But the bottom line is that once you have more than one person working on a movie, someone has to be in charge, has to have the final say. Otherwise, the film can become a mess. You've heard the saying, "too many cooks spoil the soup"? That's why restaurant kitchens have a head chef. Everyone's cooking, but there's one person who is expected to have a sense of the big picture and guide the other kitchen staff to make sure the meals are prepared properly and tabled on time. A guiding vision.

> **Ditty Bag**
>
> Short animation and experimental films are about the only forms where a filmmaker may work alone, doing everything it takes to make the film. Live action films usually require at least a few people to help as actors and/or crew.

You as the filmmaker are the head chef. The other people working on your film, whether they are actors or crew, professionals or friends, will look to you to have a plan and confidence in what you're doing. Inevitably, someone will ask whether things could be done differently or offer other suggestions. You will set the standard for how collaboration works on your set.

Being the one in charge means you have to balance what you want with an awareness of what other people need. For example, let's say you're driving cross-country and you can go for hours without a bathroom break. But maybe the person riding next to you needs to stop every hour or so.

Now, you could ignore that fact, but it's only going to cause more problems down the road (literally). So being a responsible leader means you have to take into account a number of variables, factors, and individual requests. It's not always as simple as "my way or the highway."

There are a variety of ways to be a leader. You can order people around, telling them what to do, or you can explain your goals and rally your crew and cast to help you accomplish them. You can micromanage or be hands off. You can try to do everything yourself or you can delegate. You can be a facilitator or a dictator. You can lead by example or … you get the idea; the list can go on and on. But none of these are mutually exclusive. The best leaders probably do a little of each at one point or another, tailoring their direction to the specific situation, individuals they are working with, and circumstances at hand.

The bottom line is that your guiding vision informs not just the kinds of films you want to make, but also the way in which you make them.

# The "Eyes" Have It: Looking and Seeing

The best films reveal the world around us in unexpected and meaningful ways. The purpose is not so much to show us things we've never seen, but rather to remind us of the things we have forgotten. Many of us have become so used to the everyday world that we take it for granted and no longer fully notice it.

A filmmaker can change that by showing us the usual in unusual ways, making the ordinary extraordinary or the common unique, like the kid in *American Beauty* who films the plastic bag dancing around on the breeze. In order to do this, filmmakers have to break out of the rut the rest of us are in. Filmmakers can't just look at the world around them, they actually have to see it. See the small details of life that other people miss.

## The Kitten Experiment

When I was in college, I took a course in "research design," which required us to read case studies of psychology and sociology experiments. What I remember all these years later is not how to construct a double-blinded study or the importance of control groups but rather one case study that we read: the Kitten Experiment.

Here's the way I remember it: Several groups of kittens were placed in different environments before their eyes opened. One group was placed in a room where the walls were all painted with horizontal stripes. Another group was placed in a room with only vertical stripes. The groups eventually opened their eyes and were raised in their respective rooms.

The fun began when the researchers brought the cats into a normal room filled with furniture. They discovered that the cats raised in the horizontally striped room would jump up on tabletops and chair seats and counter tops with no problem, but they kept running into chair legs—because they couldn't perceive vertical lines. As you might guess, the cats raised in the vertically striped room could navigate the most complex arrangement of table legs but could not be coaxed to jump up onto a chair or table— because they couldn't perceive horizontal lines.

The cats had been so conditioned by their environments as kittens that they could not "see" anything different. As filmmakers, we don't want to be like those cats. Instead we want to perceive what's really there rather than what we expect to see. If we can do that, we will make films that are true and authentic and revelatory.

## Live a Little

Though not true in all cases, there could be an argument made that filmmakers, as well as photographers, artists, and even writers, are more observers than participants. I've just spent several paragraphs talking about the importance of really seeing, of observing. But if that's all you do, then you're missing a crucial ingredient to being an exceptional filmmaker: living life.

The goal as a filmmaker is not just to observe but to also participate. Experience. Live. How can you make a film about the pain of heartbreak if you've never been heartbroken? How can you scare an audience if you've never been scared? Any film you make will either mimic what you've already seen or be based on assumptions that have never been tested.

I'm not suggesting you have to experience exactly what your characters do in your film, just that you have enough experience living to be able to find similar types of emotions in your own life. The role of imagination is less about making things up out of thin air than it is about finding a correlation that will allow us to understand what we haven't experienced.

The students who have the most difficulty in film school are often those who have spent all their time watching movies. Yes, watching movies is an important part in your development as a filmmaker. But movies do not take the place of direct experience.

So get out there. Try some new things. Scare yourself. Fall in love. Be a participant in life, as well as an observer. You will be a better filmmaker as a result.

## As You're Starting Out ...

If you've never made a film before, you're about to experience for the first time all the different aspects of getting a film ready for production, as well as shooting, editing, and showing it to others. There's a lot to learn, and there are a few things you can do to make the process easier and more enjoyable.

First, maximize the resources you already have. Rather than driving out into the wilderness where there are no bathrooms or refrigerators or phone service, stay close to home. Learn the basics with all the support around you that you can.

Second, start small. In film school, students often begin by making very short films, shooting about three minutes of material to edit down to one minute of finished film. The biggest problem most first-time filmmakers face is trying to do something too big right out of the gate and then getting overwhelmed. The best thing to do is to come up with a simple interaction or story you can tell in one or two minutes.

## The Film in Your Head Meets the Film You Can Make

As a filmmaker, one of the issues you'll regularly confront is the film you *want* to make versus the film you *can* make. There's always the film in our head, the near-perfect idealized form that our imagination says will be our final film. On the other hand, there's the realities of making a film, juggling people's schedules, getting equipment, dealing with weather, and simply having the skills necessary to make any film, much less the one that's in your head.

As a beginning filmmaker, the film in our head is kind of like having a train that's stationed in California. And the film we can make, based on our skills, is like a train that's stationed in North Carolina. Very far apart.

This means that the first films we actually make will probably be very different from the films we envisioned in our heads. But don't get discouraged. It's like that for everyone. The great thing about making another film and then another is that each time, your skills will get better and better, and the film you can make will start getting closer to the one you envision, kind of like that train moving from one coast toward the other. Likewise, as you begin to better understand the filmmaking process, you'll adjust the film you envision from pure fantasy to something that can be done with your resources and know-how.

## The Least You Need to Know

- An independent filmmaker rarely works alone; making a film is a collaborative effort.

- An independent filmmaker may be responsible for both the business side of making the film as well as the creative aspects.

- A filmmaker directs not just the film but also the process by which the film gets made.

- A good filmmaker draws upon his or her observations and experience to create memorable movies.

- Learning to make a film requires practice, and practice comes from making films.

# *Imitation of Life:* Moving Image Basics

## In This Chapter

- ◆ Principles of the moving image

- ◆ Types of films: narrative, documentary, and experimental

- ◆ Some distinctions between short and feature-length films

- ◆ Deciding on the scale of your film

- ◆ Why an audience will want to see your film

Years ago, people were very careful to distinguish between film and video, but nowadays, you'll hear the term "film" applied to any moving image, whether it was created with a 16mm Bolex or a DV cam or a camcorder or a 35mm Panavision or an old Super 8 camera or some technology that hasn't been invented yet.

When I use the term *independent filmmaking*, I mean the process rather than the actual format. What matters is that you're making moving images. But as you'll learn in this chapter, the images don't really move. It's just an illusion.

Intrigued? Read on …

# Creating the Illusion of Motion

Films are really like a series of still photographs or frozen moments in time. In a motion picture, each of these individual photographs is called a *frame*. To create the illusion of movement, these frames are shot and projected in a succession so rapid that when flashed before our eyes, the images seem to move.

## Photographic Medium

Traditionally, movies have been shot on filmstock, much like the unexposed film you load into a still camera. As a result, films have been historically considered a photographic medium and process. A camera focuses light onto a single frame of unexposed film, creating a latent image. This latent image can't be seen with the naked eye until after the filmstock has been processed or chemically treated.

Though a digital camera doesn't use filmstock, and requires a different kind of translation process to make the image visible, we still call the final result *photographic:* a record of what we would have seen if we had been there when the camera originally recorded the images.

## Moving Images

If each frame is a still photograph, why do the people and objects in a movie seem to move? As I've said, it's an illusion, a trick of the eye.

There have been several theories about why the human mind perceives a rapid succession of images as being in movement, but the general assumption is that the more rapid the succession of images—the more visual information you see during a given second—the less likely you are to perceive the individual frames or still photographs.

But speed alone is not enough. When you thumb through a flipbook, your eye still registers the images as a series of individual drawings or pictures. Simply flipping through the images quickly is not enough; you also have to do it at a uniform speed. Therefore, movie cameras are designed to record images—and VCRs, DVD players, and projectors are designed to play back images—at a set consistent speed.

Though there have been experiments with faster speeds and a history of slower speeds, at this point in time, this succession of images for films has been standardized at 24 *fps* (frames per second) or 24 still photographs flashed before your eyes each second. Television and many video formats have a slightly higher rate: 30 fps.

So watching a film is like seeing a good magician do sleight of hand. The movement is a trick.

We'll talk more about filmstocks and cameras in Chapter 18. For now, though, remember that films are a photographic medium and create an illusion of movement within the frame.

**Defining Moments**

FPS (frames per second) is the way in which we talk about the speed at which the film either passes through the gate of the camera or, in the case of what we're talking about here, the speed of the film passing before the viewer's eyes.

# It's How You Say It: Modes of Filmmaking

There is more than one type of film you can make, each with its own unique characteristics. Deciding which type is most appropriate for your project requires an understanding of your goals for making the film and the audience you hope will watch it. You also need to consider the relationship between form and content.

A good bartender doesn't just mix the drink (content), but also makes sure that the content is presented in the proper glass (form). White wine goes in a narrow-mouthed smaller goblet whereas red wine goes in a wider-mouthed, larger-bowled goblet. Whiskey is served in small wide shot glasses; tequila is served in tall narrow shot glasses. And so forth.

While this may seem an arbitrary decision, or one simply based on tradition, there is a reason why different drinks are served in different glasses. The shape of the glass can affect the characteristics of the alcohol and where the liquid hits the tongue. So while you can drink champagne out of any kind of container you want, a stemmed flute is not just a traditional choice but one that shapes the way in which we experience the drink. The glass affects the delivery of the alcohol and our response to it.

In film the form affects the delivery of the content. Some ideas may be more effective as fiction comedies and others may be more effective as first-person confessions. As an independent filmmaker, you want to be aware of your various options and make a conscious decision as to which mode of film is best suited to your idea or concept. In broad terms, your choices are narrative, documentary, and experimental forms, though the distinctions among these have been blurred in recent years. We now regularly see hybrids, derivations, or combinations of these in music videos, television commercials, and films. Let's take a closer look at the three basic types.

# Narrative

When you go to the nearest multiplex, most of the movies you're watching are narratives. What we mean by this is that the film is fiction—it tells a story, using actors to convey characters and dramatic situations. A common assumption is that narrative films are primarily designed for entertainment or as diversions. But there are narrative films that strive to do more than entertain, such as *Testament* and *WarGames*, which caution us about the dangers of nuclear weapons.

Years of filmmaking have standardized many of the ways for telling fictional stories in film, and I'll more closely examine some of these techniques in Chapters 5 and 6.

> **Ditty Bag**
>
> Even nonfiction films can have a narrative or tell a story, but we generally reserve the classification of narrative solely for fiction films.

# Documentary

Documentary films are in general the observation of a real event, person, or the world around us. Most of the documentaries I saw as a child were in classrooms, or maybe the high school gym, and were primarily geared as educational films.

Educational films historically have been more likely to show up on television than in a movie theater, though this is beginning to change. In recent years documentaries have become more popular, and are increasingly more likely to receive theatrical release. While they have yet to regularly rival narrative films' box office revenue, several documentaries such as *Fahrenheit 9/11* have become extremely successful.

Whereas narrative films use actors, documentary films reveal real situations and the actual people involved. These might still be for educational purposes, but many of the more popular documentaries also entertain.

Some subcategories of documentaries would include the following:

♦ *Biographical:* The film examines the life of one person.

♦ *Historical:* The film delves into an historical event.

♦ *Issue-oriented:* The film explores a particular issue.

♦ *Essay:* The film uses real events and people to create an editorial or persuasive argument.

♦ *Diary:* The film creates a view into the life of the filmmaker.

## Experimental

Avant garde or experimental films often raise questions about the physical material of film and video itself or draw intellectual connections between the process of perception and the way in which we try to make meaning from random images.

Because we live in a culture full of storytelling, whether at bedtime or in a novel or on television or in anecdotal conversations, these non-narrative films may seem more challenging for an audience. Experimental films often do not have a clearly identified story and may not even be interested in telling a story.

Over the years, many evocative images and techniques we see in mainstream films originated in experimental filmmaking. In fact, the term experimental comes from the early twentieth century when some filmmakers were truly experimenting with the then-new medium of film and how an audience responded to various shapes, lines, qualities of light, and juxtaposition of images.

# Built to Last: Duration

How long an audience can pay attention may have to do with the ways in which each type of film engages the viewer. While there are always exceptions, narratives seem to allow for a greater duration and therefore are often longer than documentaries or experimental films. This may be partly due to the fact that many narratives are meant to be entertaining rather than thought-provoking, more of an emotional experience than an intellectual experience.

Documentaries often present a great deal of information, requiring intensive thought on the part of the viewer. This might explain why they are usually of shorter duration than a narrative. And why successful feature-length documentaries often utilize certain narrative conventions.

Experimental films can be even more taxing intellectually, which might be part of the reason why they are often most successful when very short. So what's the bottom line? Evidently we can feel an emotion longer than we can think a thought.

### Staying in Focus

While there are various hypotheses about how long someone can pay attention to educational films, my favorite is that the age of the person is equal to the number of minutes he or she can remain focused on factual information. This means your average 20-year-old viewer can stay engaged by a documentary for about 20 minutes.

# It's What You Say: Telling Stories

In looking at the three broad categories—narrative, documentary, and experimental—you've probably realized that many films incorporate aspects of more than one category. For example, mockumentaries look like documentaries and may even utilize a certain degree of uncontrolled (or improvisational) filmmaking, but in fact they are fictional stories with actors creating characters. Many narrative films use experimental techniques, but incorporate them as dream sequences or subjective points of view.

Besides factors of audience duration or how long they can comfortably watch a film, we need to consider the scale of our content—how much story can be contained within a certain film length or how much time the characters experience on the screen.

In feature films, the events usually play out over the course of days, weeks, months, or even sometimes years, but we only see bits and pieces of these events during the two hours we're in the theater. Short films are often a narrower focus, a smaller moment in time. Some short films even play out as if they were happening in real time, a five-minute film literally existing as five minutes in the character's life.

Deciding the scale of your film will depend on two factors: how long a film you can afford to make and the length of film that best suits your story. In later chapters, I talk about how these two factors may affect each other, but right now, let's concentrate simply on the story's requirements.

People often describe feature-length films as being the equivalent of a novel, which would make short films similar to a short story. But novels can be made up of many more characters and story elements than can be reasonably portrayed in a feature-length film. Probably a novel's story scale is more suitable for a TV miniseries. In terms of the complexity of dramatic situations, the amount of story a feature film can cover is probably closer to that of a traditional short story, which would make short films comparable to the prose form of a one- or two-page story.

## Short Film Stories

Though you'll find different opinions about how long a movie can be and still be categorized as a short, if your film approaches the 60-minute mark, odds are most film festivals and programmers are no longer going to consider it short.

Because we don't have a couple of hours to develop a complex situation and set of characters, short films have to look for ways to convey a lot of information very quickly or to find a compressed moment that can be revealed.

The most common type of film I see beginning filmmakers try is the *skit* or *gag film*. In a way, this makes sense, because for most of us, the only short filmic moments we've seen have been the kinds of skits common to TV shows like *Mad TV* or *Saturday Night Live*. Skits or gag films are similar to a joke—there's a punch line, some sort of twist or surprise at the end. Usually in these kinds of films, the joke is on the audience; we've been misled to perceive the situation in one way and then are confronted with a contradiction at the end. Sometimes this is done for humor, sometimes for irony, and sometimes for tragedy. The risk is that such a film can fall flat if the twist doesn't feel like a logical extension of the story.

**Reel Trouble**

Bigger is not always better. A really good 10-minute film will do more for your filmmaking career than a mediocre 40-minute film.

Another approach is to make a short film that operates as a *mood piece*, creating a brief glimpse into a very specific environment or into the life of a character. Your goal here is to make the audience feel a particular emotion and create an environment, situation, or set of images that evoke that emotion. Mood films are a great choice if you're trying to keep your film under two minutes.

Though not necessary, this approach could be linked with a *character study*, creating a specific and detailed portrait of a character in just a few minutes of screen time. This study could be static, like a mood film, or it could be dynamic, showing the character at a pivotal or *defining moment*, a point where the character has to face a life-changing decision. Finding significant moments in a character's life could also serve as a microcosm for a larger story, a resonant moment that encapsulates and insinuates broader emotions and events than can be shown.

Working with meaningful moments of decision or crisis for the character in a short format is one of the best preparations for feature-length filmmaking. Longer narratives generally involve characters who grow through transitional moments to become other than what they were at the start of the film.

There are other ways to approach the short form, but no matter which approach you take, your short film has to make the most of the time you have the viewer, so the film has to be economical in its presentation of story and character.

## Feature Film Stories

Feature-length films allow for more time to build or develop characters and the situations those characters have to cope with. Character development is crucial in narrative films because it's what makes the film believable to an audience, regardless of the situation.

Feature-length narrative films often fall within very particular structures, or *genres*, such as the romantic comedy or the detective film. These are standardized formulas built around the concept that certain content requires a particular form (back to our bartender's choosing the appropriate glass for each drink). The way in which a story is told carries certain conventions that the audience has become familiar with and expects. Just as with hybrids of narrative, documentary, and experimental, specific genres can be combined to create new and unexpected ways of telling stories. Though genres can be adapted to shorter formats, they developed as a feature-length expression that requires more complex situations and setups. This may be why they remain most viable as a feature-length film.

> **Defining Moments**
>
> **Genres** are a way to classify films by their recurring use of certain conventions or specific elements, such as the femme fatale in the film noir genre, the wild and untamed landscape of westerns, or the gradual piecing together of "whodunit" in a mystery.

# Audience Participation

Films can be powerful emotional or intellectual experiences for an audience, but for this to happen, the film needs to engage the audience. Each filmmaking mode achieves this differently.

Film audiences are a bit like the people who go to an art museum. Some people love modern conceptual art and hate impressionist paintings. Others love journalistic photographs but hate abstract sculpture. You're not going to be able to please everyone, so at some point, you want to decide who it is you most want to please and make your film for them.

## Experience and Engagement

One of the primary attractions of watching moving images over reading a book or listening to a lecture is that films can sweep the audience up and provide them with an experience. Though I've noted some film modes that make their audiences work at a more intellectual level, one of the most profound effects of cinema—both narrative and documentary—is its ability to create an emotional experience for the viewers.

Traditionally, this emotional experience has been created by the effective use of characters. As an independent filmmaker, creating memorable characters is one of the most powerful tools you have to engage an audience.

Another type of engagement is to create emotionally laden situations. One of the most powerful cinematic scenes is the lights flickering out on the upended *Titanic* in James Cameron's 1997 film. In that scene we're not particularly following any one character, so part of the scene's power comes simply from the event, but if we had experienced that scene as soon as we walked in the theater, it wouldn't convey the same impact. That's because the material that has come before, where we've been introduced to characters, has allowed us to personalize the experience, to develop empathy for the people at risk. This brings added power to the scene. And this is one of the main purposes of character development in a film, to engage the audience at an emotional level so that we don't just watch the film, we experience it.

Some recent Hollywood films have begun to substitute character as the source for engagement with special effects and spectacular action sequences or visuals. The goal is the same, to hook the audience. And certainly, extreme effects can create adrenaline-pumping excitement and awe that can make a film entertaining. But whether you use effects, characters, a combination of both, or something entirely different, there has to be something that engages the audience, something that pulls them in.

## Suspension of Disbelief

The willingness to forget one is watching a film is sometimes referred to as *suspension of disbelief*. In other words, an audience knows that it is sitting in a movie theater, watching a make-believe story told in moving images. The entire movie-viewing process is inherently one of disbelief. If the filmmaker makes the story compelling enough and the filmmaking process invisible enough, the audience might become absorbed by this fabrication, but to be truly affected, the audience has to meet the filmmaker halfway, by being willing to not so much believe the story as to not let their disbelief get in the way. This applies to a movie like *Harry Potter and the Prisoner of Azkaban* as well as a film like *Sideways*.

Your goal is to make this process of suspending disbelief as easy as possible. One of the methods for doing this is by creating a world that seems credible, helping the audience to believe what's on the screen could possibly happen.

## The Least You Need to Know

◆ Movies are a series of still photographs rapidly flashed before our eyes to create the illusion of movement.

◆ Traditionally films have been classified as one of three types: narrative, documentary, or experimental.

◆ The length of your film is first determined by the size of the story you want to tell.

◆ Creating an emotional experience for the audience is one of the best ways to assure they'll want to watch your film.

# 3

# *The Poseidon Adventure: Let's Make a Movie*

## In This Chapter

- ◆ Making films within institutional systems
- ◆ Borrowing a few techniques from Hollywood
- ◆ Making films independent of those systems
- ◆ The five phases all successful films go through

Making movies is a lot like the film *The Poseidon Adventure*—your whole world turns upside down and you along with a handful of other people have to work as a team to overcome obstacles, solve problems, and find a way through. It will be scary, thrilling, exhausting, bittersweet, and life-changing.

Just because I've compared filmmaking to a movie about a sinking ship doesn't mean that it has to be a disaster. Understanding the different ways in which films get made can help you better navigate the filmmaking process. A truly independent filmmaker is open to learning from everyone, using whatever techniques work best regardless of where they came from.

# All Systems Go: Ways to Make Films

There are a lot of ways to make films. Generally, we can break these down into two major categories: films made within an institutional system and films made outside that system or independently. Let's take a closer look at each.

## Institutional Filmmaking

Institutional filmmaking is the process of making movies within a larger system that is able to provide resources. These institutional systems are simply the widely accepted or official mechanisms for making films, and depending on where you are, these could be manifested as film boards or government-owned television networks or studio systems or some other arrangement. The best-known filmmaking institution is Hollywood.

You can go to Hollywood, but you'll probably have to help others make their films for many years before you'll get the chance to make your own. Hollywood traditionally has been what's called an apprenticeship system, meaning that you get on-the-job training by working with more experienced people. Some call this paying your dues, and the dues are not so much dollars as time.

**Defining Moments**

**Indie films** is a slang term for independently made movies; you'll sometimes see this shortened to *indies*.

Some Hollywood filmmakers get a jump-start by making an independent film first, hoping to garner attention at film festivals and woo Hollywood. While not all independent filmmakers aspire to be a part of the system, those who do are extremely lucky if their *indie films* give them the opportunity to make films in Hollywood.

In the early- and mid-twentieth century, Hollywood was primarily a studio system. Large movie studios would keep a stable of writers, directors, actors, and crew people under contract, and these people would work in an assembly-line kind of process to pour out films. In the last half of the twentieth century, studios remained powerful filmmaking mechanisms but began to hire actors, crew, writers, and directors project to project.

Success in the Hollywood system is generally determined by box-office revenue—how much money the film makes. This puts pressure on Hollywood to make films that will attract the largest possible audience.

Television production is another institutionalized process, and in the United States is also based in Hollywood and shares many of the same resources. Success in television production is generally measured by how many people watch individual programs, because these numbers have a financial consequence. The more a program is watched, the more the producers can charge the broadcaster and the more the broadcaster can charge advertisers to run commercials during the show.

Another form of institutional filmmaking is industrial filmmaking—films that are made for corporate or training purposes. While these might be considered a form of documentary, they usually have very narrowly identified target audiences. (See Chapter 7 for more information about target audiences.)

A successful industrial film is not about making money or getting lots of viewers; success here is measured by whether viewers comprehend and can put into practice the skills demonstrated or the knowledge imparted.

One of newer film institutions is music video production. Though primarily commercials for songs, music videos have become a place for younger filmmakers to gain experience and demonstrate their talents in hopes of getting the Hollywood feature filmmaking industry interested.

> **Ditty Bag**
>
> The line between institutional and independent filmmaking can sometimes be blurry. National film boards such as those in Canada, New Zealand, Ireland, and Scotland could be considered filmmaking institutions, though their filmmakers often consider themselves independent because they do not receive the level of financial support or distribution that Hollywood films receive.

One of the most popular institutions for filmmaking in the late twentieth and early twenty-first centuries has been film schools. Film schools can provide a safe but expensive environment to learn the basic processes of filmmaking and the ways in which filmmaking systems work. Depending on the school, these systems may mimic Hollywood by operating as a mini-studio with highly individualized crew positions and competitive allotment of resources or embrace a more individualistic model of filmmaking as a form of personal expression and artistic exploration.

Success for films made at schools is measured by public screenings and festival awards. This is a mutually beneficial arrangement for both the student filmmaker and the school, because screenings and awards can bring attention to both. Thus the rewards are not directly about money but rather notoriety, which can open doors for the student to make more films outside of school and for the school to gain more students.

# Independent Filmmaking

As technology has advanced and prices have dropped, the average person can now easily gain access to the equipment and materials required for making films. Unsure whether to go the institutional route or convinced that right now that route's not for them, more filmmakers than ever are making movies outside these institutional systems.

Even in the most rigid institutional filmmaking systems, there is more than one way to make a film. In independent filmmaking, there are even more options. There are as many ways to get an independent film made as there are independent filmmakers. However, there are several reference points that can make your work a little easier.

The first, believe it or not, is institutional filmmaking. Many independent filmmakers decide not to reinvent the wheel and borrow from the techniques and processes that institutions like Hollywood have perfected. Therefore, you'll find that many independent production sets look a lot like a Hollywood set, with a division of labor through various crew positions, a hierarchy of command with one person in charge, and so on.

When Academy Awards are handed out to films that are called "independent," nine times out of ten the film has been shot using the Hollywood model and in fact has often received major support in one form or another from studios. That's why I consider them freelance rather than independent. These freelance films are usually made by (and acted by) Hollywood players and talent, though the financiers may have had to scramble to find money from other sources than just a single studio.

**CAUTION**

**Reel Trouble** _____

An extreme form of independent filmmaking is what's called "guerilla filmmaking." These filmmakers shoot their movies on the run with very small crews so they won't draw attention to themselves, often filming without permits or permission. This can be extremely risky; if they're caught they may have to pay fines or even face criminal charges. Most communities are excited and willing to work with independent filmmakers, and most independent films are successfully made without breaking laws or trespassing.

But there are movies that are made by people truly outside—and with no real ties to—Hollywood. These are true independent films that seem to come out of nowhere, made by people no one has heard of. They often have very small budgets and require a great deal of resourcefulness by their filmmakers to get made.

Because independent films are not made within a system and therefore do not have to conform to rigid production codes, there is greater flexibility and ingenuity in how they get made. While you might expect a Hollywood production to split all the different filmmaking duties into distinct jobs held by separate individuals, an independent film might have each person doing many different jobs.

As I mentioned in Chapter 1, an independent film might be made by one person who performs all the producing and directing chores. She might be doing this to save money or perhaps time. But she might also do both jobs because she doesn't want to dilute her vision. In independent cinema, there's no real limit to what you can do other than your own capacity to do those things well. As the filmmaker, you could write the script or act or run the camera or edit the movie. One person would rarely if ever be allowed to do all of these jobs on an institutional film, no matter how talented or skilled she is.

But some filmmakers prefer not to work in such a way that one person makes all the creative decisions. We occasionally see films made cooperatively by teams wherein all the team members assume the actual job duties, whether those are two brothers or a collective of friends. Though rare, these are films that are less likely to list a "director" or "producer" or "screenwriter" in their credits. Rather, all the key players share equal credit for making the film.

The bottom line is that in independent filmmaking, you're freer than in institutional filmmaking to figure out the ways you work best and with whom. While an institutional feature film set would expect a bare minimum of 40 people to be involved as crew, an independent filmmaker can work with far fewer people if everyone is willing to do more than one job. For example, I worked on an independent feature that was comprised of three crew people besides the director: Me as the cinematographer, who set up lights, loaded, checked, and operated the camera (each of which would be a separate job on a Hollywood film); a sound recordist who operated her own *boom* (again, separate jobs on a Hollywood film); and a production manager who also worked as a general assistant, helping wherever we needed help at any given moment. Though we all worked hard, it was one of the best crew experiences I've had.

### Defining Moments

**Boom** is the long pole that ends in a microphone and allows for microphone placement close to the action without being visible in the frame. The word also applies to the person who holds this pole, though when this is the case, "boom" is short for "boom operator."

① cinematographer
② Sound Recordist
③ Production mgr

# How Most Films Get Made

Regardless of how large your crew is and how it's organized, there are certain steps that most films go through. Many of these steps originated in and were initially practiced by Hollywood, but their prevalence is proof that they are indeed an efficient and systematic way of preparing an idea and making it into a film.

These phases or steps are development, pre-production, production, post-production, and exhibition & distribution. Please remember that while these may seem like distinct and discrete stages, the processes often overlap. These phases are not a simple progression where once you move past one stage you never go back to it. For example, screenwriting is considered a part of the development phase, but it's not uncommon to rewrite portions of the script during production or even in post-production. The boundaries between each of these are fluid and not as rigid as one might assume. With that in mind, let's look at a broad overview of the phases of production with later chapters going into greater detail about each step.

## Development

Sometimes development is called the literary phase because it is about exploring your film idea in written form. Once you have an idea for your film, you'll need to think about it and imagine all the possible ways it could be made into a story.

But imagination will only take you so far. At some point you will need to write your idea down on paper so that you can see it with new eyes and share it with others in order to get their feedback. The development phase is where you perfect your story, which means not just writing it once but revising it. And rewriting. And rewriting.

During the development phase, you may also be trying to figure out how you're going to pay for your film and trying to get other people interested in helping you either financially or physically.

## Pre-Production

Pre-production is the organizational and financial phase of production. It officially begins when you set a shooting date or start date for production. As the filmmaker, this is the point when you have to figure out how to best utilize your resources and pay for expenses based on how much money you have available (budgeting). Pre-production involves planning the specifics of making the film, such as hiring your crew and cast—I'm using the word "hire" whether you actually pay your crew or not—and scheduling when people need to be on set and what will be shot when. You'll be pre-visualizing the film so that you can shoot it as quickly and economically as possible. In independent filmmaking, this period might also include rehearsing with your actors, something not commonly done at this point on Hollywood films.

> **Ditty Bag**
>
> Unless special training is required, Hollywood productions often expect actors to prepare their characters with a minimum of guidance and before arriving on the set. In this model, any real rehearsal occurs during the production phase right before filming each shot.

## Production

Production officially begins when you roll cameras or start what is called *principal photography*, the period of time when the main scenes of the film are shot. The primary responsibilities during this phase are to capture the actors' performances on camera and to get the film "in the can" or shot. Production is all about generating the raw material that will ultimately be made into a finished film. In productions where the director and producer roles are performed by separate people, this is the one phase of production where the director is in charge, though the producer has to keep tabs on the schedule and budget to make sure that there are enough resources to finish the film.

## Post-Production

Though technically post-production would begin after production ends, the reality nowadays is that editors start working on the film as soon as possible. Post-production is where the images and sounds are reviewed to decide if there's enough material to work with, and if there is, these materials are assembled and refined into a final version of the film.

## Exhibition & Distribution

Films are made for someone to see, of course. Showing the finished film to others is called exhibition, and getting the film out in numerous venues so that an audience can see it is called distribution. This phase includes how you "sell" the film to audiences through advertising and marketing.

What's most important to remember about these different phases is that the work has to be done somewhere. If you give each phase its full due, your production has a better chance of going smoothly. But if you don't spend enough time on development, you'll pay for it either in production or post-production when you're trying to figure out how to work around a weak script. If you don't thoroughly plan the film in pre-production, you'll run into problems on the set that could have easily been avoided. If you go into your shoot without a plan of what to film, you'll be tempted to collect hours and hours of footage, and you'll have to spend exponentially more time in the editing room trying to make sense of it all. The best advice is, "do the work when it first needs to be done."

## The Least You Need to Know

- Filmmaking institutions include not just Hollywood but any well-organized or official system that supports the making of films, such as television, music video production or film schools.

- Filmmakers working outside official systems borrow techniques and strategies used in institutional filmmaking.

- Independent filmmaking allows you the freedom to make your films in the ways that work best for you.

- The five phases of filmmaking are development, pre-production, production, post-production, and exhibition & distribution.

# **4**

# *The Elusive Idea:*
# Film Ideas

## In This Chapter

◆ Pulling ideas from your own life

◆ Expressing your point of view

◆ Why do you want to make this film?

◆ Seeing is believing: why films are visual

◆ Your responsibilities when basing stories on real people or events

Being a filmmaker starts the moment you have an idea that can become a film—and you do something about it. Having the idea is not enough. A filmmaker is someone who has the commitment and ambition to see that idea emerge into a series of moving images that other people will watch.

Finding an idea that has visual story potential is as close as what you can see, touch, and hear. We've been conditioned to see the world and our lives in a particular way. The key, as always, is to look at everything with new eyes and to try to see what you've overlooked. It's less about going out and searching for ideas than recognizing the ones that are right there all around you.

# Write What You Know

Many of the best creative writing and filmmaking programs encourage students to "write what you know." The temptation of course is to copy the very films that have made you want to be a filmmaker.

Imagine standing at a photocopy machine with this book. You copy this page, and then make a copy of the copy. And then take that copy and copy it. And so on. Eventually you'll notice that the quality of each subsequent copy gets worse and worse, until the original text gets distorted and lost, harder to read, until finally you won't be able to recognize what the original document was.

That's the problem with copying other films. It reduces your chances of making something that will feel authentic or truthful. Independent cinema is so exciting because it's a study of life or the world around us that we haven't seen before and yet feels true. Independent films stand out because they are unexpected and original.

While "writing what you know" is a good first step to making original and interesting films, I encourage you to take this concept even further and "write what only you can tell." Draw from your own life, experience, and observations to help you create films that will be honest reflections and observations of the world around you.

| Ditty Bag |
| --- |
| Whenever we make films about situations or people unfamiliar to us, the danger is that we will fall back on assumptions which can become at best clichés and at worst stereotypes. Imagination alone is rarely enough to combat this problem; extensive research may help us create a film that is an accurate portrayal of unfamiliar material. Unless you have lots of time to do that kind of research, drawing on your own personal experience and observations will help you create stories that are accurate and unique. |

# Finding Your Point of View

One of the easiest ways to assure that our films are not copies of what we've seen is to allow those ideas to be filtered through our own perspective of the world. Because of our experiences, interests, and conditioning, you and I have unique views of the world around us. Both of us could choose the exact same idea to make into a film, but our two films would be different. This is because we would each see something different in that idea, and we would tell the story from our own unique *point of view*.

Point of view is why two siblings raised in the same home can have two completely different impressions of their parents and what life was like growing up. Or why two witnesses to the same crime can see radically different events.

The fable of the blind men and the elephant serves as a perfect analogy. All of them en-counter an elephant, but each "sees" something different because of where they are positioned in relationship to the animal. The same thing happens in storytelling. Rather than be ashamed of this difference or pretend it doesn't exist or try to deny it, independent filmmakers use their unique point of view to their advantage—to make distinct films.

**Defining Moments**

Point of view (POV) has a number of different meanings in film depending upon the con-text. At the moment, we're talking about POV as the filmmaker's relationship to the material, or the angle from which you see your story and what you want to emphasize and draw out.

# Choosing Ideas and Developing Themes

You may already have an idea that you're itching to turn into a movie. Or you may have more than one but are not sure if they're good. Or you might know you want to make films but you're not sure about what.

Ideas can come from many different places. Some seem to spring solely from our imagination while others are sparked by overhearing a passing comment. We see someone crying on a payphone, and we wonder why. We imagine what the world will be like in 50 years, or what it was like in the second century. We ask ourselves "what if ...?"

Many film classes start by asking their students to do a number of observational exercises. These observations can range from going someplace you've never been to carefully studying your own family to remembering events from your past. While these can generate material to turn into films, one of the primary benefits for us as filmmakers is that it trains us to pay closer attention to the world around us. This heightened awareness can open us up to finding the stories right under our noses.

You don't necessarily have to decide right now if any one idea will be your film. Your goal is simply to collect as many ideas as possible. They don't even have to be complete. They might be fragments, snippets of conversations, or a particular image you see in your head. Try not to evaluate their merits. Just collect them, see all the possibilities.

Once you have an idea you're eager to explore, try to imagine it more fully. You may find that several of your observations or ideas can be combined. This is the first step in developing our film idea. And there are some tricks that can help coach your imagination to more fully build the story.

You could first try writing down everything about the idea or story that you see in your head. Don't worry that these might be out of order or even contradict each other. Having a written record of all your thoughts makes it less likely you'll forget a good idea and also makes it easier to analyze. When you've been away from the idea for a few days or followed it down several digressions, you can reread your notes and put yourself back into your original impressions of the story.

Writing development notes to yourself can be helpful as well. When you reread what you've already written or when you're thinking about the story, you may have new insights or questions or details. Write them down for future consideration; don't necessarily try to make decisions right now or force them to fit into what you've already written.

Sometimes evoking the tone or mood you want to create in your film can help you develop the concept. For example, if you're primarily a visual person, cut out pictures from magazines or even select personal snapshots that evoke for you the atmosphere or visual look of the characters you imagine when you think about your film. Pin these on the wall near where you write.

Some people will even place physical objects on their desk that they feel evoke some aspect of the story because they can tap into those feelings by touch, and handling the object reminds them. Other people create best with music and will put on a CD that evokes the mood or atmosphere they're trying to develop.

Any of these techniques may serve to get you back into your story world and remind you how you want it to feel for an audience. As a result, your writing will be more consistent. If you ultimately lose interest in an idea, that doesn't mean you don't have what it takes to be a filmmaker; it probably means the idea isn't ready yet. Store it away for another time. Once you find the idea that's right, it won't let you go.

As you work with your idea and shape it more fully into a narrative, your initial telling of the idea in written form can be thought of as a source story—the raw material you're working with. As a source story, there's no pressure beyond doing whatever it takes to more fully understand and shape the story. You don't have to be worried about it being in correct film format; you're simply getting the story out so that you can better see it and analyze it. It could be written like a short story or a poem or an outline or a series of impressions or a journal entry or whatever form makes most sense to you.

If I ask you what your story is about, and you say "love," you've just given me your topic or subject matter. But your story is about more than just love. Your story will have a particular viewpoint about love, and this viewpoint is part of what we call *theme*—your stance or opinion or theory about love as it will be demonstrated in this story and presented in your film. You might say "love conquers all" or "love is a battlefield." Or maybe something more original. Those are themes, because they express an opinion about love.

> **CAUTION**
>
> **Reel Trouble** _____
>
> Filmmaking borrows terminology from a variety of other fields and arts, so you may find different definitions for terms such as *theme* or *premise* depending on whether you're studying theater, fiction writing, English, poetry, photography, music, or film. Don't worry about these contradictions—you're a filmmaker now. The definitions in this book will be the ones most commonly used in film.

Once you have a theme, you may want to think about whether your basic story is consistent with that theme. If not, maybe you'll want to change your theme to more accurately reflect the events of your story. Or you might decide that you really like the theme and need to reshape some of the story so that it will reflect the theme. Either way, at some point you'll want to be able to summarize your film in a premise, a one- or two-sentence summary of the basic plot structure or situation. Using our clichéd example of "love conquers all," the summary might be, "boy meets girl, boy loses girl, boy gets girl back."

# Why This Film, Why Now?

As you practice finding potential film material, you may reach a point where you have more ideas than you quite know what to do with. Figuring out which idea to prioritize can be a challenge. There are so many films you could make, so how do you decide which one to make first?

While at some point practical considerations will come into play, at this conception phase it's best to stay focused on the ideas themselves. Look at your ideas and give some consideration to what you like about each one. What draws you to this idea?

What is it about this story that compels you to tell it? Why is this idea important to you? You might like the characters or the situation. Maybe the theme behind the story expresses something you feel strongly about. There's no right or wrong answer, but understanding why you like each particular idea will help you recognize which one you're ready to work with and why.

### Staying in Focus

Writing down your answers as to why you like this idea and want to make it into a film will help you later when you write proposals to organizations or investors and have to explain why this particular film is worthy of their support.

In effect, you're looking at each idea and answering why you would want to make it into a film. If the ideas don't matter to you, and you simply want to make a film so that you can get famous or rich or call yourself a filmmaker, it's not going to be enough to sustain you. Making a film requires more time, energy, and dedication than most people realize. Independent films get made because the filmmaker passionately believes in the idea and what he wants to communicate. He never loses sight of why he wants to make the film.

Because films often take weeks, months, or even years to go from concept to exhibition, it's easy to forget why you originally wanted to make the film or what your original inspiration and intention were. Understanding your answers to the previous questions can help you find the idea that will keep you focused, passionate, and committed to finishing the film.

# That's Not the Way It Happened

The most common roadblock to writing what you know is the belief that you have to keep the events the way they really happened. But effective storytelling is figuring out what to leave out, what to leave in, and what to exaggerate. Think of the classic "Big Fish" story. Okay, maybe in real life, your sister Monica was out on the lake fishing one day, and caught a fish so small that she had to throw it back. But by the time the boat reaches the dock, and each subsequent time she tells the story about the fish that got away, that fish is bigger and her efforts to get it in the boat are more heroic.

Like any good storyteller, your sister knows to start with the truth but to then make it exciting for an audience. Start with what you know and what only you can tell, but don't be afraid to embellish and change events to make the story more memorable or powerful.

# Writing Visually

We read books, but we watch films. Films are not about words on a page, though they often start that way. A good film shows us the story through behavior and action; in other words, movies are visual storytelling.

Before deciding once and for all which idea you're going to take to the next level of development, you need to analyze its visual potential—whether or not your concept is better told with visual images or with words. If it works better in writing, then you have a book, not a film.

When writing your film ideas on paper as treatments or scripts (which I'll discuss in the next two chapters), keep in mind that films illustrate stories rather than tell them. You need to think visually when developing a film idea. Films are observable behavior, action that can be seen. Does the idea you're passionate about have cinematic properties? If not, is there a way to instill it with those? If not, then it's time for a new idea. But if so, then you're ready to start thinking how to take this idea and make it into a story.

# Being a "Good Thief"

As with all personal stories, writing what you know and what only you can tell results in stealing a little bit from your own life and from the lives of the people you know. Few of your real-life experiences happen in a vacuum. Even when you're using something from your own childhood or life as the impetus for a film, it's rare that such an event didn't involve other people.

Using *life models* as a starting point for your film ideas means that you're going to draw from events or situations that have affected not just you, but your friends or family. In addition, you may witness interactions between other people, whether strangers or family, that you think could be part of a film. Or you may be inspired by world events and from things that happen down the street.

In each of these cases you are faced with several ethical questions: do I have a right to use this material? Do I need to ask permission to

**CAUTION**

**Reel Trouble**

When drawing from your own history or situations as inspiration, be careful of choosing an event that's still too fresh. As a filmmaker, you have to be able to stand back from the material in order to fully analyze and develop its dramatic potential. If you choose something too emotionally raw, you may find yourself unable to finish the film.

use it? How will the people involved in the real-life inspiration for this story feel when they see a part of their lives in my movie?

There's a difference between being inspired by events and writing a story that is clearly based on specific events. When the story is a retelling of facts, it may be necessary to obtain legal permission. This is especially true of news stories and biographies of people's lives. You can't just retell them in film without express permission.

However, there are grayer areas when dealing with your own experiences or observations. There are certain situations I have witnessed or experienced over the years that would make very interesting films, but I wouldn't feel right using them unless I asked the other people involved if it were all right. Each filmmaker has to figure out where that line is for him- or herself. Being a thief in this regard requires a certain degree of integrity and ethics. If you're going to be a thief, be a good thief.

## The Least You Need to Know

♦ Making films about situations and characters you have some familiarity with helps to ensure that your independent film will feel honest and unique.

♦ Your personal point of view affects how you see the world and tell your stories.

♦ Subject matter is your topic; theme is a one-line position or stance you communicate about that topic; and premise is a one-line summary of the basic plot or conflict.

♦ Good film ideas are cinematic or able to be expressed visually.

♦ When basing your stories on real people and events, there are legal and ethical responsibilities.

# The Greatest Story Ever Told: Story Elements

## In This Chapter

◆ Seven common elements in film stories

◆ The importance of character and conflict in drama

◆ The scene as the basic building block for film drama

◆ The value of outlining your story

You've found a visual idea that you think has the potential to make a good film. But how do you know for sure? And how do you take that idea and make it big enough—interesting enough—to show on a movie screen to an audience?

You start by nurturing and developing that idea, which is now the source of your story. You push, shove, pull, tug, and shape it into something cinematic and dramatic, something that can become a film. This process is one of the most important aspects in the development phase of filmmaking, and you will find it easier if you keep in mind several key elements of any good story.

# Smooth Sailing: The Seven "Cs"

All film stories have certain elements in common. They have characters who face conflict and take action; and that conflict is expressed through various situations that occur in a specific time and place. Let's look at each of these seven elements a little more closely.

## Character

Characters are the "people" in our films who make the story come alive. In fiction, they're not really people, of course, but a collection of behaviors and characteristics that we recognize and perceive as being humanlike. We learn about characters based on their appearance, actions, reactions, interactions, and dialogue (what they say). In addition, we come to understand characters by the reactions around them—how other characters respond to them and what other characters say about them.

Primary characters are usually those on the screen the most. They are the key "people" at the center of your film, whether fiction or nonfiction. These characters are the ones we as an audience are going to either love or hate, agree with or disagree with, root for or root against. Those we empathize with and love are often referred to as protagonists; the characters who get in their way and serve as opposition to what the protagonists want are usually call antagonists.

Secondary characters are those who interact with the primary characters and help keep the story moving. They are important to the audience mainly because of their importance to the primary characters or the theme of the story.

In general, we expect characters to behave like real people who we might meet or know, to have an underlying psychology and coherence. We are more likely to attach to and care about a character who seems to be more like us, a person who has many facets. And if we believe the characters, we'll accept outlandish situations and scenarios. My colleague Sue Mroz once noted that an audience will go anywhere, as long as there are humans there. In *Aliens* we can accept the science fiction setting of space ships and other worlds because, at its core, the film presents us with a character with whom we can identify and understand.

Characters don't even have to be human, they merely need to exhibit human qualities for us to empathize and engage with them. We often look for human traits in other species, and this inclination is another tool that a filmmaker can use. That's why we can have a film that has animals or fish as its main characters (such as *Watership Down* or *Finding Nemo*)—because they act human even if they don't look human.

**Staying in Focus** _____

You may find it helpful to create character biographies for your primary characters. A biography might include a summary of the character's physical traits and demographics (age, gender, race, ailments, abilities, appearance), psychological attributes (mood, intellect, values, beliefs, fears, anxieties), and interactions with others (relationships, roles in society, ability to communicate and relate with others). These characteristics are not arbitrary, though; they should in some way be pertinent to the conflict and story.

There are some stories that eschew the idea of fully developed character psychology or dimensionality. Fairy tales and myths rarely create dimensional characters. And sometimes films, like *Lawn Dogs* for example, reserve the dimensionality for the primary characters and make the secondary characters more flat, one-dimensional, and one-note for narrative or stylistic reasons. Ultimately, your choice of characters and how you tailor them has a lot to do with the type of story you want to tell.

# Conflict

The term conflict is used in filmmaking to describe the core element of drama: a protagonist who desperately desires to achieve or obtain something and the obstacles or elements that oppose the protagonist's desires and therefore make this achievement or acquisition difficult. Drama = want + obstacle.

Think of it this way: You have a crush on someone. You know they like you. You want to ask them out, and so you do the first chance you get. And they say yes! Good for you, but there's no drama because there is no conflict.

Conflict and drama could occur at any point in this scenario if … You have a crush on someone, but you're not sure if they like you. Or you suspect that they don't. You want to ask them out, but you're too afraid. You want to ask them out, but you keep blowing every opportunity because of your fear or hesitancy. You ask them out, and they say no. Or there are other complications, such as your crush likes someone else. Or is dating someone else. Or has parents that won't allow dating. Or has parents who hate you.

These are all examples of conflict, because they are obstacles to what you want. If your conflict is internal, such as your fear that is keeping you down, then a filmmaker has to find a story or a situation that will allow that inner struggle to be externalized so that it can be recorded on film and an audience can see and understand.

Your main character could be in a number of different possible conflicts, though most film stories only use one or two at most. These conflicts could be against one's self (*Raging Bull*), another human (*Collateral*), nature (*Jaws*), the supernatural (*The Exorcist*), society (*1984*), or machine (the *Terminator* series).

The character's desire and the opposition need to be nearly equal so that the struggle is difficult. Conflict and drama occur when the character's sense of health, life, or welfare is threatened and they have to fight back. If there are easy solutions, there's no drama.

## Conduct

In facing conflict, the character has to take action, conducting himself in clear and observable ways. On the screen, we can only see what people do, and if what they do is motivated or psychologically understandable to an audience, the audience can infer what the character is thinking and feeling. In film, this is generally considered more effective and engaging for an audience than having a voice-over narrator or a character in direct dialogue tell us what the character is thinking or feeling.

> **Reel Trouble**
>
> Although some films, like *Amelie*, use voice-over narration in ways that don't simplify the story but rather make it more interesting and complex, there is a temptation for beginning filmmakers to rely on voice-over narration to fill in gaps of inexplicable or absent behavior on the screen. If you have to tell me the story rather than show me the story, your idea isn't ready to be a film.

The same goes for dialogue. There's nothing worse than dialogue that tells you the story or exactly what the character is thinking. Dialogue is not there for you to tell the story, it's one more example of how humans behave. Dialogue is behavior.

Many of us in real life find it difficult to talk about what's really going on inside us. We usually find other ways to reveal how we're feeling. What is often most interesting about human beings is the ways in which our words, body language, and actions can contradict each other. Someone who says exactly what they're thinking and acts on it with no ambivalence is pretty rare in the human race. People are generally more complex than that, and we expect film characters to be similar.

My colleague Chris Swider once told me that drama is when a character has overwhelming emotions but is unable to express them verbally. They want to say them, but for whatever reason, they can't. These overwhelming emotions then spill out into behavior. Once the person is able to vocalize what's going on inside, the drama is over.

Part of the drama in film is that characters are struggling to figure out how they really feel, and once they figure it out, how to reveal it. This struggle in film needs to show up in visible behavior and action.

> ### Staying in Focus
>
> Beginning filmmakers often create passive characters who observe more than they act—writers, photographers, artists. Unless your story's conflict is about one overcoming his passivity, create active characters who do things. Audiences tend to like best the characters who are most active or most dynamic. This may help explain why the Joker, Penguin, and Catwoman stole the show from the brooding reactive *Batman*. Even *Silence of the Lambs* ultimately generated more fans of Hannibal than Clarice.

Films pay close attention to what people do, not just what they say. There's a common maxim in film that says you should be able to turn off the sound and still understand what's happening. Though you might miss some very clever dialogue, this belief simply emphasizes how important it is in filmmaking to reveal behavior.

# Conditions

The conditions of your story are your setting with its corresponding scenery, location, time of day, and era. At first you may think these are arbitrary decisions, but in the best films, the conditions are integrally linked to the story's themes and situations.

For example, horror films are usually much more frightening if the story is set mostly at night, because this allows for shadows that can hide monsters or evil. You can't see what might be standing right next to you.

Likewise, the location is an important consideration. Whether your story takes place in an isolated rural community, a sprawling land of strip malls, an urban wasteland, or a gentrified neighborhood will have a huge impact on how we perceive the characters and their conflict. Each of these locations evokes certain assumptions, and as a filmmaker, you can use these assumptions to make your film more effective by finding the location that makes the struggle harder for the main character.

Finally, era is whether your film takes place in the present, past, or future. Right now, you're thinking about the ideal setting for your story. Sure, at some point you'll need to address practical considerations, because anything not set in the present involves more money for the production design's props, costumes, and sets. But at this stage, you want to give your film idea breathing room, to not limit it too quickly, until you can fully see what it is.

# Context

The conflict means nothing if it's not placed in a context that will make it come alive. For example, being really thirsty is a different issue depending upon whether I'm sitting in my living room or stranded in the desert. In selecting your context, you are looking for those situations that heighten the conflict and more fully define the characters by revealing their desires and obstacles. Finding the right context will make the film more engaging and dramatically powerful.

Effective storytelling has more to do with what you leave out than what you put in. You don't have to show everything; in fact, if you did, you'd probably bore everyone to tears. The trick is to show just enough that the audience can figure out the missing parts and understand the story. Good film stories imply more than they show.

Let's say I want to make a film about your life. Your life is the content of the film, and I've got to find a way to get everything that's happened to you over the years squeezed into two hours or less. The way to decide what to leave out is to figure out a throughline or thread that makes sense out of your life. Of course, there are hundreds if not thousands of possible threads, but I have to decide on one. What do I think your life is about? What does it demonstrate or reveal about being human? Once I figure that out, I have a general theme or context around which to build the film. Any situation that doesn't fit that theme or further develop it, I'm going to leave out. Sure, your life is much more complex than that one theme, as is any story. But I only have so much time, so I have to figure out how to say something about your life in the time I have.

There are several commonly used or stock situations I may want to consider as well. Assuming a primary conflict other than love, most feature-length narratives include a heterosexual romance for the main character. This subplot allows the audience to see another facet to the protagonist, and in many film stories, the romance storyline will intersect at some point with the main conflict. *Seven* creates one of the more disturbing intersections, but films like *Last Night* or *8 Mile* are examples of these two types of plot lines crossing paths as well. These subplots can provide a counterpoint or an echo of the main plot line, and there is usually some level of tension or conflict in both. Often times, the resolution of one helps resolve the other plot line.

Another common element of film stories is that there is usually some reason why they have to happen now, some pressure on the events to keep them moving and often accelerating. Some writers refer to this as the "ticking bomb" or "deadline." If your protagonist can take several years to solve his dilemma, well, if he is anything like you or me, he will. But in films, things have to move quickly. So the question is not whether the struggles or obstacles will be overcome, but will they be overcome in time? *DOA* is the ultimate example of how a deadline creates pressure on the protagonist and tension for the audience—the main character will die in several hours unless he can figure out who poisoned him and why and get the antidote. *Speed*'s deadline is set by the time it will take for the bus's fuel tank to run out of gas.

## Crutch

Just as we do not exist in a vacuum, to seem real, characters need to interact with the environments around them. Take a moment and think about how many objects are on your body right now—what's in your pockets? On your fingers, wrists, toes, ankles? What's around your neck? What are you holding? Now look around you; how many objects are within arm's reach? What objects are in the same room as you?

Which of these objects are more important than the others? Why are they more important? A key in your pocket may be important because it's how you get into your house or your office or your car. Or it may be a key to someplace you lived long ago and have never been able to throw away because it reminds you of that place.

We are surrounded by objects all the time; we often ignore the ones that aren't personally relevant or important at the particular moment, but we are rarely far from some object that has meaning for us.

So it is with your characters. Think about what objects or crutches might be important to them. How can those objects become a part of the story or reveal more about the character's inner world? How do these objects link the character to the external world around them?

| Ditty Bag |
| --- |
| Working with objects can be an effective tool for revealing more about your character, how they feel, and the world in which they live. In *Citizen Kane*, the story actually starts and ends with reference to an extremely important object: Rosebud. In fact, the film is structured around the mystery of what Rosebud is. |

## Configuration

There are several ways we can think about or describe a story's configuration, or structure. High or low concept. Three act structure. Plot. Stories can be told as a series of events in chronological order or they can reveal different moments based on association rather than chronology. They can exhibit a tight logic of cause and effect or be episodic. They can move forward like an arrow in flight or come full circle.

The story is all the raw material having to do with the characters, their actions, the conflict, and the situations that we have decided are important to show the audience— it is what we want to say. The plot is how we say it—how we configure, organize, sequence, and edit that raw material so that it has the most dramatic impact.

The stories you want to tell are almost always going to be bigger and messier than the films that come from them. That's part of being a filmmaker. You're pruning a tree, cutting away anything that doesn't contribute to the shape you're creating.

## Beginning, Middle, and End

All films have a beginning, middle, and end. Deciding what these are depends upon which strategy you use for organizing your story into a structure. For example, one approach is to build the material around a central question. In *Sleeping with the Enemy*, the central question is whether Laura will escape her abusive husband. The story is then configured around scenes that pose that question or seem to answer it, alternating "yes she will" and "no she won't" until there is a final climax, a point where the question is asked one last time and answered decisively: yes she will, because she's killed him. Any scene that does not either imply, ask, or answer the question would be cut.

Films can also be built around a central theme or truth, finding situations and interactions that will metaphorically illustrate that theme, such as *Pleasantville*. This kind of film might begin when the thematic material is first introduced or implied in a scene and end when the theme has become unmistakably illustrated. Or films can be built around specific events, like *Home for the Holidays*, beginning and ending with the time frame of the actual event.

Another way of thinking about where to start the film is to consider when the main conflict is set into motion. When do things start going wrong for the protagonist? When does the world become endangered? In these story structures, the film would end when your character's conflict is resolved once and for all or when things start going better for your protagonist or when the world is clearly out of danger or has been destroyed.

One of the key issues for structure is the sequence in which you show the scenes. Some stories are most effective when told in chronological order. Others may be more powerful if certain information is withheld from the audience until it will have the most dramatic impact. *Sophie's Choice* is organized out of chronology in order to delay the exposition of her choice until near the end of the film—even though she made the choice very early in her story.

## High Concept and Low Concept

In the broadest sense, we can talk about film narratives as falling into one of two general configurations: character driven or plot driven. All narrative films have plots (or structures) and characters, but many films tip the balance more toward one or the other.

Character-driven films are sometimes referred to as "low concept," and the story's events grow out of the unique traits of the character. We watch the repercussions of the decisions the character makes, and character-driven films often include some sort of recognition on the part of the protagonist. This might be seeing who he really is or gaining a better understanding of the situation in which he finds himself. Most importantly, this recognition usually provides the character with an opportunity to change, whether she takes that opportunity or not. *Garden State* is a character-driven film, but so is *My Best Friend's Wedding*, where Julianne has to realize the error of her ways and try to set her personal world right again.

Genre films are an example of plot-driven films, where the plot or situation is more important and enticing than the individual characters. Sometimes referred to as "high concept," these are film ideas that can often be described in terms of the action. For example, "terrorists hijack the President's plane." *Air Force One* is not about a president taking stock of his life and becoming a better person (which might be how a character-driven film would develop); it's about a situation that requires action. The pleasure in watching comes from the excitement of that action.

Genres are simply specific narrative configurations that have become standardized. For example, the detective genre usually starts with the arrival of the protagonist at the crime scene, and it's only through the course of the story that eventually the protagonist meets the antagonist and finally figures out that the antagonist is responsible for the crime.

But this kind of structure wouldn't work for a romantic comedy, which generally requires that the two main characters meet early on, are clearly fated to be together but either are unable to recognize that fact or are confronted with a series of obstacles that keep them apart until the end. Structurally, comedies tell their stories differently than dramas.

## Dramatic Arc

Most narrative films—and many documentaries—follow a dramatic curve or arc that incorporates exposition, rising action, climax, falling action, and resolution:

◆ *Exposition* usually refers to information you present at the very beginning so that the audience can get to know the character and story world before disaster—or drama—strikes. A common mistake is to believe that exposition needs to be all laid out at the beginning. Truthfully, the entire film is exposition—it exposes the characters and situation, creating a sense of discovery for the audience. So rather than start your film with exposition, dive right into the story. Among screenwriters there's the notion that the first ten pages have to reveal the main character, the main conflict, and a general sense of the story. In fact, if you submit a script to Sundance, for example, they ask for only the first five pages initially.

◆ *Rising action* simply means that as your protagonist surmounts one obstacle, another one takes its place, and each successive obstacle requires more determination or is harder to get around.

◆ The *climax* is the point where the protagonist engages the conflict in one last confrontation, usually with a conclusive success or failure.

◆ *Falling action* contains the immediate effects of the climax's outcome.

◆ The *resolution* is the long-term effects, usually only hinted at in the film. In the resolution, the protagonist's situation can be better than it was at the start of the film, worse, or about the same.

Most narrative film structures are a series of causes and effects, sometimes called a "causal chain." One thing leads to another. Every action has a reaction (to paraphrase Newtonian physics). This becomes a chain because each effect causes something else. And so on and so on. Another way of thinking about cause and effect is that every cause's effect is the cause of something else, so every link in the chain is both a cause and an effect.

Traditional film narratives are often highly moralistic—the characters are responsible for their own fates. For example, conflicts and obstacles get worse for the main character the more she or he is out of touch with a true understanding of self or the world around them.

As you consider the structure of your own film, ask yourself if it presents as a straight line or as a circle or as a spiral. *In America* begins with the narrator telling us she has three wishes and ends when the third one has been granted. *The House of Sand and Fog* begins and ends with the same scene, the bulk of the film an extended flashback told in chronological order. *Tarnation* begins with Jon finding out his mother has had a lithium overdose, and then we flash back to his life story until about two thirds of the way through where we catch back up to the lithium overdose, the final act moving forward in time. As you watch films, see if you can identify other types of structures as well.

# Making a Scene

While shots may be the visual building blocks for film, *scenes* are the fundamental building blocks of filmic storytelling. Scenes are units of dramatic action, a series of cause-and-effect actions or interactions that take place in one continuous space and time.

If your action moves to another space, then it's usually considered to be a new scene. Likewise, if there's been a gap or jump in time, you have a new scene even if your characters remain in the same space.

Scenes are single moments in time where either …

+ New aspects of the conflict are revealed.

+ The protagonist takes action against the conflict.

+ New obstacles are developed.

+ Important information is revealed to help the audience better understand the circumstances of the conflict or the characters' motivations.

**Defining Moments** _____

A **scene** is a small segment of a film's story, usually containing an event, moment, or interaction that helps to move the story forward. Though individual scenes may vary, the average duration for a single scene is about three minutes or three script pages.

Like the entire film, scenes have a structure and require the same considerations of the larger story: where the scene starts, where it ends, and how the drama progresses. Scenes are different from sequences and montages, which may show a series of activities that occur in different times and spaces to advance the story in a fairly rapid manner. Sequences and montages tend to show us only actions and events. Scenes show us the underlying emotional currents of a particular moment. Scenes are about more than the behavior and action we can see; they are about the emotional toll behind them.

# Keeping in Step: Story Outlines

Some filmmakers like to figure out their story while actually writing script pages, while others like to plan out the entire story as much as possible before they begin writing. There are a number of ways to do this, including some of the approaches we'll be discussing in Chapter 7. One approach is to create a scene outline; another is to create a step outline.

A scene outline generally creates one paragraph for every scene you envision in the final film. These are written in third person, present tense, and briefly describe what we could expect to see in that particular scene. Outlines usually do not include specific dialogue unless the phrasing is critical to the story or character. A step outline uses brief paragraphs or statements to summarize the major action of the story. Some of these actions might take place over several scenes, so this type of outline is less concerned about what might happen in an individual scene and instead emphasizes the general arc of the story. Either of these techniques can help you see your story in a manageable scale—in just a few pages—and can help you analyze whether the story makes sense in terms of cause and effect.

## The Least You Need to Know

♦ All dramatic film stories have certain elements in common, such as character and conflict.

♦ Most narrative films follow a dramatic arc of exposition, rising action, climax, falling action, and resolution.

♦ Scenes are the basic unit or building block for revealing this drama.

♦ Scene or step outlines can help you see the overall shape of your story.

# Chapter 6

# Something to Talk About: Communicating Your Story

## In This Chapter

- ◆ Two common script formats: master scene and split script
- ◆ Why loglines are important
- ◆ Sending out query letters to gauge interest
- ◆ How to successfully pitch your idea

By writing our film concept out in a several different ways—as a source story in Chapter 4 and as a story outline in Chapter 5—we have developed our initial idea into a viable story that we can share with others to solicit their help. The most common way to show this story to actors, potential crewmembers, and colleagues is as a script.

Getting people to read the script often depends on your ability to communicate both in writing and verbally. This chapter will provide some tips that will help you in both.

# Pen to Page: Script

There are a variety of formats for scriptwriting, but all of them have several elements in common. *Scripts* are always written in third person, present tense, and in terms of observable externalized behavior.

Because scripts are treated as blueprints for a film rather than literary works in and of themselves, they are continually being revised and reconsidered. Scripts are a sketch of what the final film will look like, not the film itself. Scripts are like diagrams to help everyone working on the film see the overall design.

As such, script formats have become standardized over the years to help make film-making more efficient and economical. As long as you're familiar with the specific format, any and all scripts in that format are quick and easy to read, allowing you to get to the issues you need to consider for making the film.

**Defining Moments**

A **script** is a scene-by-scene or shot-by-shot description of the dramatic action of your story; the script is like a blueprint in that it is not a finished piece of work in itself but rather the design that your crew and cast will use to build your finished film.

To this end, scripts are formatted to have lots of white space. Descriptions and dialogue are short and spaced on the page in such a way that the page looks more white (lots of space) than black (lots of text). The goal is to evoke the action in a handful of words, not to describe it in painstaking detail. A bonus is that lots of white space allows room for handwritten notes in the margins.

Scripts are written for your crew and actors, not your audience. Therefore, scripts need to be as clear as possible about what is happening in the story. This means that you have to give information in your script that your audience might not yet know if they were watching the finished film, such as a character's name or the fact that the scene is a dream sequence. These need to be clearly and consistently identified in your script. You wouldn't expect a carpenter to build your house based on a blueprint in which you've hidden certain design details because you want to surprise your guests when they walk in. Your house might fall down. The same goes for scripts and films.

I'm going to consider two specific script formats commonly used by independent film-makers. Shorter films that are made up of only one or two scenes might be formatted as a split script where more attention is placed on the individual shots. For longer films with sync dialogue (where actors' dialogue is synchronized with the image), the story is laid out in what is called master scene format. The primary purpose of the master scene script is to present the story scene by scene. Both of these formats differ from a shooting script, which we'll talk about in Chapter 10.

# Master Scene Format

Master scene format is a very specific and standardized method for presenting your script to others. Scripts that deviate from this method are generally perceived, rightly or wrongly, as unprofessional. Therefore, it's important to take the time to do it right.

If you've never written a script before, formatting can seem complicated and mysterious, but it's actually quite simple. The basics for setting up a page in master scene format include:

♦ 12 point Courier font

♦ Left margin at $1\frac{1}{2}$ inches from the paper's left edge

♦ Right margin set at 1inch from the right

♦ Top margin starts 1 inch from the top of the page

♦ Bottom margin varies from page to page but is usually no less than $\frac{1}{2}$ inch and no more than $1\frac{1}{2}$ inches

♦ Page numbers occur about $\frac{1}{2}$ inch from the top and about $1\frac{1}{2}$ inches from the right edge of the page

♦ The first page is not numbered, so the first numbered page in your script is page 2

> **Staying in Focus**
>
> Screenplay formatting software, such as Final Draft, can make formatting your script easy; you can also set up templates in word processing software programs such as WordPerfect, Microsoft Word, or AppleWorks to automatically set your margins and indents.

Page one of your script starts with the title centered in ALL CAPS and in quotation marks. Double-space, and from the left-hand margin, you write "Fade In" followed by a colon. You're now ready to tell your story on paper.

The rest of your master scene script is comprised of six basic elements used over and over. You'll only use the first four with any regularity. These six elements are:

1. Scene heading (a.k.a. slug line)

2. Scene description (a.k.a. action block, body copy, or direction)

3. Character

4. Dialogue

5. Parentheticals

6. Transitions

The master scene script presents each scene in the order that you intend for us to see them on the screen once the film is made. Each new scene is designated by a scene heading or slug line that tells the reader where the scene takes place, whether it's inside (INT. for interior) or outside (EXT. for exterior), the location where the action occurs, and the general time of day. Scene headings are never numbered in master scene format and begin at the left margin in ALL CAPS.

If we were going to write a scene of me sitting in my office writing this book, our scene heading might look like this:

```
INT. JOE'S OFFICE—NIGHT
```

Then there's a double space and what follows is a brief single-spaced description of environment and action. Maybe something like:

```
Joe sits in the dark, illuminated only by the glow of his
laptop. Each word he types is punctuated by the clicking
of fingers on keys.
```

This short paragraph, which also begins at the left margin, is our scene description. The goal in writing scene descriptions is to evoke the space and actions with an economy of words. In almost all cases, a scene heading should be followed by a scene description.

> **Reel Trouble**
>
> Writing dense paragraphs of description makes your script look more like a novel than the blueprint for a film. If the text on the page is long and dense, people are less likely to read your script. Write your scene description in a few short paragraphs. Tell us only what is essential.

If this is the first time the character of "Joe" appears in the script's body copy, the name should be in ALL CAPS and then after that simply capitalized as normal.

Let's say then that I start talking to myself while I'm typing. We're going to create a dialogue block. To do that, first we tab in to 3½ inches from the left edge of the paper and type my name in ALL CAPS. Then underneath that designation are the words I speak, set at 2½ inches from the left edge of the page and ending or continuing to a next line at 5½ inches from the left edge.

```
                JOE
     I need to tell them about
     dialogue.
```

When all of these elements are combined, we have the beginnings of a master scene script. Extending the scene a bit more, we might end up with something that looks like:

```
                    "TITLE OF SCRIPT"

FADE IN:

INT. JOE'S OFFICE—NIGHT

Joe sits in the dark, illuminated only by the glow of his
laptop. Each word he types is punctuated by the clicking
of fingers on keys.

                         JOE
             I need to tell them about
             dialogue.

Snapping the desk light off, Joe stands and stretches.
```

Though usually frowned upon, there is a seldom-used element called parentheticals, which can be inserted between the character name and the dialogue. For example, in our scene at my desk, if there were other people present and we wanted to clarify that I am speaking to myself, we might use a parenthetical like (to himself). Parentheticals would start at 3 inches from the left edge of the page and extend no farther than $5^1/_2$ inches from the left edge. Parentheticals should not extend to a second line. But it's better not to use them because you are doing the director's job.

There was a time when the end of the scene was designated by a transition cue, like "cut to" or "fade out" or "dissolve," but nowadays most scripts do not use transitions because the next scene heading is all we need to realize that one scene has ended and another has begun. Often times there will be a triple space between the last line of one scene and the scene heading of the next.

In general, assume that scene headings should never be the last thing on a page, nor should the character name be separated from the corresponding dialogue because of a page break. This is why in the basic page setup earlier I noted that your bottom margin can fluctuate by as much as an inch. People often assume that one script page is equal to one minute of screen time, but this can be misleading. For example, Joe's action block shown previously could be as short as two seconds on the screen or as long as ten minutes. The same is true for a script page. It takes a very precise writing style to average a page per minute. Because of this, the idea that a feature-length script should be 120 pages is no longer standard practice, and many feature-length scripts these days are closer to 95 to 105 pages.

Once you've finished writing the script, all you need in order to look like a professional is a title page that has the name of the script, your name, and your contact info. Something like this:

```
                        BORDERS
                          By
                    Josef Steiff
```

```
Josef Steiff
Address
Phone Number
E-mail Address
```

If you're feeling overwhelmed by all of this formatting, don't worry, software programs such as Final Draft can do it for you. That way you can devote all your attention to story. Because as you might guess, once you've finished your script, you'll probably rewrite it several times before showing it to others. During this process, you may find yourself going back to some of the questions and elements discussed in Chapters 4 and 5 as a way to rethink and refine your story. The goal is to make your script as good as it can be. The general assumption is that the better your script, the better your chances of making a good film.

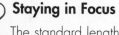

**Staying in Focus**

The standard length of a dramatic scene in a master scene script averages about three pages. If you find that your script's scenes are substantially longer, you may want to read them carefully to see if they are slowing down the pace of your story.

## Split Script

A *split script* divides the page into two columns. Down the left-hand column is a brief description of each individual shot or image; the right-hand column describes the sounds that will accompany each particular shot. This format is particularly useful when making short films that are only one or two scenes long or for making documentaries when you might use a lot of images to illustrate what a narrator is telling us. Whereas a master scene script presents the entire scene with no reference to individual shots, the split script is in effect an outline of shots in the order we would see them in the edited film.

In reading a split script, you scan from left to right across both columns so that you can see what sounds will accompany the image before you move on to the next shot. Each shot is labeled by the size or scale of the image subject:

- ◆ ECU: Extreme close-up
- ◆ CU: Close-up
- ◆ MCU: Medium close-up
- ◆ MS: Medium shot
- ◆ MLS: Medium long shot
- ◆ LS: Long shot
- ◆ ELS: Extreme long shot or wide shot

**Defining Moments**

A **split script** divides the page into two columns, the left one a sequential list of each shot. The corresponding sounds are listed in the right-hand column approximately where they would occur in relationship to the image.

We'll talk about the exact definition of each of these in Chapter 10. For now, the most important thing to remember when writing a split script is to keep the sounds in the right-hand column linked or in sync with their corresponding images in the left.

As you can see in the following example of a split script, dialogue is written as it will be spoken and indicated by the name of the character speaking in ALL CAPS. Sound effects are abbreviated as SFX, and music is noted in ALL CAPS. If you're sure of your order of shots, it's okay to number them in your split script.

---

"BORDERS"
© 1988
Josef Steiff
Address
Phone Number
E-mail Address


| | |
|---|---|
| 1. ECU of ANDY's fingers grazing along faded and peeling wallpaper. | SFX: breathing, scratchy sound of fingertips against wall; scuffling and crunching of stepping on debris. |
| 2. LS of Andy silhouetted against spots of sunlight coming through boarded-up windows. Andy stops to bend down. | SFX: continues MUSIC: pop music drifts in from some previous era, as if from an AM radio not quite tuned in. |
| 3. CU of Andy's hand brushes away powdery debris from what appears to be a broken toy. His hand jerks up and out of frame. | SFX: continues; brushing sound |
| 4. MCU of Andy standing upright, head cocked as if listening. After a moment's hesitation, he rushes into the hallway. | ANDY: Who's there? SFX: footsteps |

---

# Thumbnail Sketch: Logline

Once you have your script—or a version that you're happy with—you're ready to begin thinking about pre-production. At this point, you may want other people to read your script to see if they will help you make your film. Persuading someone to read your script can be done several ways. But the starting point is to have a *logline*.

A logline serves as a thumbnail sketch of your film's essential conflict and scenario, so that you can communicate a concise summary of your story. In many ways, a logline is like your premise. It should be a single sentence that presents the main character and central conflict and even perhaps a hint of the outcome.

**Defining Moments**

A **logline** is a one-sentence summary of the story's main conflict. It is not a statement of theme but rather a premise.

Examples of loglines are as close to you as your TV listings; oftentimes these listings summarize the essential storyline into one or two sentences that are usually fewer than 25 words. A logline for *The Wizard of Oz* might be "An unhappy farm girl who doesn't appreciate what she has is swept away to a dreamlike land only to discover that there's no place like home."

Just as you do in all other forms of film writing, you will probably need to rewrite your logline several times before you feel it's accurate. No two people will come up with exactly the same logline for any one project; the only "right" logline is the one that you feel best represents the story.

Once you have your logline, you can use it in query letters, which I'll discuss next, or when talking with people directly about your film idea. Loglines are a way in which people who have heard about your project can remember it, a kind of handle that will jog their memory.

# Query Letters

If you identify someone you think might be helpful for your production, you might write to ask her if she would be interested in reading your script or meeting with you to discuss the film. Though many people communicate by e-mail these days, unless you know for a fact that the person prefers e-mail queries, it's best to use the old-fashioned United States Post Office for this kind of letter. You're trying to put your best foot forward.

Query letters should be less than one page long with several short paragraphs, the first of which clearly states why you are writing (is it for permission to send your script or do you want to meet in person?), the second summarizing your script or film in a brief statement, and a third paragraph asking the person if you could send the script or arrange a meeting. The letter should be typed and professional looking; as with all materials that represent you or your film, be sure that it is grammatically correct with no misspellings.

Whether the result of a query letter or simply a spontaneous conversation in an elevator, another way to get people interested in helping you is to verbally tell them enough about the story that they'll want to read the script.

# Pitching Your Idea

Whenever you present your idea verbally to someone else, you are doing what we call a *pitch*. A common assumption is that pitching is done in Hollywood by screenwriters who are trying to get development executives or producers interested in their script or to get agents interested in representing them as a writer. But in fact, whether in Hollywood or independent filmmaking, pitching happens at all levels of a project. A filmmaker pitches to get money, pitches to get cast, pitches to get distributors.

There are many opinions and no surefire way to do a good pitch. Some notions of pitching have almost become cliché, such as the idea of hybrids—saying things like "it's a cross between *Terms of Endearment* and *Van Helsing*." What does that even mean? While comparisons of your story to other films may be inevitable at certain points, most people will become interested in your particular story as an independent filmmaker because of your point of view, characters, and dramatic situations, not because your movie is like someone else's. Pitching, then, is simply trying to make a connection with another person and to share with them something you love: *your* film.

**Defining Moments**

**Pitching** is the act of presenting your story verbally to others; this can be called "pitching your idea" or "making a pitch." The story itself, including the way in which you relay it, is called the **pitch**.

If there's a golden rule in pitching, it's "leave them wanting more." You're not trying to tell the whole story, just enough so that the other person will take the next step. What that next step is depends on what you want: Do you want him to read the script because you think he might invest or do you want her to watch the film because you want her to distribute it?

In some cases, you may want to state at the very beginning of your pitch the title of your project and the type of genre. I usually only do this in a "cold" pitch where the other person has no idea who I am or what my story is about. If you're pitching to someone whom you've queried by letter or already had some contact with, this info may be redundant. Also, there are times when I feel my pitch is more intriguing if I just dive right in.

**Staying in Focus**

Once they say "yes," stop pitching; you've accomplished what you set out to do. If they say "no," be gracious. You never know when your paths might cross again, and the next time they might be able to help you.

Start strong. Open your pitch with a compelling first sentence, perhaps your logline, followed by a general sense of how the conflict will escalate and the story will progress toward the climax. Bring your pitch to a close with a strong concluding statement that gives some sense of the resolution. Fight the temptation to keep talking after you've delivered the final sentence. Don't trail off; don't ramble. Just stop talking. If it helps, sit back or break eye contact or change your body position as a nonverbal indicator that the pitch is over.

Be prepared with at least three different pitches for any one film: a one-minute, a three-minute, and a ten-minute pitch. You'll rarely give the ten-minute pitch verbatim; its primary purpose is for you to have a more in-depth way of talking about your project in case someone wants to know more about the story. Always start with the one-minute. They'll let you know if they want to hear more.

If pitching has a second golden rule, it's "don't waste time"—yours or the other person's. Pitch to the right people. If you've made a horror film that you're pitching to a distributor, be sure that that distributor is interested in that particular genre. This is another prime example of how important it is to know your audience. Just as your film is more focused and effective if you know your goals and audience, your pitch will be better if you have a clear idea of what you're trying to accomplish and who you're pitching to. And practice your pitch. Know your story.

The best pitches convince the other person not just that you have a great story but that you are the right person to tell it. Never underestimate the power of your own belief in and enthusiasm for your film. Pete Jones won the first *Project: Greenlight* because in the wee hours of the morning, when he was called back to explain why he wanted to make his film, as tired as he was, he exuded passion for *Stolen Summer*. His ability to connect to the people in that room helped convince them that he believed in his story and that he was the man to make the film.

If you're not sure where to start in putting together your pitch, you can organize your thoughts by writing a proposal, synopsis, and narrative treatment, which we'll talk about in the next chapter. These have all the elements you can draw from to create a verbal summary of your story. And consistent with your script and other writing, your pitch should tell the film story in third person, present tense.

As I mentioned earlier, pitching occurs at all phases of the filmmaking process. As an independent filmmaker, you'll pitch your idea in order to recruit crewmembers, audition your cast, and raise money—all parts of pre-production. But more importantly, pitching can happen anywhere, anytime. Formal pitches might be arranged by sending a query letter, but a lot of pitching is much more informal. A person sits down next to you on the airplane and asks what you do for a living. When you say you're a filmmaker, they ask what you're working on.

> **Reel Trouble**
>
> While you need to be comfortable delivering your pitch so that you won't stumble, you don't want to sound rehearsed. There's nothing worse than a pitch that sounds like a speech. Rehearse it so you know the content, but pitching is like performing. I don't mean you need to become the characters, I mean that you have to make the pitch seem conversational. Don't get so caught up in reciting your story that you ignore the person in front of you.

This happened to a friend of mine who always has her film pitches ready and rehearsed so well that they sound like casual conversation. Ann walked off that plane with a check toward her production costs. I learned from her to never pass up a chance to pitch your film. You don't want to come off as a high-pressure salesperson or unable to talk about anything else, but part of being a good filmmaker is being able to share your vision with others.

## The Least You Need to Know

- Whether written or spoken, film stories are communicated in third person, present tense, and describe what the characters do.

- Feature-length scripts are usually 95 to 105 pages and written in master scene format.

- Writing a logline can help you concisely communicate your film's story to others.

- Query letters are useful first steps in seeing whether someone might be interested in reading your script or meeting to talk with you about your film.

- Verbally pitching your film idea is one of the most common ways to get other people interested in helping you.

# *The Picture Writer:* Communicating Your Intentions

## In This Chapter

- ◆ Various ways you can present your film concept to others in writing
- ◆ The difference between proposals, treatments, and synopses
- ◆ Identifying your themes and goals
- ◆ Identifying your audience

In the previous chapter, you developed your film idea through an understanding of various storytelling elements and methods, including writing a script. You now need to put your story into a written form appropriate to show other people whom you hope will either serve as your crew or will give you resources, such as money, equipment, or locations. This chapter and the next will discuss several ways of communicating your idea to others. Though presented in a sequential order, these methods do not necessarily need to be completed in any particular succession.

When I first started making films, I found it helpful to do each and every one of the steps described in this chapter and the next. By considering my story in these various forms, I gained a more thorough understanding of my proposed film and had more opportunities to make sure the idea was ready to produce. As I have become more experienced, I find that each film project requires a different combination or sequence of these processes. Even if you don't practice all of the following steps with every project, filmmakers are generally expected to know these various approaches and to be able to present them when requested.

No matter which of the following methods you are using, the most important thing to remember is to always tell your story in present tense and third person. Have you noticed that film reviews usually talk about the film in present tense? When we watch a film, we experience it as if it were happening right now. That's the way you should talk or write about the film as well, as if it were happening right before our eyes.

# You Don't Need a Ring for This Proposal

Grant foundations and investors that fund films often ask for a proposal, which is a brief description of your planned project. The specifics of such a proposal may vary depending upon whom you approach for funding, but there are some basic elements that are usually common to all: what the film is about, who the film is for, and why you're the person to make it.

Some grantors will provide you with a standardized form to complete. If they do, always be sure to use their form. Any time you're provided a form, make a couple of photocopies that you can use to mark up and draft your answers. Store the original someplace where it will remain clean and unwrinkled. After you have all of your answers finished and proofread, copy them over onto the original form. Double- and triple-check the form to make sure you've completed all the questions asked. Pay special attention to any checklist or request for supplemental materials, such as a script, a sample of your previous creative work, or your resumé. If any part of the form is filled out incorrectly or if you forget to provide requested supplemental documentation, you reduce your chances of being funded.

Other grantors do not require you to fill out a form but rather supply you with a list of criteria and a suggested format to follow when making your proposal. Read the criteria carefully, make notes, and then read it again. Once you feel you understand the criteria, write a draft of your proposal. Once that's done, review your entire proposal and make sure you have addressed all of their requests.

**Staying in Focus**

You want to present your film ideas in a professional manner. If in written form, this means you need to carefully proofread your proposal for typos, grammar, and coherence.

Ignoring or not following provided proposal forms and/or criteria can lose you money for your project. These forms and criteria are designed to make grantors' review processes efficient and timely by specifying exactly what information they need to make a decision. They look at many requests, and they're not going to take the time to dig for information through idiosyncratic proposals or track you down to answer a question you missed or remind you to submit a piece of information you forgot.

Some granting foundations will provide a contact person in case you have any questions about their procedures. While you don't want to be a pest, this person can be a great resource. When first reviewing the grant forms or criteria, make a list of any questions you have. Begin filling out the forms and writing your proposal based on their criteria. This process might spark more questions or answer some of the ones you initially identified. Once you feel that you can go no further without clarification or guidance, that is the time to call the contact person.

In addition, some organizations that grant money to filmmakers offer workshops to help applicants understand and complete their applications properly. This is an invaluable resource, and if made available to you, try to take advantage of it.

If you are asked to submit a proposal but have not been given any guidelines or format, you will need to create your own. Proposals work best when they're brief. There are no hard-and-fast rules here in terms of format other than to be consistent. The key is that your proposal should be easy to read, with each part clearly identified.

Here's how I write a proposal when the grantor has provided no form or specific criteria. You may want to refer to the proposal for my film, *Borders*, as an example.

"BORDERS"
© 1988
Josef Steiff
Address
Phone Number
E-mail Address

**Proposal.**

*Prime Theme:*

The inability of any border—geographic or psychological—to contain the effects of war.

*Prime Goal:*

Despite the fact that the Viet Nam War "ended" nearly 15 years ago, many families still feel the aftermath. Veterans have returned to an indifferent or even antagonistic society, no longer the children their parents remember. Families have had to deal with loss, both physical and psychological.

War is devastating enough when a family buries their sons and daughters, but funerals allow people to say "goodbye" and move on. For the families of POW/MIAs, there is no such closure.

*Borders* examines the disintegration of one all-American family when their older son is MIA, and their younger son cannot live up to their expectations.

*Prime Audience:*

People 30 years old and over who remember Viet Nam or are still living it even if no one else realizes it.

Unless it's spacing between paragraphs or headings, I always single space and limit the proposal to one page or less. A proposal is meant to be read easily and quickly.

On separate lines at the top of the page, you should center the title of your film in all capital letters (ALL CAPS) and quotation marks, followed by a copyright notice (copyright symbol and year) and then your name and contact info. Whether you bold the title of the film is a matter of personal preference, but none of the other information in this section should be in bold letters.

Because you may be submitting various documents as part of your request for funding, you need to clearly designate that this particular page is a proposal. After your contact info, triple space and type the word "Proposal" starting at (or justified with) the left margin. Another option is to center it at the very top of the page. Either way, the word should stand out, so you might put it in bold or underline it.

Double space and you're now ready to write the main text of your proposal, which usually addresses three primary areas: theme, goal, and audience.

---

### Ditty Bag

Even if you haven't filed paperwork with the Library of Congress to register your copyright, you should never distribute any information about your film without a copyright notice. In the United States, creative work is considered copyrighted at the moment of expression (written, recorded, etc.) as long as it carries the copyright symbol or the letter "c" followed by a period or the word "copyright" all spelled out and followed by the year you created it. Mailing yourself a copy of your work is NOT copyright protection and will not protect you in a legal dispute—there's no proof that the envelope was sealed when you sent it or that you didn't put your materials into it later.

---

## Theme: What's It All About?

In Chapter 4, I discussed the difference between topic, theme, and premise. As you remember, the *theme* is a central truth or insight your film implies about life or the human experience. Theme is a subtext or underlying meaning that the screenwriter or filmmaker has deliberately chosen and developed within the story.

In order for your theme to be easy to find on the proposal, you must clearly label it "Theme." Or you could note it as your "Prime Theme," which indicates that there may be more than one theme in your film, but this is the one you're primarily working with. To make your theme statement stand out, you might italicize its label or indent it. Again, there's no right way or wrong way to format a proposal—just be consistent.

If you designate your theme as prime, then you need to be consistent throughout the entire proposal and use the word "prime" before your goal and audience statements as well (as shown in my sample proposal).

Theme statements may be as long as a short paragraph, but ideally you should state your theme in a single sentence. Either way, the theme statement serves as a quick summary of the film's focus and therefore comes first in the proposal.

## Goal: Why Say It Now?

Like theme, your goal statement should be clearly identified and brief, in this case no more than three paragraphs. These paragraphs provide an overview of your rationale for developing your identified theme.

You might begin by referring to the specific context of your proposed film's setting and conflict. Depending on the project, you might include personal anecdotal information to demonstrate your familiarity or experience with the subject matter or you might summarize common knowledge or researched factual information that is relevant to the topic. Either way, you are demonstrating that you have something authentic to say.

For *Borders*, I chose to make more general statements about my rationale, but I could have approached this differently by reciting personal memories of my family during the Vietnam War years or citing statistics on how many people were still listed MIA at the time I proposed the film. I could have discussed how I wanted the audience to feel during and after watching my film.

For some documentaries and narratives, I might even want the audience to be motivated to do something; if that's the case, then I want to note it here in my goals. Any information that is important for your reader to know in order to understand why this film needs to be made is fair game—as long as you can say it in three paragraphs or fewer.

You generally want to conclude with a sense of how your particular story and approach will address, work with, or reveal your theme and goals. For *Borders*, I end with a basic plot summary of the film—my premise. This allows me to emphasize in a different way what the film is about, and along with my theme statement, provides a means for someone to remember my story.

If you're not sure how to start writing your goal statement, draw upon the work you did in Chapter 4 where you asked yourself what your film is about, why you want to make it, why it's important to make it now, and how you want people to respond to it.

## Audience: Who's Listening (and Watching)?

Films are meant to be seen. The moment of truth for a filmmaker is when the film is screened in front of an audience of strangers. Yes, you might show your film to your family and friends, but you're not reading this book in order to make a home movie. You want to make an independent film, and that means you want other people to see it. Whom you want to see it is a crucial question. And the last part of your proposal identifies in one or two sentences this ideal audience member.

Beginning filmmakers are often reluctant to identify a specific audience, fearing that they will limit who will come to see their movies. Never fear, humans love to eavesdrop and people-watch. That alone will result in some people wanting to see your movie.

Hollywood films generally have very specific demographic definitions for their ideal audience, which they sometimes call a *target audience* or *intended audience*. The target audience for most Hollywood films is what they refer to as "male adolescents." If you looked at Hollywood's specific demographics of this audience, you'd see that this general term of "male adolescent" designates Caucasian heterosexual males with an age range of early teens to early thirties.

Certainly there are other types of films, sometimes referred to as niche films, that are designed for different audiences, but Hollywood follows the money by making films for the people perceived to be the primary ticket buyers.

Now you may say, hey, I want everyone to see my film. That's a great sentiment. But for argument's sake, let's compare making a film to writing a letter. What happens when you try to write a letter that appeals to everyone? Usually you end up with an impersonal, sanitized,

### Staying in Focus

If you're not sure who your audience is, a good clue is to look at your protagonist—because your protagonist is often whom the audience is supposed to identify or empathize with. Most Hollywood film protagonists are financially well-off, Caucasian, heterosexual, youthful-looking, adult males—idealized versions of Hollywood's ideal audience.

nonoffensive surface summary of events that is safe to send everyone in your family in one mass photocopied mailing.

If I write a letter about my day, I'll use different language and tell about different events depending upon whether I'm writing to my mother, my best friend, or my boss. Knowing who my reader is affects what I write. Likewise, knowing your audience affects what you film. If you try to please everyone, you might end up with a film that pleases no one.

Don't be afraid to be specific. Rather than constraining you, you'll probably find that the more specific you are about your audience, the more focused and powerful your film will be.

Once you've completed your audience statement, your proposal is finished. Now's the time for one last look to make sure the proposal is one page or less, the format is consistent, misspellings have been corrected, the proposal makes sense, and the film's title and your contact info is easy to find.

An added benefit to having a written proposal is that it can serve as a reminder of your original intentions. Because making a film can take weeks or months or years, it's easy to get halfway done and forget why you started the project. Your proposal can refocus you by reminding you of your original theme, goals, and audience.

> **Ditty Bag**
>
> The general distinction between a synopsis and a treatment is that a synopsis is much shorter and less specific. Treatments are more detailed descriptions of the film and are therefore longer. Giving out a synopsis is good when you don't want to reveal a lot of the story's details or when you know that the other person doesn't have time to read a longer summary.

# The Doctor Is In: Synopsis and Treatment

In addition to a proposal, granting foundations often ask filmmakers to include a summary of the film's story, either in the form of a synopsis or a treatment. Synopses and treatments may also be helpful in other situations where you might be asked to show or leave behind a description of your project.

If either a synopsis or treatment is being presented along with your proposal, you should try to keep the same general format for consistency. For example, if you follow my format for your proposal, your synopsis and treatments should begin with the title of your film centered at the top of your page, with a copyright notice and your name and contact info below. Paragraphs should be single-spaced, and any bolded, italicized, and underlined elements should be consistent throughout.

As I noted earlier, films are perceived as happening right before our eyes. Films are unlike novels or short stories because they generally do not tell us what the characters are thinking or how they are feeling. Instead, films show us the behavioral results of those thoughts and emotions. Therefore, both synopses and treatments should be written in third person, present tense and generally in terms of observable behavior or action.

## Synopsis

Like your proposal, a synopsis is usually one page—certainly no more than two pages—and typed in approximately four single-spaced paragraphs with a double space between each.

The first paragraph identifies the protagonist in ALL CAPS and in psychological terms: key personality traits that help explain why the character does what he or she does. This is one of the only times you as a filmmaker will write internal information about your characters for others to read. The goal is to succinctly describe the character in a few precise terms that make him or her vivid in the reader's mind. You may include basic demographic information (age, gender), but any physical information (appearance, physicality) should only be noted if it's important to the narrative or will be part of the story. You might write a brief description of your antagonist as well.

Your next paragraph states the premise, the protagonist's basic desire, and the obstacles or opposition to that desire as discussed in Chapter 5.

The third paragraph summarizes in general terms the development or progression of the conflict toward the climax.

Your final paragraph notes the outcome of the conflict and its resolution.

You can see from this example that a synopsis is a concise overview of the narrative. It does not include dialogue or every single detail, but rather paints the story in broad strokes. Whether your film is to be feature length or short, your synopsis should be no longer than two pages; standard practice is 1 page to $1^1/_2$ pages.

"BORDERS"
© 1988
Josef Steiff
Address
Phone Number
E-mail Address

**Synopsis.**

ANDY, an impressionable 8-year old, actively creates "pretend worlds" and idolizes his big brother, KEVIN, who has been called up for a tour of duty in Viet Nam. Andy's not quite sure what that means, but he knows that his retired military DAD is prouder of Kevin than he's ever been. Though his MOM seems sadder than usual.

Moving back and forth in time between 1968 and 1988, Andy attempts to make sense of his brother's leaving for Viet Nam and never returning.

Upon learning of Kevin's MIA status, the family slowly falls apart, each member finding their own way to cope with the overwhelming loss and not-quite-extinguished hope that he might still come back. As the years pass, both parents withdraw from each other and their remaining son. Mom turns to religion. Dad finds reasons not to come home.

In a desperate attempt to keep the family together, Andy tries to replace the missing oldest and favorite son, Kevin. But with psychologically traumatic results.

## Treatments

There are two types of treatments that you might find helpful as a filmmaker. The first is an expanded version of your synopsis, and the other is a description of basic aesthetic considerations.

When people ask to see your treatment, they are usually referring to a *narrative treatment*, which is in effect an expanded synopsis. As always, the standard format is third person, present tense, observable behavior; but rather than trying to summarize the story in one page as you did in the synopsis, you can now go into more detail.

Depending upon the length of your project and what you find most helpful, your narrative treatment could be as short as 2 pages or as long as 40 or 50. The general trend over the years has been for narrative treatments to get shorter, usually under 10 pages.

If you're making a film that's not strictly a fictional story, say a documentary or experimental film, you might write a structural summary instead of a narrative treatment. This summary serves the same purpose, giving the reader a sense of how your filmic material will be revealed to the audience and in what order.

Unlike a synopsis, the narrative treatment or structural summary should begin with the first image or scene we would see on the screen and conclude with the last image or scene. In between, your treatment should give us a sense of how the film would progress in front of our eyes in a darkened theater. In narrative, this helps us see the entire arc of the story, and your narrative treatment will closely follow the step outline you developed in Chapter 5.

As you write your treatments, you want to evoke the characters, situations, and locations of your story. You're not trying to describe everything, but only enough that we can see it in our head. You're going to rely on us to fill in the details. Likewise, treatments rarely include dialogue, and then only if the piece of dialogue is crucial. Instead you might note the general topic that the characters argue about or discuss. A narrative treatment concentrates on telling us what the characters do, so that we can infer what the characters are thinking or feeling from their behavior and actions.

---

"BORDERS"
© 1988
Josef Steiff
Address
Phone Number
E-mail Address

**Narrative Treatment.**

ANDY, 28 years old, tall and scruffy, drags his fingers along peeling wall-paper. He drifts through the patches of light and dark created by beams of daylight filtering through boarded up windows. As he explores the empty upstairs rooms, unrecognizable fragments of toys crunch beneath his feet, indistinguishable from the fallen plaster and debris.

Andy bends down to look through the floor's grit more closely. He springs up, as if he has heard some unexpected noise, and rushes down the stairs to the dark hallways of the lower floor.

---

You'll notice in the excerpt from my narrative treatment for *Borders* that I do not use any "film language" such as "we see" or "close up on" or "cut to"—my descriptions alone should convey what the viewer will see. One way of making your writing more active and filmic is to use verbs that carry connotations of how something is being done rather than using adverbs. Films are about behavior and action. You might describe a painting in adjectives, but a film idea should primarily be described with nouns and verbs.

Just like you did when writing your script, the first time a character appears in your narrative treatment, his or her name should be typed in ALL CAPS, for example, "ANDY." After that, you simply capitalize the first letter of the name, as in "Andy." This draws attention to the first appearance of each character and can help you quickly tally how many different actors you may need. Some of your characters may be designated by a label rather than a proper name; treat these designations (like "Doctor" or "Taxi Driver") just like a name, putting it in ALL CAPS the first time it appears. Be consistent; each character should only have one designation.

The second type of treatment is sometimes referred to as an *aesthetic treatment*. This is a brief one- or two-page summary of how you envision the finished film in terms of key stylistic and aesthetic elements. These considerations are rooted in aspects of the technical process of making a film, but an aesthetic treatment is not about how you're going to achieve an element technically. It describes how your audience should feel as a result of that element.

An aesthetic treatment is comprised of a series of short paragraphs, each one addressing a different aspect or aesthetic choice. There is no set-in-stone rule as to format or which order you should address these. Your aesthetic treatment may vary from project to project, depending upon whether you're making a narrative, documentary, or experimental film.

Your aesthetic treatment usually begins with a paragraph about the main setting or environment of the film. You're not trying to list every single location, but the general type of environment central to the story. For example, is it a rural setting? Urban? Suburban? Is it present day, past, or future? If past, is it a specific time period? Setting also includes time of year or climate issues if they are a crucial part of the story.

Next you describe the atmosphere of the film. This is the mood or tone you're trying to create with locations you've just described and the situations you've noted in your narrative treatment. To get at this, I might ask myself if I want the film to evoke a sense of dread? Fear? Serenity? Hope? Sadness? Should the film feel light or dark? Dreary or painfully bright? Dreamy or stark? Your audience is going to have an emotional response based on the atmosphere you create. Your atmosphere helps establish a tone or mood in the film and is often determined by your theme.

What follows next in your aesthetic treatment is a summary of each of the individual components that will help create the overall atmosphere and tone of your film.

Your characters section is where you write a one- or two-sentence description of each of the main people we will see on the screen— at the very least, your protagonist and your antagonist. This thumbnail character biography might be similar to the description you used in your synopsis: a concise and precise depiction of narratively relevant psychological, demographic, and physical traits.

**CAUTION**

**Reel Trouble**

In your characters section of the aesthetic treatment, you're not trying to list every single character that will appear, just the most important ones. This probably means at least two characters, but if you find yourself describing more than five, you've got too many.

"BORDERS"
© 1988
Josef Steiff
Address
Phone Number
E-mail Address

### Aesthetic Treatment.

*Setting/Environment:*

An abandoned farmhouse, its rooms and hallways, in the present. The same house alive and well-lived in the past (1968). A small town train station, existing in that same present and past.

*Atmosphere:*

Nostalgia; sorrow; cold and desolate in the present; warm but with a sense of foreboding in the past when the family is still all together.

*Characters:*

ANDY, an impressionable 8-year old who actively creates "pretend worlds" and idolizes his big brother; doesn't understand the emotions and dynamics tearing his family apart.

KEVIN, 18, recently drafted, afraid to go to war but sees it as a way to finally win his father's approval; often seen in leather jacket that Andy will wear as an adult.

MOM would make Jackie Kennedy proud; stiff upper lip that barely hides her sorrow.

DAD, retired military; remote, imposing, but only because he doesn't know how to express his pride or love for his sons.

*Visual Composition:*

Constant reframing through dolly and tracking movements; compositions will be asymmetrical, constantly alluding to off-screen space—the inability of the "border" of the frame to contain the action or the story. This chopping off (or cropping) of the image will sometimes be accomplished by shooting through windows and doorframes as well as by placing actors at the extreme edges of the frames.

Fluid, left to right movements; slow motion, perhaps optically printed to make the figure movements more ghost-like and unreal.

Harsh lighting; the film will be shot in black & white; the nostalgia can be reinforced by tinting the images sepia.

*Aural Composition:*

Sparse. Aural motifs: train, train whistle, fragments of dialogue.

*Transitions:*

Shots linked by graphic or associational qualities; optical printing; long takes with lyrical movement and transitions. Temporal disunity. A slippery shifting back and forth in time.

At some point in the filmmaking process, you will give consideration to everything we will see in the frame, which is sometimes referred to as *mise-en-scene*. In the visual composition section you might write a short paragraph about each of the following to serve as a general guide for how you want to build the film's atmosphere with the visual look:

♦ What is the size or scale of most of your shots? For example, is the film primarily made up of close ups? Or long shots? In the early scenes of *Safe*, Carol is often seen inside her house in extreme long shots, which result in her literally being dwarfed by her surrounding environment. This is consistent with the themes and situations at work in the film—that she is not in control of her environment, and in fact, that her environment may even be oppressive or harmful.

♦ Do the edges of the frame move, either through the use of pans, tilts, zooms, handhelds, or dollys? Or is the frame static and unmoving?

♦ Within the frame, do the characters or figures themselves move? If so, how would you describe that movement? Darting? Lazy? Fluid? Jerky?

♦ Should the lighting be bright with few shadows or dark with many shadows? Should the film be filled with bright colors or should it be monochromatic?

Oftentimes as beginning filmmakers, we only think of sound as dialogue or music. But in fact, sound design is an important part of film, which can contribute to the atmosphere or mood but also allude to actions or events happening offscreen. Should the sound be dreamy or sharp? Naturalistic or surreal? Write a brief description in the aural composition section.

Finally, you may want to think about whether there should be a specific type of transition from scene to scene or even shot to shot. Do you want transitions to be abrupt or slow? Surprising or leisurely? Sum it up in the transitions section.

Each of these aesthetic treatment elements represents choices that will have an impact on the audience. You don't need to address all of them, only the ones that are clearly important for your particular film. These kinds of decisions are often made in collaboration with whomever is lighting and shooting your film or doing the sound design or editing. If you're planning on doing any of these yourself, there are a number of books, such as *Film Art* by David Bordwell and Kristin Thompson (see Appendix B), that can help you better understand how certain visual, aural, and transitional techniques can affect the mood of the audience. If you're feeling a bit lost, think about films you've seen—how did they make you feel? Try to identify the specific elements or techniques the filmmaker used to make you feel that way.

Aesthetic treatments are another tool for you to clarify how you see the movie in your head and to help you share that vision with others. This will be particularly helpful when planning the film with your cinematographer, production designer, sound designer, and editor.

## The Least You Need to Know

◆ When proposing your film to potential investors, you need to be prepared to explain what your film is about and why you want to make it.

◆ A written proposal identifies in one page or less the theme, goal, and ideal audience for your film.

◆ A synopsis summarizes your story in very broad terms.

◆ Your narrative treatment or structural summary describes—in order—what your audience will see on the screen.

# Part 2

# Buddy, Can You Spare a Dime? Pre-Production

You've got an idea. You've written it out. You're ready to start preparing to make your film. This process is called pre-production, and almost all of the work here falls under what is considered "producing."

Pre-production includes financing your film, creating a visual design, and hiring your cast and crew. You'll notice that this section of the book is the longest. There's a reason for that. The more prepared you are before you begin shooting your film, the smoother the next two phases (production and post-production) will go.

Films take a lot of planning. So let's get started!

# Chapter 8

# Take the Money and Run: Paying for Your Film

## In This Chapter

♦ Finding investors to help fund your film

♦ Creative and fun fundraising ideas

♦ Funding through credit cards and loans (beware!)

♦ Funding through grants

♦ Looking into in-kind services

♦ The right way to attract investors

There's no doubt about it: Films are expensive. To make films, you have to either rent or buy equipment plus buy all the necessary materials. Part of the reason a lot of filmmakers start by making short films is because that's all they can comfortably afford, and they hope that once people see what they can do, someone might be willing to help pay for a longer film.

There are a number of ways you can raise money to make your film. We're going to look at some in this chapter. Keep in mind that these are only options, what some filmmakers have considered in the past; you don't have to do any of these if you have a rich aunt willing to fund your trip to the big time.

# Pocket Protectors: Investors

One of the more common strategies among independent filmmakers is to find investors, people who will put up some or all of money to make a film in the hopes that if the film does well or gets sold to a distributor, they might make their money back plus a little bit extra.

While we've been talking about independent filmmaking as a sort of do-it-yourself endeavor, there are times when it's important to let the experts do their jobs. Investment possibilities are complex and mired with legal implications that can vary from state to state. This is one of those times when you'll absolutely want to have an attorney involved. It will cost you money now but can save you money and heartbreak later.

**Staying in Focus**

Besides an attorney to set up your business entity, you should see an accountant to help you set up and organize your business records. Accountants may do this for free if they know that they can expect your business at tax time.

Many cities and states have organizations of volunteer lawyers for the arts that will offer sliding fee scales or low cost legal advice for artists who meet their eligibility requirements.

One method of raising money is to set up a company in which people will invest. There are a variety of options, each with its own advantages and disadvantages. Most require state registration and fees as well as a federal Employee Identification Number. You will want to consult an attorney as to which would be best for you, but for now let's take a brief look at several options and considerations.

## Sole Proprietorships

Sole proprietorships are a simple, cheap, and prevalent type of business arrangement. You are the sole owner and therefore have complete control of the business, reporting its profits and deducting business expenses on a supplemental form attached to your individual income tax return. You are, however, personally liable for any and all business debts, which means that your own personal non-business-related assets can be used to pay off creditors and expenses if the business is unable to. You could lose everything.

You only need a federal Employee Identification Number (EIN) if you are going to hire employees. In addition, if you plan to operate your business under a name other than your own, your state may require that you file a certificate of doing business under a fictitious name. This is to assure that the public can locate the real person behind the business, and the forms are usually provided by your local county government office. Such a certificate is unnecessary if you are incorporating because this information is available as part of the incorporation documents.

## Corporations (C-Corps and S-Corps)

C-corporations and S-corporations are separate legal entities, run by a board of directors who authorize specific employees or corporate officers to conduct business on the corporation's behalf. Forming a corporation requires fees and registration with a state government. Articles of incorporation can be filed in a state other than where the business is located, which means that you may want to look for a state with the lowest registration and yearly fees.

As long as the corporation follows the regulations and rules of operation established by the state where the business is incorporated, individual investors are not personally liable for corporate debts.

Both types of corporations file their own separate income tax forms, but S-corporations' profits and losses are taxed only at the individual investor level. C-corporations' profits are taxed at the corporation level, but if those profits are paid out as dividends to the individual investors, they may have to pay tax as well. This is in effect a double-taxation, which can make C-corporations a less attractive option.

## General Partnerships

General partnerships are comprised of two or more co-owners who go into business to make a profit. Unless specified in a written agreement, all owners share these profits—and losses—equally, and all partners have equal rights and say in the management and control of the business. A written partnership agreement can specify a different set of ratios by which partners share profits, losses, and control.

**Reel Trouble**

Be careful whenever you go into business with friends. Right now you may feel like you agree on everything, but filmmaking is very stressful and even in the best of circumstances emotions can run high, disagreements ensue, and friendships can be strained. In the worst cases, you may lose your friend, your business, or both.

General partnerships are in effect an unlimited liability company. This means that each partner is liable for the partnership's debts and the personal debts of the other individual partners up to the amount of their share of the business. As a result, your personal assets, not just those you brought to the business, can be seized and liquidated to meet partnership debts. Though liability insurance can provide some protection from lawsuits, you and your partners would all be responsible for business debts and loans incurred on the business's behalf, whether you were aware of those business transactions or not.

Joint ventures are a type of general partnership, one that has been set up for a very specific project—for example, a single film. As with any partnership, there are issues of liability and control.

## Limited Partnerships

Limited partnerships create two types of partners, general and limited. One or more general partners make the business decisions and manage the company. In addition, they share in the profits and losses. As with a general partnership, there are no limits to the liability of the general partners, which makes comprehensive liability insurance and worker's compensation insurance important investments.

In addition to the general partner(s), there are one or more limited partners. In exchange for contributing money, these partners also share in the profits of the company, but any loss is limited to their individual investments. In exchange for their reduced liability, these partners have no say in the management or control of the business.

As with an S-corporation, the profits and losses for a limited partnership end up on the partners' individual tax returns, so a benefit is that they avoid the double-taxation potential of C-corporations. However, many states place a limit on the maximum number of investors that can be approached and participate in limited partnerships, so you will want to carefully review state regulations with your attorney.

## Limited Liability Companies (LLC)

Limited liability companies share certain traits with both corporations and limited partnerships. Like C-corporations they provide a similar degree of protection from liability. But they can provide the tax benefits of limited partnerships and S-corporations.

As with corporations and limited partnerships, limited liability companies are a separate legal entity. Be sure your articles of organization indicate how the partners will share (or not) in the management and control of the business.

Which of these various investor options would be best for you is something to consider with legal advice. But a lot of us aren't really interested in creating a company right now, we just want to make a film. So what are some easier ways we can raise money?

# Creative Fundraising 101

Fundraising can be as creative an endeavor as coming up with your original film idea. The key is to see beyond how you've been conditioned to think about film financing and to find the ways that work best for you.

Here are some ideas I've heard of or participated in over the years:

- ◆ "Sell" individual frames of film. Say, $10 per frame (remember, there are 24 frames per second), asking people to buy as many as they can comfortably afford. You can even provide buyers with a certificate that says which frames they have purchased.

- ◆ Sell a credit in your film, a special type of "thanks" that will run at the end of your movie just for those people who have donated a specific amount.

- ◆ For people who are unable to help you out with money, ask if they could host or provide the space for a fundraiser or donate items to be raffled or provide some service for free that will help you fundraise.

- ◆ If you have friends who are musicians, ask them to donate a performance and arrange for a venue to allow you to collect a cover charge in exchange for your friends playing live.

- ◆ If you have a friend who's a beer distributor, see if she'll provide free beer for a fundraiser at a local bar. Or see if a rental hall will donate the space for a fundraising party.

- ◆ People love merchandise related to filmmaking: hats, shirts, Frisbees, mugs, bags. Create a logo for your film and find a company that can stamp the logo and title of your film onto various merchandise that you can then sell for a profit.

♦ If you or your friends have made other films, arrange a screening and charge admission. Just be sure that the films are really good because they will reflect on your reputation as a filmmaker about to embark on a new film.

♦ Stage a public reading of your script. Besides the admission fee, you may inspire people to invest. But like film screenings, remember that the reputations of you and your film are on the line, so make sure the script is so good it will make people want to donate money.

♦ Think about friends who work in other creative fields: writers, painters, sculptors, photographers. Host an exhibition of their work and charge admission.

♦ Never underestimate the possibilities of bake sales, yard sales, bingo parties, or raffles. Your imagination is the limit for raising money for your film.

Keep in mind that besides circumventing legal and tax considerations, the only area that might be considered bad form in fundraising is to have people pay to appear in or work on your film. It's one thing to ask someone to work for free or very little money; it's another thing to ask them to pay to work.

**Reel Trouble**

Though it's tempting to try to save money by doing your own tax returns, you may actually end up losing money. A professional accountant or tax preparer can make sure that you are claiming all the deductions you are entitled to. Be sure to keep all of your receipts.

One last point: Family and friends may give you money; as long as they do not expect to make their money back, this is considered a gift. A tax attorney or accountant will be able to best advise you, but in general, gifts of money are nontaxable up to about $10,000. You are not required to report personal loans from your family to the Internal Revenue Service (IRS), but of course you are legally required to pay those loans back.

Other than gifts, fundraising income may be legally required to be reported as part of your tax return; in that case, business expenses can be deducted, so be sure to keep accurate records.

# Credit Card and Loan Options

In this day and age, we are barraged by credit card offers. As tempting as they are, credit cards are not a viable way to finance a film. You may have heard of some filmmaker who put his entire film on credit and then sold it for more than the production cost, effectively wiping out the credit card debt. But you have only heard about that rare successful exception. For every filmmaker like this lucky one, there are scores of others who face harassment or legal action.

You rarely hear about the filmmaker who's paying off her film in minimum monthly payments for 15 years or more. Or the angry phone calls from creditors when she's missed a payment. Or the long-term damage to her credit rating, leaving her unable to buy a car or home or finance another film.

Resist the temptation. Credit cards usually carry a very high interest rate, despite what any "intro" offers might promise. And as tempting as they are, they can lead you to spend more money than you can repay.

Other types of credit include personal bank loans. These require you to have collateral, something of equivalent value such as your house or car. While bank loans may give you a lower interest rate than credit cards, they carry many of the same risks, the worst of which is the potential to lose everything.

There are some banks specifically in the business of loaning money to film productions, but they will only entertain this kind of business deal if you have a signed distribution agreement with a reputable distributor who is guaranteeing to buy your finished film and distribute it. Such arrangements are extremely difficult to secure, especially for an unknown filmmaker. The odds are against your being able to secure this kind of loan.

Producing a film means being fiscally responsible. The best place to start is with your own money and resources. There's a difference between wholeheartedly believing in your film's potential success and wisely balancing financial resources with the film's costs. If you can't afford to make your film, rather than go into debt, perhaps consider a way to make the movie for less. Or put it aside and make a shorter, less expensive film first that demonstrates your talent and might help you raise money for the longer project.

# Media and Arts Grants

There are a number of private and public not-for-profit organizations that can assist filmmakers financially. Many states and some major cities have an official Film Office, and the staff there might be able to help you identify potential funding sources. For a nominal joining fee, organizations such as the Association of Independent Video and Filmmakers and IFP provide announcements of funding opportunities with deadlines and contact info. See Appendix B for more information.

Film-specific grants are available at national, state, and even regional levels. Regional media centers may exist in your state as well, providing low-cost access to equipment or facilities if they are not able to award money directly.

Films and filmmaking are often considered artistic endeavors, so check with your state's Art Council to see if they provide grants and financial awards to individual artists such as filmmakers.

Besides film-specific funding resources, you might consider whether your film's subject matter would interest other types of granting organizations. If you have a film that has a strong historical component, for example, local historical societies might be interested in contributing. If appropriate, use your subject matter as a guide to research what types of grantors might be interested, though this is often easier for documentaries than narrative films.

The advantage to grants is that, unlike loans, they are monetary awards that do not need to be repaid. The organizations and agencies that distribute grants often have a very specific application process and will usually want to review supplemental materials specific to your project. Chapters 6 and 7 can help you prepare your application.

# In-Kind Services

Besides money, people can support your production by not charging you for their services or products, often in exchange for a credit in the film. These are called *in-kind services* and can include loaning you equipment, letting you use filmmaking facilities, letting you shoot for no charge at their location, or catering your film at no cost to you.

**Defining Moments**

In-kind services are services provided for free in exchange for recognition in the film's credits. **Product placement** is when a business that has provided in-kind services or money toward your film asks to be represented in the film itself through either its product or name being featured.

In addition to a credit at the end of the film, providers might ask for *product placement*—their product or business to be featured in the film itself. For example, if the local hardware store has provided supplies for no charge, they might want the store's business sign to appear in the background of a shot. While product placement has become more prevalent in television and film production in recent years, it's up to you whether you feel such a placement is fair exchange or hurts the integrity of your film.

When preparing your budget, which we'll talk about in Chapter 16, you can count what these services would normally cost as part of your budgeted expenses and then offset those costs with the same value as part of the budget you have raised. In other words, in-kind services are just as good as cash; they are treated in your raised budget just like any money you've acquired through fundraising efforts, grant awards, or gifts.

# What to Bring to the Table

Filmmaking is always a balancing act between the resources you have and the costs of the project. While a lot of us start out by paying for everything ourselves, at some point we begin to see if there are other types of financial resources for our passion.

Anytime you ask someone to donate money or invest in your film, you want to be able to demonstrate that you are trustworthy and a professional. Documentation about you and your project can help interest people in giving you money. Depending upon the situation and the people involved, this documentation might include the following:

 ◆ A cover sheet with the title of your project, the logline, and your contact info (see Chapter 6).

 ◆ A proposal and synopsis so that people can see at a glance what your film is about (see Chapter 7).

 ◆ Resumés or CVs (curriculum vitae), biographies, and perhaps even photos of the key production personnel—at the very least, yours as the filmmaker, but also those of any of your actors who have been in other films and any of your main crew members who have film experience.

 ◆ If you've already begun production and have some dazzling footage, perhaps a video or DVD of a single edited scene so that people can see the dramatic properties of your film. If you do not have a good dramatic scene in the can but you do have a lot of beautiful shots, you could cut together a very short trailer like the ones you see in the Cineplex.

 ◆ A preliminary budget or estimate of how much you think the film will cost to make.

 ◆ Projected revenue or your anticipated box office based on how similar films have done.

---

**Ditty Bag**

For beginning filmmakers with no name recognition, your best selling points are the title of your film, the logline, and your *attachments*, which are the names of anyone well known who has committed to being a member of your cast or crew. For example, if a local celebrity has agreed to be in your film, be sure to note that in your materials. Make sure your logline is accurate and exciting, and that you have a great title.

---

All of these materials should demonstrate that you are a good filmmaker with a good idea. Besides proofreading for grammatical and spelling mistakes, be sure that your script and other materials are the best they can be and present you as a professional.

In a less formal situation, you might want to have a business card or a postcard with a photo from the film that includes its title, the logline, and how to reach you. These are sometimes referred to as "leave behinds," and the general guideline is that when leaving materials, less is more. If you have a website that carries information about the film, you could include its URL but only if the site is appropriate for people thinking about investing in your movie. In other words, don't include the URL for your blog.

## The Least You Need to Know

◆ You do not need to set up a business in order to make a film, but it can be helpful for larger projects.

◆ If you are going to set up a business, an attorney can help you choose and set up the one that best fits your needs.

◆ Good record keeping is crucial for tax purposes; an accountant can help you with this.

◆ Reduce expenses by using in-kind services or product placement.

◆ Look and act professional when asking for other people's money.

# Chapter 9

# The Secret Garden: Script Breakdown

## In This Chapter

- ◆ Analyzing the text of your script
- ◆ Weighing what you know with what you assume
- ◆ Working with subtext and themes
- ◆ Breaking the script into scenes (and the scenes into beats)
- ◆ Adding and deleting scenes

It's time to fire the writer and hire the director. Not literally, of course, but we now need to stop thinking of the film story like a writer does and begin thinking of it like a director would. This can be tough if you're the writer as well, because as the director, you now have to look at the script with "new eyes." You have to prepare the script to be performed and made into images that can be recorded with a camera.

My friend Sue compares directing to composing music. A film script is like song lyrics on a page. That's what the writer (even if it's you) has brought to the table: a poem meant to be sung. The director has to compose the melody and arrange the song so that those lyrics become a memorable experience that engages the senses and moves the audience. Even if the lyric writer and composer are the same person, these two tasks require different approaches, skills, and awareness of the song's potential.

Ultimately, directing begins with interpreting the written material so that you can better prepare it for translation to the screen. There are as many different techniques as there are directors, but here are just a few for you to consider.

# Reading the Blueprint: Text Analysis

Whether we've been writing the script ourselves or working with a different writer, we may now feel like we know the story so well, there's nothing more to do except "roll camera." But all of this thinking and reading has slowly conditioned us to see the story in only one way, much like those kittens in Chapter 1 that can only see the parts of the environment they expect. To be an effective director, we need to step back and think of the script as something we've never encountered before. We need to read the script as if we were seeing it for the first time; this allows us to do what is called "a close read." Any technique or process that we use to more closely read the script is a part of what we call text analysis.

| Ditty Bag |
| --- |
| Staged readings, or having actors read your script aloud, are one way for you to gain new insight about the material. Staged readings are not performances; actors generally sit and read from the script aloud, including one who reads the scene headings and body copy. They do not have their lines memorized nor do they act. The goal is for you to gain a new perspective on your script by engaging different senses, hearing the story rather than reading it. |

You as a director have to find a way to translate the entire script into performances and images that will convey the story to an audience in a meaningful way. Even in a short film, this can be a daunting task. But there are some techniques and approaches that can help you as a director.

One approach is to break the script down into smaller units. A carpenter doesn't try to build an entire house at once; rather she breaks the construction into more manageable tasks: pour a foundation, put up the frame, cover it with a roof, close in the sides, and so forth. While she never loses sight that she's building a house, she first concentrates on what needs to be done in each step and prepares that fully before moving on.

Rather than trying to imagine the entire film at once or as one giant whole, you can take portions of it and concentrate on those, later stringing them back together so that they create a complete, cohesive story. The script already provides you with some handy smaller units, such as scenes and characters. Your first goal in preparing your script for directing is to make sure you understand each scene and why the characters behave the way they do.

# What You Know, What You Assume

Good scripts are like treasure maps. They don't spell everything out, but they leave enough clues that you can piece together what the writer intended. When you read a script, there are things you are told and there are things you assume. Particularly with scripts you're already familiar with, you tend to skim the page and fill in the story with your assumptions.

Remember from Chapter 5 all the different ways to learn about characters? As a director, you might make a list of only those things the script explicitly tells you about each character. What are you told in dialogue and what are you told in action descriptions? You are forcing yourself to look just at what is on the page.

Based on these "facts" in the script, what are your assumptions? In fact, do you believe the facts you've been given? For example, if our character Asim says "I hate ice cream," do you believe him? If not, what in the scene or script as a whole makes you doubt his honesty here?

You could approach from the other direction and list all your assumptions about the characters and then ask yourself, what exactly on the page implies this? If you can't find evidence on the page to support your assumption, you might want to consider that your assumptions are not what the writer intended nor are they the only possible interpretation of the material.

**Staying in Focus**

If you're having trouble separating your assumptions from what is actually on the page, have someone read the script who is unfamiliar with the story. After they've finished, ask them who the main character is and what the story is about. Just let them talk, don't try to explain the story. Their responses will give you a better idea of what is actually there.

A clue that you're in the territory of assumptions is if you write down emotions, such as Asim is angry. Does Asim say he's angry? Remember from our discussion of conflict and character conduct in Chapter 5 that characters in drama have a tough time saying how they feel. And from Chapter 6 we learned that action descriptions in scripts only include observable behavior. That probably means that we're assuming Asim is angry. Then we have to ask ourselves, why? What does Asim do or say that implies he's mad? How do Carol's reactions, verbal or behavioral, imply that Asim is mad?

### Defining Moments

**Backstory** is situations and events that happened to your characters before your film takes place. This backstory shapes their behavior and sometimes may even be revealed as part of the story, but its primary benefit is to give you and the actors a way to build consistent characterizations.

Directing is an act of interpretation, figuring out what is implied by the words on the page, filtering those implications through your own point of view and interests in order to make final decisions. What you as a director create with your actor regarding Asim's behavior while he's delivering his line, "I hate ice cream," will then provide material for the audience to interpret.

As you weigh what you know with what you assume, you are beginning to put together a sense of character biography—who you think this character is. Some of the assumptions you're making about this character may be linked to things you think happened to them in the past, before your film story begins, which is sometimes called *backstory*.

In *Thelma & Louise*, one of the things we know is that Louise will not go to Texas, because she tells us in dialogue that she won't. She never explicitly says why. But as the story progresses and we see her reactions to Thelma's situation, we begin to make assumptions about what has happened in her past or her backstory. Louise never tells Thelma what happened in Texas, and we never see what happened in Texas. But whatever happened, it is part of what makes Louise the character we see in the film. The director and actor at some point considered that unspoken backstory and used it to guide the ways in which Louise would behave on the screen.

# What I Meant to Say: Subtext and Themes

We can take this notion of explicit and implicit information even further than character implications. In the best films, there are larger story implications that create a

second level to the film. The immediately apparent level is the one that overtly communicates information by literally showing us events
and character actions; we would call this the
*text*. The other level, a second level, communicates
covert or hidden information, allowing us to consider that the story's literal events (or text) have
broader implications, which we could call *subtext*.

Whenever you hear yourself saying something like
"the film is *really* about …" you're probably talking about the subtext. You're providing an interpretation of the film, getting at this idea that there
is a meaning—a central truth—beyond the events
portrayed on the screen.

> ### Defining Moments
>
> **Text** is the visible story
> or information of your film, what
> you as a filmmaker directly com-
> municate to us with your words
> or your images. In the develop-
> ment phase, this might be the
> script. But once your film is fin-
> ished, the film itself is the text, it
> is the story we see. **Subtext** is the
> underlying or hidden meaning of
> the script or film.

For example, in *The Wizard of Oz*, the text is the events we see portrayed, an unhappy
girl whisked away by a tornado from her friends and family, dropped into an unfamiliar world and struggling to find a way back home as she tries to help a scarecrow get
a brain, a tin man get a heart, and a lion get some courage. At a subtextual level, possible interpretations of the film could include that the road of life requires smarts,
heart, and bravery. Or that these qualities are within one's self even if we don't realize
it. Or as a result of being made about the time of the worker migrations from the
Dust Bowl, the film might be covertly telling people to "stay put" via its message,
"there's no place like home." Another possible subtext is that we should appreciate
our home and family because there is no place else as good. A filmmaker may be
aware of some of the subtexts in his work, but rarely all of them.

When a filmmaker or storyteller has deliberately considered and worked with a particular subtext, we call this a theme. Dorothy repeats over and over, "there's no place
like home." Like the moral at the end of a fable, *The Wizard of Oz* clearly states its
theme through dialogue. Other films might overtly state their theme in a written
quote either at the beginning or ending of the film. And there are films that disclose
their theme in the title of the film itself.

The trend these days is for films to imply the theme but not explicitly state it. The
filmmaker may still be working with a central statement of truth, but leaves it to
the audience to uncover it or figure it out. But other filmmakers may prefer to raise
moral or ethical questions that are left unanswered within the narrative, provoking
the audience to weigh the pros and cons. Films like *The House of Sand and Fog* can

leave people arguing about who was in the right and force us to examine our own values. Whether themes are conclusive positions of truth or unanswered moral questions, we expect to infer the themes from the situations, characters, and stories presented on the screen—we interpret them. Interpretation is the key concept here.

Once you know the overarching themes you want to work with, you may want to go back to your characters and story, and tweak them to make sure that they are the most effective and appropriate in illustrating this theme.

Your theme is what you want to demonstrate in this one film. You're not saying that this is the only way to think about your subject matter—or even the right way to think about it. Your theme is simply a way to organize your material so that your film will ultimately feel consistent and cohesive. In your next film, you can contradict or refute the theme you've built in your current film; you're not trying to find a theme you can live with for the rest of your life. In fact, it's common for filmmakers to start a project by building around one theme only to discover when finished that the film is really about something else.

For example, you saw in Chapter 7 that in my original proposal for *Borders*, I stated the theme as "… the inability of any border to contain the casualties of war." My story was about a young man watching as his family falls apart after his older brother has been listed as MIA in Viet Nam. However, when the film was finished, I suddenly realized that the film is really about trying to be someone you're not, trying to be what other people want you to be rather than who you are. So now when I state my theme, I might say the film says, "trying to please others by being someone you're not can have devastating results."

Does that mean I did something wrong when I started my film? No. Because my original theme allowed me to focus my story material and direct it into a cohesive experience for the audience. This was a necessary step for me to go through. But after the film was done, I realized that there were other implications in the material, subtexts that were even more powerful and personally meaningful. In that sense the best filmmaking is often about self-awareness. And self-awareness is an ongoing process.

# Breaking Down Scenes

We're now ready to look at each individual scene to see how it reveals or explores our themes and characters. Each scene, like every element in our film, has a purpose or function. In independent filmmaking, there are several possible functions or reasons for a scene to exist in our film.

The primary function of scenes in narrative films is usually to move the story forward, revealing either facets of the conflict or how the protagonist is coping with, planning for, or reacting to the conflict. Usually as the film goes on, the conflict and coping, planning and reacting become more intense or escalate, creating tension and suspense for the audience—what will happen next? Did you just see that? What can he possibly do now? In the strictest of narrative terms, if a scene doesn't progress the story, it's unnecessary.

But some independent filmmakers are interested in scenes that do something other than push the narrative information forward. Alternatively functioning scenes might be designed to create a sense of real life, where crises are not always wrapped up so neatly as they are in Hollywood films, where mood is more important than story. Or the scenes may exist as an artistic expression, perhaps emphasizing visuals over performance or surrealism over naturalism.

Narrative scenes are generally linked together by some sense of cause and effect. Non-narrative scenes step out of that causal chain and have to find other ways to connect to each other, such as through poetic association. How these different functions intertwine can contribute to the overall pacing, atmosphere, and mood of a film. Some of the most provocative films incorporate scenes that have aspects of all three functions. What often sets independent cinema apart from its Hollywood sister is its willingness to let go of some of the narrative drive and allow scenes a greater breadth of function.

But if you remember from previous chapters that audiences become most engaged to films because of character, and characters are most engaging when they are in conflict, then what a character wants in a given scene is an important way of breaking down the script.

As a segment of the film, a scene tells us some small but crucial aspect of that larger story. The specific portion of this story that the scene reveals is sometimes referred to as a throughline. The scene reveals a vital piece of information so that the audience can better understand the overall story.

We can break a scene down into even smaller units, which are sometimes called beats. From moment to moment within the scene, there can be shifts both externally and internally. The external shifts are often related to events or shifts in action from outside the character. Internal shifts are related to new insights, understandings, or decisions made inside the character, kind of like the light bulb being drawn above a cartoon character's head when they realize something new.

| Ditty Bag |
| --- |
| In film, you will hear the word *beat* applied in a variety of ways. Editors may talk about beat in terms of the pace or rhythm of an edited scene. You may also see the word within parentheses, in other words, *(beat)*, and inserted in a dialogue block—where it would direct the actor to pause, implying that there has been some sort of internal shift in the character mid-dialogue. This is generally considered bad form in screenwriting because the writer is doing the director's job. One technique for a director's script breakdown is to figure out where these internal shifts and transitions occur throughout the scene, not just in dialogue. |

Directing is sort of like being a psychologist. You're figuring out what the characters are doing and why. Internal shifts are often described in terms of what characters want at a given moment. Certainly our protagonist wants to surmount the conflict, but that's a large overarching objective and motivating force. If that's all the director and actor created, there would not be much nuance to the character or the scenes.

Just like people, we expect characters to be a complex arrangement of desires and fears, actions and reactions. People rarely move in a straight line toward what they want. Even knowing what they want is a process of discovery, the specific short-term goal often shifting as they learn new insights into their situations, conflicts, and selves. We expect the same from film characters, an interaction with the world built upon moment-to-moment realizations that evolve.

**Staying in Focus**

If you'd like to learn more about human behavior and its relationship to wants, you might find it interesting to do some research on personality theories, and in particular, the work of Abraham Maslow, best known for his analysis of the hierarchy of needs.

Each of these small shifts can be considered a beat or the marker for a beat. Beats are the smallest actable moments within a scene, and the scene's performance is built by using each of these beats to form a cohesive and coherent movement of the character, both internally and externally, from the beginning to the end of the scene.

# Editing or Adding Scenes

As you go through your text analysis, you may find that some scenes do not function within your script. Or maybe some scenes are redundant, fulfilling the exact same function of other scenes. One option is to delete these scenes, and truth be told,

I have yet to see a "deleted scenes" section of a DVD that made me go "wow, that scene was really necessary, so they were wrong to take it out." Another option would be to combine several scenes into one so that it provides new information or now has a clear function within your script.

On the other hand, you may find that crucial story information you assumed was there is actually missing from your script, which means that you have to add a new scene or rewrite an existing one to include that information.

Knowing your themes and your characters through a director's eye can give you new perspective on the best way to establish your characters. You want your main characters to come alive on the screen, and if it becomes apparent from your text analysis that their introductions are not interesting, you may want to rewrite their first scenes.

Look at the opening credits of movies and see how quickly characters are established and how much we learn at both the literal and metaphoric levels. In *Desert Hearts*, we are introduced to Kay as she throws her convertible into reverse and drives backward down the highway in order to drive side by side with her mother's car going in the opposite direction. Kay is alive, reckless, fun, and she goes the opposite direction you're supposed to—audiences attach to her almost immediately and want to know more. She's memorable.

One final trick for script analysis is to make sure you ended the story you began. For something that sounds so obvious, it's amazing how many first-time filmmakers start one story and lose track of it by the end. Your text analysis gives you one last chance to take a hard look at the overall structure of the story. Read the first ten pages of the script and then read the last two. If the two sets of pages have nothing in common, if the ending doesn't seem to be a logical extension of the beginning, you may need to do more work on your script before it's ready to direct.

## The Least You Need to Know

- Directing begins with a careful analysis of your script.

- Scripts contain explicit and implicit information.

- Themes are the implicit subtexts you choose to emphasize.

- Scenes are the dramatic building blocks for your film, but even they can be broken down into smaller units called beats.

- Text analysis will help you determine if there are redundant or missing scenes in your script that could keep your film from being the best it can be.

# Chapter 10

# The Enchanted Drawing: Pre-Visualization

## In This Chapter

- Definitions of shot size or scale

- Dividing a scene into shots

- The differences and similarities between shot outlines, shooting scripts, and storyboards

- Using symbols and metaphors

Now that you have an understanding of how each scene moves through beats—revealing more information about the characters and developing the story's conflict—you're ready to start thinking about how that information will be put on the screen. This is the first step in creating the visual design of the film.

To help with this, you'll need to break the script down even further: image by image. This process is often referred to as pre-visualization or pre-viz. This includes further breaking down the script into a shooting script, shot lists, and storyboards in preparation for filming. All of these rely on an understanding of the shot.

# Subject Size and Shot Scale

In the previous chapter, we discussed the scene as drama's fundamental building block. But most directors do not film an entire scene in one continuous take or moving image—scenes are usually broken down into a series of *shots*. As the filmmaker, you need to choose which types of shots will be most effective for conveying your story.

> ### Defining Moments
>
> Much like scenes are dramatic segments, **shots** are single visual units of continuous time in space. There are two ways of thinking about shots. One is as the material collected between turning on and turning off a camera. But in an edited film, we usually do not see all of that material—we only see a portion of it, and that single portion is called a shot as well.

Let's begin by looking at the size of the shot. I don't mean how many seconds the shot runs or how big the frame is. Instead, I'm referring to the relationship of the main subject being photographed to the surrounding environment and to the edges of the frame. The wider the shot, the more we can see the environment. The closer the shot, the more we focus on a detail within that larger environment.

If we're filming Todd and Cora and they seem to appear far in the distance as a small part of the larger surrounding environment, we would call this an extreme long shot or wide shot.

*An example of an extreme long shot (ELS), or wide shot (WS). If it's at the beginning of a film or scene, this kind of shot may also be referred to as the establishing shot (ES).*

When they appear closer to us or larger in the frame, and yet are still visible from head to toe, we call this a long shot. You can see that the relationship of subject to environment in a long shot has shifted from the previous image, with the couple figuring more prominently in their surroundings. This type of shot also allows us to see the person's entire body in movement, so we pay more attention to body language than to facial expressions.

*A long shot (LS).*

As the main subject, in this case our actors, fills more of the frame, we begin to pay more attention to them than the surroundings. The medium long shot is no longer able to present the entire standing human body. Generally in films, we as viewers are most interested in seeing people's faces, so unless the director has some clear reason to do otherwise, the medium long shot shows us the upper body and not the lower part of the person's legs. Also, a person's upper body is often more expressive than their feet, so this type of shot allows us to see their arms and hands, which in moving images is a key source of gesture and physical behavior.

The medium shot positions the couple so that they appear even closer to the audience, filling the frame more, so that the surrounding environment is less visible than in previous types of shots.

*A medium long shot (MLS) or what is sometimes re-ferred to as the American shot because of its common use in mid-twentieth-century Hollywood films.*

*A medium shot (MS).*

As the shot scale changes to make Todd and Cora appear closer and larger in the frame, we generally crop (or don't show) the lower portion of the person's body so that the viewer can concentrate on the face. This is because we look for people's facial expressions to provide us information about what they're thinking and feeling. The medium close-up relies on the facial expressions more than body language or the surrounding environment to relay information to the audience.

*A medium close-up (MCU).*

The close-up of a person usually makes the face the most important aspect of the frame. We can no longer see the person's arms, torso, or legs—all attention is on the person's facial expressions.

*A close-up (CU).*

We may want to emphasize a particular aspect of a face, such as a furrowed brow or eyes. When we show only a portion of the actor's face, this is called an extreme close-up.

*An extreme close-up (ECU).*

When composing any of these types of shots, you generally try to avoid having the edge of the frame cut across your actor right where his body segments, such as exactly at the waist or belt line in a medium shot, the knees in a medium long shot, where the neck joins the torso in a close-up or along the eyebrows or lips in an extreme close-up. Images that crop right at a body segment can look awkward and disconcerting to the viewer.

The same goes for filming objects: Try to frame them in such a way that the edges of your image do not fall right along the object's natural segments. However, when filming an object, shot proportions are less about where you crop the object and more about its relationship to the surrounding environment as contained within the frame. For example, a close-up of a penny would show the entire penny, but it would fill the frame kind of like the head does in a person's close-up.

There are several other types of shots and designations we can use as a filmmaker. The two shot is used when we want two actors in the same frame; the term *two shot* implies a medium shot in order to allow room for both actors to appear in the frame. A low angle shot means that the camera is placed below the subject and aimed up. A high angle shot means the camera is placed above the subject and looks down.

Canted angle means that the horizon line is not parallel with the bottom line of the frame, so the image seems to be tilted or at an angle; this type of shot is also some-times called a Dutch angle—*Enduring Love*'s opening scene is a great example of canted angles being used to create tension. Straight on shots are those where the camera height is pretty much equal to the height of the subject.

Whether we realize it or not, our imagination often shows us our future film as if it were a series of shots. Now that we know the common name for each type, we're ready to begin describing our script and film in these terms so that other people can help us get the film out of our head and onto the screen.

# Divide and Conquer: Shooting the Scene in Parts

Choosing which type of shot to use is not an arbitrary decision. Sure, you may have an intuitive sense of which shots you need and have a starting point with how you've been imaging the film, but now you need to make active choices as to which shots will be most effective. Your guiding vision, text analysis, and breakdown of the dramatic action into beats can help you determine which shots you'll need to convey your story.

The traditional Hollywood model for shooting can be summarized as establishment-breakdown-reestablishment. This approach implies at least four shots. The first tends to be a wider shot (such as an ELS or LS) that establishes the scene, orienting the viewer to the time and space in which the dramatic action will occur. This establishing shot is followed by a series of medium or close-up shots that break the scene up into smaller units and move closer to the actions or interactions. The scene then concludes with a wider shot (ELS or LS) that reestablishes the scene's setting.

An old Hollywood technique was to first shoot scenes in a *master shot*. In its simplest form, the camera is positioned in such a way that it best captures the overall action, usually in a wide shot scale. The camera is then turned on and runs from the beginning of the scene to the end. The resulting shot could then be used as the establishing and reestablishing shot. However, its primary purpose is to serve as a kind of spine for the scene, into which the director can then edit closer detail shots of crucial action or information. In effect, the master shot becomes the connecting material. However, this can be an expensive and time-consuming way to work.

Many low-budget filmmakers find it too expensive to shoot a master shot and then a number of smaller shots; instead they carefully plan the individual shots they will need in order to edit together a complete scene, and then they film only those shots. Instead of the spine of a master shot, they have a series of smaller stepping-stones

## Ditty Bag

Even in television, we often see an establishing shot. For example, we might see the outside of a building briefly before moving inside to see the action. This helps us know that we're in a new time and/or space from the previous scene and prepares us for new material. What's less common now in television and film is the use of a reestablishing shot at the end of a scene.

that will string together. In either method, choosing your shots is not about simple adherence to a mechanical formula. It's about understanding your story.

To tell a joke effectively, you have to set it up—make sure the listener has all the information necessary for the punch line to have the greatest impact. Scenes operate the same way; each shot helps set up the drama, making sure the viewers have a growing body of information that will allow them to understand what's going on and why the characters are behaving the way they are. Most importantly, the audience is presented the information in such a way that the scene has the most impact possible.

I usually ask myself what are the crucial shots—what does the audience most need to see in order to make sense out of what is happening? In Shot A, we see Howard standing at the parking meter. But we may not have enough information to fully understand what's going on.

*Shot A.*

*Shot B.*

*Shot C.*

*Shot D.*

However, if we break this scene down into individual shots specifically chosen to reveal information that will help us understand the story, let's see what we get.

From these shots, we learn that there's a reason Howard has to put money in the meter: the meter has expired (Shot B). We cut to Howard sorting through his money (Shot C), only to discover in Shot D that he doesn't have any quarters. Now he has a dilemma; if we wanted to heighten the tension, perhaps we'd cutaway to a police officer walking up the street.

Though this example is very basic, you can see how a few detail shots can reveal information that clarifies the story and the character's choices and actions. The number of shots in each scene will be different, depending upon the scene's content.

**Staying in Focus**

If you're not sure which shots in your scene are crucial, your beat breakdown from Chapter 9 can provide clues as to which moments in the scene need their own shots. If you can't find anything crucial in your scene, that may be an indicator that the scene is unnecessary.

Because shot scale affects how clearly and quickly an audience can see important information, I also need to figure out which scale is appropriate to the content of each particular shot. Notice the different shot scales in my example—how does each reflect the information I felt was important for an audience to see?

Once I have my crucial shots in the scene, I may need to connect them with other shots, each image revealing information that will build cumulatively in the audience's mind and help them understand the scene.

Sometimes for aesthetic reasons, budgetary concerns, or scheduling issues, a filmmaker may choose to collect the entire scene in one shot, a technique that is often referred to as the *long take* and used in films like *Straight Out of Brooklyn* or *Rope*. Without editing individual shots or images together in order to draw our attention to specific details, how do we make sure the audience sees the important action? One way is to reframe the image.

Reframing the image means that we don't have to keep the edges of the frame static or unmoving while the image is being recorded. We can adjust them to change the view of what the audience will see. These adjustments can be made either in production or post-production, which we'll talk about more in Parts 3 and 4. Each technique has a slightly different effect on the image, but the general types of reframing within a single shot are:

◆ Pan—a horizontal movement of the frame from a fixed point (the camera's tripod).

◆ Tilt—a vertical movement of the frame from a fixed point (the camera's tripod).

◆ Crane or boom shot—the raising, lowering, or moving of a camera through the air.

◆ Zoom—adjusting the lens or image so that the subject appears to be moving closer or farther away, smaller or larger in the shot; see the photo example that follows.

◆ Dolly or trucking shot—moving the camera closer or farther away from the subject; one way of thinking of this is as perpendicular to the subject; see the following photo examples.

◆ Tracking—moving the camera alongside the action, parallel to the subject; the camera is often mounted on a special wheeled wagon that runs on a track very much like a small railroad; hence the term.

◆ Handheld—taking the camera off its tripod and holding it in order to follow the action.

◆ Steadycam—harnessing the camera to a person in order to follow the action.

All of these reframings direct the viewer's attention to important visual information, much in the same way that individual shots edited together can do. In effect, reframing dynamically "edits" the image while it's being recorded or presented. Let's look at two of these types of reframings a little more closely.

Notice our three zoom shots. The zoom lens simply enlarges Cora without changing perspective. Let's compare this to what happens in a dolly shot.

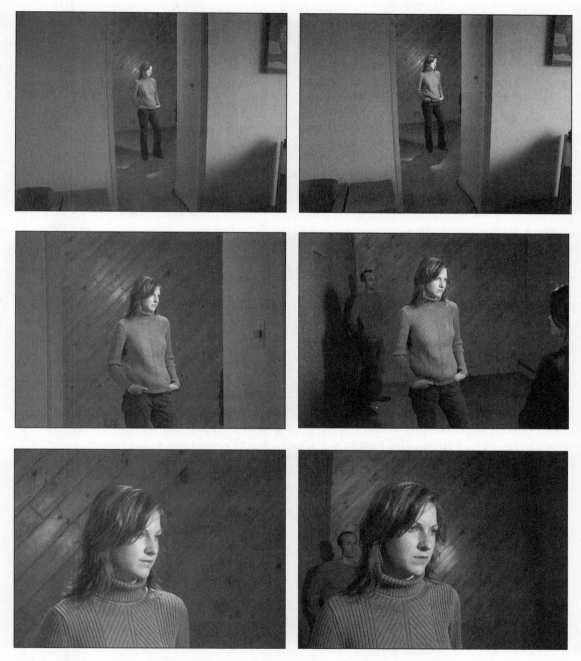

*From top: the beginning, middle, and end of our zoom and dolly.*

Notice that the general framing of Cora remains the same, but because in a dolly shot the camera is moving through space, the perspective of the surrounding environment changes, and we become aware of information we couldn't see in the zoom, such as the fact that Christine and James are in the room with Cora.

Of course, a filmmaker could still shoot an entire scene in a single shot and not reframe; *Stranger Than Paradise* includes examples of this approach. Rather than reframing in order to draw our attention to crucial information, the filmmaker can use the movement of actors. Or use lighting, much like theater productions do, to direct our eyes to certain parts of the frame. If the shot is not reframed at any point, this is called a static shot.

# Outlines, Scripts, and Storyboards

Now that you have a basic understanding of the various types of shots we can use to tell our story in film, there are several ways in which we can present that information to the people helping you.

On shorter films, this might be a *shot outline*, where you list each shot in the order that we'll see it. These shots are numbered, and each includes the size of the shot with a brief description of its visual components. Something like:

> **Ditty Bag**
>
> Shot outlines are different than *shot lists*. Outlines describe the shots in the order the audience will see them in the finished film, whereas shot lists are a listing of individual shots in the order you will film them, kind of like a shopping list. Shot lists are often prioritized to be sure crucial shots are gotten first just in case there's not enough time or money to film everything.

1. ELS    Low angle shot of the church. TILT DOWN to see the light coming from a basement window.

2. LS    The sprawling church basement, converted into a crowded maze of makeshift offices divided by modular half-walls.

3. MS    Angie rests her elbows on the desk, chin in hands, studying her computer screen.

4. CU    The hazy blue light of the computer screen glows with spreadsheets and numbers.

5. ECU    Angie's eyes dart from side to side as she scans the data.

For feature-length projects, you usually convert the master scene script into a *shooting script*. This should only be done once you feel the script is not going to substantially change before going into production. Of course, it's inevitable that there will still be small adjustments you'll need to make. But you'll save yourself a lot of confusion if you wait until your story is locked down before preparing your shooting script, which is when you number and detail the individual shots or movements within the scene.

Using the shot outline from the previous page, you might have a shooting script that looks like this:

```
FADE IN:

1. EXT. CHURCH - NIGHT - ESTABLISHING SHOT

ELS, LOW ANGLE on the church's walls, rooflines and
bell tower pointing to the heavens. TILT DOWN to the
dim glow of light from the basement windows.

2. INT. BASEMENT

LS. Fluorescent lights flicker and HUM across a maze
of desks and half-partitioned work spaces. The CAMERA
MOVES through the space, until it RESTS on ANGIE, a
young woman sitting at her desk. She rests her elbows
on the desk, chin in hands.

3. MS of Angie studying her computer screen.

4. CU of the computer screen. Spreadsheets full of
numbers. The CAMERA PANS AND TILTS UP to:

5. ECU of Angie's eyes darting back and forth as she
scans the data.

6. EXT. APARTMENT BUILDING - NIGHT

LS of Angie unlocking her door.
```

Obviously, a feature-length film will probably have several hundred shots. These shot numbers will be the way in which you organize and schedule the shoot, so once you've set them, you do not change them. However, if you decided you needed to add a shot between numbers 3 and 4 above, you would assign the new shot the designation of 3.A. If you were inserting two shots, the first would be designated as above and the second would be designated as 3.B. This allows you to be flexible and get the shots you need without throwing off everyone's paperwork and creating confusion.

You'll also notice that unlike master scene scripts, the shooting script puts any camera information, such as shot scale or reframing through movement, in ALL CAPS so that the camera operator can quickly see what will be required.

Sound cues are also designated in this way only if they are separate from the sounds the character is producing within the scene. For example, a SIREN would be in all caps, but Robert throwing a dish onto the floor with a loud crash would not. The distant BARKING of the neighbor's unseen dog would be in all caps; when we see Cari at her neighbor's door, her knocking would not. However, if the scene were set inside the neighbor's house where we can't see Cari at the door, but simply hear knocking in the scene, then LOUD KNOCKING would be in all caps. Sound cues are a quick way for the sound designer to compile a list of sounds she'll need to produce.

**Staying in Focus**

If you feel more comfortable with a mouse than a pen, there are several software programs that will allow you to create storyboards on your computer. See Appendix B for more information.

In addition to using shot outlines or shooting scripts, you can visually present each shot by drawing it into a *storyboard*. Though the storyboards we often see on DVDs or in magazines might look like works of art, you do not need to be an artist or even good at drawing in order to create storyboards that will help you pre-visualize your film.

The goal in storyboarding is to get a rough idea of how the images will be composed and how the individual shots relate to each other. This can help you catch errors or see where crucial visual information might be missing. This will also help assure that the person shooting your film—if it's not you—will be able to get the images you want.

If you're planning a feature, you may not feel the need to storyboard every single shot of the entire film, but rather only those scenes or sequences you fear may be difficult to shoot. Or those scenes that are crucial for the audience to understand the larger story.

Storyboard panels usually include a frame of similar dimensions to your final film image, called an aspect ratio (see Chapter 19), and a brief written description of the shot scale, action, and/or camera movement. Who draws the storyboards is really up to you. Sometimes the filmmaker himself will draw the boards. Sometimes he might have the cinematographer draw the boards, either working with her or giving her specific directions. Or the filmmaker might hire an artist to draw the boards. With any of these, what's important to remember is that the visual style is what people will first notice about your film. If you're the filmmaker, you get to say how the film should look. Don't have someone else draw your storyboards or plan your visuals with no input or direction from you.

# A Little Goes a Long Way: Symbols and Metaphors

A lot of beginning filmmakers often try to convey their themes or story material through the use of symbols and metaphors. Sometimes this can be quite effective, but other times it can seem at best to be amateurish and at worst laughable or pretentious.

There are a number of ways of categorizing or thinking about symbols and metaphors, some of which you've probably encountered in your high school English classes. The film *Forces of Nature* ultimately uses nature as a way to demonstrate the power of love, just not in the way Ben originally assumed. More common uses of nature in film to imply deeper meanings include the single ray of sunshine that bursts through dark clouds or our protagonist riding off into the sunset or a sprout pushing up through the barren soil or even those dark and stormy nights required by many mysteries. These are all examples of nature taking on symbolic implications.

Specific objects can also take on symbolic meaning. The crucifix. A flag. A wedding ring. Even certain shapes; for example, the shape of a cross can rarely be seen now as simply two perpendicular lines that intersect. Some of these objects and shapes may have become so widely recognized that they seem almost universal in their interpretation.

Usually the most effective symbols in film are ordinary objects or elements that take on meaning within the context of the film. These contextual symbols carry no inherent meaning beyond what they are in the everyday world. But as a result of the way in which a filmmaker uses them within the film, they take on greater meaning. This would include *motifs*—elements that are repeated in the film and begin to acquire certain meanings.

In *ET*, we are introduced to a character who may be a threat to ET and Eliot. For the first half of the film or so, we do not see this character's face, we simply see and/or hear his jangling keys. Because this sound is repeated every time we see him, it becomes our primary way of identifying the character. And whenever we hear that sound, we feel worried for Eliot and ET.

The now infamous *Jaws* music is simply a set of notes, but its juxtaposition with certain events on the screen conditions the audience to become tense and afraid every time the music plays because they anticipate another shark attack. Other motifs would include the use of each color in each film of the *Three Colors Trilogy: Blue, White,* and *Red.*

Besides objects or specific elements that develop meaning within the course of the film, there can be metaphoric levels to interactions or moments-in-time within the film. I sometimes refer to these as resonant or *metaphoric moments:* images or scenes with metaphoric value. When the women go hang gliding in *When Night Is Falling,* Camille hesitates and is told that it's now or never, that if she doesn't leap now, it'll be too late. This scene reflects not just her choice to go hang gliding but also her chance to take a risk on falling in love. One of the first scenes in *Beautiful Girls* is Paul clearing the streets of snow only to push it all into his ex-girlfriend's driveway. At the end of the film, after he's had to take a look at himself and has grown up a bit (the "recognition" I discuss in Chapter 5), he instead goes to her driveway and begins plowing the snow out of it. Sure, we could say he's simply plowing snow, but these scenes have a deeper metaphoric level that reflects his changing feelings—at the end, he's now able to let her go and move on.

Even the film's production design may serve as a metaphoric reflection of the story's themes and subtexts. The main thing to keep in mind with symbols and metaphors is that a little goes a long way. Use them sparingly, especially ones that are widely recognized—they may be so familiar or have acquired so many layers of meaning that their inclusion in a film can overpower the filmmaker's intentions or seem to hit the audience over the head with the theme and the film's deeper meanings. Symbols seem to work best when they're subtle. Otherwise they can seem clichéd or pretentious.

## The Least You Need to Know

- Shot size or scale is a way to classify shots based on how much of the frame is filled by your main subject.

- Shots can be classified by how you choose to reframe the image.

- In preparation of shooting, you create a plan for the shots you will need; this plan could be a shot outline, a shooting script, and/or a storyboard.

- Symbols and metaphors can add deeper meanings to your film, but they work best when subtle.

# Strangers in Good Company: Your Crew

## In This Chapter

♦ Who's who on the crew

♦ Finding crew members to work on your film

♦ Union vs. non-union crew

♦ Creating a legal agreement between you and your crew

♦ What's the ideal size for a crew?

If you like to surround yourself with people, now's the time. Films, especially feature films, are a team effort, a collaborative adventure. Filmmaking is labor-intensive, and it's easier and more fun if there are other people working with you. Besides, trying to do it all by yourself will send you to your bed with the covers pulled up over your head.

This is one of those times when your most important skill as a director is the ability to ask for help. Finding the right people to help is critical. Knowing what you need them to do is just as important. Let's look a little more closely at how to do each.

# Get a Grip: Crew Positions

In Chapter 1, I defined a filmmaker as someone who fulfills the duties of both a producer and a director. The producer is the person responsible for organizing the project from inception to completion, dealing with financing and other logistics to be sure the film gets made. The director is the person responsible for bringing all the creative elements—performance, setting, photography, sound—to bear, creating an environment, the set, in which each contributes to the actual filming and film.

Historically, we've thought of the director as the guiding vision behind a film, but in recent years, producers are sometimes the guiding creative force behind a film, which has resulted in a new term: creative producer.

If you are feeling overwhelmed with the task of making your film, you may want to consider whether you need a partner, either someone to produce while you direct, or someone to direct while you produce. Ismail Merchant & James Ivory, George Tillman Jr. & Robert Teitel, the Coen Brothers, Mark & Michael Polish, and Chris Kentis & Laura Lau are all examples of this kind of partnership.

As a filmmaker doing both the producing and directing chores, you'll certainly want to consider whether filling certain other specific crew positions will help you get your film made. Let's take a look at the different types of crewmembers you might find on a large film production in the general order of their involvement:

♦ Line producer   Watches the money, balancing what you need with what you can afford; negotiates deals for equipment, locations, props, and so on, by trying to find you the best deals or bargaining in order to make your money go as far as possible.

♦ Production manager (PM)   Sometimes referred to as a UPM or unit production manager; assists the line producer in finding deals.

♦ Casting director   In consultation with the director, organizes and facilitates the casting of actors, including the audition process.

♦ Location scout   Finds places that look like or evoke the settings of the script; shows the most promising to you.

♦ Assistant director (AD)   Helps you break down the script and schedule the shoot, but most importantly, communicates with everyone to make sure everyone and everything is on the set when you are ready to shoot. On larger productions, the AD will direct the extras and background actors in crowd scenes so that the director can concentrate on the principal actors.

◆ Script supervisor or continuity person   Although shot out of order, any scene in the finished film is meant to create the illusion of continuous time and space; the continuity person makes sure everything is as close to the same as possible as you shoot the same scene in separate shots or on separate days; a good camera helps to record details of costume and set; also good notes.

◆ Cinematographer (DP)   Is sometimes referred to as the director of photography (hence the abbreviation DP or sometimes DOP); oversees the lighting and visual composition of each image.

◆ Camera operator   Actually turns on, off, and monitors the camera during each shot.

◆ Assistant camera (AC)   Assists the camera operator by checking the camera after each shot, loading the camera, assisting with focus (hence why this position might also be called focus-puller) and changing any lenses or filters needed.

◆ Gaffer   Sets up the lights under the supervision of the cinematographer.

◆ Best boy   Assists the gaffer; the term no longer designates a particular gender.

◆ Electrician   Helps make sure enough electrical power is available for the lights; on larger shoots where there are not enough wall outlets, an electrician might tie your lights directly into the circuit box to avoid power overloads.

◆ Grip   An all-around physical laborer, helps move equipment or lights; a grip who specializes in working with track and a dolly for reframing shots is sometimes called a dolly grip.

◆ Sound designer   Oversees all of the film's audio elements, from production sound to post-production sound; in the same way that the cinematographer creates a visual mood to the film, the sound designer creates an aural (or audio) mood.

◆ Sound mixer or recordist   Records the sounds on set, focusing primarily on the dialogue, making sure it's audible and clear.

◆ Boom operator   Hand-holds a microphone above the actors and out of the visible frame in order to record their dialogue; to keep the operator from being seen, the microphone is attached to the end of a long pole or boom; usually headphones allow the sound mixer to communicate directly with the boom operator.

◆ Production designer   Consults with the director and cinematographer to develop an overall visual design or look for the film that reflects the story's drama and atmosphere or mood.

◆ Art director or set dresser   Makes sure that the set or location is ready for shooting, and that all of the visual details add up to an environment for filming the actors that feels authentic to the script's story.

◆ Prop person   Responsible for any objects or props that the actor will use directly in the scene or which are narratively important; this position used to be called prop master, and I've been on some shoots where the crewmember is called a prop wrangler.

◆ Wardrobe person   Makes sure that costumes are clean and ready for the actors each day that they're needed; on larger productions, the wardrobe person might also make the costumes as a costume designer.

◆ Stylist   Helps the actors with makeup and hair.

◆ Makeup artist   Creates special-effects makeup, like making the actor look scarred or burned or injured.

◆ Still photographer   Takes pictures during your production that can be used for press kits (see Chapter 27) or publicity shots in publications.

◆ Wrangler   Usually refers to the crewmember responsible for managing any animals that appear in the film; over the years, the term has become more generalized to include anything that needs to be managed—for example, if you have children in your cast, you might have a crew position called *child wrangler*.

◆ Stunt coordinator   Plans and supervises any actions in the film that might result in injury or damage, training the participants to assure the greatest possible level of safety.

◆ Transportation captain   Might personally drive or on large shoots supervise drivers who transport key cast or crew members to and from the set; the advantage is that you can ensure everyone is pretty much on set when you need them, but it can be costly; on smaller films and lower-budget features, the general assumption is that everyone can drive themselves or carpool.

◆ Music supervisor   In consultation with your sound designer, oversees the music for your film, whether hiring a composer to create an original score or trying to get legal permission to use an existing song; music will enhance or destroy a mood faster than just about anything, so a good music supervisor can help tremendously.

◆ Post-production supervisor   Oversees all phases of post-production, including the picture and sound editing as well as post-production special effects, such as computer-generated effects; makes sure everything is ready when needed and that the post-production process stays on time and within budget.

- ◆ Editor or picture editor   Actually edits your film, and may have an assistant.

- ◆ Sound editor   Edits the dialogue and collects the sounds you did not record on the set but that are necessary for the story.

- ◆ Production assistant (PA)   An all-around helper; don't underestimate the importance of having several people who can make last-minute copies, run errands for the production, make phone calls, or help you with any of the unexpected last-minute details that need to be addressed. I've learned over the years that I can combine most crew positions and get by with fewer people, but I always make sure I have at least one helper on the set as a production assistant.

While each of these jobs would be done by a separate person—often with assistants as well—on low-budget productions, it's not uncommon to have people do double or triple duty. For example, you might decide to make your line producer and production manager the same person. Or the production designer can handle props and costumes. Your cinematographer may be her own gaffer, camera operator, and assistant camera as well. Of course, the trade-off is that sometimes the shoot goes slower if you have people trying to do too many jobs at once, especially if that person is you.

In addition to these specific crew positions, I've always found it helpful to have someone on set who can serve as a reality check. Any one or several of the above crewmembers could serve in that capacity, or on some productions it might be someone I've designated as a personal assistant. The only criteria are that it's someone you trust, whose opinion you respect, someone you can confide in when you have your doubts. When you're on the set, everyone's going to look to you to know what to do next or how to handle an unexpected problem at a moment's notice—to be confident. That's a lot of pressure, and it's good to have someone who can remind you to take a deep breath, step back from the process with you, and listen as you quickly try to work out what to do.

# Finding Good Help

A piece of advice I've heard throughout the years is to surround yourself with the best people possible. A lot of us when we first start out feel safer working with people we already know, whether they're good at filmmaking or not. Certainly it's fun to work on films with friends, but there might be times when you need people who know more than you do in order to get the film made. If that scares you, remember that even though they may know more than you about some technical aspect of filmmaking, they can't know your film's story or your vision for it better than you do. This is your main strength as a filmmaker: story and vision.

If you decide to work with experienced film people, you'll have to find them. Depending upon where you live, this might be as simple as contacting a local film office or regional media arts center or your local access television channel. If there are film or video programs in your area high schools, you may find teachers, staff, or graduates interested in working on films. Colleges that teach film classes may have students interested in gaining more experience. Ask around; talk with people.

> **Staying in Focus**
>
> Some of the best films have been made by friends. If you've got plenty of time to plan or make your film, you can get by without having the most experienced crew. You and your friends can learn as you go. But for the film to get finished, you have to all be committed to the amount of time and work it will take.

Larger cities and some states may actually publish production bibles, or massive books listing all kinds of film-related services, including freelance crew-members.

Placing an ad in the local papers is a possibility as well. If you go this route, include a brief description of the film, perhaps your logline (see Chapter 6), and the crew positions you're looking for, such as "cinematographer" or "sound designer." You don't have to put a separate ad in for each crew position, just list all that you need.

## Resumés and Reels

When recruiting or hiring other people to help you with your film, their simply expressing interest is not enough. Be sure to include how interested people should apply, such as sending a resumé or sending a videotape sample of previous experience or a list of reference names and contact info or some other appropriate requirement. If your phone number is listed in the phone book and you want to avoid being barraged with phone calls at home, just list your first name in the ad with a way to contact you, such as a post office box.

Resumés will give a general sense of how many productions the potential crew person has worked on. At this point, it may not matter to you whether these have been famous films or student films, local television, or home movies. When choosing your cinematographer, production designer, sound designer, or editor, reels can be extremely helpful. Reels are often like a sampling of the person's best work, excerpts from several projects edited together so that the total tape or DVD running time is only 10 to 20 minutes.

Depending on the crew position being applied for, you'll look at different elements in each reel. A cinematographer's reel should demonstrate good technical skills in lighting, camera movement, focus, and composition. Besides the basic skill level, pay attention to each different film's excerpt to give you a sense of whether the cinematographer creates visuals that are appropriate for and reflective of the story content being shot.

With a sound designer's reel, pay attention to how clearly the dialogue is recorded, how sound effects enhance the scene, how music is used. Make note of hiss that seems to get louder and softer, especially when the actors speak. In looking from clip to clip, is the designer's work consistent and technically good?

When watching the production designer's reel, pay attention to the settings, the use of color and texture in the sets; also ask to see their portfolio as well. The editor's reel is all about how one shot transitions to another; don't get distracted by the visuals—pay attention to how individual shots are cut together. Are they smooth and seamless when cutting on matching action? Are the transitions appropriate to the mood and tone of the film?

**Reel Trouble**

If you rent a post office box, be sure to get one big enough to hold several large envelopes and videotapes so that you're not dependent on picking up applications only when the service window is open.

## Interviews

After reviewing the resumés and/or sample tapes, contact those people you're interested in talking with more. If you feel good about your phone conversation, set up a time to meet in person for an official interview. Don't be afraid to ask them specific questions about the materials they submitted to you.

In both your phone calls and your interview, an important consideration is whether or not you feel you can work with this person. Watch out for red flags and danger signs, such as the person saying things like, "everyone says I'm hard to get along with" or "I have quite a temper"—anything that implies they might be difficult to collaborate with. Try to gauge how well they will listen to you and your ideas rather than try to take over the film and make it their own.

Personally, I'll take someone with less experience and a great temperament over someone who's worked on lots of film crews but is hard to get along with. But that's me, that's my preference. Ultimately, you want to surround yourself with people you feel will get your film made the way you want to make it.

Years ago, I heard Canadian filmmaker Patricia Rozema speak, and her strategy for hiring crew has stayed with me ever since. Paraphrasing, she said she hired her crew and cast based on whether or not she'd invite them into her home for dinner. That makes total sense to me—I want a crew that I trust and feel comfortable around. If someone is the type of person I could see myself inviting into my home and spending several hours with comfortably eating a meal and talking, odds are we'll get along pretty well.

I've been on film shoots where the director or producer didn't care about crew personalities as long as the film got made. On large productions where people are being well paid, that can work because everyone's treating it like a job, a business. But independent films often feel more like family affairs, more intimate, because the crews are smaller and people's motivations are not financial.

> **Staying in Focus**
>
> Before committing yourself to a particular crewmember, make sure that he or she is available for the dates you plan to shoot. Also make sure that you have all vital contact information: home phone, cell phone, e-mail, and address.

No matter what, filmmaking is a stressful process. There will be times when you'll be frustrated, angry, depressed, and anxious. So will your crewmembers. You won't always get along, but why not hedge your bets, put the odds in your favor, by starting out with people you like?

# Paying the Piper: Union vs. Non-Union Crew

Experienced crewmembers may or may not belong to a union. Film unions require that their members be paid certain minimum amounts, have a specific number of hours off before they can come back to the set, and take breaks and meals at specific times. If any of these are violated, there can be stiff financial penalties or fines levied against the film if not outright action to shut you down. Therefore, you want to be extremely familiar with the union guidelines and rules if you're hiring a union crew.

Unlike the actors' unions, crew unions do not usually have provisions for waiving salary minimums for low-budget independent film productions. As a result, a union crew will immediately require a significantly larger budget than a non-union crew. What you're paying for is experience.

Because of the financial issues, many independent films look for experienced crewmembers who are non-union. Even then you'll need to establish how your crew will be compensated for your film in this case. There are several options.

You might ask them to work for free, which usually means that they won't make any money, but you'll feed them on the set. Or you might set a salary but ask your crew to defer it, which means that you do not pay their salary unless the film is sold or exhibited for a profit.

You might ask them to work free because they'll get a credit in the film. Of course, this will only mean something if you finish the film and show it. Another option is to hire someone who is chomping at the bit for a better credit in the film, giving them a chance to do something they've not been able to do yet. I've known assistant editors who will negotiate their rates to nearly nothing for the opportunity to be the main editor on a film. This is potentially true for people who feel locked into any one of a number of assistant or secondary positions and are looking for their break to step up to a better credit on their resumés.

You might agree to a set rate that is nominal but will at least cover their travel expenses to and from the locations, whatever you can afford, whether that's $50 a week or less or more. No, they're not going to be able to survive on it, but they can tell their family and friends that they have a paying film job. If you do pay, don't forget that you'll need to report it to the IRS.

> **Ditty Bag**
>
> If your production is non-union, it does not necessarily mean that a union crewmember can't work on it. Any union member who decides to work for less than union scale on a non-union film is generally free to do so. However, be aware that paying some crewmembers and not others can create bad feelings on the set.

# Letters of Agreement

Once you've selected a particular person to be on your crew, you'll need to both sign a written agreement that clearly spells out her crew position, the title she'll receive in the final credits of the film, her compensation or salary, if any, and the shoot dates. You may also want to specify the workweek, or how many days you plan to shoot each week, as well as the length of your expected workday. These might also be referred to as a deal memo.

Have an attorney look over your blank forms or letters of agreement to make sure they are well written and legally binding. There are certainly examples that you can use as a kind of template from a number of different film books, but you're best protected if a lawyer has helped you write or at least approved the forms you're using.

Both you and the crew person should keep a copy of your agreement with original signatures. If you haven't already, create a large file or box to contain all the paperwork for your film: releases, permits, receipts, contracts, letters of agreement, and so on. Your copy should be filed with all of the other important paperwork for your film.

# Skeleton Crew: The Bare Minimum

Finally, let's spend a little time thinking about how many people it really takes to make a film. The long list of possible crewmembers at the beginning of this chapter may be a little intimidating, but that list is just to give you an idea of the different jobs that need to be done to make a large film. In independent filmmaking, it's not uncommon for people to do more than one job, thereby cutting the size of the crew.

How many people do you really need to make a movie? Well, the answer is, however many it takes! There is definitely a point of diminishing returns. I've worked on some crews that are so big that the production bogs down and loses momentum simply from so many people standing around or trying to get so many people from location to location. I've heard of feature films being shot by one person who does their own camera and sound while directing the actors. Somewhere in between is the ideal for you.

Bigger is not always better. Figure out which jobs need to be done on your film and whether any can be combined into one crew person; go for the minimum number of people it will take to do these jobs and still make your film effectively.

## The Least You Need to Know

♦ There are many different possible crew positions on any given film; the key word is "possible"—choose only the ones you need to make your film.

♦ When people express interest in helping on your film, ask about their previous experiences and to see their resumés or reels.

♦ If you can afford to hire a union crew and you do, be sure to read the fine print—know all the rules and regulations that apply to your situation.

♦ Have signed written agreements with every crewmember and keep these agreements in a safe place.

♦ On smaller productions, it's not uncommon for each crew person to do more than one job; this can help keep your crew size small and manageable.

# Big Fish: Your Cast

## In This Chapter

◆ Why casting friends and family may not be a good idea

◆ Finding professional actors through actors' unions

◆ Auditioning potential cast

◆ What you need to know about release forms and legal permission issues

In many ways, your film will succeed or fail on the basis of its performances. Whom you cast is one of the most important decisions you will make as a filmmaker. A lot of us when we first start out feel a lack of confidence and may be afraid to work with actors. We may start by making films that star our friends and family, and that can be a fun and safe way to learn. But as a filmmaker, you need to know how to audition actors and choose the people who will best bring your characters to life. Especially if you're making a feature, this is one of those times when you need to think about what's best for your film.

On large productions, there may be a person designated as the *casting director* who works alone or with a small team of people. A good casting director can make your work easier by sorting through all the people interested in being in your film and showing you the most likely candidates. Even if you want to be involved in all stages of casting, it can be extremely helpful to have a person who can place the ads, field the calls, and handle all the details of auditioning your film. One of the advantages is that this other person, whether a casting director or not, gives you someone to discuss your options with, someone to test your opinions about which actors might be best for the film.

# Wanna Be in a Movie?

When filming over a period of several days, weeks, or months, you need people who are committed to the project, people who will stick it out. At first glance, you'd think that your friends and family would be the most likely people to do this—and even work for free. But you may find out the hard way that friendship and family loyalty will only carry you so far. Eventually your everyday relationship begins to intrude, assuming you won't mind if they miss this one day of shooting or that you'll understand that they have to leave early today or that you'll be fine with them loudly disagreeing with your decisions on the set.

If you're working with friends and family, you need to be prepared for these possibilities so that you're not too disappointed or angry if they let you down. This is not to say that all friends and family should be avoided. But you need to be as realistic with them as to how much time the film will require and how boring acting can be. There's an adage that film sets are all about "hurry up and wait." That goes doubly for actors. You and your crew will be busy setting up shots, filming them, breaking down equipment, and moving on to the next shot. Your actor is really only busy for the few minutes you're actually rolling cameras. Experienced actors know to bring a good book or their own work to fill in the time between shots—they're prepared for this fact.

**Staying in Focus**

If you're casting non-actors, you can hedge your bets by casting to type, picking someone who already behaves, talks, or looks like the character he'll be playing.

But the most important consideration is whether or not your friends and family can act. There are a lot of directors who have had great success working with non-actors. But it's not as easy as it might seem. There's a difference between non-actors and bad actors. Keep in mind, too, that you may not be the most objective eye on this. You may find it hilarious and compelling to watch your best friend or parents on the screen, but would an audience of strangers find them just as interesting?

Friends and family work cheap. That's their primary advantage. The disadvantage is that they might not be able to act. And they may not realize just how much time and work a film requires, ultimately leaving you in the lurch.

# Look for the Union Label: SAG and AFTRA

If you decide to cast experienced actors, you may run into the issues of unions. Not all experienced actors are in a union, especially in smaller communities. And non-union actors can provide you a bit more flexibility in terms of arranging compensation. On a non-union film, there are several ways you can save money. You can ask the actors to defer their salaries, meaning they work now for free and get paid later if the film gets sold or makes money. Or you can negotiate with them to volunteer their time and work on the film. Or you can pay them as little as they're willing to work for.

But union actors are bound by union rules regarding how they are to be paid and how much. In Canada, the Alliance of Canadian Cinema, Television & Radio Artists (ACTRA) represents union actors. The major acting unions in the United States are the Screen Actors Guild (SAG) and the American Federation of Television and Radio Artists (AFTRA).

SAG actors working on large-budget union films are guaranteed certain minimum standards and rates, just as union crewmembers are (see Chapter 11). However, SAG does provide several special arrangements for independent filmmakers working with smaller budgets. These arrangements include special dispensations for student films, experimental films, limited exhibition films, modified low-budget films, and low-budget films. Each category has stipulations as to how high the budget can be in order to qualify and whether all cast have to be union or not.

Whether they belong to a union or not, experienced actors can be found in a number of ways. One of the best is to attend plays on a regular basis, keeping the printed program and making notes to yourself as to any actors you think would be good for film. If there are acting training programs, whether high school drama clubs, college courses, or community theater workshops, check them out and attend public performances of student work to see if anyone catches your eye. Network with other filmmakers in your area, watch their films, and make note of any actors they've cast that you think you'd like for your film. Finally, the most tried-and-true method is to place an ad or press release in your local papers announcing auditions for your film.

> **CAUTION**
>
> ## Reel Trouble
>
> Beginning filmmakers are routinely warned not to have children or animals in their films, because both can be difficult to control and both can slow your production down. While children who belong to the union may have restrictions (length of work-day, tutors on set), they are generally a little better prepared for life on the set than children who don't belong to the union. Usually at least one parent will be on set as well, which may either help or hinder the child's work. Either way, you'll want to have one or two crewmembers whose sole jobs are to deal with the parents, entertain the children, and help ensure they'll be ready when you need them.

# The Audition Process

Auditioning potential cast members is your first chance to see the director/actor relationship at work. Even if you plan to cast your friends or family, be sure to audition them first. This will help establish a new kind of relationship and let them know that you're treating your film as a professional endeavor (and encourage them to do the same). Some directors choose not to audition actors but rather simply meet with them to discuss the project. This works best if the actor is well known, with several films in release so that the director already has a general sense of how the actor looks and acts on camera.

There are two types of auditions: open calls (sometimes called *cattle calls*) and scheduled appointments (which more experienced actors usually prefer). An open call is when you advertise hours that potential actors can drop in and audition on the spot. Scheduled auditions are when you ask actors to contact you beforehand and schedule a specific appointment time.

## Getting the Word Out

Before you can hold an audition, you need to have some idea of what you're looking for. This involves another kind of script breakdown, this time by character. You'll want to prepare a brief description of each character you plan to cast, certainly any-one who has a major speaking role. This shouldn't be more than a paragraph or two, a brief summary of the character's key physical or psychological traits. Your aesthetic treatment from Chapter 7 might help you prepare this.

Once you have basic descriptions for each of your characters, you'll then want to distill these down to one- or two-sentence summaries of their visible demographic information: gender, race, ethnicity, age, general look. You might also include an adjective or two regarding their visible demeanor. This is the information you'll use to advertise what types of actors should audition.

Because ads cost by the word, the goal is to be succinct but clear enough so that you are only looking at people you'd consider casting. Besides a brief character type, include the logline in order to give prospective actors a sense of what the film is about. Also let them know if there will be pay or if you're expecting them to work for free. Be sure to include your contact information.

### Staying in Focus

To keep everything more organized and separate from their personal lives, film-makers will often buy cell phone services, create a separate e-mail address, set up a website, or rent a postal mailbox just for the production. All of these cost money, however, so you have to budget for them. But they can afford you a little bit of privacy, and these expenses, if used exclusively for your film, are tax-deductible if you keep all your receipts.

If your local community has a theater newsletter or an actors' hotline, definitely place your ad there. Some local newspapers also have classified sections specifically for actors and musicians; if yours doesn't, you could place an ad in the "help wanted" section knowing that you may get a lot of calls. You could also post an ad on the bulletin boards at local college theater departments or community theaters.

When posting fliers on bulletin boards, make the bottom edge of the flier a series of small tabs that can be torn off, each with a reminder of the ad's content, such as "actor wanted," and the phone number or address to contact you. This will help keep interested people from taking the entire flier or not contacting you because they didn't have a pen and paper to write down your info.

You'll need to decide whether this first call should be just for resumés and *headshots* or whether you want to go ahead and schedule the actors for an audition time or whether you want to create an open call for drop-ins. If you just want the actors' resumés, you should only include a mailing address in your ad; if you want to go ahead and start seeing people in person,

### Defining Moments

**Headshots** are the standard format for actors' resumés. They're called headshots because one side is usually an 8"-by-10" black and white glossy photo that emphasizes the actor's face, usually similar to a close up, medium close up, or medium shot. The photo is backed with a written resumé of the actor's experience.

you'll want to include your phone number and ask them to bring a headshot with them to the audition.

Before you can actually schedule appointments with your actors, you need to figure out where to hold the auditions. The ideal audition space will provide access to restrooms, a small check-in or reception area where actors can wait if they get there early, and a separate room where the actual audition takes place. Your home is an inappropriate and unprofessional location for auditions. If you have set up a production office outside your home, and it's big enough, that might be okay. Otherwise, you'll need to rent or borrow a room for the auditions. Many local municipal buildings and libraries will rent meeting rooms for a nominal fee, as will some high schools, colleges, and churches. Even community theaters might have a stage or meeting room they'll rent.

Never hesitate to see if you can bargain the price lower or exchange free use of the room for a credit in your film. The worst they can do is say no. Any rental fee you do have to pay should be included in your budget as an expense of the film.

## Using Your Audition Time Productively

For the actual audition, you'll want to book actors back to back within a specific block of time. In order to make it as convenient as possible for interested actors, you may want to schedule your auditions in such a way that people can make either day or evening appointments. Let the actors know whether they should come prepared to present a *monologue*.

**Defining Moments**

**Monologues** are usually a one- to five-minute excerpt of dialogue from a published play or film script. Actors usually have several prepared that they feel best show off their talents. Some casting directors don't like using monologues; however, they can be a valuable way of seeing how the person performs something he has memorized.

If you're doing an open call, be prepared to have a lot of down time. Bring some other work for you to do. Even with scheduled appointments, many actors will not show up. Don't take it personally. They may have gotten paid work at the last minute or forgotten about the audition, or they may have had difficulty getting there. For this reason, I usually schedule more appointments than I can comfortably see in one hour; for a first call, I might schedule people every ten minutes, assuming some of them will not show, which will allow me more time with the ones who do.

If an actor misses the audition and calls asking for a second chance, he or she is still worth seeing if you haven't found the perfect person for that role yet. On the other hand, you want to keep an eye out for any indications that not showing up or being late is a pattern rather than a special one-time circumstance. If it's a pattern, your film will become a frustrating and potentially expensive experience while you wait for the person to show. For any actor who misses more than one audition or meeting, it's probably a pattern.

At the audition space, have a reception area set up with a desk and staffed by a friend or crewmember, who is there when the actors arrive. This person welcomes the actor and has him sign in, checks the actor's name against the appointment list, collects the actor's headshot (if brought), asks the actor to print his name in bold letters on a blank sheet of paper, and has the actor fill out a questionnaire or calendar sheet with either his availability or any scheduling conflicts during the days of the film shoot. In addition, the greeter provides the actors with any materials that will help them better understand the film or prepare for the audition. These materials might include the one- or two-paragraph descriptions of each character you prepared earlier or a brief synopsis of the film. These materials might also include *sides*, which are several pages of dialogue from your script. These sides will allow you to see the actor delivering some of the character's lines, giving you a better chance to see if this is the right fit. You'll have different sides for each character, and actors who want to audition for more than one character may want to review all of the relevant sides.

Some filmmakers are reluctant to let any of their script out at this stage. If you prefer, you can create one- to three-page sides that have dialogue and interactions similar but not identical to your script. The actors are not expected to memorize the sides before coming into the audition, but it gives them a chance to think about their performance rather than just read the scenes cold. It is worth noting that some filmmakers and casting directors will ask actors to do cold readings of material they've never seen before as a way to gauge the actors' natural instincts and ability to work quickly.

## Inside the Audition

Inside the actual audition room, I try to have at least two other people with me: someone to help keep notes and a person to videotape each audition. You don't want to have so many people that the actor feels overwhelmed, but you also want to have the viewpoint of at least one other person you respect. Either of these people could be a casting director or some other crewmember, and any of you might go out and bring each actor in.

You will usually sit at a table with the video camera behind you or beside you so that it captures the audition from your visual perspective. You should have copies of the sides in case the actor didn't bring hers in or in case you want the actor to read for a part she hadn't considered.

The first thing to do is turn on the camera, have the actor hold up his piece of paper with his name printed in large bold letters while he says his name aloud. This is sometimes called *slating* the audition and will allow you to quickly find a particular audition on the tape.

### Staying in Focus

Videotaping the audition can help you make your final choices. Some people who are incredibly charismatic in person can look lifeless on film; likewise, someone might seem nondescript in person and yet almost glow on the screen.

If you've asked the actor to prepare a monologue, listen and watch. If you're using sides, anyone at the table can read the other lines so that the actor has the give and take of dialogue. Whether you have the actor do one or the other or both, after each, you might ask if the actor could do it again, but with an *adjustment*. For example, if the actor presented her monologue as if she were giddy and excited, I might ask her to do it again as if she were depressed or sad. If he's reading his sides as if he's just lost his best friend, I might ask him to read the lines as if he's just found out he won the lottery.

What I'm looking for is whether the actor is able to make adjustments in the performance. Directing is working with the actor to adjust his or her performance to make the character come alive on the screen; in effect, I start this process right in the audition. What I learn from this is how well the actor can make adjustments and how well we work together. Before they leave, thank each actor for auditioning.

### Ditty Bag

When actors submit headshots via mail, they usually expect to only be contacted if the filmmaker or casting director wants to set up an audition. At your auditions, if you let everyone know that you'll be phoning for callbacks or casting by a specific time and day, anyone who has not heard from you by then will assume you are not interested. Certainly, it's polite to call everyone, but it's not always feasible. For actors you've seriously considered and brought in for several callbacks, it's expected that you or the casting director will telephone them whether they got the role or not. Yeah, it's tough to tell someone he didn't get the part. But it's part of the job.

## Callbacks

After the first auditions, which might take place over several sessions, review your notes and watch the videotape, deciding which people you want to see again. Those, you invite for a callback, a second audition. One of the advantages of callbacks is that you can have the actors work with each other in various combinations, looking not just for the best individual performance but the best interactions that will make the characters seem more real. This callback process might take a number of sessions as well, as you hone in on the people you want to cast.

## Casting

Once your auditions are over, you will need to verify that the actors you want are available for the dates that you'll need them. You may also need to give your actors some guidelines about how much they can change their appearance before shooting begins. For example, you may have cast someone partly because of his beard or because of her black hair. You don't want any surprises on the set if he shows up the first day clean-shaven and she arrives a blonde.

Finally, you might be tempted to cast yourself. Sure, you work cheap and you know the characters better than anyone. Trying to direct the film and be its star at the same time is hard work. My experience is usually one of two things suffers, either the directing or the acting, especially for directors who haven't made a lot of films. If you do decide to act in your own film, you'll want to have exceptional crewmembers who can do more than their fair share on the set, in effect making your job as director as easy as possible.

# Getting Written Permission

Before you ever put your actors on set in front of the cameras, you must have their express written permission to use them in your movie. This is often called a *release form*.

Every film school has stories of good films that have never been shown because the filmmaker forgot to get signed permission from the actors. Years ago, one of my students made a short film that required her female actor to be partially undressed. Though the film was tastefully done and quite good, the actor had second thoughts afterward and said she'd sue if the film were shown or submitted to film festivals. Unfortunately, the student filmmaker did not have a release form from

**CAUTION**

**Reel Trouble**

Keep in mind that release forms, deal memos, and contracts are only binding if signed by a legal adult. If you're casting underage actors, you'll need to have their legal guardians sign these forms on their behalf.

the actor, and she's never been able to show her film for an audience. As you can imagine, it's heartbreaking to make a good film and then not be able to show it.

A release form can be as simple as a one-page letter signed by your actor that gives you the right to photograph the actor and use his or her voice in any form or medium and to use these images in connection to the exhibition of the film.

In addition, you'll need a written agreement with each actor as to how he or she is to be compensated for being in your film. This could be a contract or deal memo. Contracts are often several pages long, whereas deal memos in independent filmmaking are often a single page. There are a number of ways you can address the issue of compensation. If your actors are in a union such as SAG, you'll need to be sure that your compensation arrangement is allowable according to union rules. Even if your actor is non-union and working for free, this arrangement needs to be in writing.

With any legal work, it's always best to have a lawyer help prepare the documents. There are a number of books available that have basic legal documents and contract templates, and those can save you some legal fees, but even with a template, it's a good idea to have a lawyer check them before you enter into a legal agreement with your cast.

Finally, file your actors' release forms with all other legal documents and important paperwork associated with your film. Do not lose this paperwork—and never throw it away—because a distributor will need proof that you have these legal permissions and rights before they will buy or distribute your film.

## The Least You Need to Know

- While it may be an inexpensive option, casting friends, family members, or even yourself in a film may not be a good idea.

- The Screen Actors Guild (SAG) will allow their actors to work for less than union wage if your film production meets certain criteria.

- Auditions are a good way to gauge an actor's talent and see how well he or she can work with you.

- Release forms, deal memos, and contracts give you the written permission you are required to have in order to use an actor in your film.

# Chapter 13

# *The Searchers:* Location Scouting

## In This Chapter

♦ Finding the right location for your film

♦ Space, sound, and other practical matters of a location

♦ Securing permits and release forms

♦ Other considerations to ensure smooth shooting

Your film could be set on Mars, but you'll probably have to shoot it here on Earth. Setting and location are two different things. One is where your story takes place, the other is where you shoot the film. Like so many things in film, the setting is often an illusion. An abandoned asylum passes for a medieval castle. A small school passes for a mansion. The point of location scouting is not to find where the story takes place, but to find a location that evokes the story's setting.

In thinking about your settings, you need to consider not just the physical space or buildings but also the atmosphere or the mood this space is supposed to convey to the audience. The best location scouts understand that the goal is to evoke the story's world, not necessarily find its literal correspondences. In order to do this, the scout has to be able to look beyond what locations are and see them for what they can be made into.

# The Look and Feel: Essence of Place

As you prepare to find locations for your film, you or your location scout will first want to make a list of all the settings in your film. You will want to pay attention to the way each of these is described in the script, not so much for its physical details as much as its essence. From there you'll begin to hunt for and compile a list of locations that could serve as each setting.

Keep in mind that your main character's home in the script doesn't have to be shot in one house in real life. Maybe you like the exterior of one location, but you like the living room in another, the bedroom of another, the stairway of another, and the laundry room of a fifth. With a little care while you're shooting, in the finished film these can all be edited together in such a way as to seem like they're one big continuous house. Only you and your cast and crew will know otherwise.

**Staying in Focus**

If your city or state has a film office, they may have a file of people who have registered their homes or businesses as possible film locations. Usually anyone listed in this file will expect to be paid, but many owners are negotiable, especially if you explain that yours is not a Hollywood film but rather a low-budget independent.

Think of location scouting as mix and match. Begin now keeping a journal or record of interesting houses, buildings, cemeteries, parks, forests, beaches, and other places you pass by or see and think might be interesting film locations. Take pictures of them or sketch them, being sure to record their addresses or directions on how to find them again. Squint your eyes and ask yourself what they remind you of, what they make you think of, what they could pass as.

Independent filmmaker Sam Sanders needed to film a scene of gypsies in the desert for *Gypsy Blood*. Within driving distance of her home was a series of dunes that served that purpose perfectly. Likewise, filmmakers in the Midwest regularly use the Great Lakes for scenes set on an ocean. Be imaginative.

Sometimes, though, a real location will not be enough to convey the essence of the setting that you want. You may decide that you need to create the setting from scratch, either by building sets or creating a virtual location. I'll talk about each of these options more in the next chapter. But if this is the case, your location scout may need to help you find a warehouse or stage space large enough that you can build those sets you need or put up a *green screen* for filming actors for placement in a virtual set.

The bottom line is that your location scout is first and foremost looking for a location that will create the illusion of authenticity. In film, if it can be made to look like a duck, it is a duck.

After your location scout brings you photos and descriptions of all the possible locations that would work aesthetically, you'll need to decide which ones will be best to use. This is where several practical considerations come into play.

> **Defining Moments**
>
> A **green screen** is a type of backdrop that actors sometimes perform in front of. In post-production, the solid color of the backdrop is replaced by computer with a superimposed image, making it appear as if the actors are in a setting that would have been too expensive or fantastic to create in reality.

# Room to Move: Having Enough Space

Assuming you love the look of the place, one of the first questions you'll have to ask yourself is whether the space is large enough to hold all of your crew and your equipment. You need more space than just the area that will appear onscreen. You'll also need a staging area, someplace where all the lighting, sound, and camera equipment can be unpacked and left with their respective cases when not in use. This area needs to be big enough that it will allow your crew to check, prep, and work on equipment as needed. If you're outdoors, this area will need to be protected from the weather and secure, or guarded to prevent theft.

If you're planning on using camera movements, you'll need to make sure there's enough room for the camera to move through the space—with a crew person attached. If you're planning on a tracking or dolly shot (see Chapter 10), is there enough room to lay the track the camera needs to roll on? Likewise, is there enough room to set up any lights you need so that they won't be visible in the frame? Take measurements of the location or have your cinematographer accompany you.

# I Can't Hear You: Sound Considerations

Assuming there's enough room to shoot, you then need to evaluate the location for sound recording. Trying to film a dialogue scene along the flight path of a major airport or underneath an elevated train line is going to be impossible because of the constant loud interruptions.

Spend some time there and really listen to the location's environment. Can you hear traffic? Is there a frat house next door and you're planning on shooting on a Saturday night? Are there major appliances, equipment, or machinery that hum while running and cannot be shut off? You might find it helpful to visit the location during the time of day you plan to shoot. Some locations are very quiet during the daytime and noisy at night and vice versa.

Microphones used for collecting sound are very sensitive, but the well-trained ear can pretty accurately tell whether there will be sound problems at a given location. If you're in doubt, have your sound designer or recordist come out to the location and check it herself.

# Power Play: Electricity

If the shots you're filming at this location will require lights, is there electricity? In Chapter 19, we'll talk about how to figure out how many lights you can plug into a circuit, but for the moment, figure out if the location has accessible electricity and where the fuse or circuit breaker box is located.

If you're shooting an exterior location or in a building that doesn't have electricity, you'll need to add the price of renting a generator to your budget. Generators are big, usually a truck or a large trailer that has to be driven to the location. And they're noisy, so before deciding on your location, you'll want to make sure you'll be able to park the generator far enough away that it won't interfere with recording sound and yet close enough that you can run the necessary cables to provide power on the set.

You may decide to forego a generator if you're shooting exteriors or in an interior location that has big windows that let in a great deal of natural light. However, in these cases, you're at the mercy of the hours between sunrise and sunset, and the sun and clouds will change the quality of light as they move across the sky, disrupting continuity. To get around this, you may set up lights to simulate the daylight and keep it consistent throughout the day. If windows will be visible in your shot, you may have to light the environment right outside the windows to resemble daylight; this will work best if there's an obstructed view out the window and you're not trying to light an entire open field. If you're shooting an exterior area in tight close-up with little background visible, you might be

### Staying in Focus

Many things we take for granted require electricity, ranging from charging cell phones to making coffee. Even if you decide that you don't need electricity on your set for lights or other equipment, you might need power for these other things.

able to get by as well with lights simulating daylight. Bottom line: It's a rare scene and location that doesn't need any electrical power.

# Green Rooms, Restrooms, and Craft Services Areas

Besides a staging area for your equipment, you'll need areas for your cast to relax between shots. Ideally this green room, the theater term for this kind of space, needs to be far enough away from the set that the actors aren't distracted by all the chaos of setting up shots and getting the set ready. But it needs to be close enough that they can get to the set very quickly when you need them for a shot.

Ideally this area should be warm if it's cold weather, cool if it's hot weather, dry, relatively comfortable, and have easy access to restrooms and running water. In addition, it should be relatively close to craft services.

Craft services is not just about catering, or the meals prepared for cast and crew; craft services is a daylong obligation to make sure there are refreshments, food, and snacks. Crews and casts work best when they're not hungry, and most will work hard if they're well taken care of in this department. It's not uncommon for the craft services costs in an independent film to be one of the most expensive items on the budget, as you'll see in Chapter 16. I'll go into more detail about what kinds of things to feed the crew in Chapter 21. For now, though, keep in mind that many of the food items for craft services need to be kept either cold or hot, so if you're on a location with no electricity, you'll need to figure out how to accomplish this.

# Release Forms and Permits

Once you've settled on a location, you need to have written permission to shoot there. Verbal permission is not enough. Your location manager or production manager can do a lot of this legwork.

For residences, businesses, and private property, you need the owner's permission. A manager cannot legally give you permission to shoot in a restaurant. Generally, with privately owned locations you'll need a release form, a one-page statement similar to an actor's release (see Chapter 12) but specific to the location and signed by the owner. This release should include permission not just to shoot on the location but to use the location's image and likeness in your film.

Sometimes private owners will want to be paid a fee. Whether or not you can afford or want to pay for your locations is up to you. You can sometimes barter for a film credit or agree to pay a nominal fee.

Public areas are a slightly different matter. If you're planning on shooting on a street, road, park, forest, or beach, you will need to have a permit from the entity that oversees that area, whether it's a city, county, or state agency or office. For example, parks may come under the jurisdiction of a city or county's park and recreations department. State forests or beaches probably come under the jurisdiction of that state. Streets may require approval from city hall.

Permission for all of these kinds of areas usually requires you to apply for a permit, and there's almost always a fee involved. Depending on the location, fees can run from $50 to several hundred dollars. However, you may be able to bargain for a lower fee by explaining that yours is a low-budget independent film or by offering a credit in the film.

Permits are time limited; in other words, they're not good indefinitely. Permits will specify how many days you can shoot at a particular location, and what hours you can shoot there on those days. Ask for dates and times on your permits after careful thought and try to have your permits extend a few days after you think you'll be done shooting just in case things go slower than you expect.

Filing for permits takes time. You usually can't decide on a public location today and shoot there tomorrow. Pick up the necessary forms and find out about the fees as soon as you think you might want to shoot at a particular location. These fees and any costs associated with location scouting in general should be included in your budget.

Once you have the permit, make several copies of it and file the original away with your film's other paperwork. Make sure you and at least one other crewmember, such as your assistant director or production manager, have the copy with you at all times while filming at the location. This will save you time and frustration if a police officer asks to see proof that you have permission to shoot there.

### Reel Trouble

Having permission to shoot at a location, such as a grocery store or park, does not include permission to film customers or people at that location. This is why you may want to try to control who is visible in the frame by blocking off the area or shooting when the business is normally closed. Whether you've cast them or not, you must have a signed release form from anyone who appears in your film. I usually make sure that we have a stack of blank ones with us at all times, especially if we're shooting in a public location.

Finally, be aware that some areas that you might consider public are actually privately owned or governed by a municipality; for example, subway trains and platforms, suburban and national rail systems as well as their train stations, plazas and shopping centers. My friend Dana once spent several hours in the middle of the night being questioned by railroad security because she was filming at a train station without a permit. Guerilla filmmaking is great until you get caught. The test for any location is, do you have written permission? If you don't, you need to find out who has the right to give permission. Trust me, there is someone.

# Making It All Work

There are a few other considerations when thinking about locations: proximity, parking, security, trademarks, and insurance.

Proximity has to do with how close the location is to your other locations or where you and your crew live. The longer it takes you to drive to a location, the less time you have there to shoot, and in some cases you've just paid your crew and cast to ride in a car. If your location is several hours away from where you all live and you'll be shooting there several days, you may want to consider renting a motel or finding friends' couches you all can crash on so that you're not making the trip (and losing that travel time) every day.

Whatever your location, you need to ask yourself if it will be easy for your crew to get there and, once there, will it be easy to park. If you're shooting in a city, will your crew carpool or drive individually? If they're parking at meters, are you expecting them to pay or will you be paying? How convenient is it to feed the meters throughout the day? (If your crew has to regularly put money in their meters, designate one crew person to do this for everyone. This will help prevent your entire production from stopping because all your crew leaves the set for 10 or 15 minutes every two hours.)

Keep in mind that some municipalities do not allow cars to park in the same spot for more than two hours at a time, so crew parked in metered spaces may have to regularly move their cars. If they have to park in parking garages or pay lots, who will cover those costs—them or you? You'll also need to set a policy about whether you'll pay for parking tickets or not; I usually don't.

Some cities will allow you to mark off meters or a part of the street if you have a permit to shoot. For example, Chicago will provide permitted filmmakers with "no parking" signs they can post. And if you're willing to pay the towing charges, the city will even tow cars from your location if necessary. Oftentimes, the signs are enough. I've never towed a car that disregarded our "no parking" signs.

Permits to shoot may allow you a certain degree of permission to momentarily disrupt traffic, but if you're planning on completely blocking a street for several hours, you need to make sure that your application for the permit clearly states this and whether there are any additional stipulations.

If you're shooting on sidewalks with a permit, you may want to station a crew person at either end of the set to prevent pedestrians from wandering into your shot while you're filming. Whenever you're done with the shot and getting ready for the next, these pedestrians can be allowed through if they haven't already decided to go around by crossing the street.

> **Ditty Bag**
>
> Some municipalities may require you to hire off-duty police officers to control car and foot traffic if you're blocking a road or street. At that point, you'll have to decide whether you have enough money in the budget to do that. If not, you'll need to find another location or rework your shots so that you're not blocking traffic.

Depending on where you're shooting, you may want to hire or assign someone to watch the equipment and make sure nothing gets stolen. In larger urban areas, you may want to consider contracting with a security firm, especially if you're shooting at night. In more rural areas where there's less foot traffic, you might be able to simply have a crew person keep an eye on things.

When considering your locations, pay attention to the larger environment. Recognizable commodities, landmarks, and large chain businesses have often trademarked their images, names, or logos; if these appear in your scene's background, the owners of those trademarks may have the right to stop your film from being distributed. This is a similar issue to using well-known and trademarked items as props in your scenes. When in doubt, you should obtain written permission before using any trademarked image in your film.

Finally, you must have insurance coverage for your location. The owner's or municipality's insurance is not enough. Location insurance is often a general liability policy and quite inexpensive; you'll be provided a certificate of insurance that you can then copy and give to the owners so that they have proof that you're covered. Depending on where you live, you may be near an insurance company that works with film insurance on a regular basis. The company I use in suburban Chicago will even fax copies of my certificate of insurance to all of my locations so I don't have to worry about it.

Choosing your locations is the fun part. Securing them is the hard part. Trying to shoot without legal permission can result in your film being stopped at best and your being arrested at worst. Whenever you approach an owner or government official to ask for permission to shoot, try to be as professional as possible. Have a brief description of the film that you can leave with them if they ask, but in meeting with them, tell them a little bit about the film. Stress that it's low budget. Many private individuals hear the word "film" and assume all films have the Hollywood-sized budgets they hear about on TV. Also, having a film made in your home can sound glamorous, but unless you've been through it, you usually can't imagine how stressful it will be. Explain to the owners of private property what will be involved, which specific rooms you'll need and especially how many days and how many hours each day you'll need to film there. Don't lie because you're afraid they'll say no if they realize how long it will really take; you run the risk of them throwing you out with only half the shots you need.

Sometimes the owners may ask if they can hang around while you're shooting. This is your call, but many directors, if they can afford it, will pay for the owners to be away during the shoot—whether that's admissions and refreshments at the local movie theater or a day at an amusement park or several nights at a motel. Your ability to do this will depend on your budget. The risk in having the owners there is that they may start interrupting your shoot to complain about your rearranging the furniture.

Regardless, you should always leave a location as good as—if not better than—when you found it. This means that you need to be as careful as possible when shooting and replace anything you break. If you've badly scuffed the walls, this may mean repainting them if you can't wash the scuffs away. You'll probably want to make more films. You don't want future location owners to say no because you treated someone poorly now. Basically, as independent filmmakers, we're at the mercy of our reputations.

## The Least You Need to Know

- The right location for your film creates an illusion that matches your script's setting, tone, and mood.

- Locations are not just about the look, but also the practicalities of shooting: room for your crew, cast, and equipment.

- You need legal written permission to shoot at a location and to use it in your film.

- Always leave your locations in as good or better shape than when you arrived.

# Chapter 14

# *Design for Living:* Production Design and Art Direction

## In This Chapter

◆ The goals of production design

◆ Set construction and dressing

◆ Props and objects that are important to your story

◆ You are what you wear: costume considerations

When we first think about the visual look of our film, we often consider how we'll light the scene, how we'll compose the images, and how we'll move the camera or reframe. But one of the most important factors in the visual look of our film is its production design.

You may still hear it referred to as art direction. That's partly because as novice filmmakers, we're more likely to have heard this particular term. But art direction nowadays is considered only one small part of production design.

## An Eye for the Details: Production Design

The production designer is responsible for all the physical three-dimensional design elements that will ultimately be filmed and appear in the frame. This means overseeing the set designs, set decorations, props, and wardrobe, perhaps appointing another individual over each specific area.

Preparing the production design varies depending upon the designer. Films create illusions. Sometimes that illusion is of reality, sometimes it's of fantasy. The designer has to balance the creation of a three-dimensional illusion with the practical concerns of shooting a film.

The designer starts by reading, rereading, and studying the script. Here are all the clues that he or she will need in order to build a three-dimensional world for the characters to live in. Rarely will a production designer see the job as simply following the specific details in the script—there aren't enough there anyway. Like many other aspects of filmmaking, production design is an act of interpretation.

The story's subtexts and themes may provide inspiration or strategies for approaching the overall design of the film and the specific designs of each scene. The production designer is looking for ways to metaphorically reflect the story with architecture, color, texture, and objects. Research is another important aspect of production design, especially for films that are set in a specific time period or environment.

The designer will do his own breakdown of the script, developing a system to keep track of every set and the other elements it will require. The script's scene headings or slug lines provide a good initial summary of the sets that will be needed, but sometimes there are other sets that are buried within the script, such as a mock TV show that is supposed to be running in one scene.

The production designer works closely with the director and cinematographer to make sure that all required settings have been discussed and agreed to. As locations are secured for shooting, the designer will probably want to visit and review them, taking measurements and verifying which parts of the location will or might possibly appear in frame.

The goal is to come up with an overarching strategy for the visual design. This strategy will help the feel and tone of the film remain consistent and reflective of the story's action and deeper themes. In some ways, finding a strategy is as simple as finding one thread, one image, one metaphor that will allow you to build the entire look of the film.

---

### Ditty Bag

If already at work, the production designer may be able to provide the location scout with general impressions of the type of locations that will fit into the overall design. For example, the script may call for a bank. But not all banks look alike. As the designer works, she may begin to imagine and build around a particular style of architecture. This kind of information could be helpful to the location scout.

The designers in shows like *Trading Spaces* will every once in a while reveal their inspiration for all the various colors or textures used in redecorating the rooms. The show's room makeovers often start with one very small inspiration, like a flower or a rock or a photograph or a painting or a theme. That's what a production designer is looking for, too—the one small inspiration that will lead to a consistent strategy and approach to shaping the story's physical world.

# Faking It: Sets

In production design, it doesn't matter what things are, it's what they look like that counts. Film has always been about that. That's why Hollywood back lots have streets that look like they've come right out of the old west, but if you walked into one of the buildings, you'd find it's just a wall—there's nothing really behind it.

We use the word *set* to mean either locations where you're shooting in a previously existing environment, such as someone's home, or settings you've specially built under controlled conditions, such as on a stage, in a warehouse, outdoors, or with computer software.

Sets that are on location probably allow less flexibility for radical changes. After all, once you're done shooting, the owners will want everything pretty much back the way they left it. But remember, production design and art direction are about the appearance on the screen, not the materials used on the set.

Production designer Manuel Peña Perez once taught me that if you need to change the look of a kitchen, you don't necessarily have to paint the cabinet doors or put on new ones. You can use construction paper cutouts inset in the doors. No, you wouldn't want to live and work in a kitchen that has construction paper on the doors, but on film, the material doesn't matter—just how it looks. Suddenly a kitchen or interior door looks as if the individual inset panels have been painted a different color. And after the shoot is over, you can easily remove the changes and restore the kitchen to its original look.

Even on locations, you may be able to get permission to paint the walls as long as you agree to return them to their original colors after the shoot. If you decide to do this, it may be worth paying professional painters so that your crew isn't wasting time they could be spending shooting your film. Either way, don't repaint too quickly—you may find when you watch the *rushes* or when you start editing that you need to go back and re-shoot a scene.

**Defining Moments**

**Rushes** are film, video, or digital copies of your unedited footage so that you can review what you've shot without damaging the camera original. The term comes from the days before video, but still applies today when shooting film. Because you can't view what you've shot until it is processed by a lab, you have to have a print made. So you don't have to wait several days, some labs provide overnight processing so that you can see what you accomplished on yesterday's shoot—these rushed prints are often called *dailies* for obvious reasons.

If you build a set, you're going to need carpenters and electricians who can make everything functional, look real, and be safe for your actors and crew. Building sets physically allows you to plan for more complex production possibilities, such as creating walls that can be removed to allow plenty of room for the camera for certain shots but then replaced when the camera is facing the opposite direction. Or having no ceiling or a ceiling that can be removed for overhead camera shots or to allow lights to be hung from above to illuminate the scene.

## Flats

Sometimes sets are built in segments that allow for easy maneuverability of the camera and crew in order to best film the action. Sometimes these segments might be referred to as *flats*, which are often about 3' by 8' and designed in such a way that they can be linked together to create a longer wall. If you've seen a high school play, you've probably seen flats. You'll notice that some may be solid walls and others might have a window cutout or a door. The advantage to flats is that they can be combined in a variety of ways to create different looks. The disadvantage is that the seams where they join can show.

**Staying in Focus**

Whether you're shooting on a constructed set or at a location, have a member of your production design crew photograph the set in detail. This way, if you later need to come back and re-shoot or *pick up* a shot you've missed or are not happy with, your crew can recreate the set fairly quickly and easily.

To get around this problem, sometimes set builders will use the same idea but on a larger scale, building sections of walls that extend beyond the planned framing of the shots. Another option is to secure smaller flats together and then cover them with wallpaper or some other material that will hide the seams and make the flats look like one continuous wall. Either way, these constructed temporary walls need to be well braced from behind so that they won't tip over or shake if a door is slammed. Besides the actual brace, grips will usually put sandbags along the brace to give the entire structure more weight and a low center of gravity, reducing the chances of it falling over.

Just like painting or restoring your location, don't be too quick to *strike* (or tear down) your built set. Even if you don't expect to, you may find that you need to shoot additional scenes or shots on it.

## Virtual Sets

With the advent of better and cheaper computer software programs, virtual sets like the ones used in some music videos or the film *Sky Captain and the World of Tomorrow* are becoming more and more commonplace. Working with these kinds of sets often looks best when your actors work in front of a green screen, which serves as basically a large blank canvas that can be filled in by computer later. If you're using virtual sets, you will need an indoor space large enough to erect a green screen big enough to encompass the action and shot scales you imagine.

Regardless of the set, don't expect your production designer to spend the whole day watching you shoot. The production designer is almost always working at least one day ahead, making sure that your next set is available and ready when you get there to shoot.

# Power to the Props

There's a difference between set dressing and props. Set dressing includes any objects and materials that make the set seem more authentic to the story's world. Props are objects specifically used in the scene by an actor or that are relevant dramatically. The production design team is responsible for both, though usually two different people will handle these. The art director will take care of organizing and keeping track of the set dressings.

Any prop that is narratively important has probably been clearly indicated in the script, and a prop person makes sure that any props needed for that day's shoot are on set. Once the props are no longer needed, this crew person makes sure that the objects are properly stored and easy to find the next time they are needed.

If possible, I try to have multiples of the same prop. For example, if I need a baseball for a particular scene, I try to make sure I have several. This helps prevent a frantic search and a halt to production if the one we've been using gets lost. This is especially important for breakable objects. And if the script calls for a prop to get broken, keep in mind that you might want to shoot that scene several times. You'll need to have plenty of the same prop so that you can keep breaking one until you've got the shot you want.

Have you ever noticed that presents on TV or in films are rarely wrapped the way you wrap? The actor simply removes the lid, bow and all, to see what's in the box. This saves time because the lid can be put right back on and the shot redone immediately. On the set of *Rhapsody*, we staged a wedding reception that required the bride to open a large gift that was a blender. Blenders don't come in boxes with removable lids, so we wrapped the present over and over, everyone having to wait while we rewrapped the box between each take, until the director had the shot he wanted. If we had been smarter or had the money, we would have had at least two or three blenders wrapped and ready to go. That way, we could have grabbed the unwrapped box out of the scene and rewrapped it while the director was using one of the others for the next take.

# Clothes Make the Character: Costumes

Another crucial aspect of the production design is the costumes worn by the actors, or the film's wardrobe. Just as with props, there's usually one person in charge of all the costumes, though he or she may have assistants.

On large-budget films, the wardrobe person may actually be in charge of making the costumes, but for independent films, we usually can't afford to make clothes and often ask our costumer to scrounge secondhand stores and the actors' own closets to see what can be used for the film and not cost us a lot of money.

But designing, making, or buying the clothes is not the only wardrobe issue. If the actors need to wear the same costume for several days or longer, the wardrobe department has to either wash the clothes or send them out to be cleaned. Though it's not necessarily glamorous, having someone who can wash the costumes can keep the air on your set a little fresher. On really low-budget films where the actors are wearing

> **Ditty Bag**
>
> Even if the costumes need to look dirty on the screen, this—like so many other things—is an illusion. The wardrobe person stains or distresses the clothes so that they can be fresh for your actor but still look a mess in reflection of what your character has gone through.

their own clothes, it's not uncommon to ask them to wash them. But do you really want your actors coming to work tomorrow exhausted because they didn't get enough sleep because they had to wash their costumes?

If your budget allows you to buy some of the actors' wardrobe, one way of getting around having to do laundry every night is to buy three or four of the same shirt or pants or dress.

Another common option on low-budget films is to have the actors wear their own clothes for the film. This assumes that your characters would wear the same kinds of clothes that your actor owns, which is not always the case. Because a single scene may be shot out of order over the course of several days, you will still run into issues of cleaning and making sure that the clothes do not get dirty, torn, or ripped in such a way as to break the continuity of the film.

No matter how you decide to handle the practical aspects, wardrobe is an important component not just of your production design but also of your actors' performances, the creation of their characterizations. Audiences learn about your film's characters by how they act, talk, and look. A major part of the character's look is how he or she is dressed.

## The Least You Need to Know

- ◆ Production design is an overarching strategy for creating the look and feel of your film.

- ◆ The production designer works in collaboration with the director, cinematographer, and location scout.

- ◆ Props used by the actors are important to the story or to their characterizations.

- ◆ Because your characters are further defined by the clothes they wear, costumes are another important consideration of a film's overall design.

# *Rushmore:* Scheduling Your Film

## In This Chapter

- ◆ Why it's important to time your script
- ◆ Breaking your script down into trackable elements
- ◆ Creating a reasonable workday
- ◆ Establishing a shooting schedule
- ◆ Backup plans
- ◆ Call times: getting everyone on set

You're almost there, and you're eager to get started, get on the set, and start rolling camera. But there are two critical interrelated steps you need to complete to be sure you have enough money and enough time to finish your film once you start shooting: your budget and your schedule.

Budgeting and scheduling are linked, and in effect, both are budgets. One budgets your money, and the other budgets your time. To accurately budget your money, you need to know how much time it will take to make your film.

# Timing Your Script

Until now, you've had a ballpark guess as to how long your final film will be. You certainly know whether you're trying to make a feature or a short. But to accurately schedule and budget your film for production, you need more than a guess.

Most of us use our script's total number of pages as an estimate for how long the final film will be, relying on the old film adage that a page of script equals one minute of screen time. But as I noted in Chapter 6, writing one page per minute is a very specific writing style, one that takes some practice. Therefore, we may need to time our script to get a more accurate sense of how long the finished film will be. Timing your script may seem unimportant, but it can save you headaches not just with your budget, but also in post-production.

---

### Ditty Bag

Years ago I directed an infomercial script that came from a major advertising agency. I assumed that the script had been timed by the agency—big mistake. When we got into the editing room, we discovered that the first 5 pages of the script actually took 20 minutes of screen time. We had to choose between squeezing 25 pages' worth of content into the remaining 10 minutes or doubling our editing costs by going back and reediting those 20 minutes of screen time down to 5. If either the producer or I had timed the script ourselves, we would have saved hundreds if not thousands of dollars in the editing room.

---

There's no one way to time your script. You will need to try several different methods and learn which ones are most accurate for you. In other words, this first time out, it'll be a bit of trial and error. This is why maybe making a couple of short films before tackling a feature-length film can be helpful.

Some of the methods I've used to time my script include sitting down with my shooting script, shot outline, or storyboard. I take each shot (or sometimes the scene) and fully imagine it, using a stopwatch to time how long the shot or scene plays in my head. The danger is that my imagination tends to speed up the action to get to the important parts. I have to force myself to think through each action or interaction fully, and having the storyboard or shot descriptions in front of me can help keep me focused.

Another technique is to read the script out loud, body copy and dialogue. Again, not perfect, but when I read the script silently to myself, I tend to read it much faster than it will actually play on the screen. Reading out loud slows me down to something closer to the amount of time the scenes and images will require.

Though I'm sure my neighbors wonder what's going on, I have also locked myself in my apartment and acted the whole script out, dialogue and action. Of course, I have to pretend I'm driving a car or doing any other actions that are too big for my apartment.

Staging readings of the script with actors or friends can also help me figure out how long it is. Those readings might be in my living room or at a theater; it doesn't really matter. Probably one of the most accurate methods is to use my rehearsals as an opportunity to time the script. If my actors and I have been rehearsing, before they leave, I have them run through the portions of the script we've been working on that day and write down the amount of time that section took in my script.

Finally, there are professionals who charge to time your script. But keep in mind that none of these methods are perfect. Your best bet is to try different methods and find what works best—or is most accurate—for you. I'm now at a point that I can pretty much look at my script and know how long my final film will be. But that's because I've made enough films to learn the particular relationship of my words on the page to the images on the screen. With experience, you'll be able to accurately estimate how long your finished film will be, too.

# Bits and Pieces: Breaking Down the Script for Production

Obviously, it takes longer to shoot a film than to watch one. On the set, we need to allow time for setting up lights, prepping the camera, rehearsing the actors, and doing shots over. Everything we've been doing so far is about getting the film down into manageable units that we can deal with. In Chapter 9, we broke the story down into scenes, and those scenes into beats so that we can work with our actors more effectively. In Chapter 10, we broke the script down into individual shots so that we can be sure the visual information necessary is presented.

At this point, we're ready to break the script down further into specific components. Our starting point is to divide each script page into eighths. This allows us the flexibility to shoot portions of scenes and to carefully examine exactly what will be needed for those portions.

Take one of your script pages and fold it in half horizontally across the middle. Now fold it in half across the page again, and now again until you have a long narrow rectangle. Unfold it and look at the text; each fold marks one eighth of the page—a very small amount of the scene. We're going to schedule our film by how many eighths of a page we can shoot on a particular day.

How many eighths of a page you can shoot on any particular day will depend on a number of factors. You have to build travel time into your schedule, because driving to distant locations will leave less time for shooting. Different sets will require a different amount of setup time. Some actions will take more time to film than others. Complex lighting designs, camera movements, and stunts require more time because you'll need to either rehearse them on set or retake the same shot over and over till you've got it as close to perfect as possible. Depending on these and other factors, you may shoot anywhere from one eighth of a page or more in a single day, though probably the average is about two to four pages per day if you're lucky.

Moving the camera, adjusting the lights, or going to another location all take time, and you have to schedule accordingly. On large productions, it's not uncommon to get only about 10 shots per day. Of course, it depends on the shot.

You will rely on your key crewmembers to accurately estimate how much time they will need to have everything ready for you to shoot the scene. Always assume that everyone, including you, will be more optimistic than realistic about what can be accomplished. This is especially true of beginning filmmakers, but even experienced crews can underestimate how much time they need. The bottom line: Figure everything will take longer than you planned.

# Juggling Where, When, Who, What

Once you know how many eighths of pages you'll be trying to shoot on a given day, you need to prepare breakdown sheets for that day's work. These sheets include the name of the production, the specific date of this shoot, the setting, location, scenes covered, number of pages broken into eighths, the scene or shot's number, and a short synopsis of the scene. After this basic information is a series of boxes large enough to fill in a series of details to help make sure everything and everyone you need is on the set.

These boxes are broken into various categories, any or all of which can be used for detailing the relevant requirements of the scene—what we will see in the scene. The first category is CAST, which lists the characters numbered in the order that they appear in the scene. If appropriate, you may include a list of BITS, or bit parts, which usually means nonspeaking roles or people who serve as doubles (DBL) for your main actors. ATMOS. stands for atmosphere and involves background characters or extras who will be needed to fill out the scene. An important category is PROPS, specific objects that are required to be in the scene. Additional categories may include LIVESTOCK, VEHICLES, and Special Effects (which are special effects that have to be generated on set, such as fog or smoke).

Scene # 3

Script Page:     4

Page Count:    2-5/8

**MaryKnoll**

Breakdown Sheet

Date:    12/08/04

Int/Ext:    EXT

Day/Night:    DAY

Scene Description:   Scene 3 series.

Setting:

Location:

Story Day:         Notes:

| Cast | Extras | Bits/Doubles |
|---|---|---|
| 3. IRAM<br>4. MIKE<br>5. TOR<br>6. KYLE | | |

| | Elec/Grip/Crane | Wardrobe |
|---|---|---|
| | | |

| Props/Set Dressing | Communication | Stunts |
|---|---|---|
| | | |

| Special Effects | Trans/Pic Vehicles | Permits |
|---|---|---|
| | | |

| Hair/Make-Up | Music/Snd/Camera | Wranglers/Livestk |
|---|---|---|
| | | |

*A typical breakdown form created with computer software, in this case Mindstar's Cinergy Suite, which imports your script and generates a breakdown for each scene.*

*(Courtesy of Cinergy Suite, Mindstar Productions.)*

You might have several breakdown sheets for any one day of shooting. Each day's sheets should be separated with a cover sheet that summarizes what day of the shoot it is (first, second, third), as well as the day of the week and calendar date for the shooting day and the total number of pages to be shot to the eighth of a page (such as $2^3/_8$ or $1^1/_8$ or 4).

If preparing these sheets by hand rather than computer, the information will probably be all handwritten onto blank forms, similar to the form in the previous figure, but eventually the production manager or assistant director will make sure they're typed up into a day-by-day shooting schedule sheet. These typed sheets may be more than one page. Each new day's shooting schedule always starts on a new page.

```
Shooting Schedule                                                          PAGE 1
                                          CIG
                               Maryknoll - PROD# 12345

PRODUCER:                                              FILM SHOOTS - 22 DAYS:
DIRECTOR:                                              Monday January 3, 2005
PRODUCTION MANAGER:                                    -- THROUGH --
1ST ASST. DIRECTOR:                                    Tuesday February 1, 2005

                    Shoot Day 19: Thursday January 27, 2005

Scene 38      EXT. SUBURBAN TOWNHOUSE BACKYARD - NIGHT                    1/8 pg.
              Scene 38 series.                                           :08

Scene 1       EXT. SUBURBAN TOWNHOUSE FRONT YARD - AFTERNOON (SUMMER 1999)  2-1/8 pgs.
              Scene 1 series.                                            2:08
              Cast
                1. JOEY
                2. MRS. BANKS

Scene 52      EXT. THE "GATE" - NIGHT                                     2/8 pgs.
              Scene 52 series.                                           :15

Scene 10      EXT. THE "GATE" - NIGHT                                     5-3/8 pgs.
              Scene 10 series.                                           5:22
              Cast
                3. RAM
                4. MIKE
                5. TOR
                6. KYLE

              END OF DAY 19: - Total Pages 7-7/8 pgs.
```

*An example of a day's shooting schedule, also created with Mindstar's Cinergy Suite software.*

*(Courtesy of Cinergy Suite, Mindstar Productions.)*

If you do not get everything shot in one day that you had hoped, you will need to carry over any incomplete portions of the page to another shooting day. When that happens, you're starting to get behind schedule, which means that your shoot may go longer than you had planned, which means that your film may cost more than you had budgeted.

# All Work and No Play: A Reasonable Workday

If you're anything like me, you may lose all track of time on your set. Even my bio-logical clocks of hunger and full bladder can get ignored as I reach "the zone" and get swept up in the joy of creating. This push to do just one more thing before breaking is a common one for filmmakers caught up in the momentum of the set.

On the flip side, your crew is rarely going to be at the same level of intensity because they have a different investment in your film—it's less personal for them. Don't feel bad about that; it's the nature of any artistic endeavor where one person's guiding vision pulls together a group of collaborators.

The important thing to note here is that your crew may not be able to put off going to the bathroom or having a short break or eating lunch. If they try, there's a certain point where the crew is no longer able to work their best or may begin resenting the work. And if you're not paying your crew very much or at all, you are relying on their goodwill to carry them through and keep showing up each day.

The sad truth for you as the person in charge is that you will rarely get to take a break when your crew does. Whenever they're on break, you'll probably be frantically preparing for the next few shots or troubleshooting problems that have arisen while you were busy shooting the previous ones. If you're lucky, you may be able to catch a quick break here and there when the camera crew is setting up for a completely new shot, but don't count on it. Likewise, most directors I know eat on the run. But there is something to be said for sitting down and eating at least one meal a day with the crew, even if for a few minutes. Eating a meal together can bond people.

Psychologically, people feel better going home early than working long after they were supposed to be done. I usually pad how much time we need crew each day. For example, if I figure we should be done by 5 P.M. today, I tell the crew we'll be done by 8 P.M. This gives me a buffer so that if things don't go as well as I had hoped, I have time to catch up. But if things do go well, then I can let my crew go home early. Even if by half an hour, leaving early makes them much more willing to show up the next day. Working longer days than scheduled should be the exception, never the rule. As the production progresses, if you see that there's an upcoming day that will need to go longer than scheduled, alert your crew ahead of time. They are far less likely to become frustrated if they go in knowing that the day will be long.

Also make sure that there's enough turnaround time between leaving the set one day and returning to work the next. Figure at least eight hours, because even in the best of circumstances, the crew has to drive home, unwind, go to sleep, get up, shower, and drive back to the set. With an eight-hour turnaround, your crew will still be lucky to get six hours of sleep. If you know that your call time tomorrow for crew is 6 A.M., try not to have today's shoot run past 9:30 P.M. I've actually been on projects where one day simply ran into the next, kind of like pulling a double shift. This is not an ideal situation, but if that happens, try to wrap early the second day so people can get some rest. Or let nonessential crew go home for a few hours. Also try to avoid shooting every single day for weeks on end. Allow your crew and cast at least one day off each week if possible.

**Staying in Focus**

Don't be alarmed if crew members catch catnaps on the set. If they've done their work and are simply waiting until they're needed, there's nothing wrong with them getting some rest. The main thing is that the AD or their department head can quickly find them when they are needed.

When shoots go way over schedule, especially for novice filmmakers, it's often due to lack of preparation. As much as possible, try to make sure that you're not the reason everything is grinding to a halt. Don't keep your crew waiting for you to tell them what to do. Delegate and trust them to do what needs to be done. Likewise, use every moment to its fullest advantage—keeping in mind that sometimes, the best advantage is to walk away for five minutes and clear your head.

When scheduling your film, keep in mind that it usually takes several days for a crew to "gel" and find the most efficient way to work together. Don't try to shoot your most complicated scenes right off the bat. Start light, because the first couple of days will be your slowest no matter what. On the other hand, don't save the hardest stuff until last. Try to put the more difficult scenes, shots, and sequences near the middle of the shoot when you can take full advantage of your crew working like a well-oiled machine and before momentum starts to dwindle toward the end of the shoot. Your first and last days of shooting should be your lightest in terms of workloads.

Your reputation as a director on set is based in small part on first impressions or your first few days, but in large part to last impressions—how your last day of shooting goes. This will be the freshest experience in your crew's mind, and if it's hell, that will color your crew's summary of the entire shoot when they tell others about working on your film. Absolutely do not go over on your last day. Better to schedule an extra day of shooting as soon as you realize it will be necessary than to have your last day run hours and hours after you were supposed to wrap.

Finally, one way of maximizing your time is to have a second unit or a small crew you can assign to collect images that do not involve dramatic action from your actors. These could be establishing shots of the settings or special material you need.

# Putting Together a Shooting Schedule

Figuring out what to shoot which day is like putting together a puzzle. Generally, you try to lump together all the shots that need to be filmed at one location and those shots that involve a specific actor. This will save you travel and set-up time if you have to go to the location, dress the set, and set up equipment only once rather than multiple times during your shoot. And in the film business, saving time is saving money.

Besides saving time, there's another reason to try to schedule all of the scenes at a given location together. If you shoot some scenes at a location and then come back months later, you may find that the location has radically changed. The owners may have redecorated, added on, or even torn the place down. You can avoid this pain by shooting everything you need at a specific location at once.

Likewise, filming all the scenes with a specific actor as close together as possible is, in the Hollywood system, a way to save money. If you're paying your actors a weekly salary, but there are many days they're not in front of the camera, you're losing dollars. Even if you're not paying your actors, there's a benefit to scheduling the filming of their scenes as close together as possible: actors are more likely to keep showing up if they feel a certain momentum that comes from shooting multiple days in a row. If your actor is only needed for three days of shooting spread out over five months, their commitment may have diminished enough by the third shooting day that they forget to show up or arrive late or look drastically different.

### Reel Trouble

One of the most common mistakes is to schedule a day shoot right after a night shoot. On your board it may look like two different days, Monday and Tuesday, but a night shoot means that you began shooting Monday night and wrapped on Tuesday morning. To schedule a day shoot for Tuesday morning means your crew has had no sleep. Allow at least a full day between the two so that your cast and crew can get the rest they need; in this example, their next workday would be Wednesday. Likewise, try not to keep shifting back and forth between day and night shoots; lump them together so that the crew and cast have time to readjust their sleep patterns.

On the film *Rhapsody*, we had to halt production for several months. When we resumed shooting, one of our lead actors showed up on the set 50 pounds lighter and with a shaved head. We had to become very creative in filming because the new scenes had to edit seamlessly with the old ones. Padding, loose clothes, and wigs were not the ideal solution but were all we could do. Some ways we could have avoided this was to shoot the film in as compressed a schedule as possible, not allowing for long gaps between the shoots; or to shoot the film in complete segments that occur in the film around the same time so that any gaps in production correspond with gaps in time between scenes in the script.

You'll never be able to schedule everything perfectly, but the ideal is to come as close as possible. As you figure out a general progression of what you'll be shooting when and where, you begin building a production board. Production boards are so named because they used to be large boards hanging on the wall that allowed everyone to easily and quickly see the film's schedule. Nowadays, the basic design of the board remains, but in a smaller form—on the page, and many producing software programs allow you to easily create these.

| | | | N | N | N | N | N | N | N | N | N | N |
| | | | 1-3/8 | 6-2/8 | 6-3/8 | 1/8 | 1/8 | 1-3/8 | 5/8 | 6/8 | 3/8 | 2 |
| | | | EXT. MARYKNOLL - NIGHT 11 | EXT. FIELD -CONTINUOUS 12 | EXT. MARYKNOLL - BACK SEM RHELL - NI 13 | EXT. MARYKNOLL - NIGHT 14 | EXT. "THE GATE" - NIGHT 15 | INT. MARYKNOLL MAIN FLOOR WEST WI 16 | INT. MARYKNOLL MAIN FLOOR INT RISE 17 | INT. REST ROOM - CONTINUOUS 18 | INT. MARYKNOLL MAIN FLOOR INT RISE 19 | INT. MARYKNOLL MAIN FLOOR HALL WA 20 |
| Character | | No. | | | | | | | | | | |
| JOEY | | 1 | | | | | | | | | | |
| MRS. BANKS | | 2 | | | | | | | | | | |
| IRAM | | 3 | 3 | | 3 | | | | 3 | 3 | 3 | 3 |
| MIKE | | 4 | | | 4 | 4 | | | | | | |
| TOR | | 5 | 5 | | | 5 | | 5 | 5 | | | 5 |
| KYLE | | 6 | | | 6 | | | | | | | |
| KATIE | | 7 | | | | | | | | | | |
| ANDREA | | 8 | | | 8 | | | | | | | |
| OPERATOR | | 9 | | | 9 | | | | | | | |
| SERA | | 10 | | | | | | 10 | 10 | 10 | | 10 |
| MOTHER | | 11 | | | | | | | | | | |
| DOCTOR | | 12 | | | | | | | | | | |
| MR. BANKS | | 13 | | | | | | | | | | |
| TV ANNOUNCER | | 14 | | | | | | | | | | |
| "MARYKNOLL" | | 15 | | | | | | | | | | |

*A production board allows you to see at a glance whether the scene is night (N) or day (D), how many pages are in the scene, the scene number and location, and which actors need to be present.*

(Courtesy of Cinergy Suite, Mindstar Productions.)

A board is basically a series of vertical columns, each one detailing the location, time of day, and shots to be filmed. These columns are often color coded in such a way that you can see at a glance which shoots are day or night, interior or exterior. The specific colors matter less than simply having a consistent system.

# Making Contingency Plans

As you're putting together the schedule, remember that if you're shooting outdoors, the times of sunrise and sunset will be an important factor. In the winter, you'll need more days to shoot the same number of exteriors as in the summer because there are fewer daylight hours in winter.

Likewise, if you're shooting outdoors, you're somewhat at the mercy of weather. If you need a sunny day but it rains instead, is there something else you can shoot at an indoor location? Or can you shoot the scene and make the rain work for you? For example, *House of Flying Daggers'* climactic fight scene was not supposed to be shot in the snow, but on the morning of the shoot, the ground was blanketed. The director ultimately chose to shoot the scene in the snow rather than wait. Anytime you wait, you're in effect taking longer to make your film—and paying more in crew or location fees.

For these reasons, build a time contingency into your schedule. Schedule your crew longer than you think you'll need each day. Once you know how many days you think it will take to shoot the entire film, add several more days to the schedule. These extra days can serve as a buffer so that you have time to pick up any shots you did not have time to complete before. In fact, it's not uncommon to call these *pickup days*.

As an independent filmmaker, keep in mind that all we've been talking about so far is scheduling how many shots or how much of the script we'll shoot each day. You'll also want to make sure that you schedule time for production meetings with your key crewmembers to go over the schedule and plan the shoot. And as an independent filmmaker, you'll probably want to schedule rehearsal times with your actors. Usually, the more you rehearse with your cast ahead of time, the faster production goes on the set.

# Hear Ye, Hear Ye: Letting Everyone Know

Once you have your schedule set, you need to let everyone know where and when you'll need them. This is where the assistant director can prove invaluable. Basically, assistant directors are part of the producing team—despite the name, they're not next in line to direct, but next in line to produce. Assistant directors help keep the director organized and make sure that everyone and everything is on the set before it will be needed.

This means that the crew and cast need to know which days and what times they need to be on set. If someone doesn't show, the assistant director needs to know how to reach him or her. So the assistant director makes sure everyone knows the schedule ahead of time and then may remind them again the day before they're needed. This is done through *call sheets*, or a day-to-day listing of who needs to be on set and at what time.

Also, when you set call times, or when people need to be on the set, remember your crew usually needs to be there before your cast. Your crew will need time to set up lights, cameras, sound gear, and dress the set. This time is generally wasted for the actor unless he needs hours of makeup, so schedule actors to arrive on set so that they're ready about half an hour before you plan to use them.

### Staying in Focus

Your assistant director and other crew people need to have all the contact information for each cast and crewmember. Many computer software address books will allow you to print out pocket-sized hard copies. Once all the names and numbers have been entered, print out copies for you, your assistant director, your production manager, and your production assistant so that there's at least one person on set all of the time with everyone's contact info. I usually include our vendors, such as equipment rental houses, insurance company, and craft services caterers in this address book as well.

Just like you had to juggle a lot of different factors to get the schedule set on paper, you will need to juggle a variety of different timelines while you're filming. Each day's shoot is kind of like preparing a large meal. Some dishes take longer to prepare while others take longer to cook. You have to make sure that all the dishes are ready at the same time so that they can be served together at exactly the right temperature. The same principle applies on a film shoot.

## The Least You Need to Know

- To accurately prepare your schedule, you need to time the script.

- Break the script down into individual elements that will be required on the set in order to better plan each day.

- Maintain good working conditions for your cast and crew by setting reasonable workdays and making sure there's enough turnaround time.

- Always have a backup or contingency plan for shooting.

- Make sure everyone involved with the film knows where they're supposed to be and when.

# Chapter 16

# *Money Train:* Budgeting Your Film

## In This Chapter

- ◆ Above the line and below the line expenses
- ◆ How to put together a budget
- ◆ The usual most expensive budget items
- ◆ Last-minute and incidental expenses
- ◆ Tips for keeping good records
- ◆ Working within your shooting budget

All fundraising efforts—whether telethons or door-to-door collections—have a goal, an amount of money the person or organization needs to raise. Can they get by on less? Probably. Would they like to raise more? Absolutely. But having a tangible amount, a realistic assessment of how much money they need, helps motivate and focus their efforts. You'll set a dollar-amount goal for your film as well.

While having an overall financial goal will help you get started with some of the basic fundraising ideas discussed in Chapter 8, investors will want to see an actual breakdown of costs. In other words, they will want to see how you arrived at that overall dollar goal. This breakdown of expenses is what we call a budget.

However, a budget is not something you develop once for investors and then file away. It is a "living document," constantly changing as you troubleshoot and deal with the changing conditions of making your movie. When you first start preparing and thinking about how much your film will cost to make, you create what is called a preliminary or estimated budget. This budget serves as your "best guess" as to the resources you'll need and how much they'll cost. Inevitably, this preliminary budget will be revised throughout the production and post-production phases.

# Lining Up: Above and Below the Line Expenses

Traditional film budgets are divided into two major categories, above the line and below the line. This "line" actually existed in traditional budgets as a bold horizontal stripe across the page, dividing the costs incurred before production and associated with the creative talent from the costs of production and post-production and the physical labor of making the film. Even without the bold stripe, this differentiation is still a standard way of breaking down a budget.

Above the line costs include story expenses (acquiring the rights to the story if necessary or purchasing a script outright) plus salaries for the producer, director, writer, and talent (or star actors). These costs are usually much more expensive for a Hollywood film than for an independent feature. Below the line items are the salaries and operational costs required to make the film and edit it, such as staff and crew salaries, film or tape stock, equipment rentals, facilities, and so on.

**Reel Trouble**

Each hour or day you go over your original schedule potentially increases your budget. Increasing your budget means either you have less money to finish your film or you have to find additional resources. If you are both producer and director, you have to be able to tell yourself no or find workable compromises when what you want to do is too expensive.

The budget is influenced by a number of factors, not the least of which is scheduling. The more days you take to make your film, the more expensive it's going to be. So figuring out a realistic schedule is an important component (see Chapter 15).

Besides scheduling, you need to research the costs of each aspect or individual element of your film, from equipment rental to location fees to transportation to catering to salary compensation for the people helping you. We've already discussed each of these specific areas in preceding chapters so that you have a better understanding of what each entails. Now's the time to make final decisions about these areas, and how much those decisions will cost you.

Some elements may have set prices or formulas that you will have to follow; others are negotiable. For example, if you're using a union crew, you will have to pay union scale and follow union rules and formulas for breaks and overtime. If you're not using a union crew, you will have more flexibility in negotiating individual compensation for each crewmember.

Whenever you negotiate a deal, be sure to have it in writing. For example, if your non-union actors are going to defer their salaries, you need to write up a deal memo that details the terms of this agreement that both you and the actors sign and keep copies of. The same holds true with any negotiated expense.

Figuring out the cost of each element may require Internet searches, phone calls, letters, e-mails, and conversations to work out and confirm prices. Most vendors and crew people will have a day rate but will also offer a discounted weekly rate if you need them more than just a day or two. Though it varies from place to place, a weekly rate is commonly equivalent to the total cost of three or four days at daily rate. In other words, if your cinematographer has a day rate of $100, you may be able to hire her for a weekly rate of $300 to $400. Be sure to ask for both the day rate and weekly rate.

Once you've done your research and agreed on specific prices for goods and services, you're ready to put a dollar amount to each of these items. Simply, you multiply the day rate for any given element by the number of days you will need it. Or if you're dealing with weekly rates, multiply by the number of weeks necessary.

> **day rate × the number of shooting days = total money needed**
>
> **weekly rate × the number of shooting weeks = total money needed**

If your shoot runs three weeks and two days, then you'll figure the cost at the weekly rate for two weeks and add that to the total of two days at the day rate.

If you want to build a contingency plan into your budget, one way to do it is to estimate all your costs as day rates, knowing that you'll often be paying a weekly rate—which will leave you a cushion of money for unexpected expenses. And there are always unexpected expenses, which I'll discuss in a few pages.

Not all services or goods will have a day or weekly rate; they will be charged as flat or fixed rates instead. For example, art direction or catering may simply be a flat cost for the whole project. As with your variable rates above, you will need to establish the cost for these goods or services and confirm those in a deal memo. Once you have, you're ready to include them in your preliminary budget.

**PRODUCTION BUDGET**
**CIG**

DATE  12-8-2004

TITLE:  Maryknoll

PICTURE NO.  12345

EPISODE: n/a

PREPARED BY:

DAYS

| | | | |
|---|---|---|---|
| Shooting: | 22 | Producer: | |
| Travel: | 0 | Director: | |
| Holiday: | 0 | 1st AD: | |
| Rehearse: | 0 | UPM: | |
| TOTAL: | 22 | Finish Date: | February 1, 2005 |

| ACCT. # | DESCRIPTION | TOTALS |
|---|---|---|
| 1100 | STORY, RIGHTS & CONTINUITY | |
| 1200 | PRODUCER'S UNIT | |
| 1300 | DIRECTOR | |
| 1400 | CAST | |
| 1900 | ATL FRINGE BENEFITS | |
| | Total Above-The-Line | |
| 2000 | PRODUCTION STAFF | |
| 2100 | EXTRA TALENT | |
| 2200 | SET DESIGN | |
| 2300 | SET CONSTRUCTION | |
| 2400 | SET STRIKING | |
| 2500 | SET OPERATIONS | |
| 2600 | SPECIAL EFFECTS | |
| 2700 | SET DRESSING | |
| 2800 | PROPERTY | |
| 2900 | WARDROBE | |
| 3000 | ACTION PROPS: PICTURE VEH | |
| 3100 | MAKE-UP & HAIRDRESSING | |
| 3200 | LIGHTING | |
| 3300 | CAMERA | |
| 3400 | PRODUCTION SOUND | |
| 3500 | TRANSPORTATION | |
| 3600 | LOCATIONS | |
| 3700 | PRODUCTION FILM & LAB | |
| 4000 | SECOND UNIT | |
| 4100 | TESTS & RESHOOTS | |
| 4200 | STAGE RENTAL EXPENSE | |
| 4300 | PROD PERIOD FRINGE | |
| | Total Production | |
| 4400 | SPECIAL PHOTOGRAPHIC EFX | |
| 4500 | FILM EDITING | |
| 4600 | MUSIC | |
| 4700 | POST PRODUCTION SOUND | |
| 4800 | POST PROD. FILM & LAB | |
| 4900 | MAIN & END TITLES | |
| 5200 | POST PROD FRINGE BENEFITS | |
| 5300 | STOP MOTION PHOTOGRAPHY | |
| 5400 | PUPPET MANUFACTURING | |
| | Total Post Production | |
| 5500 | VISUAL EFFECT | |
| 6500 | PUBLICITY | |
| 6700 | INSURANCE | |
| 6800 | GENERAL EXPENSES | |
| 7400 | ALL OTHER-FRINGE BENEFITS | |
| | Total Other | |
| | GRAND TOTAL | |

*A budget top sheet; notice the division between above the line and other expenses.*

*(Courtesy of Cinergy Suite, Mindstar Productions.)*

In showing your budget to investors, the top sheet (or summary page) is enough. This top sheet summarizes the expenses of each key element in one page or less, whereas the entire line-by-line budget might run a number of pages.

# Putting Together Your Budget

If you're not sure where to start in terms of putting together your budget, use the phases of production to help you organize, creating a separate list or file for each one.

For example, in the development phase, your list might include any expenses related to getting a script ready for pre-production. If you're doing an adaptation, this would include what you had to pay to secure the rights for the original material. If you paid someone to write a script or bought a pre-written script outright, those costs would be itemized here as well. If your film idea required research, any costs associated with that would be included. Generally, in development the only salaries that might be relevant would be the producer's and the writer's.

In the pre-production phase, you'd include the costs of preparing the shoot, getting everything ready. These expenses would include location scouting, which might involve mileage and/or a fee for the persons performing that task. You may need to rent facilities for auditioning, casting, or interviewing crew. Casting expenses would include photocopying of any materials for the actors or your assistants, and if the casting sessions run all day, you'll need to feed any of your working staff. If you're videotaping the auditions, you may need to rent a camera and buy blank videotapes. If you begin rehearsing before production begins, paying your actors or providing refreshments or renting locations ahead of time are all budgetable items.

Pre-production costs might also include those associated with setting up a production office, a central location for all the business activities of making the film; this might include phone and fax capabilities separate from your home resources. As you break down and prepare the script, there will be additional costs associated with photocopying, storyboarding, scheduling, and budgeting. At some point in this period you may begin paying for a production manager and other crew people who help prepare the production.

Your production phase costs are primarily equipment, consumable materials, catering, and salaries. This might also include airfare and other transportation costs related to getting crew and/or cast to locations. If you're shooting remotely for more than one day, you'll need to find or pay for lodging. Different locations may require fees or permits. Included here also are any supplies or materials needed for the production design, including costumes, stylists, set construction, and so on. Besides the preceding chapters, Part 3 of this book will help give you an overview of the production phase.

Post-production costs entail picture editing, sound design, and finishing costs. Processing and other costs associated with getting your film ready to edit would go here, as would purchasing the legal rights to any music you might want to use. This section would include salaries for any people who will be editing picture and sound or assisting those editors. Even if you can do a lot of the work at home, at some point you may need to pay for an online edit or syncing sound to picture or a finished print. Many of these issues will be discussed in Part 4 of this book.

# Big-Ticket Items

So far I've given you an overview of many of the possible areas of expense in making your film, but there are a few "big-ticket" items that we need to note.

Salaries are rarely as simple as handing someone money or a check. The individual crewmembers are supposed to report to the IRS anything you pay them as income. In addition, if you're operating as a business and paying your crewmembers a salary, you are required to follow guidelines regarding payroll taxes and withholding at the federal and state (and possibly county or city) levels.

**Staying in Focus**

If a potential crewmember has his own equipment, you can rent his equipment package rather than pay him a salary. However, if he is not incorporated as a business and you pay more than $600 for the rental, you'll need to issue him a 1099-Misc tax form. This form will require you to have his name, address, and tax ID number (either EIN or SSN). Paying as a rental eliminates your need to treat the money as payroll and will save you some tax dollars.

If a group of friends are working on your film for free or deferred salaries, then you do not need to worry about these issues. But you will need to feed them. Never underestimate the power of food in keeping crew and cast happy, especially if they're not getting paid or getting paid very little. Craft services—providing meals and snacks on set—will be one of the most expensive items in your budget. In fact, on really small low-budget films, it's not uncommon for craft services to be the single most expensive line item.

Equipment rentals or purchases will be another major expense. Almost all rental houses will provide some sort of weekly or long-term rate, and many are willing to negotiate beyond their officially stated rates. They're usually not going to give you stuff for free, but if you request a reasonable discount, they'll often consider it.

All rental houses will require you to prove that you have insurance before letting you leave with the equipment. This is only one type of insurance that you'll need to budget for, and as far as film expenses go, insurance is usually a pretty good bargain. Your local, regional, or state film office may be able to suggest insurance companies. Rental houses may share what companies they regularly work with.

You'll want to make sure you have insurance coverage for the loss, damage, or theft of equipment, props, or wardrobe as well as location insurance to protect the owners where you're filming. You'll need insurance protection for injury on the set, and if you're issuing a payroll, you'll need worker's compensation. In addition, you may have heard of errors and omissions (E&O) insurance, which provides some protection in the event someone sues you for using their trademarked or copyrighted material accidentally, but for most low-budget films, that's really more an issue at the distribution stage, and something you don't have to pay for now. In fact, if a distributor buys your film, they'll likely pay for it.

> **Reel Trouble**
>
> Be careful of the "boys and their toys" mentality. There's a temptation to see equipment rentals as a chance to work with the latest or most expensive gear simply for the coolness factor. But as the producer, you have to choose the most affordable way to get the job done.

Another major area of your budget will be consumables, particularly unused blank filmstock and tape stock that I'll call rawstock. In Part 3, I'll talk about these materials more specifically, but in terms of preparing your budget, be aware that your origination format (what you shoot on) and release format (the primary method you exhibit your film) will have a major impact on the total cost of your production.

There are two factors that determine how much rawstock you'll need: the length of your project and your shooting ratio. Obviously, a ten-minute film will probably require less rawstock than a two-hour film.

The other critical factor in this determination is the shooting ratio, which can be thought of several different ways, such as the number of minutes of film you shoot to get a single minute of finished film on the screen or how many times you shoot the same action that will appear only once in the final film. If you shoot each action once, your shooting ratio is 1:1 or one to one. If on average you shoot two takes for every single shot in the final film, this would be a shooting ratio of 2:1. Shooting ratios are averaged over the entire film, so any individual shot might be taken fewer or more times; this means you might shoot one shot in a single take and another shot in three takes—the average is two takes per shot, or a shooting ratio of two to one. At first glance, it may seem that shooting in single takes is your best choice to save money, but in fact, a one-to-one shooting ratio brings many challenges that can cause headaches, delays, and greater expense in post-production.

One of the determining factors in your shooting ratio will be the complexity of your individual shots. For example, any shots involving camera movement will usually take longer to set up and practice and are more likely to "go wrong" and need to be re-done. This takes more time, which means more money.

I'm calling your attention to these particular areas because they are often the most expensive elements in your budget. But remember that a complete budget takes into consideration everything needed to make your film. Besides the big-ticket items, your budget will need to include the costs of many smaller expenses, expenses related to each of the previous chapters, such as location scouting and production design. You'll be surprised how fast they add up.

# Petty-Cash Expenses

Another part of your budgeting process is to determine an amount of cash to have on set for unexpected last-minute expenses. This is sometimes referred to as petty cash or a slush fund, and it can save you from having to stop the shoot in order to send some-one or personally go to the bank. I usually try to make sure we have at least $200 in cash on the set, including two rolls of quarters. Basically, this money is to handle what-ever small incidentals need to be paid during the day. There are no hard-and-fast rules for handling petty cash other than it can only be used for production film-related expenses, any money taken out has to be replenished, and these transactions have to be documented. I usually appoint a well-trusted crew person such as my production man-ager to handle the petty cash, so that I can focus on working with the actors and crew to get the shots. Whenever the production manager takes money out of petty cash, she writes a note or better yet exchanges the money for a receipt of whatever the money was used for, later "billing" it against the specific budget item and replacing the money, so that each day we start with enough cash to handle any unforeseen emergencies.

# Accountability: Keeping Records

Keeping accurate records is one of the most important aspects of producing a film. These records are what will afford you tax breaks as well as making sure you have enough money to finish the film. If you can afford an accountant or negotiate with one to help you set up your business expenses for free (usually in return for preparing your taxes), by all means, do it. But if you can't, here are some general concepts and tips to help you.

I usually ask another person I trust with my life to assume the primary responsibility of keeping track of the bills and money; I then periodically double-check to make sure I know how much money we have to spend at any given moment. Trying to do it all yourself usually means something will suffer—either you'll lose track of money or not do your other jobs well.

As part of your record keeping, you want some sense of how much money you have in comparison to how much money you're spending. This is a balance sheet, an accounting of both your expenses (or liabilities) and your income (or assets). Your assets include money you've raised for the film, minus any taxes you've had to pay on it. But your assets also include any in-kind services you've received, such as your crew working for free or a restaurant donating their craft services. I talked a little bit about in-kind services in Chapter 8. Basically, in your ledger, you list the dollar amount of these services or products with the notation that they are "in-kind." They are considered an asset because in effect, they're as good as money in getting your film made and contribute to your overall income. These are offset, of course, in the expenses or liabilities side of the balance sheet, as if you had paid for them. Your ledger sheet lets you know how much it really cost to make your film and how you paid for it, either with donations of in-kind services or with money you raised for the film.

With all that has to get done, it's easy to lose track of the details on a film set, but if possible, try to balance your accounts daily. If not daily, at least once a week, though if there are any errors, you'll be surprised how difficult it is to reconstruct what happened a day or two before, much less a week ago. Again, you can have someone else do that for you, but be sure to take a look at the balance each day.

If you can negotiate with a local bank to provide you free checking, creating a separate account with checks or an ATM card specifically for the production is a great way to keep records of your production costs. You'll know that all deposits and checks written on that account are for your production, and it will make your record keeping easier.

> **Staying in Focus**
>
> You may find it helpful to keep a running list of when bills need to be paid or, if you have a pledge of money from an investor, when you can expect to receive it. Never assume how much money you've got or how it's being spent.

However, if you can't find a bank to provide free checking, you may decide it's simpler to use your own account. If so, consider ordering a set of checks with a distinctly separate series of numbers so that they stand out on your bank statement from your personal finances.

Deposits to your personal account will be trickier, so be sure to keep an accurate detailed log of each and every deposit. Itemize each check; do not lump them together into one massive deposit, but deposit each check separately so that the actual deposit will be easy to confirm on your statement.

Another option is to use one particular credit card for all production expenses, in effect using the monthly bill as a method of record keeping. The problem of course is that it's tempting to spend more money than you've got, so I only recommend this if you are disciplined enough to pay off the balance each and every month. That way you're not wasting 20 percent of your assets or budget on interest charges.

With all receipts, including ATM withdrawal and deposit receipts, always clearly mark what the receipt is for and enough info that you can easily understand the reasons for it months later. Keep in mind that some receipts fade with time, so I often photocopy them or write in pen the amount, date, and reason in the margins or on the back just in case.

Besides accounting to your investors and making sure you're spending your money in ways that will assure completing the film, good record keeping will save you hours if not days of work when it comes time to file your taxes.

**Staying in Focus**

Whenever I begin a film, I create a clearly labeled box to hold everything that has to do with that particular production—bank statements, receipts, actors' headshots, deal memos, release forms, permits, and copies of my budget and production materials. As I begin working with individual vendors, I then create a separate envelope for each one to hold all of that vendor's receipts and bills. I add to this box throughout the entire project.

# Having Enough Money to Bring It Home

Every once in a while, you will hear of a filmmaker diving in before they have all the money they need. Or sometimes, a filmmaker will severely underestimate the production costs and run out of money mid-shoot. Rarely do these kinds of situations have happy endings, though *Narc* is one film that did. Reaching the finish line is easier if you keep a few things in mind:

◆ **Prices vary.** Different places charge different prices for the same goods or services within the same town or from town to town, so compare and find out who has the best deals.

- **Convenience isn't always affordable.** A few years ago I needed to rent a Super 16 camera in Chicago, but the prices were more than my budget would allow, so I called a place in Milwaukee and found a Super 16 package at almost half the cost. Yes, I had to drive two hours to pick it up, but ultimately, my time and gas mileage was a better deal than renting closer to home.

- **Newer isn't always better.** For example, in Chicago, there are equipment rental houses with the latest equipment that charge 25 to 50 percent more than rental houses that have older equipment; of course, if you're using older equipment, it's extremely important to check and make sure it works properly.

- **The price is not necessarily the final price.** Many places are willing to negotiate a better deal if they consider you a good risk. Deals are not always about money but sometimes specific equipment, so if they insist the price can't be lower, see if you can get more for that price. The key here is to be reasonable in your request; ask for discounts, especially if you're a student.

- **Nothing beats a good bargain.** Some vendors, especially small ones, and some crew people may be willing to barter or exchange services with you, kind of the "you crew for me on this film, I'll crew for you on your film" notion.

- **The best things in life are free.** In-kind services are the lifeblood for independent filmmakers; these can include you doing your job for free.

- **Better late than never.** Deferring salaries for cast and crew basically means you'll pay them later if the film makes money; deferring your own salary or personal costs can help keep your budget manageable.

- **Burning bridges will cost you.** Follow through on your promises, pay your bills on time, and don't bounce checks. It's impossible to predict who'll come through for you in a pinch or who you may need down the road, so make sure no one has a reason not to help you when you really need it.

Finally, any good budget anticipates the fact that unforeseen circumstances are the very nature of filmmaking. Equipment will break, a location will fall through, weather won't cooperate, and you'll need to reshoot some scenes. Therefore, most budgets include a contingency line item of 10 to 15 percent. I'd like to think you won't need it, but my experience is that very few films come in under budget.

# Final Destination: Your Shooting Budget

As I've mentioned, your budget changes throughout all phases of your film, from pre-production through production and post-production and on to exhibition &

distribution. While your preliminary budget is a good starting point for letting investors know how much the film will cost, right before you begin shooting you'll need to prepare a final shooting budget. This shooting budget is the point where you have to take a hard look at how much money you have and how much money you need. My guess is these two numbers will be different, and not in a good way. I've met very few filmmakers who felt that they had more money than they needed to make a film.

---

### Ditty Bag

When people say that a film showing at the local multiplex was made for an unbelievably low amount, such as $10,000, $50,000, or even $100,000, be skeptical. They usually mean that's how much money it took to get the film "in the can"—or simply shot. That figure rarely if ever includes the full post-production costs, which are very expensive as well—usually at least some of those have been picked up by the distributor—and none of the distribution costs. Some filmmakers will talk of negative costs, or the amount of money the film cost before distribution.

---

If you don't have all the money you'd like, there are a couple of things you can do. You could always start shooting and hope that you can find more money later, in post-production, after you have something to show people and interest them in investing. This is risky. There's nothing much worse than having boxes of exposed film in your fridge because you can't afford to process them. Or having your film held hostage by the lab because you can't pay the bill. A smarter way might be to rethink how the resources you have can be used. This means compromise—which is just a nicer way of saying you need to let go a little bit of that ideal film in your head and embrace the film you can make.

## The Least You Need to Know

◆ Films always cost more to make than you expect.

◆ Preliminary budgets are prepared early in the process and estimate how much money the film will cost.

◆ Keeping accurate records is essential.

◆ Before you begin shooting, balance your budget by making sure your costs are not significantly greater than your resources.

# Part  3

## Ready for My Close-Up: Production

There's an old adage for filmmaking that goes "plan the shoot, shoot the plan." Now that you've completed pre-production, you're ready to put your plan into action.

This stage is about directing and running your set. To be as prepared as possible, you'll learn about rehearsing your actors and coordinating your crew. Throw in a little lighting and sound, and your job is complete.

Lights! Camera! …

# Chapter 17

# *The Miracle Worker:* Directing

## In This Chapter

- ◆ Collaborating with actors
- ◆ Rehearsals as an important aspect of independent filmmaking
- ◆ Crewmembers as advisors
- ◆ Keeping everyone informed through production meetings
- ◆ Running the set

Would you prefer sitting for hours talking with a stranger or would you rather spend that time playing with gadgets? Are you more comfortable with people or machines? The answers to these might give you a glimpse into your potential strengths and weaknesses as a director. Either way, the temptation for many of us is to spend the most time and energy on what we like or think we do well and to avoid the areas we're less confident in.

This means that if you're more confident in your ability to work with machines than with people, you may be tempted to focus all your directing energies on the technical aspects of making your film: visual design, lighting, sets, and so on. If you're more confident working with people than setting up your computer, you may tend to focus all your directing energies on the actors and leave your crew to figure out the technicalities of making your film. The ideal film director falls somewhere in between these two extremes.

# Acting Up

When I first started making films, I was nervous about working with actors. I wasn't sure how to direct them, what they would want from me, and whether I would be able to provide them anything meaningful. I didn't always understand the terms they used or how they went about creating a performance. As a result, I was tempted to let them figure out the performance on their own, and if they asked me questions, I'd defer to their judgment.

As a director working with actors, like many things in film, it depends on where you want to do the work. You can do it before you reach the set, on the set, or in post-production. But one way or the other, you'll have to work to get the dramatic action revealed in your film. Besides the technical aspects of how you present that action, the primary conveyers of the drama are your actors.

Some directors see most of their work with actors as occurring in the casting process, thinking that if you cast the right person, you have to do very little on the set because they'll intuitively give the performance necessary for the film. Some directors see most of their work as being on the set, and they may cast for general look rather than acting ability with the idea that they'll direct every single movement as if the actor was a manikin that the director is posing. Some directors figure that they'll create the performance through editing by choosing the best takes and shots to construct a character, taking much more time in post-production. Other directors see the actor as an active collaborator and do a great deal of work or rehearse with the actor before production begins.

Just as directors work differently, so do actors. Part of being a good director is figuring out how your actors work best and providing a situation in which they can do their best work. For example, some actors immerse themselves and heavily research their roles while others rely more on their intuition and instincts. Or some actors need to warm up and will get better with more and more rehearsal, while other actors give their best work in their first effort. The real challenge is when both of these actors are in the same scene!

Because there are so many demands for my time when I'm on the set, my general bias is to work with the actors before production, during the rehearsal process. This isn't always possible on Hollywood films, due to conflicting schedules and budgetary considerations such as paying the actors to rehearse. But for independent filmmakers, rehearsal is a staple and can save you money in the long run. The general idea is that the more you rehearse the actors and hone the performance, the fewer takes you'll need on the set to get the shot you need.

In a way, I think of the rehearsal process as research. Or archeology. We are uncovering the story, backstory, and characters as a team. Even if I've written the script, I learn new facets of my story through this process, which ultimately informs my aesthetic decisions and helps me make a better film.

Rehearsals are also the place where the actors and I establish our working relationships, which will carry over onto the set. We find the ways to communicate with each other most effectively and establish a common vocabulary. In a way, rehearsals are a conversation between me and the actors.

We may start the first time with what is sometimes called a *table read*, which simply means getting everyone in the same room and reading the script aloud. The idea here is not to start acting, but to simply read as a group the entire story in one sitting so that each of us gets a sense of the overall arc of the story and each character.

From that point, we begin working with individual scenes, and in fact, the smaller beats within that scene (see Chapter 9 for more information about beats). Using text analysis and working in smaller units helps us understand the moment-to-moment aspects of the scene, allowing the actor to construct a performance that can be shot out of sequence (as most scenes are) and edited together for a cohesive presentation and dramatic action.

Improvising character interactions not in the script can sometimes be a useful tool for actors and directors who are comfortable with the technique. This process might help the actor and me gain more insight into the character. Improvisation is a very specific technique; you might want to take a class or learn more about it before trying it as a directing approach.

Within an individual scene, one of the most important questions for you and the actor to ask is simply, why doesn't this character leave? What makes the character stay in that moment and interaction? The answer needs to be a psychological motivation, which will help you get to the wants and needs of the character—not simply because the story will fall apart if the character leaves.

I see my role in working with actors as guiding the performance, letting the actors do the work they love. Rather than me doing the work by micromanaging their performances, I try to

> ### Ditty Bag
>
> There are a number of misperceptions about acting and how actors achieve an emotional performance. One thing to keep in mind is that acting for film is not about therapy for the actor, it's about creating a character who will appear on screen as three dimensional, which means psychologically complex.

guide the establishment of parameters and story world in which the actors can explore and develop the characters. Rather than saying, "cry here," I try to create a safe environment for them to create an interior world where the character will feel the emotions that might result in tears.

This kind of work can be scary for the novice, especially if you don't feel so comfortable working with people. We live in a culture that often tries to avoid conflict and intense emotion, but dramatic stories are about conflict, and those conflicts are engaging for an audience because they are expressed through the emotional life of the characters.

Actors are best able to do this work if I'm doing my work of listening. This means rather than telling them how I see the role, I ask them questions about how they see the role. This process also helps us begin to establish trust and an environment for them to experiment and explore in order to arrive at their performance. My ideal is to make them less aware of themselves than they are of the characters they're portraying, which is part of the reason that I usually don't want actors to watch dailies or scenes they've already shot while we're still in production. The risk is that they'll become self-conscious.

### Defining Moments

When you **block** a scene, you are choreographing the actors' movements within the space and in relationship to each other, ideally revealing behaviors that will allow the audience to better understand the characters and the dramatic moment. Blocking on the set adds the camera to this mix so that choices are made as to how it moves or is placed in relationship to the actors' physical interactions.

Often on the set (and most common in Hollywood filmmaking), there are run throughs or mini-rehearsals where the camera crew is all ready and you as the director have the actors go through the scene or shot several times right before filming it. This is a good place to make minor adjustments in *blocking*, because you'll rarely have the luxury of rehearsing extensively on your set before the day of filming. But again, this may depend on whether you're working with an actor whose performance gets worse the more she practices it. Also you may do more than one take of the same shot so that you can choose the best in the editing room. If you are doing multiple takes, make sure you have a reason. If you're simply getting the same performance over and over and are not adjusting the image at all, it's a waste of rawstock (blank film or tape) and time.

Experienced actors are accustomed to the idea of *adjustments*, or fine-tuning the performance to your suggestions between each take. Usually with these adjustments, I try to keep the actor in the story world as much as possible and build off the points of reference we've developed during the rehearsal process. Therefore, I might suggest shifting the goals or wants of the character with phrases such as "as if" or "like you're" rather than stating "get angry." Directing actors is in many ways a facilitation process, and you can use metaphors and analogies to help the actor find the character's internal truth. This is often more effective than asking them to mimic your way of saying the line or your gestures.

# Crewing Up

Delegate, delegate, delegate. Whether there's one other person helping you or five, fifteen, or fifty, don't try to do everything yourself. Hire people you can trust, meet with them, communicate your guiding vision and then stand back and let them do their jobs. Concentrate your time and energy on those production responsibilities that only a director or producer can carry out.

Traditional sets usually operate as a hierarchy, a series of departments each with its own manager who answers to the director (who in turn answers to the producing concerns of budget and schedule). These key department heads coordinate the work in their various areas. Though it might seem odd to think of your film production having departments, I'm going to use that term to refer to major crew areas (such as cinematography, production design, and sound design) whether you have several people in each area or just one.

This set hierarchy also dictates a certain flow of communication. When we talk about directing your crew, what we usually mean is that you give direction to your key department heads rather than personally direct every single person on the set. Think of your department heads as middle management. For example, you as the filmmaker wouldn't tell the gaffer to move a light—you'd tell the cinematographer what you need to be done, and the cinematographer assigns the task. Likewise, if the gaffer has an idea about the lighting design, he would take that idea to the cinematographer rather than you. While it may seem unnecessarily rigid, this communication model is designed to reduce confusion or even chaos on the set. Too many individuals coming to you with ideas or needing information, or worse yet your crewmembers receiving multiple (and sometimes contradictory) orders from you and/or your department heads, is why a structured communication model makes sense.

> **Ditty Bag**
>
> Oftentimes, you as the filmmaker will only hire department heads, such as the cinematographer, who in turn will hire her own gaffer, electrician, and grips. This is because cinematographers, production designers, and sound designers often have crewmembers that they regularly work with, making for a more efficient team.

This doesn't mean you only speak with your department heads and ignore everyone else on the crew. While you won't be directly telling grips or boom operators what to do, you should still follow the common courtesies of saying "hello" and knowing their names, regardless of their function on the set: production assistant, best boy, set dresser, grip. This can go a long way toward instilling loyalty and hard work, especially if you're not paying much.

On small shoots, a rigid hierarchy may not be practical and may seem too impersonal, especially if everyone is doing more than one job. Many independent filmmakers work with very small crews and the same people over and over. As a result, communication on the set may be less formal and quicker because everyone's pitching in and knows what to expect.

The bottom line is that a well-working set has good clear communication, from you to the department heads, and from the department heads to the individual crewmembers and vice versa.

## Who's on First

As the filmmaker, you will want to involve your production designer, cinematographer, and sound designer as soon as possible. These are your primary collaborators who will help you bring your guiding vision to life and will serve as your key production department heads, managing all the different tasks it takes to make your film.

Your department heads need to have some idea of their budgets, especially your production designer and cinematographer. Being a filmmaker who is both the producer and the director can be tough, especially at this point, because your department heads may ask for things you can't afford. For example, your cinematographer may be advising you that your film absolutely needs to be shot in 35mm film. You may be convinced and yet you know you can't afford it. You now have an inner conflict. In order to pay for what the cinematographer wants, you either have to raise more money or cut the budget somewhere else. One requires more time and the other means another part of your production will suffer.

> **Staying in Focus**
>
> As a director, no one is expecting you to be an expert on everything. But it helps if you know a little bit about everything, so that when your crew has questions or suggestions, you have a general idea of what they're talking about. Chapters 19 and 20 will give you a better understanding of basic cinematography and sound issues on the set.

The solution is coming up with compromises you can both live with. Perhaps you can shoot in another format, such as Super 16, regular 16mm, 24 P, or HDTV that is closer to what you can afford. When weighing your options, you want to consider that each format will probably require different costs in the post-production phase, so making your decision based on budgetary concerns, you need to figure not just the difference in rental and rawstock production costs, but also your editing costs.

If you as a filmmaker are both producer and director, you have to keep an eye on the practicalities, such as budget, as well as your dream. Having another perspective on the budget can be extremely helpful, and if you're producing/directing the film, you will want to hire a line producer or production manager early as well.

Another person helping you with the budget can take some of the pressure off and help you say no to requests. I used to get annoyed when the cinematographer or sound designer would regularly ask for more than what was budgeted—more equipment, more expensive equipment, more time—until I realized that part of their job is to ask for everything they think will make their work easier and the film better, no matter what the cost. Part of my job is to weigh those requests with how much we have to spend and make a decision.

> **Staying in Focus**
>
> You may feel like you're under pressure from your key department heads to make your film a certain way. Keep in mind that they are advisors. You as the filmmaker are the decision maker. Sometimes the decision is no. And when it is, your advisors need to come up with another way to accomplish their tasks that will work for the film and that you can afford.

## ADing It All Up

On the actual set, your lifesaver will regularly be your assistant director (AD). Your AD makes sure cast and crew are where they're supposed to be when they're supposed to be there. If there's anyone on the set who never stops, it's your assistant director. A good AD has to keep an eye on what's going on now as well as what's coming up three hours from now and tomorrow. A good AD keeps you from having to handle all the little details that have to be taken care of in order for you to roll cameras.

Your AD will make sure you have all the materials for a shoot the night before, will schedule and confirm all the necessary people, keep track of everyone on the set throughout the day's shoot, and make note of anything that didn't get finished that has to carry over to tomorrow (or another day).

Your production manager (PM) makes sure that all the equipment and services are ready and available when needed. If a piece of equipment breaks or needs to be replaced, the PM is the person who calls around looking for the best prices.

Small independent films may sometimes merge the jobs of assistant director and production manager. This is because despite the name, an assistant director is part of the producing team, not the directing team.

# Productive Production Meetings

While much of the actors' preparation work occurs during rehearsals, most of your crew's preparation for the shoot occurs during production meetings. These are often a series of meetings involving different personnel as appropriate and are one of the primary aspects of the collaborative process. Production meetings are the place where you and the key crewmembers lock down details and plan the shoot, clarifying what's needed and who's doing what.

I may initially meet with just my production designer and cinematographer to map out the visual look of the film. As we begin laying out the logistics of shooting, these production meetings may include members of my producing team, such as the assistant director or production manager, as well as the sound designer.

Ideally, each meeting has a specific set of goals to be accomplished and serves as a clearinghouse of information that crew need in order to more effectively and efficiently prepare for production. In effect, these meetings are a primary source of communication, and hopefully everyone leaves with a better idea of the tasks at hand and who is responsible for what.

> **Staying in Focus**
>
> Like films, meetings have their own duration threshold. I've always heard that once a meeting goes past about two hours, people can become overwhelmed and tune out. Now, if everyone is caught up in a creative task and energized, you can probably go a little longer. But there is a point of diminishing returns. Try to keep your meetings efficient. Don't waste people's time. Be prepared, have clear goals for the meeting, guide the discussion to keep it focused on what's relevant, and summarize at the end what needs to be done before the next meeting.

These meetings are also a great opportunity to anticipate problems before we get to the set. As a result, you may want to think of these meetings as a two-way communication. You have information about the shoot that you may need to impart, but also make sure you allow time to hear and consider crew questions or suggestions. Of course, discussion takes more time than simply telling people what to do. But discussion is an important element in the planning phases, because it's by hearing other people's ideas and concerns that you better prepare for shooting.

With a large crew, I might hold meetings with my department heads who in turn meet with their own respective crewmembers. These meetings address the practicalities of shooting and make sure everyone is prepared so that things on the set will run as smoothly as possible. However, I have found it helpful to schedule at least one meeting fairly close the first day of shooting that is open to every single crew person. My goal at that meeting is to give an overview of the production strategy and schedule, share my guiding vision, and help build momentum (and hopefully excitement) for everyone to work together.

There's no way you'll be able to anticipate every possible eventuality in a production meeting. The goal in these meetings is as much to develop a unified strategy and approach for making decisions quickly on the set as it is to foresee and solve potential problems. Believe me, even on the best-planned shoots, something (or many things) during production invariably goes differently than you expect. Good planning gives you an anchor to keep you from getting swept up in the chaos of shooting.

# Calling the Shots

On the set, there are certain protocols that help keep people informed of what's going on. Every shot is preceded by a general organized chaos that with experience you will take for granted and learn to tune out.

---

### Ditty Bag

Common set courtesy requires that you warn people when you might be doing something that could momentarily interfere with their job or even harm them. For example, whenever you or a crew person walks through the frame while the camera operator is prepping the shot, you should say loud enough for the operator to hear: "crossing." When changing power cords, you might yell out "repatching" so that the cinematographer doesn't wonder why a light isn't turning on. Before turning on a light, the gaffer or grip should call out "eyes" as a warning not to look his or her direction because the bright light can hurt your eyes.

---

As you're preparing to film a shot, you might be working with the actors to make sure they're ready to film this particular part of the scene and are comfortable acting in the space. This process might include any last minute adjustments to the blocking or performance. You may designate certain points in the blocking by number, as in "one" for where everyone starts, "two" for a significant moment during the shot, "three" for a second significant moment if necessary, and so on.

Meanwhile, your cinematographer and gaffer are probably fine-tuning the lights and getting everything ready to actually record the actors' performance. This includes positioning the camera, and the camera operator will need to see the action run through a couple of times to make sure that the camera is properly placed and that the framing is correct.

Whenever a new lighting setup is being done, your assistant director will check in with the cinematographer to get an estimated time of arrival (ETA) of when the camera crew will be ready to shoot. This can help the director know how much time he has to work with his actors without tying up the production, but also this can help the production manager and/or assistant director see whether the shoot is staying on schedule and whether any adjustments need to be made in the day's work.

Once the camera position is set, that's when the location sound recordist and boom operator place themselves to get the best possible sound while remaining out of the camera's framing. The sound team will need the actors to run through their lines to be sure the levels are set correctly. The boom operator will need to figure out how close she can place the microphone without it appearing in the frame, which requires her talking with the camera operator. (I'll discuss cinematography and sound concerns in more detail in Chapters 19 and 20.)

When these run-throughs are completed, you're ready to roll camera. There are generally a series of calls that are made to assure everyone is ready, and these are usually done in a specific order.

Most times your AD will make the first call, because it usually has to be shouted and you may need your voice later on:

> **"Quiet on the set."**

This lets everyone know to stop making noise. The assistant director will then indicate whether this is a run-through (a rehearsal of the shot) or a take (the actual filming of the shot).

> **"This is a run-through"** or **"This is a take."**

Because sound media has traditionally been less expensive than filmstock, you usually call for sound to start rolling first. You or in some cases your AD will say:

> **"Roll sound."**

If it's a take, once the sound mixer or recordist is sure that the sound is recording, she will call:

**"Speed."**

Then you (or sometimes your assistant director) will call:

**"Roll camera."**

Your camera operator will then start the camera; once the tape or film is clearly moving through the camera at standard speed, he will call:

**"Speed."**

The next step is to slate the shot, providing visual information about the scene number, shot number, and take number. The person slating may also shout out this information so that the sound crew can record it as well. Slating will help your editor identify each shot in post-production. The person slating will usually do it without a prompt, but if necessary, the AD might call out "slate." When the person slating finishes identifying the shot, he usually calls "mark."

Then you (never the AD) will call:

**"Action."**

Generally, you as the director will want to match the tone of the scene with your call for action. If the performance is to be loud and lively, then you might want your "action" to be energetic. If it's a somber scene, you may want your "action" to be more subdued. This helps the actors set their performance, just as a barbershop quartet might match their harmonies to a first hummed note by one of the members.

After the action is completed, you (never the AD) will call:

**"Cut."**

At that point, your camera operator may need to check the camera to make sure there were no problems in recording the shot, and your sound recordist may double-check to make sure the sound was recorded well. The camera operator may call "clear." Either way, you should check with both to see if there were any

**Staying in Focus**

In order for the actors and crew to get used to the calls, you will make all of these calls during a run-through as well, though in that case, your sound and camera people might respond "sound" and "camera" rather than "speed" so that there's no confusion that they're actually recording.

problems. If there were, these should be recorded where appropriate (either on the camera log for the visuals and the sound log for the audio) as well as with the script supervisor.

The script supervisor or continuity person keeps a running record of every single shot, noting what part of the scene it has recorded, a general sense of what appeared in the frame, how long the take was, and any notes about quality, whether mechanical (such as audio or visual) or performance (flubbed lines, dropped or omitted lines, and so forth).

> **CAUTION**
>
> **Reel Trouble** _____
>
> A common mistake for beginning directors is to say "action" and "cut" too quickly. Some of the best reaction shots I've gotten are after the action of the scene is over but before I call "cut" and even sometimes after the camera has set but before I call "action."

If you need to retake the shot, no one moves from their locations except the actors, who you may ask to "go back to one," meaning they should go back to the first blocking point or starting positions for the shot. Or you may decide that the first part of the shot is okay, but you need to redo the ending, and so you begin filming the retake further in, asking the actors to go "back to two." Of course, doing this means that what you originally envisioned as one shot now has to be able to be cut into two shots, but this may not be an issue if you're planning on cutting in another shot in the final edit between the beginning and end of the take.

Each take is numbered separately, which is reflected on the slate, the camera log, sound log, and continuity script. The identification of each shot on each log needs to be the same, which requires quick and efficient communication among all the people keeping logs. And then you start the whole process again.

In order to let your crew and cast know that they're released to go home at the end of the day's shoot, after the last shot your AD calls:

> **"That's a wrap!"**

## The Least You Need to Know

- As director it's important to delegate; explain what needs to be done and then let your cast and crew do the jobs you've hired them to do.

- Treat your cast and crew as collaborators.

- Use production meetings and rehearsals to share your vision and to establish working relationships with cast and crew.

- Set protocols help keep shooting organized and efficient.

# Through a Glass Darkly: Camera and Lens

## In This Chapter

- ◆ The difference between film, analog video, and digital video
- ◆ The effect of generation loss on the image
- ◆ Wide, normal, telephoto, and macro lenses
- ◆ Ways to view your image while you're filming

Though we've been using the terms *film* and *filmmaking* to refer to moving images that might originate on either filmstock or videotape, it's time to look at each of these a bit more closely.

I now need to be much more specific and precise in my terminology, so I will be distinguishing between film, analog video, and digital video (DV) in this chapter. I will use the term *filmstock* to designate unexposed Super8, 16mm, or 35mm film and *videotape* to refer to blank videotape, whether it's DV or analog.

## Machine in a Box: Cameras

Film, analog video, digital video: These are the three primary ways of collecting moving images in the early twenty-first century. The one thing these all have in common is that they require a camera in order to produce a photographic image.

Cameras are simply machines that expose a series of still photographs—or frames—that can be viewed later. All cameras are a combination of optics (or lenses) and mechanics—and in most cases, electronics, as well—that work together to record these images.

The mechanical system drives the filmstock or videotape through the camera and in front of the lenses (or optical system) in order to render an image. The electronic system helps regulate the speed of the mechanical system as well as automate certain functions of the camera, such as control of exposure, focus, and/or in-camera effects. Because film, analog video, and DV media are each a little bit different, they require different types of cameras and render their images on different materials.

# Latent Images: Film

Film is still the standard by which movie images are measured, and film cameras are classified by the width of the filmstock they use. This width is gauged in millimeters (8, 16, 35, 65). The wider the filmstock, the better your image quality. Of course, wider filmstocks require larger cameras, which means that 35mm filmstock will render a better image than 16mm, but it will also require a bigger (and heavier) camera.

Though you might run across an old Super8 or even an older 8mm camera at a yard sale, both are pretty much obsolete because of the difficulty finding raw filmstock or a lab that will process it. Most independent filmmakers dream of shooting on 35mm like the big Hollywood films but usually can only afford to shoot on 16mm film. For this reason, Super16 has become a popular variation of the 16mm format because it is designed to create the size and scale of image we often associate with widescreen 35mm film projection (see Chapter 19). However, Super16 requires a specially designed camera and can only be projected as a finished film sound print if it's blown up to 35mm, which can be very expensive.

A 100-foot load of 16mm film is a little less than 3 minutes' worth of screen time; a 400-foot load will give you about 10 minutes. With 35mm filmstocks that come in 400- and 1,000-foot loads, figure you'll get about 1 minute of screen time for each 100 feet.

When ordering filmstock, order it all at the same time if possible so that it will be from the same batch number. Though the production of raw filmstock is automated, there can be slight variations from each production run, or batch. On the other hand, if you don't mind these potential variations and you're trying to save money, you can order what are called *short ends* or other people's leftovers—parts of rolls they didn't shoot—that have been sold back to the vendor.

## Perfs

All filmstocks are pretty much like the film that you'd use in a still camera, just on a longer roll. The edge of the film is made up of *sprocket holes* or *perforations* (sometimes simply called *perfs*). These allow the camera (and a projector) to move the film. The image area is called a frame. In 16mm film, the perfs occur at each frame line (or the top or bottom of the frame). In 35mm film, there are four perfs per frame. In addition, there is an edge number that can assist with editing, which I'll talk about a little more in Chapters 22 and 26.

Depending on the format, raw or unexposed filmstock may be *double perf* or *single perf*. Double perf means that there are perforations along both edges; single perf filmstock only has sprocket holes along one edge. Most 16mm filmstocks are single perf to allow for use in Super16 cameras. Super16 creates a wider image than regular 16mm by extending the frame into the area that would have been used for the second row of perfs. Even if you shoot double perf filmstock (such as in 35mm), once a sound track is added, your composite (or combined sound and visual) print will only have one set of perfs because the sound track will be along the opposite edge of the finished film. For this reason, projection prints are single perf.

## Layers

Filmstock is made up of several layers. The thickest is a transparent *base*, which for many years was made of cellulose acetate (hence the slang term *celluloid* for film) but is now made of polyester. The base has to be strong enough and flexible enough to wind through the camera, because it has a very important cargo: an even coat of *emulsion*.

The emulsion is where the latent photographic image is created. This layer is a gelatin-type

| Ditty Bag |
| --- |
| If you're holding a piece of film or videotape, the emulsion side is where the visual information is stored. This layer or side will be a little less shiny and feel just slightly sticky or tacky to the touch. The base side will be shinier and smooth. To protect the image, try not to touch the emulsion or allow it to get scratched or dirty. |

substance that contains light-sensitive particles and/or dyes. As light hits each frame, it causes a change that we will not be able to see until the film goes through a chemical process in the lab. After processing, the remaining particles on the print are called *grain* and appear as small textures that seem to dance around the image as it's projected. The light of the projector shines through this grain, creating the picture we see on the screen.

Because the base layer is so reflective of light, there is a danger that light can pass through the emulsion and through the base, only to be reflected back up into the emulsion from the base's shiny outer surface. This can cause halos around bright light sources. To help prevent this from happening, there is an *anti-halation layer* (sometimes called a rem-jet coating) along the back of the base. You'll also sometimes hear people talk about the *subbing layer*, by which they simply mean the "glue" that holds the emulsion to the base.

## Types of Filmstocks

Most feature films are shot on negative filmstock, so when the film is processed in the lab, the resulting image is a negative. In order for you to be able to see the images like they appeared in front of the camera, you need to make a print, or positive image, much like you do with a still camera.

However, just as still cameras can shoot slide film, where the *camera original* is a positive rather than a negative, you can buy movie filmstock that when processed will develop as a positive image. This is called *reversal* film.

For movies bypassing film prints and going directly to DVD, some independent filmmakers will shoot on reversal and digitize the camera original as soon as the film is processed. But most of the cinematographers I've talked with do not recommend this. For theatrical projection, you'll have to make a negative print from your reversal camera original and then a positive print from that negative, losing quality with each step. By the time you're finished, you would have been better off shooting negative filmstock to start with. An added benefit to negative filmstocks is that they have a greater exposure latitude, meaning more tolerance for over- and under-exposure—a good thing for inexperienced cinematographers.

> **Defining Moments**
>
> The **camera original** refers to filmstock that has actually run through the camera. If you're shooting negative film, your negative would be the camera original. If you're shooting videotape and then putting it in your VCR to watch, you're watching the camera original.

As you know from still photography and watching movies, filmstocks also come in color and black & white. If I held up a strip of unexposed b&w filmstock and a strip of unexposed color filmstock, they'd both look the same; the difference is in the emulsions, the way each responds to light, and the way each is processed. Deciding which to choose is usually considered an aesthetic choice—whether b&w or color images are more fitting for your story and the mood of your film.

## Sensitivity to Light

Films are rated by their sensitivity to light, and we call this rating *film speed*. The more sensitive the film is to light, the *faster* it is, and the less light is required to create a usable image. As you might expect, then, *slow filmstocks* require more light to expose a usable image because they are less sensitive to light. The science of measuring an emulsion's sensitivity to light is called *sensitometry*, and the actual measurement of this sensitivity is referred to as the film's EI or exposure index. The manufacturer recommends an optimal EI for each film stock produced, usually written as an ASA (the American standard), though an ISO (International Standards Organization) number will include the metric equivalent, or DIN, after the ASA. These numbers help you calibrate your light meter so that you're able to better control your exposures. The higher the number, the faster the filmstock. Therefore, a filmstock rated at ASA 500 is faster and requires less light than a filmstock that has an exposure index of 100.

Though there are exceptions, and high-speed filmstocks are becoming better and better, the general bias is that images created with a slower filmstock will have less contrast and less grain, and they will be sharper with a higher resolution than images created with faster filmstocks.

Because film camera bodies are fairly small and unable to hold the amount of film needed, you usually have to load your unexposed filmstock in what's called a *magazine* that attaches to the top of the camera. If you've ever seen an old-fashioned movie camera that seems to have mouse ears, those ears are the magazine—one "ear" is the roll of unexposed film and the other "ear" is the take-up reel, where the filmstock goes after it's been exposed.

Unexposed filmstock is extremely sensitive to light, so it's often wrapped in a black bag and sealed in a can. After shooting, return the exposed film to its bag and can, carefully labeling it so that you won't accidentally re-open it. Whenever you're handling unexposed or unprocessed filmstock, you have to keep it away from light. Any light will destroy the image. For this reason, large film rolls are loaded in the dark, most often in a light-tight sack called a *changing bag* or *changing tent*. You place the unopened film canister and the magazine inside the bag, zip the bag shut, and then insert your hands up past your elbows through the sleeves, which are designed to create a light-tight seal around your arms. Then by feel, you open the can of film and load your magazine. Once the film is loaded and the magazine is sealed shut, you can unzip the bag and attach the magazine to the camera. There will be a small loop of film hanging out of the magazine that you can then thread through the camera body. Once threaded, the camera body is closed and creates a light-tight seal. You are now ready to shoot!

---

**Staying in Focus**

One-hundred-foot loads of 16mm film can be purchased on *daylight spools*, which help protect the film from light. Daylight spools allow you to load a camera in a lighted room without exposing more than just a few feet of the film. You can also unload the camera after the film is shot, and only expose the last few feet. If you are still shooting a scene when the film rolls out, though, you'll want to be sure to unload in complete darkness so that you can salvage as much of the last shot as possible. The drawback to daylight spools is that they are noisier than standard film cores, which can be a problem if you're shooting sync sound.

---

## Intermittent Motion

While you're filming, here's what's happening inside the camera. Each frame of the film is pushed into the film gate by a *pull down claw* (completely misnamed, since it really pushes the film) that enters each perf, one at a time. While the film is being positioned, a shutter—which looks a little bit like a circle with about half missing— spins around to block the light coming into the gate through the lens. The pull down claw briefly holds the frame in place (sometimes with the help of a registration pin for added image stability) while the shutter rotates out of the way, allowing light to reach the frame while it is stopped in the film gate. The shutter spins around, blocking the light, and the pull down claw releases the perf and enters the next one, repeating the cycle. This synchronized movement of the claw and shutter is what we call *intermittent motion*, which simply means that there is a rapid start/stop cycle.

For sync sound film, this start and stop movement happens so fast that the camera can take 24 still photographs per second, which we call 24 fps (frames per second).

# Magnetic Fields: Analog Video

Videotaping has been made simpler over the years with the introduction of camcorders, or a camera and videocassette recorder (VCR) combined. Before camcorders were available, the actual videocassette recorder was a separate deck linked to the camera by a cable.

When you hold a piece of processed film or negative, you can see individual rectangular frames, each a small picture. When you look at a strip of recorded videotape, you won't see a photographic image with your naked eye. This is because the image has been recorded in the arrangement of magnetic particles. However, if we could see individual frames without the assistance of a monitor, we would find that the video information is recorded diagonally across the tape. Along one of the videotape's outer edges is the soundtrack, where the audio is recorded as an analog signal as well, and along the other edge is what we call the *control track*, which ensures that each frame of video can be accurately located.

Just like newer filmstocks, videotape is comprised of a strong, durable base layer made out of polyester, and like filmstock, this layer is shiny and smooth to the touch. Attached to this base is a fine oxide coating or emulsion that is susceptible to magnetic fields.

Visual information is converted into electromagnetic energy, which then realigns the magnetic particles in the oxide. When played back, these particles are converted back into a video signal that we can then see with a television monitor. With that said, a TV monitor in the United States cannot show a video recorded in Europe because there are different video and broadcast standards around the world. The two most common are NTSC (National Television Systems Committee), which is used in Canada, Japan, Mexico and the United States; and PAL (Phase Alternating Line) in Europe and China.

In NTSC video, the image is comprised of 525 horizontal lines in two fields, scanned in an interlaced pattern. This simply means that every other line is scanned from top to bottom (the first field) and then the scan begins again, taking in the alternate lines ignored in the first scan (the second field). The video image that we see results from these two fields being interlaced into one image (or full video frame) thirty times a second, or at a speed of 30 fps.

Video cameras acquire light and color on CCDs (Charge-Coupled Devices), which are tiny electronic circuits that are sometimes called *chips*. The CCD converts the patterns of light into an analog signal, which is then recorded on videotape.

Most professional cameras are three-chip, or have three CCDs. As the light comes into the camera, a prism splits it into three colors—red, green, and blue—and each color of light is sent to its own CCD. Whereas in films the filmstock determines how much light will be needed to create an image, in video it's the sensitivity of the CCDs that determines how much light will be needed to create an image.

The cassette compartment is the area of the camcorder or the video recording deck where the videocassette is inserted or loaded. When this compartment is open, the insides of the image-making and recording mechanism are exposed. Dirt, smoke, and moisture can damage the recording and playback heads of the compartment and ultimately ruin the video image.

Rollback occurs in both the camera recording mechanism and in VCRs. Whenever a videotape is started in either of these types of machines, there is a slight delay before the tape is at the right speed for proper recording or playback. During this time, the tape actually rewinds a few frames, a process that is sometimes called rollback. Because of this, allow a minimum of five seconds of tape (or *head roll*) to pass through the mechanism before calling "action" to ensure that you'll record the beginning of your scene. Some camera operators call out "speed" to let the director know when the head roll has been completed. Likewise, run five seconds of tape after the cut has been called (as *tail roll*) to assure that you don't lose the end of your shot. These heads and tails will give you plenty of room to edit.

There are several different types of analog video systems. The one you're probably most familiar with is *composite*, where the video signal contains a combination of all the *luminance* (or light) and *chroma* (or color) information. You probably know it better by the name VHS (Vertical Helical Scan or Video Home System). The disadvantage is that the quality of the image diminishes significantly with each generation or copy.

> **Reel Trouble** _____
>
> Traditional video editing requires you to *dub* or copy the image from one tape to another. Before it's over, you'll make a copy of that copy, and a copy of that copy, and so forth. With each copy, or generation, the signal becomes more corrupted and the image quality diminishes. This is called *generation loss*. In a way, it's like my photocopying analogy in Chapter 4. A release copy of an analog video project can end up being several generations away from the original, so each generation loss is a major worry and consideration for videomakers.

A second type of video format is sometimes referred to as *Y/C* but is probably better known as S-VHS (or Super-VHS); here the signal is split so the luminance information is separate from the color information, even though S-VHS can record on standard VHS tapes. The primary benefit of this split signal is that there's less generation loss than with VHS.

In terms of analog video, the industry standard is *component video* also known as Beta SP. In this format, the light or luminance is separated from the color as it is in Y/C, but the color or chroma is split into separate components as well. This allows for the most analog generations before losing its resolution, and therefore it's the industry standard for broadcast.

# Ones and Ohs!: Digital Recording

Like analog video cameras, DV cameras operate at 30 fps and acquire light and color on CCDs as well, but in this case, they convert the patterns of light into a digital signal that uses binary code—signals made up of a series of ones and zeroes, kind of like a series of light switches that are either on or off. As with film and analog video, DV tapes are made up of a base, but instead of one magnetic layer, the DV tape has two that are sandwiched between the base and a diamond-like carbon layer that protects the oxide. In addition there is a black coating and lubricant layer that helps the tape move more smoothly through the camera. Timecode data that allows each individual frame to be easily located is written in the control track area. Even though I've been told that DV cameras do not experience rollback, most camera operators still wait five seconds before calling "speed" to avoid any timecode problems.

MiniDV, the lower end of DV cameras, has an image quality that rivals Beta SP, the highest end of analog video cameras. And better yet, because the visual and audio information is stored digitally, one of the most significant features of digital video is that in theory there is no generation loss. Each "copy" is as good as the original.

Besides MiniDV, there are several proprietary DV formats that for the most part are not compatible with each other or MiniDV. But the big news in recent years has been the development of a digital 24 progressive cinema camcorder (or 24P for short). Using MiniDV videotape, this camera comes the closest to being an affordable

**Staying in Focus**

Whenever shooting a professional project on video, even DV, it's best to use a brand new tape rather than rerecording over other material. The reason is that videotapes eventually wear out and the emulsion will eventually be unable to faithfully maintain its ability to store data. Even though DV is a digital process, it's recording the binary code on a magnetic medium that is subject to wear and tear.

way to make movies that are shot on DV but look similar to 16mm or 35mm film. They're relatively inexpensive (under $4,000), and before you rent a 35mm film camera it might be worth comparing the quality and purchase price of a 24P.

No matter what your origination format, you can convert your images to another medium. Digital video can be converted to analog video or blown up to film. Analog video and film can be digitized to be edited on a computer or released as a DVD. Currently, most independent films originate either on film or DV. But if you're short of money, don't be afraid to use any cameras or media at your disposal.

# Optic Nerve: Lenses

Lenses are a series of optical elements that concentrate, disperse, or change the direction of light rays to form an image. The distance from the center of the lens to the point where light rays converge and focus is called the *focal length*.

Traditionally, lenses were designed with a fixed focal length; a lens was either wide angle, prime, or telephoto. Almost all video cameras and many film cameras, though, have a variable focal length lens or what is more commonly called a zoom lens. The advantage of zoom lenses is that they can be adjusted to serve as either a wide angle, prime, or telephoto lens; one variable focal length lens can eliminate the need to carry several fixed focal length lenses.

By changing the focal length on shots, the camera operator can alter the perceived magnification, the depth of field, and the scale of objects in the image. Lenses are usually distinguished on the basis of their effects on perspective:

- A *wide angle* or short focal length lens gives a wide field of view and exaggerates depth. At this focal length, a lens tends to distort straight lines at the edges of the screen, bulging them outward. In 35mm film, a wide angle lens would be anything with a focal length (and number) less than a 35mm focal length, and in 16mm film, a wide angle lens would be any lens that has a focal length of 16mm or less.

- A *prime or normal* lens is a medium focal length lens that minimizes perspective distortion and comes closest to approximating the perspective of the human eye. When shooting with a 35mm camera, the prime lens is 35mm to 50mm in length; in 16mm filming, it would be a 25mm lens.

- A *telephoto* or long focal length lens generally flattens the space within the image; depth of field is reduced and the objects from foreground to background seem flattened or squashed together. What makes a lens telephoto is that its

focal length is greater—and therefore a higher number—than the focal length of the prime or normal lens. In 35mm filmmaking, telephoto lenses range from about 75mm to 200+mm, whereas 50mm to 75mm would be a standard range of telephoto focal lengths when shooting in 16mm film.

◆ A *macro* lens allows the camera operator to photograph extremely small objects by moving the camera within one or two inches of the object and still obtaining a sharp focus.

Each of these different focal length lenses affect the depth of field, or the range of distances within which objects appear to be in sharp focus. Generally the wider the lens—the smaller the focal length—the greater the depth of field. The greater the focal length of the lens or the more it is set for telephoto, the less depth of field you will get. In the case of a telephoto lens, the depth of field is called *shallow*, meaning that fewer objects between the foreground and the background are in focus. Wide angle lenses are better for creating a deeper depth of field. See Chapter 19 for examples and more information about focus and depth of field.

> ### Ditty Bag
>
> If you're shooting filmstock, depth of field can also be affected by the size of film you're shooting—the smaller the millimeter, the greater the depth of field. With all other settings (aperture, focal length, focus) being the same, a 16mm image will have greater depth of field than a 35mm image.

For DV and video cameras, the wide angle, normal, and telephoto focal lengths will vary from camera to camera depending on the size of the camera's CCD. For this reason, many DV lenses will include a "35mm equivalent" rating to help you figure out how each lens will affect the perspective of the image.

One other aspect of a lens system is its aperture, a mechanism much like the iris of the human eye that can be opened or closed to let in more or less light, just as the pupils in your eyes grow larger or smaller depending upon the lighting conditions. Some cheaper video cameras have automatic apertures that cannot be adjusted. But most video and film cameras designed for filmmakers do have variable apertures, which are adjusted by f-stops.

We measure the amount of light coming through the lens in f-stops. But somewhat the opposite of what many people would first think, the smaller the f-stop number, the larger the aperture and the more light that enters the lens. F-stop numbers are marked in white and are wrapped along the barrel of the lens:

1.4    2    2.8    4    5.6    8    11    16    22    32

As you move from one number to the next, you're either doubling the amount of light entering through the lens or you're cutting the amount of light in half. The higher the number, the less light enters the lens; the lower the number, the more light. In other words, an f-stop of 8 allows twice as much light as an f-stop of 11 but only half as much light as an f-stop of 5.6; of course, the lens is like a dial, so it's possible to set your aperture somewhere in between each of these numbers as well.

Also, you may see some oddly numbered variation of the f-stop number at the bottom end of the range. This is because of that particular lens's optics. In addition, some cameras will have t-stops (usually marked in red), which are considered more precise.

Aperture affects depth of field as well. The more light there is, the smaller the aperture (and the higher the f-stop number), the greater the depth of field. In other words, as you stop down (or let more light in by increasing the size of the aperture), the less depth of field you're able to render in the image.

Just as filmstock can be assigned a speed based on its sensitivity to light, lenses are also assigned a relative speed based on how much light-gathering capability each has. A lens that can open up to f1.4 can gather more light—and therefore can shoot in less light—than a lens that can only open at most to an f2. Of these two lenses, the first one would be the fastest.

Besides helping to create the image on filmstock or videotape, the optical system of the camera also directs light to the viewing system, which allows the camera operator to see what image the camera is collecting. Most viewing systems on professional cameras are through-the-lens, known as a reflexive or reflex system. You see the exact image that is exposing the film or rearranging the magnetic particles on video or being converted into ones and zeroes for DV.

On film cameras, this image is projected onto a ground glass; video cameras display this image on a small television-type monitor. The camera operator is able to view this image through an adjustable eyepiece called a diopter. For comfort, most diopters include a rubber eye cap; and for convenience, they can be focused without affecting the focus of the camera lens, allowing camera operators who wear eyeglasses to videotape or film without their glasses on.

---

**Ditty Bag**

Like old-fashioned still cameras, there are some older movie cameras that may have an auxiliary viewfinder with its own lens attached to the side or top of the camera. Because you're not seeing through the same lens that's directing light to the film frame, there's a slight difference between what you're seeing and what is actually being filmed. This is called a *parallax view*.

With a video camera, the diopter magnifies the small television-type monitor in such a way that the camera operator can place his eye directly to the viewfinder and see the image clearly. But the video diopter is often hinged so that it can be flipped out of the way, allowing the camera operator to monitor the image on an external screen attached to the camera without having his eye directly pressed against the diopter.

Unlike video cameras, the only way to monitor the image on a film camera is with your eye to the diopter. As a result, some cameras are equipped to connect to a video monitor. This is called *video assist*. Because movies shot with 16mm and 35mm film cameras are often released at some point in formats for viewing on a television, the diopters of some film cameras will include TV-safe lines so that the camera operator can compose her images knowing that when shown on TV—which loses an edge of visual information all around the frame—the movie will still look good and the audience will be able to see everything they need to in order to understand the story.

This consideration of what the audience will actually see in the frame brings us to issues of aspect ratio (the dimensions of the image), image quality, and lighting, which I'll talk about more in the next chapter.

## The Least You Need to Know

- In 16mm and 35mm, the speed of the filmstock determines how much light is necessary to render an image.

- In analog and digital video, the camera's CCDs determine how much light is necessary to render an image.

- Beta SP is the broadcast standard for analog video filmmaking.

- Because of the way digital video (DV) records the image, there is no generation loss as you edit and copy your movie.

- The amount of light entering a lens is controlled by the aperture and is measured in f-stops.

- When shown on a television monitor, visual information in the edges of the film frame will be lost.

# Chapter 19

# Visions of Light:
# Cinematography

## In This Chapter

- ◆ Why add light to your film?
- ◆ Four qualities of light you can control
- ◆ Three-point lighting as a foundation
- ◆ Qualities of the image you can work with
- ◆ Continuity editing: maintaining the illusion of continuous time and space
- ◆ Tips to look like a pro

Cinematography is all about getting the shot, and a good one at that. Due to the expense of filmstock and processing, directors shooting their movie in film rarely have the luxury of using multiple cameras. Occasionally you might see an exception for those stunts or scenes that cannot be easily repeated. But most of the films we see are shot with a single camera, moving the lights and camera for each shot. As a result, we try to make the filming more efficient by shooting everything at once that requires a particular lighting or camera placement or setup. In most cases this means that we have to shoot the scene out of order.

Television, on the other hand, is often known for its multiple camera shooting, capturing the action from a variety of angles, and in effect, decreasing the amount of time it takes to film because you get most of your reaction shots and your detail shots simultaneously. Of course, this requires many more lights so that you can illuminate the entire area to be filmed at once.

With DV becoming so affordable, you may decide to shoot multiple cameras; if you do so, just remember to sync all the cameras to the same timecode to make your editing easier. But multiple cameras may not be practical when shooting in confined locations or with lights. And the more footage you shoot, the more footage you have to sort through in the editing room. Most independent movies are still shot "single camera," and as a result, there are some production techniques that have been developed to minimize the chance of mistakes on the set that can cause problems in the editing room.

# Light and Shadows

In cinema, lighting is not about light, it's about shadows. Because most movies are two-dimensional representations of a three-dimensional world, shadows and light become our biggest clues for perceiving depth in the frame, allowing us to use our imagination to fill in the third dimension. Shadows cast by an actor can help us figure out her relationship—how near she is—to the objects and environment around her. Shadows attached to an object help us perceive its shape and texture, giving it depth as well as height and width.

Of course, the starting point in lighting for movies is that you can't film in total darkness—you won't get an image. So you need a minimum amount of light to simply create a recognizable image. Once you have a minimum of light on the set, everything else is about effect.

I've talked earlier about the idea that every element in a film has a function. Lighting can function to draw attention to visual information that we need to see in order to make sense of the story. Other functions can include creating a sense of realism or affecting the mood of the film.

With CCDs and filmstocks becoming more and more sensitive to light, we are able to shoot in increasingly lower light conditions, and many novice filmmakers assume that camera operators simply shoot with whatever light is naturally available. But cameras cannot "see" as well as the human eye; they are unable to

| Ditty Bag |
|---|
| Besides providing a sense of objective realism, lighting (just like all aspects of production design) can be used to reflect or present a character's interior reality or emotional state of being. |

register images in extremely low or extremely bright lighting conditions, even in situations where the human eye can make out details.

Many times the cinematographer, gaffer, and lighting crew have worked hard to create the illusion that the light on the screen is from natural everyday sources. This kind of lighting design uses the natural light sources in the shot or scene, such as lamps or a sunny window, to determine the quality and direction of the set lights. Some people refer to this as *motivated lighting*, in that the direction and quality of the light is motivated by the light sources in the frame or that we would expect to see in this setting.

If there is not enough light present for the CCDs or filmstock to produce images that are relatively free of color distortion, noise (in video and DV), or grain (in filmstocks), we call the image *underexposed*. At the other end of the exposure continuum, there are times when so much light is present that details of the image tend to wash out or disappear in the brightness; we would call these images *overexposed*.

Figuring out how to set the aperture (or f-stop) so that you get just the right amount of light requires a light meter. There are three primary types that you might see on a film set:

- Incidence light meters measure the light falling on a subject.

- Reflective light meters measure the light being reflected from the subject.

- Spot meters allow you to quickly measure contrast ratios within the frame by measuring the reflected light in a very small specific area.

Because we're often shooting the shots within a scene out of order, we need to have an overall lighting plan so that as we move the lights for each new set of shots, our general qualities of light remain consistent. This *lighting continuity* helps assure that when watching the edited film, the audience will believe the scene is taking place in continuous time and space. Lighting continuity does not require that the light be realistic, just that it be consistent from shot to shot in a given scene.

# Qualities of Light

One of the first considerations when lighting a scene is the intensity or brightness of each light and each light's relationship to the others on the set. This relationship among the lights establishes the amount of contrast between the brightest areas of the frame and the darkest areas. We sometimes call this the *contrast ratio*. Shots that are brightly lighted and have very little contrast are called *high key*. Shots that filled with shadows and have a great deal of contrast are said to be *low key*.

*Left: high key lighting. Right: low key lighting.*

The contrast ratio is sometimes referred to as the key/fill ratio, meaning the difference in lighting that's created when both the key and fill lights are on compared to when the fill light is on by itself. The key light is the main lighting source in the shot and therefore often the brightest. The fill light is a softer and less intense light that is often used to fill in the shadows so that they won't appear too dark. Since each f-stop doubles or halves the light, depending on whether you're opening up (making the aperture larger) or stopping down (making the aperture smaller), the contrast ratio is expressed as doubling or halving. A contrast ratio of 2:1 means the difference is 1 f-stop; in other words, the amount of light produced by both the key and fill lights is double the amount of the light produced by the fill light alone.

Though we can see a far greater range of contrast with our eyes, filmstocks and camera CCDs are far less sensitive and cannot render detail in their images if the contrast ratio is too great. For this reason, you generally never want more than five stops (or a contrast ratio of 32:1) between the brightest and darkest areas of the frame when shooting video. Filmstocks are generally better able to handle a greater lighting contrast than video, so you might be able to comfortably shoot a contrast ratio of 128:1.

We can control the intensity of each light, thereby manipulating the contrast ratio, by either moving the light farther away or closer to the subject. We can also make the light less intense by adding *scrims* in front of it; in fact many lights have a holder just for this purpose. Scrims are small circular screens that absorb light by a specific amount.

Whether high key or low key, any lighting setup begins with a decision about the angle and direction of the light. Just so we can see the differences more clearly, let's look at examples that only have one light source, so that we're better able to see the direction and angle.

*Top lighting.*

Top lighting usually looks the most natural to us, because we're used to the sun and ceiling lights; however, we usually experience light coming from above on an angle. In this image, the key light is not at an angle but is rather shining straight down on Christine and so it seems a bit unusual.

*Side lighting.*

Side lighting positions the key light directly to one side or the other of the subject. While it's somewhat unusual in the natural world, except perhaps at sunset and sunrise, we usually don't find side lighting quite as disturbing as under lighting, but it can still create a sense that there's something not quite right, something that we can't quite see.

*Under lighting.*

When we see light coming from below, which is called under lighting, we usually find it disturbing and unsettling. We're not used to seeing attached shadows going up the face.

Besides contrast and direction, we can also control the light's specularity—whether the light is hard (creating sharply defined shadows) or soft (creating less defined shadows), as James is demonstrating in the next photos.

*Hard light. Notice that James's shadow is dark with distinct edges.*

*Soft light. Now James's shadow is softer and the edges less sharply defined.*

We can soften the light by using *diffusion*, which scatters the light further. You can think of the effects of diffusion as similar to the difference between a bright sunny day (hard shadows) and an overcast day (soft shadows); the cloud cover acts as diffusion for the sun, scattering the light more evenly and diminishing shadows.

Another way of diminishing shadows is to *bounce* the light or aim it at a light colored wall or ceiling or even a piece of bounce board (basically just a white piece of foam like you can buy at art stores and also sometimes called reflective board). The reflected light is much softer and will not produce harsh shadows. Bounce board can also be effective when you're shooting outdoors in the sun and don't have any lights to reflect some of the sunlight back into your subject's face in order to reduce the contrast ratio (much like a fill light would do if you were on a set).

Other ways to direct or control the light beam include using barndoors, which are metal flaps that can fold across the front of the light and help you keep light from spilling into areas of the frame you don't want it. Scoops and snoots are kind of like a metal lampshade that directs the light to a specific area. Flags or gobos are flat panels that can be attached to a C-stand and used to block or direct light. Cookies are cutouts that create patterns on your set when light shines through them.

Another consideration in the quality of light is its color. Sunlight is a different color from fluorescent light, which is a different color from the light generated by household light bulbs. Whenever we are in an environment that is lighted by one of these major sources, we usually interpret that light as white because our eyes adjust to it and make allowances for it.

---

### Ditty Bag

Gas cookstoves usually have a blue flame, but when a pot boils over, the flame will become yellow or orange. This is because the liquid from the pot is cooling off the flame. It's the same in color temperature: the hotter the light, the more blue it appears; the cooler the light, the more orange or red it is. Sunlight is bluish, fluorescent light is often greenish, and tungsten or household light is reddish.

---

We usually describe these differences in terms of *color temperature*, which is measured in degrees Kelvin. Midday sun on a clear day is about 5,600 degrees K. Fluorescent lights are about 3,600 degrees K. The lamp by your bed is probably less than 2,800 degrees K. Why is the color temperature such a big deal? Because white is the reference for getting all the other colors correct. Unlike our eyes, filmstocks and CCDs have to be told which type of light to treat as white and can only reproduce accurate colors when properly balanced for the specific light source.

There are several ways we can compensate for these color differences. 16mm and 35mm filmstocks are rated as either daylight ("D" for shooting outdoors) or tungsten ("T" for shooting indoors with movie lights). Daylight-biased film will treat 5,600 degree K light coming through the lens as white. Anything cooler will look more yellow-red, and anything hotter will appear bluish. Tungsten film is rated at 3,200 degrees K, which means that's the temperature of light that will appear white.

However, there may be times when all you have is tungsten film, and you want to shoot outside. In that case, you'll need to filter the light; otherwise your exteriors will appear more blue-gray than you'd expect. An orange 85B filter will cool the daylight to about 3,200 degrees. Using a filter for this purpose is sometimes called color correction or color balancing.

### Staying in Focus

Each type of filter absorbs a different amount of light. Anytime you use a filter, you have to compensate for the light absorbed by opening up the aperture or setting your f-stop at a lower number. Many filmstocks will make this computation for you by setting a different ASA depending upon whether you're shooting daylight or tungsten and with or without a filter.

Correcting daylight film for use indoors is rarely done, because by the time you either filter the light (blue 80A filter) or gel the lights blue, there is so little effective illumination reaching the lens that you can't get a good exposure. For these reasons, the lights that you use for filmmaking are not quite what you would find around the house. They're brighter, hotter, and usually require more electricity. And they'll have funny names, like HMIs, babies, tweenies, inkies, and soft lights. Some use a halogen quartz light bulb that produces light at a color temperature of 3,200 degrees K, while others use a halogen metal iodide bulb in order to produce light at 5,600 degrees Kelvin. If you try to film using your household light bulbs, you may have trouble getting enough light for a good exposure, but even if you could, you'll find that the light given off is a murky orange that can look brownish. Never fear—there are special light bulbs made to use in lamps that appear in the frame that give off 3,200 degree light, called *practicals*.

For video and DV, we color correct by setting the *white balance*. Manually setting the white balance is accomplished by aiming the camera at a plain piece of white paper or poster board under the lights you'll be shooting. You then press the white balance button, in effect telling the camera that the piece of paper in front of its lens should be recorded as true white. By setting the white balance in this method, all other colors will appear true or accurate during the shoot. If the white balance is not set properly, the camera may record the images with a blue or red tint, ruining the footage. Unfortunately, the white balance needs to be set each time the camera is moved into a different lighting situation.

Some video and DV cameras are equipped with automatic white balance, wherein the camera itself determines what type of correction needs to be made for colors to be recorded as true. Other cameras may have presets for daylight/outdoor and tungsten/indoor, which the camera operator has to choose in order for accurate color representation. The bottom line is that white balance is a term used to describe the balancing of the video camera's electronics to reproduce white light, and hence colors, accurately.

# Three-Point Lighting

Though lighting is limited only by your imagination and budget, much film lighting is based on a series of principles easily demonstrated by what's known as a basic three-point lighting setup, but as you can see, we're going to actually use four lights.

Let's now look at each light in turn to see exactly what it is doing.

*Here is a "behind-the-scenes" view of a classic lighting setup. The movie camera would be placed at the right edge of the frame. Use this as a reference as you see the various effects below.*

*Here is what the lighting would look like if you were looking through the camera.*

*Light from the* key light *will appear through the camera to be the main illumination in the scene. It is often the brightest light on the set and is approximately 30 degrees to side of subject-camera axis. Unless motivated otherwise, the key light is usually above the subject and aimed downward at a 30- to 45-degree angle.*

*The* fill light *is next to the camera, at camera height, and may be scrimmed so that it is less intense than the key light. Fill light may be unnecessary on anything wider than a medium shot, but in medium close-ups to extreme close-ups, the fill light softens the attached shadows and keeps the contrast from becoming so dark that we lose the detail of the face.*

The back light, *sometimes called a separation light or rim light, separates the subject from the background, which is especially important if the background is dark. The back light is usually directly opposite the key light and aimed down. Barndoors keep the light from spilling anywhere in the scene except for the actor's back. Because we're only seeing a small edge of the light, the back light is usually as bright as or sometimes even brighter than the key light. If the back light is aimed upward from a low angle, you might call it a* kicker.

The set light *helps make the background more interesting; often a set light will be aimed through a cookie in order to create patterns in the background.*

In some cases, you may set up a very diffused fifth light at the subject's eye level and aimed from the camera to get rid of shadows around the eyes. This can also create a sparkle in the actor's eye, particularly helpful if you have an actor with very dark irises.

# Qualifying Image

Besides lighting, there are other issues that affect the quality of the image and therefore fall within the considerations of cinematography. One of the most apparent image qualities is its aspect ratio, or the relationship of the width of the frame to its height. Not so long ago many films and all television programs had a squarish aspect ratio of 1.33:1. But over the years, movies have developed wider compositions, ranging from what is called *widescreen* to *cinemascope*. Notice how the aspect ratio changes how much we see and the compositional aspects of each of the following images.

*The traditional aspect ratio of standard television screens and standard 16mm and 35mm film is 1.33:1.*

*A widescreen aspect ratio of 1.85:1 is the most common for feature-length films, including independent movies.*

The aspect ratio can be determined by the camera you use to shoot your film, or if properly planned for while shooting, it can be created in post-production by masking part of the frame. Besides the aspect ratio, there are other qualities to the image that we may want to consider. These might affect which format we ultimately decide to shoot our movie on. These qualities are:

◆ Sharpness, or the filmstocks' or CCDs' precision in rendering a straight edge or line in the frame. Oftentimes, as grain or video noise increase, sharpness decreases.

◆ Resolution, or the ability to record fine detail and texture; unless stylistically motivated to be otherwise, most independent films strive for the highest resolution or best detailed picture the budget will allow.

◆ Saturation, or the filmstocks' or CCDs' ability to reproduce color; saturated colors will be deep and vivid; desaturated colors appear paler as if washed out, making the image seem more monochromatic.

Like editing and mobile framing, focus is a technique filmmakers can use to direct the audience's attention and even shift (or *rack focus*) during a shot. Depth of field can be affected by whether you're shooting 16mm film, 35mm film, analog video, or DV as well as the amount of light, the focal distance of the lens, and the distance between the subject and the camera.

*Deep focus means that everything in the foreground, middle ground, and background appears in focus.*

*The depth of field in this photo is very shallow, allowing Cora to remain in focus even though Todd, while standing right next to her, is in soft focus (or slightly out of focus).*

Focus can become an important element to your film's composition. Shallow focus can make DV look aesthetically warmer and more like film, which is often considered dreamier looking and less harsh than video and DV images. Several factors can influence the depth of field and how much of your foreground, middle ground, and background are in focus, such as your aperture setting or the focal length of your lens. One common generalization says that if you measured the distance between your camera and your subject—let's say it's nine feet—and you set your focus for that distance, one third of that distance—or three feet—in front of your subject will be in focus and two thirds—or six feet—behind your subject will be in focus. In reality, this is dependent upon which lens you're using and the like, though the distance from camera to point of focus can also affect the depth of field.

# Directing the Eye

Production—shooting your film on the set—looks back to pre-visualization (see Chapter 10) and ahead to editing (see Chapter 22), with many of the concepts that are required at those stages affecting what you shoot now. An important factor in editing is the concept of screen direction—knowing where people are in relationship to the space around them. Television sports programs do not have a problem keeping the viewer oriented to the action within the space because, even though there are several cameras taping, they are all kept on one side of the stadium in order to prevent problems with screen direction. Keeping all of the cameras on one side of the action is sometimes called the 180-degree rule; this rule simply means that an imaginary line of action is drawn between two objects or people in the scene. This line might be created by two people standing across from each other, or one person looking a particular direction or a person walking or running through the environment, or in sports, from one end of a court or stadium to the other. In order to keep all the screen directions consistent, the camera operators videotape from one side of this action line.

The only time when a camera might be placed close to the 180-degree line is when shooting two people talking, setting up what are called reverse shots (see Chapter 22 for an example). Reverse shots imply a point of view and are often over-the-shoulder shots (OSS) of the person listening; they are also sometimes called reaction shots. In these cases, the camera may be very close to the 180-degree line, but it still does not cross it, and the editor may cut back and forth between close-ups of both people in the scene.

As you might guess from having a maximum angle—180 degrees—you can move your camera before disrupting continuity, you also have a minimum distance or angle the camera has to move. If you don't move your camera at least 30 degrees between two shots that will appear next to each other in the edit, you'll create what is known as a *jump cut* (see Chapter 22).

*This diagram illustrates the 180-degree and 30-degree rules.*

## Look Like a Pro

As the filmmaker, no one expects you to be an expert on cinematography, but here are a few practical tips and common practices that can help you get through some of the more technical aspects of shooting your film:

♦ Avoid blowing a fuse by knowing how many lights you can plug into one outlet. The formula is $W = A \times V$ (watts equal amps multiplied by volts). Because the standard electrical voltage in North America is 110 volts and most circuits in the average house are either 15 or 20 amps, you can figure out how many watts the circuit can comfortably handle. 110 volts × 15 amps = 1650 watts; 110 volts × 20 amps = 2200 watts. If each of my lights is 750 watts, I can only plug in two of them safely; a third will overload the circuit. If you have the light's wattage, you can also figure out how many amps you'd need on a given circuit by inverting the formula like this: amps = watts ÷ volts.

♦ If your subject casts more than two shadows, change your lighting. The ideal is one shadow, although audiences often will not notice two; a third is another story. We often try to light from above so that any shadows will be cast toward the floor and out of the frame. And shadows appear most strongly against light backgrounds.

> **CAUTION**
>
> **Reel Trouble**
>
> Movie lights get very hot; be careful about placing them too close to the ceiling or the wall. I've seen a couple of scorched ceilings that had to be repainted at the production's expense. And they were lucky that a fire hadn't started.

◆ When you're shooting on a location with fluorescent lights, turn them off and use your own lights. This will prevent the camera from picking up any flickering of fluorescent lights that the human eye can't see. If you have to use the fluorescents because they're going to show in your shot, use your light kit to flood as much tungsten light as possible so that your lights overpower the fluorescent ones. They may still flicker a bit when the camera is aimed directly at them, but at least your whole scene won't be strobing.

◆ When handling lenses and filters, always hold them by their edges. Never touch the surface of the lenses or filters. The oils from your fingers can etch your finger-print into the surface and distort your image. Never use lens tissue on a dry lens—add lens cleaner or breathe heavily on the lens so there's moisture before brushing the dirt away in circular motions.

◆ When replacing quartz bulbs, be sure not to touch the glass of the new bulb directly. The oils from your fingers can weaken the glass and cause it to explode when it gets hot. If possible, wear gloves. While you don't need to worry about your oils on the glass of the old bulb, it can remain hot for a long time, so be sure to let it cool before removing or wear gloves as well.

◆ To ensure similar lighting from shot to shot, always light your wide shots first, especially when working with a limited number of lights. The danger in lighting close-ups first is that you may end up using all your lights to illuminate a small part of the frame and then realize you don't have enough lights or wattage to duplicate that lighting design when you need to light the wider shots. When edited together, this will make the lighting look inconsistent and destroy the illusion of continuous time and space.

◆ Check out the location before the shoot and create a floor plan or an overhead view of the set. Mark where you intend to place and direct the lights so that when they arrive on set, you know what you're doing or at least where to start. Sure, you can fly by the seat of your pants and a certain degree of flexibility is required, but good cinematographers plan ahead.

◆ Keep a ditty bag of essentials on hand. A basic cinematographer's kit might include a pair of work gloves (heat resistant to safely handle hot lights, barndoors, and scrims), a light meter, clothespins (called C-47s on some sets) for attaching gels and diffusion to the lights, an orange stick to clean the gate of the camera if you're shooting film, lens tissues, lens cleaners, a blower brush, a small flashlight, and a small piece of white foam core that can be used for white balancing or to bounce light. It's also a good idea to have a couple of different kinds of light meters plus some of your own sandbags, batteries for the flashlight, diffusion, and gels.

## The Least You Need to Know

◆ Once you've met the minimum amount of light needed to expose an image, your lighting becomes about effect.

◆ Figuring out your contrast ratio helps ensure that the difference between the brightest and darkest parts of your image is not so great that you lose visual detail.

◆ Color balancing in film and setting the white balance in DV and video is crucial for rendering accurate colors in your image.

◆ Three-point lighting is just one example of how movies often use more than one light to create shadows and depth to the image.

◆ The 180-degree rule helps maintain screen direction so that the viewer can clearly understand the action in the scene once the individual shots are edited together.

◆ Following common industry practices can make the technical aspects of shooting your film easier.

# Chapter 20

# *The Quiet Earth:* Gathering Sound

## In This Chapter

- ◆ Recording location sound
- ◆ Single-system and double-system sync sound recording
- ◆ Analog versus digital audio recording
- ◆ Types of microphones used in film
- ◆ Ambient and wild sounds

Of all the technical aspects in filmmaking, sound is the one most likely to be taken for granted. After all, novice filmmakers are often advised to watch films with the sound turned off so that they can concentrate on the visuals. So film is a visual medium, right? Well, yes and no. Film is a combination of visual and audio information that the audience experiences over the course of time. When the audience sits down to watch a film, their eyes *and* ears are engaged. Sound makes the film experience more complete because it makes the world of the story seem more real by engaging more than one of our five physical senses.

Bad sound will keep your film out of distribution before bad camera work will. Film audiences are more forgiving of an unclear image than they are of an unclear sound. Fuzzy images can seem artistic. Fuzzy sound just seems like a mistake. So while your audience might take your sound for granted, you cannot.

# A World of Sound

Sound design is the creative process by which all the individual elements of a film's audio—dialogue, presence, sound effects, and music—are brought together. While much of this work is done in post-production (see Chapter 23), it begins on your set with *location sound*.

## Defining Moments

**Location sound** is simply any audio that you record or collect while on the set or location. The person responsible for recording this sound is usually referred to as the *sound mixer* or *location mixer*.

Dialogue is one of the most important location sounds your mixer will collect. There are other types of location sound as well, which we'll talk about later in this chapter.

Though you don't technically need a sound designer before shooting, your location sound mixer will be better equipped to collect the necessary sounds if she is thinking ahead to post-production. Your sound designer can help provide that perspective.

Though it rarely takes as long to set up sound as it does lights, sound recording is often the first thing to get sacrificed or compromised when the day is running behind schedule. A common way this happens is for the director to decide to film some of the shots without sound, which is called MOS. (In early Hollywood, many cinematographers were from Eastern Europe, where the letter *w* is pronounced like an *m*. When these Eastern Europeans called for a scene to be shot "without sound," their heavy accents made the phrase sound more like "mit out sound" which got abbreviated on the camera log as MOS.)

The problem is that recreating in post-production all of these sounds that are occurring naturally on your set is very expensive. In terms of dollars, your cheapest audio minute is the one on the set. For small-crew, low-budget independent films, you're better off to take a couple of more minutes and let your mixer record the sounds. Even if later you decide not to use the sound collected for these shots, at least your sound designer will have a reference point from which to create new sounds. Collect as much of your sound on location as possible.

# Read My Lips: Sync Sound

If all you've ever used before is a video camcorder for home movies or weddings, you may think sync sound is a no-brainer. When you watch the tape, the people's lips match their corresponding sounds—everything is in sync. In effect, your camcorder is what we'd call *single-system* sync sound—both the image and audio are recorded simultaneously on one format that keeps them synchronous when played back. This is because the camcorder has a built-in (or "on board") microphone, but the audio you get from this usually isn't going to be good enough to use for a movie to be distributed. You can often hear camera noises such as the tape drive or any automated features, such as auto focus. If you are manually changing focus during a shot, you may hear your hand turning the focus ring. Your voice as you mutter under your breath will probably be louder than the voices of the people in front of your lens.

If your camera has an auxiliary mic (microphone) port, you are able to plug in an external microphone that will usually cut off or override the camera's internal mic. But this is a far from perfect solution.

> **Staying in Focus**
>
> While it may seem simpler to collect your sound with the camera when shooting in video or DV, every time your audio crew wants to collect sound independently of the image or listen to an audio take to be sure it's okay, they're tying up your camera. The best advice is to never rely on the sound mechanism of the camera.

For these and other reasons, professional films—even those shot on DV—collect the visual and audio material on two different machines. This assures complete control and monitoring of each, and is called *double-system* sync sound recording. The challenge in double-system sync sound recording is that your audio has to be collected at the exact same rate as your visuals or you have to create a corresponding reference on each that can be lined up. Even if they're plugged into the same outlet or if both are using battery power, cameras and recording decks will run at slightly different speeds—just enough to make syncing lips to words virtually impossible.

The solution early in 16mm and 35mm filmmaking was to physically connect the camera to the audio recording deck via a cable. As you might guess, another cable on the set was the last thing anyone needed, and *cable sync* was eagerly replaced by *crystal sync*. No more cable was necessary because a crystal in each motor—the camera's and the recording deck's—assured both machines ran at the same speed. Since then, with the application of timecode to film production and the development of smart slates (which I'll talk more about in a moment), synchronizing film and audio from two different machines is about as simple as lining up their corresponding references—their timecodes—in post-production. Timecode works on the same basic principle as edge numbers on your filmstock; it's simply a method to allow you to quickly locate a specific and individual frame of film or video.

Even though both the camera and the recording deck are running at the same speed, you still need some way to match a particular frame of picture with the exact corresponding point in the audio.

The traditional method has been to use a clapperboard: a board upon which you write the details of the production, date, scene number, shot number and take number. A hinged stick at the top of the board is opened wide and then slammed down, making a sharp sound. Pausing a split second so as not to blur the image of slate, the person then quickly pulls the closed slate out of the frame. The dialogue editor will later match the sound of the slate closing with the frame where the stick slams tight against the top of the clapperboard.

However, there are more modern ways to slate. Electronic slates are usually small handheld boxes that are connected to the recording deck. Turn on both the camera and recorder, aim the light bulb toward the lens, and when you press the button, a light will flash at the same time a beep is put on the audio track.

Another method is making sure that the visuals and audio have the same timecode numbers. Though some film cameras will now generate their own internal timecode that can link with the audio deck, you do not need a timecode camera in order to use timecode syncing. Because sync sound film runs at a fixed rate of 24 fps, timecode slates can be placed in the frame at the beginning of your shot so that the editor can see the exact timecode when the beep occurs on the soundtrack. A smart slate generates its own timecode that it sends to the recording deck; dumb slates can't generate timecode and have to receive it from an external generator, such as the recorder.

## Reel Trouble

Don't slate the shot and then turn off the camera; if you do, you've just defeated the whole purpose of doing a sync slate. Picture and sound will only sync up in editing if both the camera and recorder are turned on before the clap and then run continuously after the slate until you call "cut." However, to save some time and because the verbal slate can't always be heard due to microphone placement, some mixers will preslate their audio, turning on the audio deck to verbally identify the scene, shot, and take number and then turning it off until it's time to record the clapperboard slate.

Forgetting to slate your shot can cause a number of hardships in the editing room. However, if you do forget and the camera is still rolling, you can do what is called a tail slate. At the end of the shot, before you call "cut" and stop the camera and sound deck, call for a "tail slate." The person slating dashes into the shot, holds the slate upside down (but with the printed info facing the camera) and snaps the stick closed if you're using a clapperboard. An upside-down slate lets the editor know that the sync point is at the end of the shot rather than the beginning.

# Rearranging Particles and Turning On or Off

Just as we can now record moving images either as analog video or digital video, the same is true of sound. Though both use meters to help you set your levels (or how loud the incoming sound will be), there are some differences that might be helpful to know.

## Analog Recording

Analog recording tends to be more forgiving of overmodulation, or when its loudness has overpowered the microphone or recorder's ability to process the sound without distortion. When setting your VU meter for analog recording, you want the needle to spend most of its time (or average) around the 0 mark, knowing that it's okay for the needle to occasionally peak into the red because you have some audio headroom. If you're going to err in analog recording, err toward the needle going into the red (or recording "hot").

The drawback with analog recording is that the recorder itself creates a certain level of analog tape noise, which is sometimes called the *noise floor*. If you record your primary sound so softly that you have to make it louder in the mix, you will be making the noise floor louder as well. Therefore, we try to record sounds as loudly as possible so that any volume adjustments in the mix are more likely to be turning the sound down.

As a result, *recording optimally* in analog is about getting the loudest possible sound without any distortion in order to create as much distance from the noise floor as possible. In addition to the noise floor, there is the risk of a 60 Hz hum created by AC current if you plug the deck into a wall outlet, which is why most sets run their recorders on battery power.

Many analog recorders will give you several options as to what speed to record. Analog sound quality is always better the faster the tape travels through the recorder, so if at all possible use the fastest speed settings, which are usually measured in IPS (inches per second).

# Digital Recording

Digital recording is more of an all-or-nothing kind of endeavor. The drawback is that once you cross the threshold into overmodulation, the sound becomes unsalvageable. Therefore, you do not want to ever cross that 0 point on the meter. In order to prevent this, set your levels so that the sound averages about -10. The advantage to digital recording is that you don't have a noise floor to worry about, so it's better to err toward recording the sound a little too softly.

Though digital recording has been up to this point primarily on tape and other forms of removable media, location digital hard drive recording is on the horizon. In the meantime, Nagra, the industry standard in analog audio recording, now markets a digital recorder that uses flash cards to store the audio. The amount of audio each card holds depends on the size of the card (measured in megabytes) and the recording's sample rate (or number of times the audio is sampled as it is converted into binary code; generally the higher the sample rate, the better the sound quality). While it may be tempting to buy the largest flash card possible, if something goes wrong, you run the risk of losing a lot of audio material. For this reason, you may be better off using smaller cards. Some mixers even use a separate flash card for each new roll of film or videotape put in the camera.

Regardless of whether you're gathering your sound as analog or digital recording (and some productions collect both as a failsafe), never ride the gain control (or adjust the volume) during the recording. Set your levels by having the actors perform or run through the scene as they will perform it but without filming it. Then leave the settings alone until the take is over—whether it overmodulates or seems too soft or looks just right. Adjusting the levels during the actual take just complicates the work in post-production and may make the audio unusable.

**Staying in Focus**

Though some mixers will disagree, my general stance is that if possible you should leave all EQ (or altering sound by manipulating its frequency) and filtering of sound for the sound mix in post-production. For the most part, any manipulations you do to the sound during its recording cannot be undone, whereas if you do them in post-production, they're nondestructive and can be undone.

You will always want to clearly label your audio media both in writing on the storage container and also recorded through a microphone at the beginning of each day's shoot. This is called slating your roll, and it usually includes the title of the production, the director or filmmaker's name, what number roll or tape it is, current date, your name as the mixer, and perhaps the name of your boom operator; if appropriate you'll want to include any information that will assist in post-production, such as the sample rate, tape speed, and any other pertinent information. Recording a notation on the audio whenever the camera is reloaded can also be helpful.

# Types and Placement of Microphones

We primarily use our eyes to orient us to our environment and more specifically to the sounds in our environment. In a crowded room with everyone talking it can be difficult to understand anything anyone is saying ... until we look at a specific person. Suddenly, we can hear what he is saying above the din of noise. We are using the process of looking to help our hearing isolate a particular sound. We are concentrating on certain sounds to the exclusion of others.

Unfortunately, neither a microphone nor a recorder has this capability; neither can give priority to particular sounds; they record all sounds equally. This inability of audio recording to differentiate individual sounds can result in the audience hearing only a jumble of voices. Therefore, we artificially create the effect of selective hearing with microphone placement: the closer the microphone is to one specific sound source, the better we hear that particular sound source and the less we hear other background or ambient sounds.

In addition, we expect what we see and what we hear to match. If we see a close-up of a person talking, we expect his voice to match in its apparent "closeness" to the microphone. If instead his voice sounds far away, it seems incongruous.

Microphones are usually classified by their pickup pattern, the directions from which they gather sounds. This pattern is also sometimes referred to as the mic's polar pattern, and there are a variety of possible patterns and microphones, though I'm only going to talk about the three most common for film shooting.

*Omnidirectional* microphones pick up sounds from all 360 degrees surrounding the mic—sounds that are in front of, behind, and beside the microphone. Most video cameras' internal mics are omnidirectional, which makes it crucial for the camera operator and other crew members to be silent during videotaping if you are using the onboard mic. This kind of microphone might be good if you were trying to collect sound from a large crowd or environment or perhaps if you were simply recording a *scratch track* you plan to later replace. But they are poor for isolating a specific sound and are rarely used on sets for recording dialogue.

*Unidirectional* or *cardioid* microphones are most sensitive to the sounds directly in front of them, therefore recording most clearly any sounds coming from the direction where the mic is pointed. These microphones are less likely to pick up sounds from behind or to either side, though if a sound is loud enough, it will still be recorded.

**Defining Moments**

A **scratch track** is a track of sound that is never intended for inclusion in the final soundtrack of the film, but rather serves as a guide to help in syncing up replacement sounds. For example, if we were going to replace a series of gunshots, syncing these visually by searching for each frame where the gun goes off would be extremely difficult; but if we recorded a scratch track on set, we can use its sound or waveform to indicate exactly where each replacement gunshot sound needs to go.

An extreme unidirectional microphone is sometimes called a shotgun and is good at isolating only those sounds directly in front of the microphone. However, if it's aimed just slightly *off-axis*, meaning that the microphone isn't pointing directly at the sound source, such as an actor's mouth when recording dialogue, there can be a noticeable drop-off in the sound because the ratio of ambience to dialogue is getting greater. Shotgun mics are also very susceptible to handling noise, such as any sounds that might occur while the *boom operator*—the person holding the microphone—aims the mic or turns it to follow the action.

Because cardioid and shotgun microphones usually require a small battery in order to operate, the sound mixer will want to have a backup supply of batteries on hand.

Outdoors, wind noise can wreak havoc with recording sound, and oftentimes microphones will be suspended inside zeppelins or covers that help shield the mic from wind and reduce the noise.

A third type of microphone is sometimes referred to as a body microphone or *lavaliere* or *lav*. There are two types: wired and wireless. Wired lavs basically tie your actor to your recording deck and can get caught on a variety of things, causing noise in your audio. Wireless lavs can ruin your sound by picking up radio wave interference, so many filmmakers try to avoid wireless microphones unless absolutely necessary.

You often see these kinds of microphones in news magazine interviews and reality TV shows, but in a narrative film, you wouldn't want to see the small wire and microphone sticking out of your character's shirt collar. Therefore, you usually try to hide them in the person's clothes.

In theory these allow you to get the actor's dialogue in tough sound conditions, such as a stormy beach, because the microphone is right up against his body. They can also be handy if you have an extremely wide shot and there's no way to get your boom operator close enough to the actor to record his voice with a cardioid. The drawback is that if there is a lot of character movement, you may get unwanted fabric noise that's recorded louder than his voice.

Even if you're using wireless lavs as a guide track for a wide shot, as soon as you get the print take, take the boom right then and record the actors on location giving their lines wild (without the sync camera running)—doing it right then assures that the ambience will match, and you may not need to replace the dialogue later in post. Ask the actors to run their lines three times, so you've got some variety of pacing and intonation. Because replacing the dialogue in post-production can be so expensive, collecting the sounds wild on set will sometimes provide you close enough sync in editing. You don't need to do this on every take, just those where there's doubt that you're going to have good sound.

When placing mics, a starting point is to consider the framed shot and the point of view of the audience member. Though mixing the soundtracks in post-production will enhance a sense of sound perspective, you can begin the process by placing the mic so that it's consistent with the perspective of the image. For example, if you know that the image will be a medium shot, having the mic so close to the actor that we can hear him breathe may sound inappropriate. However, if we're shooting an ECU of his mouth and nose, we will want the microphone close enough to get the breathing sound.

Because of the narrow pick-up pattern of cardioid mics, which tend to be used most often for dialogue on the set, the boom operator needs to be sure that the microphone is perfectly aimed at whoever is speaking. The mixer can help because the mixer will be hearing the sound in the headphones and will notice any shifts in quality as the mic goes off axis.

In scenes where two people are talking, there is still usually only one microphone, and the boom operator has to quickly re-aim the mic for each line of dialogue without creating handling noise. Booming is a real art and takes a lot of strength and endurance to hold the pole out over the action.

Regardless of the mics you use and where you place them, the mixer will wear headphones to monitor the sound as it is recorded. This helps assure that the necessary sounds are being recorded optimally. Even if you know the sound won't be able to be used, you still need to record it as a guide track for later automated dialogue replacement (ADR), which I'll discuss in Chapter 23.

**Staying in Focus**

For difficult sound recording situations, be sure to allow the sound team time to set up, place the mics, and do a sound run-through to make sure there are no problems before filming the shot.

# Don't Be Afraid of the Wild

If you were filming a basketball game, you would notice that your audio track includes the sounds of people cheering, the buzzer, the ball hitting the court, the squeak of shoes on the floor, and so forth. These are *ambient sounds* of that particular environment, the natural sounds that occur within a certain surrounding or setting, just as the traffic noises of a busy metropolitan street would be considered the ambient sounds of a city.

Ambient sounds are always present. Whenever you record dialogue, a low level of ambient or background sounds will be recorded also; the goal is to place the mic so that the ambience does not overpower the dialogue. But it will still be there.

To help make the dialogue edit as smoothly as possible in post-production, you need to collect the ambient sounds of the location environment. Many production crews will say that you're collecting presence or room tone, but most sound designers and post-production sound teams will consider the sound you collect to be ambience. It's not worth arguing over, so whatever your crew calls it, as long as you're talking about the same thing and you're consistent, you should be fine.

Ambience should be recorded at the exact same level that the dialogue was recorded at—in other words, do not turn up the gain for ambience; leave it set the same as when the actors were talking. In digital, the meter may not even move and you may think that nothing is being recorded, but it is.

For every location, you want to record at least 30 seconds to a minute of ambience. Listen for any rhythmic or sharp distinctive sounds; these will cause problems when you try to use the ambience in post. You want the crew and actors to remain on the set if possible while you're collecting ambience because their bodies and breathing affect the acoustics of the room. Consulting with your sound designer or post-production supervisor will help you plan for the sounds you'll need to collect on the set.

### Defining Moments

**Wild** sounds are those that you record independently without being synced with the camera.

Always try to get the best sound on set possible. Don't fall victim to the belief that you can fix bad sound in the mix or that it'll be easier to create your sound effects later. Even if you can, it'll be expensive. So collect as many sound effects on location as possible. Even if you think a shot can be MOS, try to record sound even if you didn't have time to perfectly place your mics. Your crew is already there, so use them. The worst that will happen is that you will have a guide track from which to sync the effects. If recording a car chase, after the shots, if you're waiting for the camera crew to set up the next shot, ask the drivers to drive around and let you record the sounds of the cars *wild*.

Ambient sound is different from *presence*. Ambience is the natural sound of the environment where you filmed. Presence is constructed in post-production. Presence tracks are less about the actual ambience recorded with the image than the types of sound an audience would expect to hear with a particular image. This realization allows for a great deal of creative flexibility in the sound design and edit. An editor enhances the ambience from a location by building presence—adding tracks of effects to the scene that were not originally recorded with it. These sounds appear to be generated from the environment or the events depicted within the image and yet can give the scene atmosphere and mood.

## The Least You Need to Know

- ◆ Location sound is your cheapest audio minute, so collect as many of your sounds on location as possible.

- ◆ Double-system sync sound is the preferred method of recording visual and audio material.

- ◆ Sound can be recorded in analog or digital formats, although digital audio recording is rapidly becoming the standard.

- ◆ The closer the microphone is to a specific sound source, the better we hear that sound and the less we hear other background sounds.

- ◆ Wild sounds are those without a corresponding image that you collect on your own without being synced to the camera.

# Chapter 21

# Guess Who's Coming to Dinner: Taking Care of the Cast and Crew

## In This Chapter

- Making the most of your collaborators
- The importance of good communication with your cast and crew
- A well-fed crew is a happy crew
- How to tactfully deal with problem crewmembers

You could be a saint and still lose your cool on a film set. Hard work and long days coupled with pressures regarding time and money is a recipe for ... well, if not disaster, certainly some stress. Even the most mellow person can become a bear under the wrong conditions.

Some sources of stress are beyond your control, such as weather, equipment failures, and illness. Having contingency plans and thinking ahead (such as watching ten-day weather forecasts) can help diminish their impact, but there are certain stresses you have to live through rather than remedy. However, there are some stresses that you can control, remedy, and possibly eliminate with just a little common sense and effort.

# The Filmmaker's Responsibilities

In Chapter 1, I talked about the fact that the filmmaker is responsible for both the film and the process by which the film gets made. Your guiding vision is one of the touchstones that will allow you to make consistent decisions, especially as you work through the minutiae required to make the film.

The other touchstone is collaboration. People often talk about filmmaking as a collaborative art form. Collaboration means more than simply having several people that you boss around. Collaboration implies working with people to see your vision develop and be expressed as a film we can all watch.

As the filmmaker, you are the final word on all decisions regarding the production. But in order to make the best possible decisions, you need two things:

- All the information necessary to make an informed decision

- A consistent strategy for how you make decisions so that you can make them quickly

Having all the information necessary usually means that two heads are better than one. No one person can see every aspect of filmmaking in fine enough detail to anticipate all possible situations or needs. So don't even try. As the filmmaker, you are expected to have an overarching view of the entire process, but you're going to need your crew and cast to help you fill in the details. This is one of the primary advantages of working with others.

### Staying in Focus

When shooting sensitive scenes where the actors may feel particularly exposed or vulnerable, you can ask for a closed set (which means that only essential personnel are there for the filming of the shot).

While asking for suggestions and input from your crew will slow things down on the set or in your production meetings, this discussion can be invaluable for seeing things you would have missed and for making the crew feel more personally involved in the filmmaking process. This doesn't mean you have to listen to every single crewmember all the time, but your department heads can serve as advisors. For example, if your production manager discovers that the camera your cinematographer had been counting on is not available for rental, rather than trying to figure out alone what to do, ask your cinematographer for suggestions on how to proceed. Perhaps another camera will suffice. Or perhaps you'll need to consider rescheduling the shoot for a time when the camera will be available.

With that said, everyone will look to you to be the final word—which is where having a consistent strategy for how you make decisions can be helpful. Decisions about the visual design, whether lighting, shot scale, art direction, or costuming, can be based on a thorough understanding of your themes and your guiding vision. Decisions about technical issues can be guided by that vision as well. Obviously, another consideration in some cases is a financial one—what you can afford.

As we've talked about before, effective directing requires awareness and communication. Communication is one of those things we often take for granted but is more fragile than we might first think. Part of communication in film production is clearly delineating responsibilities as well as seeking advice when necessary. I usually hire my assistant director very carefully, because I need her not just to be well organized in helping me stay focused, but also because I count on her to be able to keep me apprised of the morale on the set or to pull me aside if in my excitement I forget to give the crew breaks. In effect, she's a reality check for my awareness, and as a part of her job, she sees all aspects of the set and interacts with more crewmembers than I might during the course of the day. She keeps me from developing tunnel vision.

Finally, a maxim for being the director on set is: "be firm and decisive but open to ideas." In other words, be flexible and able to take in new information and changing situations quickly. But also be able to problem solve and make decisions effectively and stand by them.

> **Staying in Focus**
>
> If you and a crewmember radically disagree on how to solve a problem or issue, try to step back and make sure you're doing what's ultimately best for the film. There are compromises you will have to make in order to see your film finished. Pick your battles wisely.

# The Way to a Crew's Heart: Craft Services

You've seen the guy standing along side the road with a handwritten sign that states "will work for food." Truer words have never been spoken for the crew of a low-budget film. A film crew will put up with a lot of things, but they won't put up with hunger. Food is a necessary expense for your production.

When I first started making films, the food costs were often more than any other budget item. And we're not just talking meals (which would be catering). We're talking about snacks, soft drinks, coffee, and chewing gum as well as meals—hence the term "craft services."

You need a crew person (or two) who simply handles craft services. They need to have food on the set before crew and cast arrive, and they need to replenish the food throughout the workday. If you run out of food, they need to go and buy more. You may need to ration expensive items by setting specific meal and break times, but there should always be something to drink or nibble on between official breaks and meals.

> **Ditty Bag**
>
> Whenever your crew seems to be getting short-tempered or distracted, odds are one of three things is happening: they're tired and need a break, they're exhausted and need to go home, or they're hungry and need to eat. Nine times out of ten, it'll be hunger.

Your craft services people need to survey the entire crew and cast for any special dietary needs before the first day of the shoot. If you have vegans on your crew, or if someone has food allergies or food sensitivities, you need to make sure there are foods they can eat. Here are some ideas for what to serve:

♦ If you're having an early morning shoot, you'll definitely want to have breakfast foods available, such as fresh fruit, bagels or muffins, yogurt, individual boxes of cereal and milk, and caffeinated and decaffeinated coffee, tea, and juice. The general idea with breakfast foods is to offer things that can be grabbed quickly, eaten without a plate, and easily carried around and munched on while the crew works.

♦ Lunch should probably come somewhere between four and five hours after breakfast, though you may have some flexibility on this—unless you have a union crew whose contract will specify meal times and intervals. Lunch can be sandwiches, salads, celery and carrot sticks, dip, and so on, along with soft drinks, bottled water, and other beverages.

♦ Include at least one hot meal a day to give your cast and crew a chance to actually sit down. This will probably be your third meal of the day, but it doesn't necessarily have to be. For this hot meal, pizza doesn't count. Sure, pizza once in a while is fine, but day in and day out, it gets old, even for the heartiest of fans. Inexpensive hot meals can include baked lasagna, macaroni and cheese, spaghetti, and other dishes that are easy to fix and keep warm.

Coffee, hot water for tea, and soft drinks should ideally be available throughout the workday, and if you're working late into the night, you'll want to put on a fresh pot of coffee.

If you have a kitchen on set, you can cook there, but often if you're shooting on location, your craft services people will have to go pick up the hot meal from somewhere else. Here's a great way that friends and family can contribute to your film, either by cooking and preparing your meals from groceries you provide or even buying the groceries as well. But the meals can get expensive, so it's a lot to ask one person to prepare all the food for a shoot for free, particularly if the shoot is for more than one or two days. Maybe have a group of people preparing food, a different person each day. This assures variety in the menu and keeps the burden from getting too great on any one person. The other option is to approach local businesses to provide the food, either as a donation or for a fee. Maybe your local grocer will donate some food if you buy from them. Or a local restaurant might donate a meal to your production.

> **CAUTION    Reel Trouble**
>
> Snacks like potato chips, donuts, and brownies are easy for crewmembers to grab and eat while they work, but they can be messy. Try to include some healthy choices like pretzels and cut-up fruit or vegetables. They're still easy to eat but won't leave gummy handprints on the set or equipment—and crewmembers won't have to waste valuable time running to the bathroom to wash their hands.

If you are going to budget to pay a catering fee, shop around, compare menus, and get estimates. One of the best hot meal caterers I ever used was a neighborhood tavern that served food. We chose them because they gave us the best price, but the food was unbeatable and we couldn't have done better in terms of quality.

Keep in mind that high glucose content foods (sugary snacks, cookies, potatoes) can result in a "crash" or sleepiness shortly after eating. You'll want to strike a balance between energizing healthy foods and crew favorites that may have high carb or high sugar content. If you have a crew that loves Double-stuff Oreos and you refuse to provide them, well, you just might have a mutiny.

One craft services person I worked with, Jean, quickly figured out everyone's favorite foods and made sure that at least one meal during the project was built around each crewmember's favorite foods. Granted, we were a small crew so it was fairly easy to do—but believe me, we never felt so special.

I've only seen crews walk off a set and stop working for two reasons: an unprepared director and poor craft services. This is not as petty as it sounds. Your crew is giving you anywhere from 4 to 16 hours of their time each day—they trust you to take care of them. If the director is unprepared, the days become much longer than they need to be, and if there are poor craft services, it can be a sign that the director is not taking care of her crew.

# Expressing Your Appreciation

There are a number of ways you can show appreciation to your crew and cast for all their hard work. Certainly pay is one of those, but for most of us independent film-makers, especially when we're first starting out, this isn't a realistic option. Because we may not be paying salaries or a union scale of wages, clearly demonstrated appreciation is one of the things we can do that keeps our crew willing to show up for work each day.

> **Staying in Focus**
>
> Besides saying "thank you," a common courtesy and sign of respect is to say "please" when asking a crewmember to do something. Also, giving praise when someone does something well goes a long way.

Appreciation is based in (and an indicator of) respect for the people you're working with and who are helping you make your film. This appreciation can be as simple as knowing everyone's name on your crew and cast and acknowledging them with a "hi" or a smile when you see them each day. Say goodnight at the end of the day. Thank them for their work that day. This doesn't necessarily have to be a personal message each time, but simply calling out "thanks" and "good-night" as you see people packing up and leaving leaves them with a good feeling.

Though it varies from film to film, I've sometimes found it helpful to shake each cast and crewmember's hand when I first hire them or, in the case of crew hired by my department heads, the first time I meet them. This might happen at our first rehearsal or a production meeting, or the set on the first day of the shoot. Shaking hands may seem corny, but in fact, human touch is a very powerful bond for most people.

Usually once the film has finished shooting, you'll want to throw a wrap party for the entire crew and cast. I've been to some wrap parties where the filmmaker shows some of the rushes (or unedited footage) of the film, but keep in mind that some cast and crew may feel self-conscious seeing their work so soon after shooting it and may not be able to relax and simply celebrate being done. The wrap party is a thank you and a celebration. Any disagreements should be left on the set. Here's your chance to hang out and just be a real person with the people who have worked so hard for you.

Finally, one of the standard ways of expressing appreciation is to give the cast and crew (at the very least the department heads) a copy of the finished film, which may be months or in some cases years after the initial production. The actors and crew can use this as part of their professional reel, which in turn might help them get other (better-paying) jobs.

# When You Have to Fire a Cast or Crew Member

In the ideal world, everyone pitches in, works hard, and is a pleasure to work with. But under the stress of making a film, sometimes people hit a breaking point. This can show up a variety of ways, either shutting down completely and withdrawing from the work or exploding on the set and contributing to an atmosphere where everyone is walking on eggshells or taking over the shoot and telling you how to do your job in no uncertain terms. You as the filmmaker don't have the luxury of doing any of these. But you may find a crewmember who is intentionally or unintentionally making the shoot more difficult.

For the most part, firing someone should be a last resort. I believe everyone should have the opportunity to adjust or improve his work. So while your first impulse might be "get him off the set," you want to approach the situation calmly and consider whether the crewmember has a clear understanding of his job, what you expect, and the requirements of the task. Especially with inexperienced crews, you have to be prepared for mistakes to be made.

> **Staying in Focus**
>
> You may have heard that first-time directors in Hollywood are usually advised to fire someone on the first day of the shoot as a way of establishing authority. However, your authority on the set best comes from your being prepared, knowing what you want, clearly communicating your guiding vision, and working as hard as your crew.

Think about how you would want to be treated if you were making an honest mistake in your job. Probably you'd rather not be called out in front of the whole crew. So if you're having difficulty with a crewmember, try to discreetly pull him aside at the first opportune moment and talk directly about the situation. If it's someone other than a department head, you may want to first let the department head know about the concern and let her try to address it; if that's unsuccessful then you may need to become involved.

Either way, try not to think of it as an argument or a win/lose situation. If the person becomes upset, do not engage or become equally upset—things will generally just escalate and get worse. The best option is to calmly point out what you think could be improved in the crewmember's work and see if he understands why you think it might be a problem. Then ask him how he (or both you and he) might make the situation better. If you can arrive at a plan, then go back to work, and treat him no differently. A good guiding philosophy on the set is to never hold grudges.

If the situation or work improves, end of story. However, if things do not improve or in fact get worse, then you may need to talk with the crewmember again. At this point, you may have to decide whether the crewmember's presence or work is causing too much distraction, unease, or danger for the crew. If so, you'll need to let the person go. If it's a union crewmember, consult the union contract to be sure you follow proper procedure.

If it's a skill issue and not an attitude issue, you may want to consult with your production manager to see if there's a better job fit. If you do need to ask the person to leave the project, try to have this conversation at the end of the day so that the drama behind the scenes doesn't get in the way of your shooting the drama in your scene. This is the kind of conversation that should be held in private. If appropriate, you may want to include the department head who is affected or a member of your producing team, but the fewer the crew people, the better.

The next day, simply make a brief statement that the crewmember will not be returning, but try to do it in a way that is not sensational and leaves the crewmember with some dignity. Refrain from talking behind his back or giving details; this can only unsettle and divide your crew.

If you're very lucky, you won't have to fire someone. But as you make more films and work with more people, there may come a time when you have to ask someone to leave. Frustrations can sometimes run high, and if someone has a short outburst directed at equipment or work in general, it is not worth firing a crewmember as long as the storm passes quickly and they agreeably settle back into work. Firing someone may be an option you have to explore if you have a crew person verbally abusing you or other crewmembers or putting them at risk or making the set a difficult place to work. Some warning signs of crewmembers who may not be able to make it through the long haul are anyone who says no to most of your requests, someone who explodes and takes hours to calm back down, someone who regularly shows up late or leaves early or can't be found on set, someone who acts as if he is the only expert. Basically, all of these are unprofessional behavior. Generally try to model the kind of behavior you want from your crew.

## The Least You Need to Know

- Your cast and crew are there to help; think of them as advisors and collaborators.

- Good communication helps your set run smoothly.

- Don't underestimate the power of a full stomach to keep a crew working and relatively happy.

- Treat all cast and crew members with respect.

- If you have to fire someone, do it tactfully.

# Part 4

# Don't Worry, We'll Fix It in ... Post-Production

A fallacy so common that it has become a cliché and a joke, "we'll fix it in post-production" is like saying, "yeah, we have a flat tire, but we'll just keep driving on the rim." By the time you get to the tire shop, repairs will take longer and be more expensive. Fixing the tire when it first went flat would have been easier and less expensive.

Walking out of production, you now have the raw footage that will ultimately become your movie. The post-production phase begins with editing your picture and ends when you have a final version of your film with sound that you can show an audience.

# Chapter 22

# Edward Scissorhands: Editing Your Picture

## In This Chapter

- ◆ What is film editing?
- ◆ The difference between linear and non-linear editing
- ◆ The different services provided by film labs
- ◆ Understanding the process of editing
- ◆ Continuity editing
- ◆ The aesthetics of editing

Some filmmakers make their film in the planning, some in the shooting, and some in the editing. Though every filmmaker will approach each stage differently, over the years I have come to realize that I make my film in post-production. Everything before that has simply been a process of collecting raw material for me to edit.

In some ways, editing is like building Frankenstein's monster—you take all these pieces that you've collected and now have to figure out how to put them together in a way that gives them life as a single entity. Another way to think of it is that editing is the final rewrite of your movie. When you're sitting in the editing room, you're face to face with what you actually filmed, not what you wanted to film. Sometimes it's difficult to clearly separate what you achieved from what you intended, but in editing, this perspective is critical. The temptation of course is to rush back out for reshoots, if you find that your achievement falls short of your intention. But reshoots are expensive and time-consuming. Before going that route, it might prove more helpful to really take stock of what you have and decide whether with some adjustment it's already a viable film.

# The Final Cut

Early filmmakers shot their stories in one long take. Rather quickly, some realized that they could tell stories that occur in more than one place or time. These filmmakers would plan carefully and shoot their films in the order the stories were to be presented to the audience. We now call this process *editing in camera*.

Eventually, filmmakers began to realize they could physically cut and splice the film in order to rearrange the sequence in which it had been shot before presenting it to an audience. This process of taking shots apart and putting them back together in a new order is known as *editing*.

There can be a variety of goals and strategies for how to sequence your shots, but in the broadest terms, we can think of editing as a way to tell a story, make an audience feel, and make an audience think. An independent film may embrace a little of each of these philosophies, but the priority in most narrative features is on creating a clear story and an emotional experience for the audience.

# Linear vs. Non-Linear Editing

Editing, as a film term, is both a noun and a verb. When we talk about editing as a noun, we are talking about the concept of editing: the rationale behind linking one shot with another and the relationship between the two. These relationships can be varied, ranging from graphic cuts to continuity editing which we'll talk about a little later in this chapter. The verb editing is the act of assembling images and audio into a particular order. It is the physical labor of editing. We usually use the terms *linear* and *non-linear* to distinguish how that work is done.

Imagine laying a long line of bricks in concrete, alternating red bricks with yellow bricks. When you get done, you realize that you accidentally put two yellow bricks next to each other. You can't insert a red brick in between them because all the bricks are set in the cement. And you can't take one of them out, because you'll now have this gap in the dried cement where it used to be. While not a perfect analogy, this is kind of like linear editing, where each brick would be a shot.

Traditional video editing, which requires dubbing shots from one tape onto another, is considered a linear editing system because you have to assemble the shots in order. You can't go back and insert anything new unless you cover up a previous image. And the only way to take something out is to cover it up.

But let's say we created the same line of bricks, only this time we don't place them in concrete, but simply lay them next to each other. Now we can add a red brick in between the two yellow ones or take out one of the yellow bricks and move all the following bricks so that no one can tell we made a mistake. This represents what happens in non-linear editing.

> ### Ditty Bag
>
> Still confused? Maybe this will help: Writing this chapter on a typewriter would be a linear process; writing it on a word processor would be a non-linear process. Linear editing is virtually obsolete at this point. Non-linear editing is now the industry standard.

Physically cutting and tape splicing 16mm and 35mm workprints is a non-linear editing system, because you can go back and insert, take out, and rearrange your shots in a variety of combinations—nothing is locked in as you go. Computers make non-linear editing even easier and quicker, and better yet, they allow us to create several different cuts of the same material so that we can compare our different options.

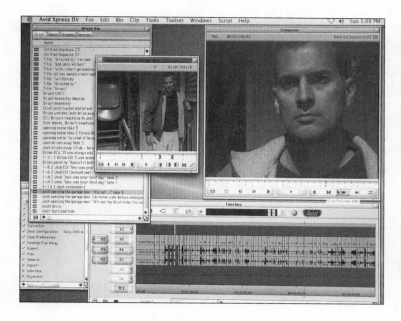

*Editing software like Avid's Xpress Pro (pictured here, courtesy of Avid Technology, Inc.) turn your computer into a post-production suite, allowing you to keep track of your information in moveable windows and to create multiple video and sound timelines (or tracks).*

*(Film frames of Robert Garabedian from* Brush, *directed by Chris Peppey, written and produced by Josef Steiff. Avid is a registered trademark of Avid Technology, Inc., in the United States and/or other countries.)*

# Working with a Film Lab

One option for an independent filmmaker is to shoot on a digital camera, transfer the footage from the camera right into a personal computer, edit and mix the film digitally, and then burn a DVD copy for people to watch. In this case you're basically an entire studio, post-production facility, and lab all rolled into one. However, if you are shooting your movie on 16mm or 35mm film—or if you're shooting on DV but plan to release your movie on film—you're going to need to work with a lab to process your negative and/or make your prints. Film labs offer the following services:

◆ The lab can strike what is called a workprint, which will allow you to manually edit the film with a pre-computer-era editing machine, splicer, and splice tape. Workprints are cheap copies of your negative and therefore it doesn't matter if they get scratched or dirty—their primary purpose is to help you work, to give you a copy of the film to edit so that the original stays clean and safe.

◆ The lab can "print" your negative directly to an analog or digital video format through a telecine. This makes sense if you're planning on editing digitally because you need a video copy of the rushes to digitize into your computer and begin editing.

◆ The lab can copy your film to VHS or 3/4" U-matic video if you're doing a linear editing on an analog video system. If you plan to finish up with an on-line edit (see Chapter 26), this analog copy can have the timecode burned into a small box at the bottom of each frame so that you can see it on your monitor—(this would be called a *window dub*).

◆ Some labs can digitize your rushes to a hard drive or removable media that you can simply insert into your computer; this allows you to immediately begin editing digitally.

**Staying in Focus**

Finding a lab is as simple as an Internet search (Appendix B will give you a head start). Don't worry if there are no film labs in your region. Labs are used to dealing with customers from all around the country.

◆ After you've finished editing, labs can print your finished movie as a 16mm or 35mm film. This usually involves several steps that I'll discuss more in Chapter 26. Whether making a film print from negative or digital video, you want to make sure your source material for the print is as good as possible—if you're printing from a digital master (DV or computer edit), make sure your digital movie is at the highest possible resolution.

Each lab service will cost a different amount, and prices can vary from lab to lab, so comparison shop. Labs are also sometimes willing to negotiate types of services and costs.

# Frame by Frame: The Editing Process

Just as most scripts go through a series of development steps and rewrites, editing is usually easiest when treated as a process of incremental steps. Perfectly editing a film in one try is virtually unheard of. Instead, editing is a trial-and-error process, trying different combinations of shots and durations until one has found the perfect edit. Let's take a look at each of the steps involved in editing in the order that we would do them.

## Syncing Rushes

Before you can start editing, you need to sync your rushes, making sure that the sound of your actors speaking is synchronous with the images wherein you see their lips moving. If you have filmed in double-system sound (see Chapter 20) you will need to either sync these yourself or have the lab sync them.

If you are syncing yourself, you will use the slates of each shot to match sound with picture, by finding the exact frame where the clapper snaps shut and aligning that with the specific point in the audio track where you hear the snap. With electronic slates, find the frame where the light flashes on and match that with the beep. With smart slates (or digital slates), simply match the time code numbers.

## Logging the Footage

Logging the footage, making a record of every shot in the order it appears in the raw footage, can be a tedious job, but if done well it can save you a lot of time and money in the editing room. The log ideally notes the exact length of each shot. If you have had the lab create a work print for manual splicing, use the edge numbers. If you're editing digitally, use the time code reference numbers, though computer editing programs make the process of logging almost as easy as typing labels for each shot.

The continuity script as well as the camera and audio logs can help with the logging process, but keep in mind that on set errors might have been made in the notations. These production materials are simply an additional reference.

In the following excerpt from a continuity script, each shot is marked by a vertical line drawn directly on the script and labeled at its beginning with the scene and shot number as well as a brief note of shot scale and content. Look at shot 1-9 (CU Josh) on the right-hand side of the script. You'll see that the beginning and end of the shot are indicated with a horizontal line. Where the vertical line is straight, we'll see this action or dialogue on the screen; the squiggly line indicates dialogue or action that is out of the camera's view. If the shot continues onto another page, this is indicated by an arrow at the bottom of the page (see shot 1-8 in the example). The advantage to making a continuity script while you shoot is that you can easily see if all your essential dialogue and action are covered by your shots.

*An excerpt from a continuity script.*

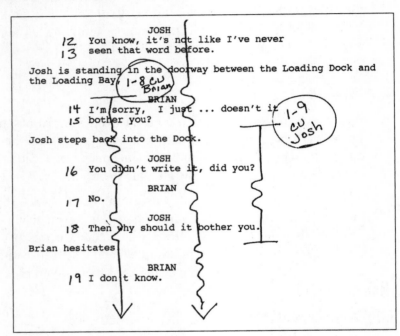

## Pulling Shots

Pulling shots is the process of deciding which shots and takes are usable and separating them from the footage you do not intend to use. When physically cutting film as a work print, you'll actually hang these shots in a bin or roll them onto film cores for easy storage. If editing digitally, you'll place these shots in a virtual bin or separate folder.

## Paper Edit

Before putting the shots together, some filmmakers make a list of each shot in the order they plan to use it. This paper edit helps them organize and maximize their time in the editing room, especially important if you're renting a facility and paying by the hour or planning to rent editing equipment. An added benefit is that creating a paper edit allows you to make early editing decisions sitting somewhere other than in front of a monitor.

## Assembly Edit

Once you've got the general sequence of shots figured out, you assemble them in order as complete takes (from camera on to camera off). If you're unsure which take of a specific shot is best, leave both in for now. If you're cutting a film workprint, you string master shots with close-ups and cutaways immediately following. With non-destructive digital editing, it's tempting to go ahead and roughly place them as you go along. Either method is okay. If you didn't shoot master shots, then you assemble shots in the order scripted.

This is also the stage where you add your head and tail leaders and SMPTE count-down with beep, especially if you're working in a 16mm or 35mm film workprint. The "2" frame of the countdown is synced with an audible "beep" on your sound-track; this will help keep your dialogue and picture in sync and will be the reference point for the lab when they sync your final sound mix to your conformed or on-line picture for a composite print (see Chapter 26). If you are splicing film, place all shots with their emulsion side down so as not to chip away or scratch the emulsion while you're cutting and splicing.

## Rough Cut(s)

Now you make final decisions about which takes to use, and "tighten up" shots by figuring out roughly where each should begin and end. With a physical workprint, you want to keep all of these trims, or if you're cutting digitally, be sure you're editing in nondestructive mode, because you may later realize that you cut a little too much and need to reinstate some of those frames. In the rough cut stage, you begin intercutting more closely and incorporate your close-ups, insert shots, and cutaways into the master shots, being sure to keep the dialogue in sync. Your film will probably go through several rough cuts as you try to find the best pacing and juxtaposition of shots.

### Staying in Focus

As you put the shots and action in the order that you had scripted, you may find that the scenes do not work as well in editing as you had thought they would on the set. Don't be afraid to rearrange shots (or even entire scenes) while editing to make the story clearer or to create greater dramatic impact.

## Get Feedback

At some point, you'll be too familiar with the footage to have a clear perspective on how your edits are working. Getting feedback from others can help, though feedback can sometimes be overwhelming—everyone will have a different opinion.

Generally, I pay more attention to the trends in feedback rather than the specifics. One person may hate a particular edit and that can be personal taste. But if several people are confused or disturbed by the edit, I need to look at it more closely. That doesn't necessarily mean I'll change it. Ultimately, the decision of whether or not to make adjustments based on feedback is yours.

Anytime you're soliciting feedback, it's good to allow your test audience the opportunity to make some general comments and observations, but it's also important to ask about any specific shots or edits that you're unsure about. Always include at least a couple of people in each of your feedback sessions who have never seen the film before.

Finally, feedback is not about explaining or defending your film. It's about collecting the observations of an unbiased audience. If I can't understand the film's story from the rough cut, you verbally telling me the story won't be helpful—you won't be able to do this with every audience member who sees your film. All that will speak for you in a theater is the sequence of images you provide. So in these feedback sessions, spend most of your time listening and taking notes, even if your first reaction is that you disagree with the comments. You can later consider them more carefully.

After you've considered the feedback, revise your rough cut as you see fit. Repeat these two steps as necessary until you arrive at your ...

## Fine Cut

A true fine cut or final cut is that point when you're happy with the picture edit and have no plans to make any more adjustments. This is called *picture lock*. Now you can begin finalizing elements of the sound design, such as music score and sound effects. If you begin editing sound tracks before you have picture lock, every change in your picture edit requires that you change every sound track (and there can be a lot of them before you're done) the same number of frames. Otherwise, you throw your sound out of sync. See Chapter 23 for sound editing considerations, but right now, you're only editing picture and any sync dialogue that goes with that picture.

# Continuity Editing Makes the Story Clear

In Hollywood (and many independent) films, the goal is for the audience to become so absorbed into the story that they forget they're watching a film. This requires that the filmmaking processes become invisible so that the audience doesn't pay attention to the edits or camera or sound instead of the story.

When watching a movie, I'll sometimes point out a great edit, and the person sitting next to me will say, "What edit? I didn't see a cut." That's the goal—that the audience won't notice the edits.

Films are shot out of order. Even individual shots within a single scene are filmed out of order. But when we watch a movie, we are usually unaware of this fact. This is because most television shows and movies rely heavily on a style called *continuity editing*. This is simply a method for putting shots together so that they imply continuous time and space—even if the shots were filmed months apart or in different locations.

Editing that creates a clearly established continuous time and space helps the audience make sense of the images—and more importantly, the story—they are seeing by establishing the spatial relationship of objects or people in the frame to each other and to their environment. Good continuity editing requires thorough planning in pre-production, getting enough shots (or *coverage*) on the set, and a skillful editor.

To create this illusion, and to keep audiences from noticing the film's edits, a variety of techniques and principles have been developed and standardized, such as the 180-degree and 30-degree rules I discussed in Chapter 19. These rules about the placement of the camera help keep the edits from diverting the audience's attention. For example, the 180-degree rule is responsible for maintaining screen direction, one of the most important aspects of keeping the audience oriented to the space of the scene.

Another trick for hiding edits is to cut on an action rather than when everyone or everything in the frame is stationary. This is sometimes called matching action or match on action shots. A simple example would be a LS (long shot) where we see a basketball player shooting a foul shot and then cut to a CU (close-up) of the ball going through the basket. The motion of his actions and the ball minimize the viewer's awareness of the edit because their attention is drawn to the movement. While filming, the two shots that are to be edited together need to extend or overlap the action so that the editor has plenty of room to find the perfect point to cut. All this means is that the director wouldn't call cut on the first shot until after the ball had gone in the hoop; and the second shot would start before the ball enters the frame. This is why you'll also hear this kind of cut sometimes called *overlapping action* even though in the final edit the action won't necessarily overlap. Matching action shots can be even more subtle than this example, and when done well are virtually invisible to the average audience member.

On the other hand, jump cuts are edits that do catch our eye because they do not seem to flow, making the second image seem to pop or slightly jump out at us. These usually occur when the two shots being edited together are too similar in terms of shot scale and background, something that can happen if the camera hasn't been moved more than 30 degrees between the two shots.

Other ways to hide edits include changing in the image size (or shot scale) or camera angle from one shot to the next (as long as it's more than 30 degrees and doesn't cross the 180-degree line). A sound effect bridging the edit divides our attention between hearing and seeing, taking our full attention away from the visual, and often making the edit less noticeable as well.

**Reel Trouble** _____

Using the same shot more than once can cause problems later, especially if you're conforming negatives where you ultimately only have one of each image to work with (see Chapter 26). Though reusing a specific image has become easy to do with video and digital editing, most audience members recognize a reused image, and this recognition can confuse them or distract from the story. Many editing software programs allow you to set a preference that will prevent you from using the same shot twice or help you detect duplicate uses of the same image.

The flow of the narrative can create audience expectations and pique their curiosity, helping to mask individual edits also. For example, if we see Howard opening a box (Shot A), we expect the next shot to show us what he sees in the box (Shot B). His POV (point of view) is reinforced by the camera angle and height as well. If we cut back to the original Shot A, this type of edit would be considered an *insert edit* and is different from a *cutaway*, which might show us another aspect of the scene.

Or you may decide for narrative purposes not to show us Howard's POV shot of what's in the box yet. Maybe your next shot will be from the box's POV of Howard's reaction upon seeing what's inside (Shot C). Or you might cut to another scene. But any action is going to create a certain curiosity in the audience, and you need to be aware of how you're working with that curiosity and audience expectation for dramatic effect.

*Shot A.*                    *Shot B.*                    *Shot C.*

POV extends also to the issue of eye-line matches. Let's say Namita and Arturo are having a conversation. If Namita is standing, looking down at Arturo who is seated on the floor, we expect Arturo's eyes to be looking up in any shots, and in fact, we may expect the camera height and angle to reflect his POV as well. Likewise, Namita's shot would have her looking down. If these eye-lines don't match, and there's no narrative explanation for why they don't match, the audience will be confused and again pull out of the story while they try to figure out why these two people conversing are not looking at each other's faces.

A related method of editing for story and POV is to use *reverse shots.* Christine and Cora are sitting talking with each other. In the first shot, we see Christine from over Cora's shoulder (sometimes called an OSS or over-the-shoulder shot). Without crossing the 180-degree line, we then cut to Cora. If we're cutting specifically to see her reaction, we might call this a *reaction* shot. We could then cut back to Christine and so forth. This method is also referred to as *shot/reverse shot.*

Of course, audiences are aware that there may be gaps in time between scenes, so when we talk about continuity style of editing, we mean those techniques that ensure the illusion of continuous time and space within individual scenes and an understandable overarching chronology from scene to scene. See Chapter 24 for more information about different types of transitions we can use between scenes.

> **Staying in Focus**
>
> Remember the fundamental principle in continuity editing: Every transition should be motivated by dramatic necessity. Whether an action or a reaction, an expression or a gesture, editing allows you to guide the audience's attention and reveal dramatic information when it will have the most impact or relevance.

*Left: over-the-shoulder shot; right: reverse shot. Look at their eyes in each image: We can see that the screen direction has been maintained because Christine's eyes are looking screen right, while Cora's eyes are looking screen left. We have kept our camera on one side of the 180-degree line and therefore it seems as if Christine and Cora are looking at each other.*

# Temporal and Spatial Distortions: Aesthetics of Editing

One of the considerations an editor has to make is how long an individual shot needs to remain on the screen in order to relay necessary information to the audience. The scale of the shot or image size may determine how long a shot needs to remain on the screen. For example, an extreme long shot requires more time for the audience to take in all the visual information than a close-up does. The degree of movement within the frame may also influence how long the image should remain on the screen.

Despite its prevalence for conveying a narrative, continuity is simply one style of editing. Besides placing one shot next to another for clarity of story, there are other approaches. Though the word montage has several different definitions, you're probably familiar with the type of montage made popular in music videos, where a series of images are edited together that are obviously not continuous. Music videos edit some of these images on the beat. But if every image is cut on the beat, the video can soon feel mechanical, becoming so predictable that the audience may grow restless watching it. Therefore, music videos incorporate several different editing strategies. One strategy is to edit shots together based on the graphic qualities of the linking shots—qualities like color, screen direction, movement in the frame, shape, or texture. Examples of graphic editing would include a shot of a round red balloon being cut with a round red button on someone's lapel or a shot of a car driving from screen left to screen right with an athlete running the same direction.

Despite the fact that graphic cuts can be visually creative, an entire film of montages can become monotonous. But many successful films use short montage sequences to reveal basic story information rapidly or to compress a lot of time in the characters' lives into just a few minutes for the audience.

Ellipses are created when two shots leave out some degree of time. For example, if in one shot Kjersti tells Peter that she wants to take a train ride, and in the next shot we see them at the train station, we accept the missing time as related to their finalizing the plans. And we make a reasonable guess about how much time is missing. We assume that getting to the train station wasn't narratively important, so we accept its absence. In this way, time has been compressed—more time has passed for the characters than for the audience. Most films compress time by showing us only those moments or actions that are crucial for understanding the story. We don't need to see every single thing these characters do in their lives, only those things that relate to the story being told.

Some ellipses can be vague and run the danger of confusing the audience, distracting them from the story while they try to figure out just how much time has passed. *Closer* is an example, because it's not always clear how much time has passed between each scene.

In addition, we can expand time in our editing. Inserts and cutaways may expand time slightly. Slow motion expands time. Whether in conjunction with story elements or not, using any of these technical methods of connecting images—graphic cuts, match cuts, shot/reverse shot, and so on—as well as the duration of each shot will set up visual rhythms, almost like music. These rhythms are sometimes referred to as *pacing* and ideally give the film and story momentum that keeps the audience interested and involved.

## The Least You Need to Know

◆ Editing is the process of taking shots apart and putting them back together in a new order.

◆ Non-linear editing allows for the most flexibility in post-production.

◆ Film labs can help prepare the materials you will need in order to edit or release your film.

◆ Editing includes several stages that shape the film into its final form.

◆ Continuity editing is designed to keep the audience oriented to each scene's time and space so that they can concentrate on the story.

◆ Besides telling a story, editing can make the audience feel emotion, think, and guide their attention.

# 23

# Sounder: Sound Design

## In This Chapter

◆ What makes sound *sound* the way it does?

◆ Four elements of sound design

◆ Creating a plan for identifying the sounds your film needs

◆ Using music in your film

◆ Getting the right mix

You're trying to talk to the person next to you in a crowded party, with the music thumping, scores of people talking, the hallway clock chiming and a blender grinding away. You notice that whenever you look away, you have trouble hearing what he's saying. But if you look at him, you seem better able to hear his words.

Now close your eyes and listen to the room around you right now. My guess is that it's probably a lot quieter than the party I just described. In fact, your first reaction may be that it's silent. But if you keep your eyes closed for several minutes, you'll probably become aware of many sounds. First the sounds nearest you, but then gradually, the sounds filtering in from farther away, perhaps the next room. Or down the hall. And then perhaps sounds from outside; depending on where you are, these new sounds might be the soft murmur of traffic, children, birds, or crickets; the wind through the trees; the crashing of waves.

Though we may be unaware of them, we're surrounded by a multitude of sounds all the time. A truly silent environment is rare. Listening is a matter of perspective and what we choose to hear and concentrate on. This is why a mother can hear her baby make the slightest noise upstairs, even when everyone else says they didn't hear anything.

# Getting an Earful: The Art of Sound Mixing

When your eyes were closed, it's not that you weren't hearing those quieter sounds before, it's just that you weren't aware of them. In the noisy party, you were bombarded with so many sounds it was more difficult to differentiate among them, though by focusing your attention you had a better chance.

Our brains create our own real-life sound mix by distinguishing among all the sounds we hear and calling our attention only to those that may be important. We're able to do this because each sound has certain acoustic properties.

You've probably heard the term *sound wave* before. Sounds are vibrations in the air—often compared to ripples in a pond—that our ears are able to perceive; these waves are made up of peaks and valleys. The height or depth of these peaks and valleys determines the sound's *amplitude* or loudness. Amplitude is measured in *decibels* (abbreviated as *dBs*), and we generally interpret louder sounds as being closer to us.

The number of complete waveforms, or cycles, that occur per second determines the sound wave's *frequency*, which we perceive as a tonal range or *pitch*, something completely different from what we were talking about in Chapter 6. Treble tones have a greater frequency and therefore a higher pitch than bass tones. Frequency is measured in *hertz* (abbreviated as *Hz*); one thousand hertz would be called one *kilohertz* and written as 1kHz.

We rarely experience pure tones, or sine waves. Most of the sounds we hear include *harmonics*, which give the sound a distinctive quality that helps us to recognize its source. For example, we can usually tell if a musical note—such as middle C—has been made by a piano or a human voice or a trumpet. This is because each source creates a different set of harmonics. We call this distinction *timbre*.

These sonic qualities help us distinguish among all the sounds we hear. But as I noted in Chapter 20, microphones are not able to make this distinction. They record all sounds indiscriminately, and if we simply play this indiscriminate recording with our movie's visuals, the sound track will be a muddle. Therefore, the sound mixer (in post-production, called the *re-recordist* in order to differentiate him from the location sound mixer) and designer have to help us out. They're kind of like our brain, selecting which sounds need our attention. At least within the film.

The goals in the sound mix are to enhance the story, creating an interpretation of the material as well as contributing to the audience's belief that the characters are living in a world that's real to them.

# Almost Never a Quiet Moment

Sound designer Ric Coken often says, "people say a picture is worth a thousand words, but I can give you a sound that's worth a thousand pictures." Just as we want to say the most with every word choice in a script, a sound designer wants to say the most with each sound he or she chooses or creates for the mix. Basically, sound design is built around four elements: silence (or a lull in the sound), dialogue, music, and sound effects (sometimes abbreviated as SFX). The mix is where you bring these elements together.

Because dialogue is considered an essential element of character behavior and story, we usually foreground (or emphasize) the dialogue tracks when mixing. One way we can do this is by slightly lowering the volume of music and the other soundtracks whenever a character is speaking; this is called a *dipped mix*.

There may be times where the dialogue recorded on set can't be used. In those cases, we might ask the actors to watch the projected film and, along with the scratch track recorded on set and audio cues, rerecord their dialogue, trying to match performance as well as lips. We call this ADR (automated dialogue replacement), and this will be your most expensive audio minute. Originally designed as a "fix" for those occasional scenes where sync dialogue from the set couldn't be used, ADR is now quite prevalent in Hollywood films. But for the independent filmmaker, the cost is often prohibitive, so it's better to get a first-rate dialogue recording on the set if at all possible.

Good ADR tries to match the ambient sound quality of the original shot by recreating its perspective and acoustic properties. There's nothing worse than seeing a beach scene and hearing lip smacks we wouldn't be able to hear over the waves because the ADR microphone was so close. Or hearing slight room reverb on a scene that takes place outside.

For shots with groups of people shouting or talking en masse, you might do what is called a *loop group*. Unlike ADR, you're not trying to sync a specific line of dialogue but rather you're creating an aural environment. To keep the words indistinct or if you plan on marketing your film internationally, you can either play the track backwards in the final mix or collect *walla walla*.

After inventorying and listening to the sounds collected on the set, the sound designer makes a list of sounds that will need to be created. Then a sound creator may

### Defining Moments

**Walla walla** is, believe it or not, a technical term for collecting the sound of human voices without getting specific words. You have everyone simply say "walla walla" in a variety of intonations and volumes, and when mixed low over a crowd scene, it will sound like the indistinct murmur of voices.

gather these from a sound library or make her own either in wild recordings (recording isolated effects) or by doing Foley (creating sound effects synchronously while watching the film). The work of Foley artists is another example of the illusion of film: coconut halves can become horse hooves hitting the road, a bite from an apple can become the snap of a whip, and so forth.

Any or all of these sounds may be combined with other sounds to make them more unique to your film. This process of choosing the specific sounds to use and then combining them is highly interpretive, and when done well resonates with the film's story.

For example, merging the sound of wild animals with the sound of a blazing fire might subliminally reinforce the idea of fire as alive and ferocious. Sound design is about creating a subjective experience of the story, adding another layer to the director's and cinematographer's interpretations. Sounds can also reveal or add aspects to your characters; for example, the gunshots from a protagonist's gun will often sound different from the gunshots fired by the antagonist.

Finally, never underestimate the power of silence or quiet moments (sometimes called *lull*) in your film's soundtrack. Elements in film are most prominent when in contrast to other elements, and the same is true for your sound mix. Well-placed silences can help give individual sounds a greater impact.

# Mainly on the Plane: Sound Relationships

If you don't have film footage to look at yet, the script can give you a head start on the sound design issues. I usually make a copy of the script that's just for sound notes and use colored highlighters to mark any sound cues or potential sound sources written into the script. My marks are color coded by types of sounds; for instance, SFX that have to be created will all be marked in the same color. If I see in the body copy that the character starts a car, I highlight "starts the car" since I'll need to create a sound for that. Then I might draw vertical lines on the script that serve as designations for how long general types of sounds will need to run. Not all sounds run through the entire scene, much less the entire film. Ideally these lines are color coded as well, consistent with the colors that I used to highlight corresponding text in the script. I might handwrite notes along these timelines so that I have a bit more detail as to what these sounds will involve.

Once I have the film, I try to study at least one frame per shot to make sure I've thought out all the necessary sounds and considered issues of *sound perspective*. Let's say I've got a shot where a couple is talking at a beach party, kind of like this:

The first thing I do is imagine this two-dimensional image as it would be in three dimensions by dividing it into a series of planes—foreground, middle ground, and background—as shown in the following figures. I then study each plane one at a time, looking at all the possible sound sources in the frame. In the foreground, we have our couple talking, and because they're so close, we'll expect to hear their dialogue clearly; but I would ask myself if there are any other sound sources along this same plane. As drawn, there don't appear to be, but the sounds of their bodies, clothes, and footsteps as they move would exist on the same plane as well. Whether I need to include those is open for debate, depending on how I construct sounds for the middle and backgrounds.

The middle ground has a lake—what sounds would be associated with that? Perhaps waves lapping against the shore, or swimmers splashing in the lake? The wind blowing through the trees? The person playing with a dog? Also, if I imagine that there are more people at the lake than we can see in this image, I may want to include those sounds as well.

What potential sound sources do you see in the background? Maybe the jet in the distance? Perhaps there are boaters on the lake?

I then use these planes to consider each sound in relationship to the others. For example, if I'm able to hear birdcalls from the background or the lapping waves from the middle ground, then I'd probably be able to hear *fabric noise* in the foreground.

### Staying in Focus

Sound design is about filling in the illusions. This means that sometimes the designer will include subtle sounds that you might think one wouldn't hear in real life. For example, you might consider walking on grass or in sand a nearly silent endeavor, but in many movies, we actually can hear these kinds of footsteps, especially if the action is in the foreground.

Because the couple and the sounds they make are very close to me, in perspective to the distant sounds, it might seem odd that I can hear lapping waves but not their footsteps.

In the same vein, if I can hear distinct words from the people in the middle ground, then it's going to seem odd if I can't hear the conversation in the foreground clearly and loudly—more loudly than either the birds or the other people.

If the image is very dense with a lot going on, then I might double-check myself by dividing the full frame vertically into thirds, studying each third carefully to make sure I haven't overlooked a potential sound source. I may do this horizontally as well.

Besides the sounds that we would expect to accompany particular actions or objects on the screen, sound can also allude to the *off-screen space*, the world that exists for these characters beyond the frames of the film. For example, if a car drives by our couple, we don't expect to only hear it while it's on the frame—we'd expect to gradually become aware of the sound while the car was still off screen and then hear the sound continue after the car has left the frame. Just as the picture can fade in and fade out, sounds in the film's mix can fade in or fade out or even "dissolve" into one another, which we call a *crossfade*. In addition, there are times when a sound designer may play with the relationship of sounds to each other as a way to "pull focus" or draw our attention to a particular part of the frame.

As we consider the sounds that we may want to build into our soundtrack, we can play with how congruous the sound is or how closely it matches the sound source. For example, if we see the image of a dog barking but hear the sound of a cat meowing, the sound is incongruous. If this is not being used for clear creative effect, it can distract the audience.

# Make Your Own Kind of Music

Within a few days of first seeing *Star Wars*, I ran across a record of its music for sale. I couldn't figure out how this could be, because I didn't remember any music being in the film. How did I miss John Williams's score? Because I was so drawn into the story— and his music reflected the ups and downs of the narrative—I didn't even hear the score, and it wasn't until I saw the movie a second time that I realized there was music.

*Star Wars* is a good example of what we call a *musical score*, a piece of original music created specifically for your film. Because of this, it usually fits perfectly with the movie, enhancing the viewing experience.

In this day of synthesizers and home recording software, you may have a first-rate com-poser living right next door to you and never know it. Music programs at high schools, colleges, and universities often have students who would love to write music for a film. If you do go with the idea of a musical score, be sure to have a signed release form from your composer and the musicians that you have the right to use the music and the recording as part of your film.

Besides a musical score, many films have a *soundtrack*, a collection of popular songs that have been chosen to reflect the moods, themes, or actions of the film. *The Big Chill* is an example of this type of film music, and this kind of film music probably works best for more contemporary film stories.

Soundtracks can be a more expensive proposition because you have to get legal permission to use pre-existing songs and recordings, and most times this requires a fairly hefty fee. You pay this fee for every *needle drop*, or every time we hear the song (or fragment of the song) in your film. The music fees will also vary depending on whether you plan to show your film only in film festivals or to distribute it theatrically, on cable or as home video/DVD. Many independent films negotiate first for the cheaper festival music fees and then later if a distributor is interested, renegotiate to pay the theatrical fees. To avoid fees, some filmmakers will select older music that is in the public domain and no longer copyrighted. However, if they are using a pre-existing recording of the song, that recording may be copyrighted; more people fall victim to performance rights violation than copyright violation. Both have to be cleared for you to be able to use a song from a CD or record.

### Reel Trouble

Never use copyrighted music that you do not have the rights to. I've been on several film festival juries where we had to disqualify a great film from screenings and awards because the filmmaker did not have clearances to use the music. If you try to show your film without these permissions, the copyright holder can take legal action against you. For more information on obtaining legal permission to use popular music in your film, check out the BMI and ASCAP websites listed in Appendix B.

Rather than using songs you've seen on MTV or heard on the radio, how about checking with local bands who write their own material? Or ask them to record a song that's already in the public domain. Just be sure to get their written permission to use their songs and recordings in your film. This is where a music supervisor can help.

The one thing to keep in mind is that music—especially popular songs—will date your film faster than just about any other element. This is okay if the story is meant to evoke a very specific moment in time with a variety of cultural references, but for a story that's simply meant to be contemporary, next year's instrumentation and mixing techniques can make today's popular music sound old and feeble. This is why some filmmakers will use classical music, which audiences tend to accept as more timeless. Another option is not to use music at all but rather build a soundtrack of natural environmental sounds that is dense and layered, creating its own rhythms, tempos, and narrative emphasis.

# Mix Master

In the past few years, creating a great sound design and mixing your film has gotten much easier with computers and software. Whereas years ago you had to rent a studio by the hour in order to mix your film, computer software like DigiDesign's ProTools has become more and more affordable. But whether you create your sound design at home or at a studio, let's look at a few tips that will make your job easier.

Building your soundtracks and mixing will be easier if you've made sure during production that the camera log and sound log correspond. While these won't match perfectly, because there will be some camera shots that might be MOS (or without sound, heaven forbid!) and times when your location sound crew collected wild sounds for effects, good logs from both departments will make your job easier.

**Staying in Focus**

Before you begin mixing, be sure the titles and credits sequences have been edited into the picture or at least have been timed so that you know exactly to the frame how long your soundtrack needs to run.

Create a logical layout to your tracks. We usually divide the sound design into three categories: dialogue, music, and SFX. The goal is to keep all the tracks in each category next to each other; in other words, all of your dialogue tracks should be next to each other. This is incredibly easy now in the world of digital mixing.

If possible, assign a separate audio track to each major character in your film just for his or her dialogue. That way you can make general EQ decisions (altering the sound by manipulating its frequency) once and not need to make radical adjustments during the mix. Secondary characters who are only in one or two scenes may not need their own track and can be combined with characters who speak elsewhere in the story; within a given scene, though, the ideal is that each speaking role will have its own track. Your dialogue tracks may also include ambience tracks built from sound collected on set to help smooth out your editing of the dialogue in the scene.

You may need several tracks for music as well. Generally it's a good idea to separate music that the characters experience from within the scene, such as coming from a radio or an iPod. If your music tracks include a score as well as pop songs, then you'll probably want to separate these as well. And within each of these types, perhaps even subdivide again. By putting each type of music on a separate track, you won't need to continually reset or adjust levels and EQ.

Your sound effects or SFX tracks are usually subdivided and grouped according to their prominence in the mix. Background tracks might include *presence*, which is different from the ambience or naturally occurring sounds you collected on set. Presence tracks are sound effects that are deliberately constructed by the sound team in post-production to simulate the sounds we would expect to hear in the scene's environment. As a result you might have multiple tracks of presence. Other background tracks might include off-screen sounds.

Your other primary group of SFX tracks would be foreground tracks, such as your Foley and any individual or separate sounds you've added. Keep all of these sound effects on adjoining tracks.

Though computers allow us to start and stop and change settings at precise moments, this kind of segment-to-segment mixing can be very time-consuming. As a result, it's still a good idea to maintain plenty of space between individual sounds on a single track so that the re-recordist has time to respond and make adjustments "on the fly."

Often you'll mix groups of tracks respective to each other before the final mix, such as your background tracks. Whenever you do this, it is called a *premix*. This technique helps ensure you have a reasonable amount of tracks to mix at any one time. It's easier to keep tabs on what's happening on six tracks than sixty. The bottom line is that there has to be a logic to how you've laid out your tracks, and that all the tracks being mixed can be seen on the screen at once.

Now that most mixing is done on computer, *log sheets* or a detailed map of all the tracks and the location of each sound are no longer necessary. However a re-recordist will appreciate a general one-page summary of what each timeline is. In Chapter 26, we'll talk about finishing up your sound mix and marrying it to your visuals.

## The Least You Need to Know

◆ The sound mix makes sure we can hear what is important, usually dialogue.

◆ Sound design is built around silence, dialogue, music, and sound effects.

◆ Sounds within a scene exist in relationship to other sounds and the image; we expect sound sources in the foreground of the frame to be louder than sound sources in the far background.

◆ Music helps reflect the moods, themes, or actions of the film.

◆ Organizing your tracks by type—whether dialogue, music, or SFX—will make your mix go easier.

# 24

# *Strange Brew: Special Effects*

## In This Chapter

- Fades, dissolves, and other special transition effects
- Using green and blue screens
- Computer animation and modeling techniques
- Special effects using makeup and other materials
- A handful of other special effects

Part of the magic of films is that they show us what we can barely imagine and portray the everyday world in ways that make it unforgettable. Just like an illusionist, a filmmaker can allow us to look at what we might turn away from in real life or to safely experience danger.

Films are a controlled illusion, and the phrase *special effects* (often abbreviated as *FX* or *SPFX* to distinguish it from the abbreviation for *sound effects*) has become a catchall term for a number of different manipulations of the film or video image. These manipulations or effects can be accomplished "in camera" or achieved on the set or created in post-production.

## From Here to There: Transitions

As I mentioned in Chapter 22, *transitions* are the connecting point between two shots. The most basic transition is what we call a *straight cut*, where the last frame of Shot A is placed right next to the first frame of Shot B. While straight cuts are almost always used for all the edits within a given scene, there are ways to make this transition more gradual, especially when it's from one scene to the next. Transitions between scenes—one thing ending and another beginning—are natural punctuation points within your film. The type of transition you use will either emphasize or smooth that punctuation point. The best films use transitions that are conscious choices that feel consistent with the tone of the film and reflect or reinforce the story or theme. Let's look at some common transition effects in use today.

# Fade

The simplest of these transitions is the *fade*, and the effect is exactly what the word implies. The image either fades in, starting from a blank screen and gradually appearing in full detail, or fades out, gradually fading and becoming dimmer and less distinct until the image finally vanishes into a blank screen.

Remember how the first words of a script are "fade in"? That's because many films' first images fade in from a blank screen, even if it's such a quick fade that we barely notice. Similarly, the very last image of many movies fades out, sometimes slowly to create a lingering feeling or quickly to sharply punctuate the film's last few moments.

Fades can also be used within the film. Between scenes, these fades to black or white can draw attention to the passage of time and divide the film into segments that feel like chapters. The screen does not need to be fully blank for very long to register with an audience—a second or two is probably more than enough.

When posting in 16mm and 35mm film, fades are created in the lab. As the image is being printed, the machines are in effect stopping down for a fade out, gradually decreasing the amount of light hitting the print. They need time to reset or open back up to allow full light to expose the print again. As a result, the lab settings often dictate how long your fades can be and how much time you need between effects. In film, and depending upon the lab, fades are often in fractions or multiples of 24 frames: 6 frames, 12 frames, 18 frames, 24 frames, 36 frames, 48 frames. When these kinds of effects are created in the lab, they are called *optical effects*.

Fades can also be created in camera during production. Many 16mm and 35mm cameras allow you to adjust the aperture while filming, letting more or less light in to expose the filmstock, in effect creating a

> **Ditty Bag**
>
> When you see the term "fade in" or "fade out," the implication is that the blank screen is black. But you can also fade to white or another color. Generally, these would be noted as "fade to white" or "fade in from white."

fade. Many digital cameras also offer this feature. But once you've done an effect in camera, it's pretty much there forever. If you don't like it, about all you can do is edit it out. You have the most control for perfectly timing and placing your fades during post-production, so filmmakers generally avoid doing in-camera fades.

## Dissolve

The second most common type of effects transition is to overlap a fade out with a fade in, which we call a *dissolve*. In the center of the dissolve there is a brief moment when both images are on the screen simultaneously, which can create startling connections between one shot or scene and the next.

Like fades, dissolves can be done both in camera and in post-production. For 16mm or 35mm film to create a dissolve effect in camera, you would have your first shot fade out and then rewind the filmstock back to the point where the fade out began. Then you'd shoot your next shot while slowly fading it in, exposing the film twice. Of course, if you didn't expose correctly or rewound an incorrect number of frames, or if your second shot needs to be redone, you have to go back and redo the first shot as well, but you won't know until after the film has been processed.

Even more than fades, dissolves are best to do in post-production, because if you don't like the effect, you can redo it or adjust it without damaging your original shots. Especially now with computer editing, you can easily and quickly try out a wide variety of transitional effects that are non-destructive and leave your original image intact.

> **Ditty Bag**
>
> A very quick dissolve, so quick that the eye can't really see it, is sometimes called a *soft cut*. This kind of edit from one shot to the next softens the edit, making it less noticeable to the eye than a hard cut, or an edit where one shot butts right up against another shot.

## Wipe

If you've seen the *Star Wars* films, you will have noticed that many of the transitions from one scene to the next look like the shots are sliding across the screen or as if the new shot is pushing the previous shot off the screen. This effect is called a *wipe* because the new shot wipes across the screen, replacing the previous shot.

Wipes as a film effect are much more difficult to achieve than fade ins or dissolves and cannot be done in camera. For 16mm and 35mm film editing, wipes require a laboratory process known as optical printing, where the two images of the transition are reshot, kind of like what would happen if you took a photograph of a photograph.

For digital editing, computer software programs can achieve this effect much more easily, and it is a fairly common option. However, because wipes are a rare type of transition in contemporary films, when they are used they often make a film feel as if it were from a different era. *Star Wars*, for example, harkens back to the 1930s serials. *Desert Hearts*, which also uses wipes, is set in mid-twentieth century Reno. In both of these cases, the wipes contribute to each film's feeling of nostalgia and age.

In theory, wipes can move across the screen from right to left, left to right, top to bottom, bottom to top, or even from any corner across the screen to the opposite corner. The most common, though, are from side to side.

## Freeze Frame

While it may seem odd to call it a transition, another type of effect that is sometimes used as a transition is the *freeze frame*. Freeze frames are another post-production effect that in traditional film editing would require optical printing but which are easy to achieve in digital editing. Basically, this effect is where the image freezes and in effect becomes a still photograph that remains on the screen. It may eventually straight cut into a new shot or it might fade out or it might dissolve into another shot or it might simply "restart" and continue on. *Lock, Stock and Two Smoking Barrels* uses freeze frames within the scene and shot to allow time for the voice-over narrator to fill us in on particular details that relate to the frozen image.

## Superimposition

Though not quite a transition, another type of effect is a *superimposition*, the movie equivalent of a double exposure. Though primarily a post-production effect, it is actually possible to create a superimposition in camera when shooting 16mm or 35mm film, but as with all in-camera effects, do so at your peril.

Besides these effects, there are a number of ways one scene can move into the next, and one of the best ways to learn about transitions is to watch films and pay special attention to those points when one scene becomes another. *Blood Simple* has some amazing transitions. *Rope* cleverly disguises its transitions, making the film seem as if it were shot in one long, continuous take. It hides its transitions by having someone or something briefly obstruct the camera, filling the image and making at least one frame black, then cutting into a new shot that starts with something obstructing the frame and moving away so that the image reappears.

# It's Easy Being Green

In Chapter 14, I mentioned the idea of virtual sets—film locations that exist only in your computer upon which your actors are superimposed. *Sky Captain and the World of Tomorrow* is an example of such a film. And back in the 1990s, MTV went through a brief period where its VJs did their between-video banter in front of frequently changing or spinning virtual sets.

Virtual sets are a type of special effect, and in some ways they are a variation on the traditional matte painting and rear-projected backdrops. In classical Hollywood, one of the ways to create imaginative landscapes and settings was to create a painting that could be mounted to the front of the camera (in a matte box) or superimposed over the image of the actors in post-production; part of the painting would be clear or left out, and this area would perfectly line up with a constructed set where the actors would perform. Matte paintings allowed for relatively small sets to be built and yet on film to look as if they were huge vistas.

A similar cost-saving and production-easing technique has been the use of backdrops. Scenic backdrops, are large panels painted to resemble a particular environment. *Charlie's Angels* (the first movie) has some fun with a scenic backdrop. The problem with scenic backdrops, of course, is storage, so sometimes they would be painted on the side of a studio lot building. An easier solution to storage that offers a wider range of backgrounds is to photograph or film a backdrop and then *rear-project* it on a screen behind the actors. Basically, green screens and blue screens are a similar idea, only applied in post-production. Your actors perform against a blank screen that can be covered up with another image in post. Because neither the actors nor their costumes are the same color as the blank screen, the superimposed image will not cover them up and will simply fill in the block of green or blue. Your actors will look like they're in front of the added image in the final composite.

This effect can become more complex by creating blue or green screen objects that can be in front of your actors or that they can use. Later this blank object can easily be replaced with another image. Also, wires supporting actors can be green or blue to ease in their later removal from the image, making the actor appear to be suspended in the air. This is a similar process to how an actor can appear to be missing a limb.

Green screens have become more prevalent than blue screens because their particular hue is less likely to show up in the actors' clothing or in any set elements that need to be retained in the final image.

These effects are getting better and better, though creating a background that merges perfectly with the actors' action is still a challenge to do completely convincingly. Before committing yourself to this kind of production, you may want to do a series of tests to be sure that the results are what you want. Despite one or two notable exceptions, blue and green screens are not used to shoot an entire film but rather for special shots or scenes that would be too difficult or too dangerous to create physically.

## Computer Animation and Modeling

You may have some scenes in your film that are panoramic views of action that don't require the presence of actors. These might be space battles or a burning building or dinosaurs walking the earth or a city collapsing under a tidal wave or you name it. Traditionally, many of these kinds of effects were done with models and miniature sets that were created to scale and filmed in stop action, a method of shooting one frame at a time, moving the objects just a little bit between each frame.

As computer animation programs have become more sophisticated and less expensive (see Appendix B for some examples), you can render many of these kinds of scenes in your computer. Animation always takes longer than you think it will, but when done well, the effect can be impressive. We've come a long way since *Tron*.

> **Ditty Bag**
>
> Stop action is a common animation technique. *Rudolph the Red-Nosed Reindeer* and *Chicken Run* are examples of films made this way.

## Creepy Special Effects on Set

Not everything has to be done in camera or during post-production. You can physically create certain special effects right on the set with makeup and other materials. I remember hearing long ago that chocolate syrup made the best-looking blood if you were shooting in black & white film. Evidently it was quite convincing. Though I never used it, what I learned from this is that like so many things in filmmaking, it doesn't matter what something is (chocolate syrup), it only matters what it looks like on film (blood).

Makeup effects can create bloody wounds and decaying bodies as well as horrific-looking monsters and creatures from other planets. Experienced makeup artists who have a good budget often work with latex foam to create special pieces that can be applied to the skin (hence their often being called *appliances*), creating different shapes, lumps, and textures. Once these are covered up with additional makeup to help hide the seams, the effect can be quite amazing.

Local theatrical costume shops, Internet costume sites, and Halloween specialty stores often will sell fake blood (or theater blood) as well as scar applications and a variety of molded materials that can look like just about anything you can imagine.

However, you can achieve impressive effects with materials available from your local grocery store. One part corn syrup, two parts red food coloring and a touch of blue will make for pretty convincing blood, though it'll look darker in the bottle than on the skin, so don't be afraid to add more food coloring so that it looks convincing. Split pea soup—alone or in combination with other soups or foods—has made for some pretty realistic-looking vomit (for example, in *The Exorcist*). Glycerin dabbed on the skin can sheen like sweat or resemble the watery seepage around a wound.

**Staying in Focus**

Whenever mixing up your own makeup materials, make your cleanup easy by using disposable cups and containers.

My friend Gary Schultz is great at creating makeup effects, and I asked him to help me out with a few I could show you. First we gave Clint a scar by using rigid collodion, a smelly clear fluid that draws the skin into a shallow crease as it dries. It works best on areas where the skin is looser. You want to be very careful when applying it near the eyes; be sure to read the label for warnings, and you'll want to have some Spirit Gum Remover on hand to clean it off.

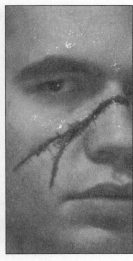

*Before.*               *After: healed scar.*               *After: bloody and fresh cut.*

Turning the scar into a bloody cut simply required a créme- or grease-based makeup to create a black highlight in the deep part of the crease. Then Gary used a stipple sponge to apply very thick homemade corn syrup-based blood to make fine scratch marks across the scar. The sheen around the edge is a little glycerin applied with a cotton swab.

Now take a look at Bill's arm before and after. Though it may be hard to see in a black-and-white photo, Gary first applied grease-based misty violet and brown makeup to resemble bruising and to give the skin a mottled appearance. Then using Plasto, Gary molded individual lumps onto the skin and used a cotton swab to smooth and reshape the bumps.

Other kinds of skin effects are as simple as mixing up a box of plain gelatin and food coloring to create a wide range of gruesome effects, such as Bill's burned face.

**Reel Trouble**

Because many makeup effects dry on the skin, they will pull body hair as you remove them. To prevent that, either have the actor shave or use a thin layer of petroleum jelly on any hair first. Also, using créme- or grease-based makeup rather than cake makeup can help.

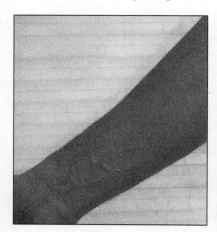
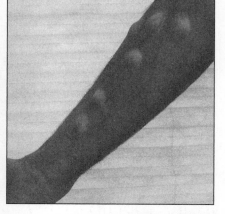

*Bill's arm, before and after.*

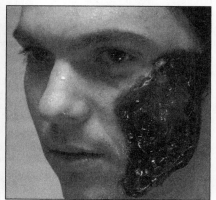

*Bill, before and after.*

You have to apply the mixture fairly quickly—Popsicle sticks work great—using different strokes to create the varying textures. The gelatin is very sticky and will dry quickly, and will stick to the skin for several hours. After you're done, it's easy to peel off.

Even with the best makeup artist in the world, the makeup effects require proper lighting and editing to work to their full potential. And it's not always what you show, but what you imply that will affect an audience. Because of that fact, sound design can play a huge role in how effective a makeup effect will be.

Besides makeup, there are other things you can use to change the look of your actors. Scleral lenses, a type of contact lens, can make human eyes look blind or as if they should be those of an animal. But, and it's a big but, scleral lenses can be dangerous for the wearer if they have not been purchased and fitted by an eye-care professional. Ignore the cheap ones you can buy in novelty shops or in the back of magazines, unless you want to potentially damage your actor's eyes. If you must have the effect, go to an optometrist.

In the same way that changing a person's eyes can radically change his appearance, changing his teeth can have a similar startling effect. The simplest technique is to black out a tooth in order to make it seem like it's missing. But only do this with materials such as tooth wax that are designed for this purpose.

Besides doing makeup on one of your actors, you can also create replicas of animals or human bodies in order to shoot scenes that would be too risky or unnecessary for a real animal or person. In *There's Something About Mary* they used a replica rather than the real dog for many of its mishaps. *Jaws* used a mechanical shark for most of its scenes.

When figuring out how to do makeup effects, have fun, be creative, be safe, and do camera tests to be sure that the effect looks good on the screen.

# Other Special Effects

Hollywood and big-budget films create a variety of effects on set, such as explosions, fires, car wrecks, and near-impossible physical feats of the characters (such as leaping between buildings or falling from great heights). Keep in mind that these kinds of effects are created by trained and experienced technicians. These might include stunt coordinators, stuntmen and -women, pyrotechnicians as well as a fire-fighting crew, and an emergency medical team on set.

To create the effect of someone getting hit by a bullet and bleeding, special effects artists usually use what's called a *squib*, a small pouch of red fluid that is wired to explode or burst open upon a signal from a remote control. Each squib can be pretty expensive, and while it might sound simple, you want an expert doing this work so that the effect doesn't become real.

If you must have potentially dangerous stunts, fire, or explosions in your film, remember that the keys to success are careful planning, camera tests, rehearsals, and a crew trained and qualified to achieve the effects safely. Also, depending on the effect and the location, you may need additional permits. At the very least, you want to be sure that local law enforcement and other appropriate services are aware of what you're doing. My best advice for these kinds of effects, though, is to bite the bullet (so to speak), pay the money, and hire professionals.

Less dangerous are the additional effects you can create by manipulating the image as it's being recorded or in post-production. Common techniques include filtering the image or changing its speed. Let's look at each a little more closely.

## Filtering the Image

While many of the filters we talked about in Chapter 19 are used to help compensate for lighting conditions and color temperature, there are *effects filters* designed to be placed in front of the lens in order to create a certain effect on the image. On some cameras the filter can screw directly onto the lens, while other cameras require that the filter be placed in a special holder, or matte box, which can be attached to the front of the camera. Depending on the filter, they can be used to help create the illusion of fog (a scenic fog filter) or make the highlights of the frame seem to sparkle (a star filter) or even help darken the sky while leaving the lower half of the frame at full exposure (attenuated or graduated filters).

> **Staying in Focus** _____
>
> Attenuated filters are sometimes used for shooting *day-for-night*, which means that you shoot a scene in the daylight that can pass for night in the film. One tip for making day-for-night look good is to shoot the scene on a bright sunny day. It sounds counterintuitive, but once you've underexposed the shot and tinted it blue, the deep shadows will resemble the kinds of shadows created at night in moonlight. Recent advances in filmstock speeds and digital camera technology allow us to shoot in lower lighting conditions than ever before, so shooting day-for-night is now more a stylistic choice than a necessary one.

If you're shooting on filmstock, the effects of these filters will usually be more pronounced in 35mm than in 16mm. Also these effects can now be easily created in post-production with computer software, and going with the idea that it's always better to have the most control over the effect as possible, that may be a better choice for you.

## Slowing Down and Speeding Up

Slow motion is a common effect in films to emphasize the emotional impact of a particular moment for the audience. Back in the old days, when film cameras were hand cranked, this effect became known as overcranking, which simply meant that the camera operator turned the crank faster, allowing more film to run through the camera than usual. When processed and projected back at normal speed, the action would appear to be slower than normal—in other words, slow motion. You can also undercrank, which means running the film through the camera slower than usual so that when projected, everything appears to be moving faster than normal.

Though we no longer hand-crank cameras, these terms have stayed with us over the years as a label for the resulting effect. Though motorized 16mm and 35mm film cameras still require you to adjust the speed of the film in order to create slow or fast motion as an in-camera effect, you can also create this effect in post-production either through optical printing or with computer software. Likewise, digital cameras will often allow you to do slow or fast motion in camera, but with computer software allowing you to easily manipulate the speed of the image in post-production, it makes more sense to do it there.

## Throwing It in Reverse

Let's say that you want to have a car speed up to your actor and quickly stop just before it would nudge the back of his knee. There are a couple of ways you could create such an effect. Because film is a two-dimensional space, you could shoot the scene in profile and, with careful staging and use of lenses, actually have the car and actor not really near each other. For example, the car could be in one lane and the actor in another—proving once again the illusion of film. Or you could green or blue screen the action and create a composite image as we discussed earlier.

**CAUTION** **Reel Trouble**

Anytime you're mixing people with machines such as cars, you always want to be extremely careful so that no one gets hurt. That's why Hollywood has specially trained experts to do stunts.

Another option would be to reverse the footage. In other words, I could start filming with the car's bumper up against my actor's leg and then have the car drive backward quickly away from him. Then in the final film, I reverse the images.

Before computers and digital images, if I wanted to reverse the image in a film, I had two options. I could either do it in the lab with an optical printer or I could shoot it on the set by turning the camera upside down. In the rushes, my image would appear upside down as well, but I could cut it out and insert it in my footage so that the image would seem right side up. If there was lettering in the frame or it was obvious that the steering wheel and driver were on the wrong side of the car, I'd also have to flip the film over so that these would appear not just right side up but also oriented correctly left to right.

Nowadays, computer software for film editing will often allow you the option of reversing the footage with the flick of a keystroke or a mouse click. Reversing the image can be used for a number of interesting narrative effects, but like any good effect, it needs to add something to the story. Just looking cool isn't enough.

## The Least You Need to Know

- Fades, dissolves, and wipes are all ways in which one scene or shot can transition into another.

- Filming your actors in front of blue and green screens allows you to create settings and backdrops that would be too expensive or difficult to build in reality.

- Computers now allow us to easily accomplish many effects.

- Realistic makeup effects can be made with items around your house.

- Whenever doing special effects on your set, think safety first and leave the dangerous stunts to the pros.

# Chapter 25

# *Safe:* Titles and Credits

## In This Chapter

◆ Giving your film a title

◆ Different types of title and credit sequences

◆ Basic design considerations when creating your title sequences

◆ Knowing how long to leave each credit or title on the screen

First impressions are important. The title of your film is literally the first thing audiences will see. Finding the perfect title can be difficult, and some filmmakers use a working title until they decide on just the right name for their film. The independent film *Southside* became *Dirty Work* because the latter title is more intriguing. *Almost Famous* started life as *Untitled* (in fact, the director's cut DVD of the film is released as *Untitled*). Working titles are also sometimes used to keep people from knowing too much about the film while it's being shot.

Titles cannot be copyrighted, though having a title too similar to that of another film can sometimes cause legal problems, as well as confusion for the audience. As a general guide, shorter titles are easier to remember. The title of your film ideally evokes the story and tone without giving it all away. Bad titles are those that are so general they don't create an image in the prospective viewer's mind. Good titles are memorable, creating an immediate snapshot in our brain and arousing our curiosity: *sex, lies and videotape, She's Gotta Have It, The Decline of the American Empire, The Evil Dead, Blood Simple, I've Heard the Mermaids Singing, Tomb Raider, Boys on the Side, The Opposite of Sex,* and *Resident Evil,* to name a few. Of course, audiences can get upset if your title promises something it doesn't deliver, so your title has to relate to the story somehow.

Besides the title of your film, you credit all the people who helped you. On larger films, personal name recognition and association to familiar people or films are very important in marketing. Star power simply means that a person's name may bring an audience in. And star power is not limited to actors like Julia Roberts or directors like Quentin Tarantino. Other films that were released before yours and proved popular also generate star power. This is why some films are advertised as "from the producers of …" or "from the director who brought you …." But odds are that for now, you'll have to bank on the title of your film more than your name recognition.

# Reading Lessons: Text That Can Appear in Films

Not to confuse things, but the term *titles* (with an *s*) doesn't mean the name you've chosen for your film, but rather is used to refer to a number of different types of written text that can appear in a film. Digital technology has made this process simpler than ever before, allowing us not only to edit our film on computer but to also create our own title sequences. With the click of a mouse we can add text in a number of different fonts and effects, easily moving the words and letters across the screen in a variety of ways.

The *main title sequence* usually occurs at or near the beginning of the film and includes the title or name of the film as well as the names of key people or companies involved with the film. Because of this early placement in the film, this sequence is sometimes referred to as the *opening credits*.

For many years, films would run the main titles before the movie began. Television shows often run a teaser before the opening credits as a way to hook the audience (and keep them from changing channels), and some films emulate this technique as well, such as *The 25th Hour*. In recent years, there have been more and more films that begin with no main title sequence and instead run the main titles at the very end of the film. This can be an effective way to throw the audience right into the action without any preparation.

> **Ditty Bag**
>
> Most films we see have the titles and credits move across the screen; the most common movement, especially for the credits that come at the end of the film, is what is called a *scroll* or *crawl*, where the titles move up the screen. The credits at the beginning of a film might move horizontally across the screen rather than vertically, or they might simply fade in and out.

For features, there is a traditional order in which these opening credits are arranged. Usually the title sequence begins with the names of the distribution and production companies that have provided primary financing or support.

If the director has been more than just a director for hire, in other words, she has been a guiding force throughout the filmmaking process, then you may see the credit, "a film by" and then her name. This is sometimes referred to as a *possessory credit* and is traditionally reserved for the director. If you're assuming the producing and directing duties of your film, then you should definitely include this statement in your opening credits.

**Staying in Focus** _____

Short films have shorter main title sequences. If you're titling a short film, you will want your opening credits to be succinct. "A film by [your name]" after the title of the film may be all you need. *Bambi Meets Godzilla* is a witty spoof of films where the credits are longer than the actual film. However, if you have a particularly well-known actor starring in your film, you may want to include his or her name in the opening credits.

After these opening credits, we usually see the principal players or the names of the actors who are playing the most important characters in the film. The actual order of the cast's names (and sometimes even where the name is placed on the screen) is determined in the actors' contracts.

Following these, the crew department heads each receive a title. You may see some variation from film to film as to the exact order, but watch the opening credits for several movies and make note of the sequence each uses. What you'll probably see is that the last two credits before the film actually begins are "screenplay by" and "directed by." The director's credit is always the last credit of the sequence, and in a traditional titles sequence, the last credit we see before the film begins.

Main title sequences are often shot or prepared by a separate crew on large films. In fact, an entire industry has developed wherein filmmakers create the title sequences. One of the most famous opening credits sequences is for the film *Se7en*.

Besides the opening titles, there is a credits sequence at the end of the film, and this is often referred to as the *closing credits* or *end credits*. These credits are a list of all the people who worked on the film in some technical or advisory capacity. Usually the closing credits begin with a summary of all the speaking roles and the actors who filled them. These might be in the order of appearance (and designated as such) or in the order of importance (the main character listed first, second most important character second, and so forth).

Following the cast are the nonspeaking and background roles, usually listed simply as a broad category headed by the word *with* or *extras* and the individual actors' names listed in alphabetical order. No character names are designated, since many of these parts may have been unnamed background characters.

Following the cast names are the names of all the crew. Even more so than the opening credits sequences, you may see variations from film to film as to what order these credits occur. Besides the technical crew positions, and especially in independent films, there are a series of "thanks" near the end of the end credits. These acknowledge the people who advised or offered in-kind services or assisted in supporting the production either financially or by donating time, services, locations, or goods. Be sure that you list everyone who has helped or supported your film—this is their official and public "thank you" and recognition, and it means a lot.

> **Reel Trouble**
>
> As you're preparing your credits, do one last check to make sure you have signed releases for every actor. Without signed releases, your actor can potentially prevent you from showing or selling your film.

*Subtitles* are usually text that appears near the bottom of the screen and either translates the actors' words if spoken in a language other than the audience's or gives information that is not obvious from the image, such as a location, date, time, and in documentary, a person's name or title/occupation.

*Innertitles* are also known as title cards and refer to written text that is inserted between shots or scenes. We're probably most familiar with this type of titles in old silent films where dialogue or story material would sometimes be written on the screen.

# Setting the Mood: Choosing the Right Font and Size

Besides the actual name of your film, the opening credits are usually the audience's first indicator of the mood and tone of the film. A professional-looking title sequence not only encourages people to take your film more seriously but also prepares them for watching your movie.

I learned the hard way how titles prepare an audience. Though my film *Borders* is shot in black and white, my opening and closing credits are in color. The titles created an expectation in the audience that the film would be in color, and this incongruity distracted them. Once you lose your audience, even for a few moments, it's difficult to get them back.

Creating credit sequences is more than simply listing people's names, jobs, and the title of the film. The style of the lettering, its font and size, can indicate certain information about your film, such as its tone and intent.

living room

*living room*

**LIVING ROOM**

living room

*living room*

*Notice how the same words imply different moods simply by changing the font and style of the lettering.*

When reading a list of jobs and the names of who performed those jobs, a viewer will usually have an easier time distinguishing these if the job titles use a different font, size, or color than the names of the people. Basically, the contrast between name and job will make it easier to read and comprehend.

In a similar way, it's usually easiest to read text when it is in stark contrast to the background. White letters on a black background would be an example. And in general, white is considered the best choice for any type of text in the frame because it usually provides the greatest amount of contrast with most backgrounds. The exception, of course, is if the background is a light color—then white lettering might be hard to read, and black or another color might be more appropriate.

When subtitling films into another language, there's nothing more frustrating than being unable to read the translation because there's not enough contrast between the text color and the background color. Because many films will include visual compositions that include both black and white in their frames, you may find it more effective to subtitle in a color like bright yellow, which is relatively rare in compositions and is more likely to be read against both black and white. Another option is to outline the subtitle text in black so that if the white letters fall against a light colored background, the outlines will make the text legible. For films that are letterboxed on DVD, the black region at the bottom of the screen is the perfect place to put subtitles because the contrast remains constant.

> ### Ditty Bag
>
> Black letters on a white background are rarely used in 16mm and 35mm film because as film is projected, it inevitably gets scratched. These scratches are dark and therefore easily show up on white backgrounds, but would be less visible against a black background. This is why most titles and credit sequences have dark backgrounds. Of course, if you're going to release your film as a DVD or for broadcast only, you don't need to worry about scratches created by projectors.

When titling your film, remember that most of your audience is ultimately going to watch the program on television sets rather than giant movie screens. Even if your film is initially shown in theaters, at some point you will probably distribute it in a format for viewing on television (either broadcast by a cable company or released as a DVD). Therefore, it's important that the letters in your titles are large enough to be read on the average TV screen. But if they are too large, they will seem to burst out of the frame, which may prove distracting to the audience.

# Choosing the Right Placement

There are a variety of theories about how to "read" (in other words, view) and compose an image. Not all parts of the frame are created equal, at least in terms of perception. Some cinematographers and filmmakers study classical painting for visual composition, drawing on concepts like the *Golden Mean*.

> ### Defining Moments
>
> If you divided the frame into thirds by drawing two equally spaced vertical lines and then drew three equally spaced horizontal lines, the points where these lines intersect are sometimes considered the **Golden Mean**. Some painters and cinematographers feel these are the most important viewing points, and any detail of importance would be placed there to draw attention to it.

But there have been studies that indicate we scan images based partly on cultural training. In western cultures we've been trained to read a page of text from left to right, top to bottom. When looking at an image, this training persists. Our eyes usually start in the upper left quadrant of the frame (near the Golden Mean) but then scan the image like we'd read a page, ending up and resting in the lower right-hand corner of the frame—just where you'll end up on this page before turning it to the next one.

Because the human eye rests briefly in this lower right quadrant, some filmmakers feel this is a more important area to place crucial information than the upper left intersection of the vertical and horizontal thirds. Notice the opening credits of *New York, New York* where our protagonist in extreme long shot enters a crowded bustling street and exits in the lower right-hand corner of the frame. His presence is even more emphasized by having a neon sign shaped as an arrow pointing to where he'll come out of the crowd.

Some magazines even charge more for full-page ads that fall on the right-hand page than the left-hand page. This tendency of the human eye in Western culture to rest in the lower right quadrant of the frame is why if two actors' names appear side by side in the same frame, the right one will often be slightly higher than the first. The belief is that this placement will help to combat the left to right, top to bottom scanning that would result in the name in the lower right area of the frame getting more of the viewer's attention. This impression that things in the right half of the frame draw more of our attention is sometimes referred to as *asymmetry of the frame*.

So are we doomed to only look at the lower right quadrant of the frame? No, we can direct the viewer's eye with compositional elements, such as placement, lines, shapes, movement, contrast, and so forth.

Generally, the eye will be drawn to whatever is different in the frame, whatever stands in contrast to the rest of the image. For example, at the beginning of *Deceived*, we see a sea of black umbrellas moving away from the camera. But there is one bright one that comes into view, so it stands in contrast because of its color. And this umbrella is moving toward us, so it stands in contrast to the movement of all the other umbrellas moving away from the camera. As you're watching films, notice where your eye is drawn and ask yourself why that part of the frame has gotten your attention.

When placing text in the frame, there are few rules other than doing what will make the text legible. Of course, subtitles are meant to be unobtrusive and usually run at the bottom of the screen (remember, they need to be large enough to read on a TV screen) and are ideally one or two lines in length—three at the maximum.

When superimposing your titles over images, try to treat the text as part of the overall composition. Create a title and image that are attractive and pleasing to the eye.

Finally, you almost always lose some of the frame's edges when you show a film on a television or computer monitor. Therefore, it's important to allow enough room around the edges of your frame for this. Just as many cameras have a TV-safe outline in the viewfinder that assures all of your action will appear on a TV screen, there is often a second outline inside that one that serves as a TV titles safe box. Film editing and titling computer software often has this kind of indication as well, and if you're shooting your titles the old-fashioned way on an animation stand, the field guide also has the TV safe and TV titles safe areas marked.

# Timing Is Everything: Titles on the Screen

How long should a title remain on the screen? Well, scrolling is a popular way of handling closing credits (which is usually the longest title sequence of a film) because each name is on the screen the entire time it takes it to scroll. You may have seen some scrolls that are so fast you can't really read any of the information. This may make sense when a film has to fit into a set broadcast length, but for your film, your credits are the place where all your crew and cast—who have worked for free or very little money—and your supporters get their reward, their recognition. Don't rush through these. The scroll doesn't have to be so slow that you can read every single name and job, but a viewer should be able to comfortably scan and read at least half of the names (and if they're a speed reader, all of them). Most computer programs for titling will have several set speeds from which to choose, so you don't have to guess.

> **CAUTION**
>
> ### Reel Trouble
>
> Before finalizing the credit sequences, review your crew and cast's release forms and deal memos. These forms hopefully had them print their names as they want them to appear in the film's credits. Don't assume you know. Sometimes people go by nicknames in everyday life but use a different name for their professional credits. Likewise, double-check all spellings. Triple-check by having someone else go through every name carefully. You wouldn't want your name or the title of your film misspelled. Your crew feels the same. Their name in the credits is a huge part of your payment to them for all their hard work; it should be right.

For the opening credits (name of film, your name, and any key personnel) and individual credits that appear on the screen by themselves, the name of your film probably needs to stay on the screen the longest—after all, it's the most important piece of information for the audience at this point.

Your and key personnel names should be on the screen long enough to read out loud one and a half times. Why out loud and one and a half times? Because you're already familiar with what the text says, so when you read it either to yourself or out loud, you're going to read it faster than a person who's never seen the information before. Reading it out loud slows you down some, but one and a half times slows you down a bit more, hopefully approximating how long it will take the average viewer to read the info to themselves while watching your film.

Make sure that the job responsibilities each person is being credited for are accurate and agreed upon—your deal memos and release forms should be the starting point for this kind of info, though sometimes during the shoot some crew may have shifted or taken on more jobs that you want to credit them for. The easiest way to deal with credits is to keep a running list throughout the production of any job changes or any additions.

Of course, all of the individual credits that appear on the screen separately need to be paced as a group so that no one credit gets more attention than comparable information. For example, it may be okay for the title of the film and your name as the filmmaker to be on the screen *slightly* longer than any of the other individual credits, but all of the main actors' names should be on the screen the same amount of time and perhaps slightly longer than supporting actors, who as a group should each be on screen the same amount of time. Likewise, all of your key crewmembers should get the same amount of screen time.

## The Least You Need to Know

♦ The title of your film needs to be interesting enough to make an audience want to see your movie.

♦ There are other types of titles that can appear in your film: opening credits, end credits, subtitles, and innertitles.

♦ Design credits that are easy to read and are part of your composition.

♦ Give your audience time to read the titles.

# Chapter 26

# The Conformist: Finishing Up

## In This Chapter

- ◆ Different types of release formats for your movie
- ◆ Creating a final sound mix for your composite print
- ◆ Conforming and on-line editing
- ◆ Optical and digital soundtracks
- ◆ Release prints
- ◆ Archiving your master film

Let's say you shot your movie on a digital camera, downloaded the footage right into your personal computer, edited the film, and mixed the sound digitally. Or maybe you shot your movie on 16mm film, had the footage processed, edited a workprint, and mixed the sound at a studio. Or maybe you did some combination of the two.

Either way, you've probably been watching your film on a computer screen or in editing suites or in the mix studio where it's okay that each component (image and audio) is separate and may even exist on multiple tracks or timelines. The average movie theater or home entertainment system, however, has to have all of this visual and audio material combined into one finished format that can be easily shown to an audience—a *composite*. Let's look at some of the ways you can create a composite, assuring that you can show your film to others.

# Choosing a Release Format

The release format you choose for your film will affect the choices you make in production (shooting) and post-production (editing). Even though you're reading about finishing up as part of exhibition & distribution considerations, you ideally want to choose your release format before you start shooting.

There are a number of ways you can release your finished film, and you're probably familiar with or at least aware of most. You can release your independent movie in any one (or a combination) of the following formats:

◆ 35mm film print

◆ 16mm film print

◆ DVD

◆ Beta SP

◆ DV master

◆ VHS

> **Reel Trouble**
>
> Super16mm film format is a single perf filmstock that allows you to expose part of the edge of the film for a widescreen aspect ratio. The problem is that in order to put a soundtrack to the film, you have to blow it up to 35mm. So while you can shoot in Super16, you can't release your film in Super16.

Any of these release formats can include material that was originally shot as Super 8, 16mm, Super16, 35mm, VHS, 3/4" U-matic, Hi8, Betacam SP, MiniDV, Digital8, DV, 24P, HDTV, and so forth. Which you choose to shoot depends on your budget and what is readily available.

Some of your decision as to which release format you want is going to be based on where you imagine seeing your film. Most movie theaters are not equipped to project 16mm, DVD, or video (whether analog or digital). Your typical multiplex movie theater can pretty much only show 35mm film prints without having to bring in extra equipment. Galleries, museums, and some smaller locally owned film venues that specialize in independent and short films are more likely to have 16mm projection capabilities or DVD and video projection.

If your primary goal is for your film to be broadcast on television or cable, Beta SP is still the primary release format, though depending upon the network or company, you may be able to submit a DVD or DV master.

Though yet to fully catch on with the average consumer, several companies have been distributing short films in streaming video on the Internet. In order to keep the amount of memory needed at a manageable level on the server, most Internet movies are low resolution, compressed into a format like MPEG, which wouldn't look good on the big screen but is just fine when viewed in a small window on a computer.

Before choosing your release format, imagine an audience watching your film. Are they sitting in a big-chain movie theater? In front of a TV? Huddled at a computer screen? This will give you a clue as to which release format is for you—the exhibition venue will determine your release format.

Once you've figured out your preferred exhibition method, you need to figure out the best way to create material for that release format. You'll probably have more than one option, and the determining factor may ultimately be which one costs the least.

---

### Ditty Bag

While 16mm and 35mm prints can be projected almost anywhere, broadcast and home video standards vary from country to country. Aside from the issues of NTSC and PAL, DVDs are generally designed to be compatible only with the players in certain regions (which are designated by number). Region 1 DVDs will only play back in DVD players found in the United States, Canada, and U.S. territories; Region 2 DVDs can only be viewed in Japan, Europe, South Africa, and the Middle East. Region 3 in Southeast and East Asia, including Hong Kong; Region 4 in Australia, New Zealand, the Pacific Islands, the Caribbean, Mexico, and Central and South America; Region 5 in Eastern Europe, India, Africa, North Korea, and Mongolia; and Region 6 DVDs will only play in China.

---

If you're planning to release your movie only for broadcast or DVD but you want it to have a film look rather than a video look, shooting on 16mm is much cheaper than 35mm but can look just as good as 35mm when converted to a digital image. Early on, a lot of music videos were shot in 16mm, but released for broadcast as a Beta SP. I've shot several of my projects on film, only to release them as videos. On the flip side, many films that are released as 35mm prints are ultimately released in DVD format for home viewing. And just because you shot your film on DV doesn't mean you can't release it as 35mm film. *28 Days Later* was shot on DV, edited digitally, and later transferred to 35mm film. However, blowing up analog video to film usually looks awful. You're better off shooting film, DV, or HDTV formats if your ultimate release print is to be film.

# Sounding Off

Before *striking* or creating your release print or format, you need to finish up your sound mix. Through the process of premixing (or mixing in combination) various audio tracks, you ultimately arrive at what is called STMS (pronounced "stems"), which stands for *six track master mix*. This master allows you to easily mix out the dialogue tracks for an *M&E* (music and effects only), also known as an international mix. By separating out the tracks that carry your film's dialogue, another country can easily dub your film in their language.

---

**Ditty Bag**

When you mix out the dialogue for your M&E mix, you lose all of the audio of the production track. If when you were editing you left in sounds collected during the action (such as footsteps or door openings) instead of replacing them with sound effects, your M&E will have missing sounds that will make the film seem incomplete. If so, you now have to go back and do another Foley session to replace those missing sounds. Once finished, you will have what's called a *fully filled M&E*. Some smaller international markets may accept a less than full M&E; if you have a distribution deal, you may have been able to negotiate for the distributor to pay for it.

---

Final sound mixes have moved from the days of simply being stereo, or *discrete*, with left and right channels. *Cinema stereo* added a center speaker for dialogue, but most movie theaters at this time are wired for *surround sound*, which simply adds rear mono speakers to the cinema stereo arrangement. If you're planning to strike a 35mm film print to be shown in movie theaters or for broadcast, you'll want your master mix to be either in discrete, cinema stereo, or surround sound.

As you probably know, home entertainment systems—and a handful of movie theaters—are able to provide even more separation of the audio. This format, called 5.1, means that there is a left, center, and right speaker plus a subwoofer and rear stereo speakers. If you're planning to show your movie as a DVD, you'll want a 5.1 master mix.

Why all these speakers? Because they help create sound perspective, helping to establish a more three-dimensional experience for the audience by letting us hear sounds from behind and beside us as well as from in front of us. And more complex sound mix configurations are on the horizon.

# Matching Picture: Conforming and On-Line Editing

A composite print is simply a copy of your movie in which the picture edit and the sound mix are combined. In 16mm and 35mm film, this is commonly referred to as a *married print*. Your composite is your first chance to see all the pieces together as a whole, and if you're happy with it, this composite will serve as the master from which you'll make copies of your movie for release. Creating this composite is different in 16mm and 35mm film than in analog and digital video.

## Negative Cutting

If you've been editing with a workprint, once you've reached picture lock (or are completely done editing the images), and while your sound designer and re-recordist are mixing the sound, you can now have the negative cut to match your edited workprint. This process is called *conforming*, and you are literally matching each shot in your edited workprint to its corresponding negative original. The workprint is like a road map for editing the negative. Because there is only one negative, and it is basically the source for all release prints, cutting and handling the negative has to be done extremely carefully.

I've conformed a couple of films, and the pressure is on to make no mistakes, because if you cut in the wrong place, you can't really put it back together without your mistake showing. Similarly, any dirt that gets onto the negative will show up on all of your film prints. I usually work in a room with no ventilation, and I cover the walls and ceiling with plastic so that dirt and dust are kept to a minimum. I wear gloves made especially for handling film negatives.

I know where to cut the negative because the editor has prepared an edit decision list or EDL. When working with workprints, this EDL is based on the edge numbers along the side of the print and lists every shot in order by its edge numbers and frames. I find the corresponding numbers and count the corresponding frames along the negative. In order for the cement splices not to show, conforming the film requires an extra frame and a half at the heads and tails of each shot. The shots are alternated between two (or sometimes more) rolls, a process called *A/B rolling*, with black leader filling in between, creating a sort of checkerboard pattern. Save yourself the agony and hire a negative cutter.

EDLs are easy to generate when editing on a computer. Once you've got a finished edit, most software programs can generate an EDL that you can print out and hand your conformer. If you are planning to conform film negative from a digital edit and computer-generated EDL, you'll want to make sure that the EDL has compensated for the difference between film frames being 24 per second and video frames occurring 30 every second. Otherwise, your cut negative will have a different running time and throw your sound mix out of sync.

The first positive print of your conformed negative is called an *answer print*. Answer prints are usually very expensive (tens of thousands of dollars for a feature film) because they are *timed*, meaning that a technician adjusts the printing machine from shot to shot to make sure that the exposures and colors are consistent within each scene. You or your cinematographer may have provided timing notes from having looked at the workprint, making suggestions of shots that should be lighter or darker or adjusted in terms of color.

> **Ditty Bag**
>
> To save money, rushes or work-prints are usually not timed but simply printed to the exposure and color information provided at the head of a film roll as a color chip chart or if there is no color chip chart, to a best guess exposure based on the first shot of the roll. This is called a one-light or best-light print.

After reviewing the answer print, if you are satisfied with the exposures and colors, it's time to add the soundtrack. If you are not satisfied, then you would make a new set of timing notes and have another answer print struck. One way to save money is to add your optical soundtrack (which I'll discuss a little later in this chapter) when making the answer print; that way, if your answer print is good, you already have a film you can show people.

Making multiple copies of your film will eventually wear out your negative, therefore you may have an added expense of creating an *inter-positive* (IP) of your negative from which you can create a new negative (or *inter-negative*, abbreviated IN) if you plan to make more than 5 to 10 copies (or *release prints*) to show in theaters. Your IP and IN can cost nearly as much as your answer print. You'll definitely want to shop around and compare prices before choosing a lab.

# On-Line Editing

If you're editing on a computer, one of the issues you have to deal with is memory. For a short film, this may not be an issue—your computer or external hard drives give you enough memory to edit the film at its best quality with room to spare for the soundtracks. However, for a feature, you may have had to edit the film at a lower resolution than you'd want people to see it. While this low resolution can allow you to fit more footage on your hard drives, once you have your finished edit, you need to somehow get the film image back to its best quality.

This is where an on-line edit becomes important. If you have enough hard drive space, you can do your own on-line edit, but many filmmakers—especially if they've shot a feature—will go to a post-production facility or *post house* that specializes in on-line editing. You'll need to take all of your raw materials, such as the original footage, along with a digital copy of your edit decision list (EDL).

You can do an on-line edit for a movie you've been cutting on analog video as well. Once again, you need an EDL and your original footage.

> ### Staying in Focus
>
> If your on-line edit is for broadcast, you'll want to use drop frame (DF) timecode. This is because even though we always talk about video being 30 frames per second, the video format used in North America (called NTSC) is actually 29.97 fps. Despite the name, DF does not omit frames of video, but rather adjusts the way we count each frame to compensate for this slight difference, assuring that one second of broadcast time is one second of video time. Computer editing software will usually give you the option of running your timecode in DF or ND (non drop).

If your final release print is to be DVD or Beta SP, you can program in your digital EDL, and the on-line computer editing system will shuttle through your raw footage, finding each shot and digitizing it at high resolution and then assembling it into a final version. Just as in a film answer print, you may go through this on-line edit of your movie scene by scene, adjusting the color rendition and making sure everything is okay.

At this point, you may decide to make a film print of your movie; if so, you'll go through some of the (expensive) steps I described in the previous section.

# Dense Area: Optical and Digital Tracks

Once you have a master version of the picture, either as a conformed negative, an answer print, or an on-line edit, you're now ready to marry sound with picture.

For most 16mm and 35mm films, the sound mix is converted from an analog or digital signal to what is called an *optical sound track*. This sound track is actually two wavy-looking lines that run along one side of the film where the audio information is now represented photographically. The nuances of the sound track create varying thicknesses in each line, affecting the amount of area each of these lines take up, which is the reason it is sometimes referred to as a *variable area* optical soundtrack.

In a movie theater where the film hasn't been matted correctly for the screen, you can sometimes see these lines at the far left edge of the screen. Or sometimes when the film breaks or comes off the projector, it will slide across the screen and you can see the optical soundtrack's two parallel squiggly lines.

### Staying in Focus

While 35mm optical sound tracks can provide good-quality sound when projected, 16mm optical sound is not nearly so good, and your goal when mixing a soundtrack for release as 16mm optical is to make the dialogue as clear as possible.

When the film is projected, a special lamp shines through these lines and each variation in the lines' area creates a corresponding variation in the beam of light, which is then converted to an electrical signal that can be converted through speakers into acoustic sounds that we hear in the theater. This method of marrying sound to picture is sometimes referred to as 4-2-4 because the original mix was four tracks converted into two optical tracks that are then decoded by the projector back into four separate tracks of audio distributed among the speakers in the theater.

In recent years, some 35mm films are released with what is called a *digital optical soundtrack* where, in addition to the variable area optical sound track just described, digital information that can be read optically will fill the spaces between the sprocket holes as a series of small dots or speckles.

Creating a composite print of your film in DVD format is much simpler because both picture and audio are digital, and home theater systems allow for the full 5.1 audio. However, your on-line edit pulled the original sound for each shot as well as the picture, so you now need to *layback* your master sound mix, syncing it with your finished film.

If you want to release your movie as a DVD with menus and options, you'll want to do what is called DVD authoring. There are companies that will make multiple copies of DVDs for bulk prices, if you need to make a lot. Or if you have a DVD burner, you can make your own DVDs off your computer, assuming you have enough memory to store a full high-resolution version of your film on the hard drive.

If instead you are planning to take your on-line edit and blow it up (or copy it to) 35mm film, you'll probably strike a test print, or answer print, to be sure that you do not need to make any further adjustments to compensate for this change of formats. If you're happy, you're ready to start showing your film.

# Please Release Me

Film release prints are inexpensive in comparison to the answer print, inter-positive, and inter-negative costs I talked about earlier in this chapter. A feature-length 35mm film release print from an inter-negative might only cost $1,500 to $3,500 depending on the lab. Even DVDs can seem expensive if you've exhausted your budget. But if you want to be able to show your film more than one place at a time, you'll need additional copies or *release prints*. Of course, if you've been lucky enough to sign a distribution deal, they'll pay for all of those costs (plus advertising). If not, then for your bank account's sake, only make the minimum number of prints you need.

Any film release print struck from negative or a film copy of the negative will suffer a slight loss in quality, or generation loss, just like the video we talked about in Chapter 18. Though in theory digital copies do not experience generation loss, the fact that the source material is recorded on videotape does leave it vulnerable to some problems, especially the more that original videotape is played.

# Shelf Life: Archiving Your Film

You never want to send out or show your only copy of the film. Just like you would back up your data on a computer, you want to have a master copy of your film tucked away someplace safe.

All media have a shelf life. Over time, every medium degrades. Therefore, it's important to keep your masters carefully maintained and stored, whether they're picture negative, Beta SP, or even digital video and DVD. Some labs provide archiving services if you've been working with them throughout the production and use them for striking your release prints.

Film is sensitive to high temperatures and extremes in humidity. Videotape is a magnetic medium, which will over time degrade just from the impact of various stray magnetic fields, including the Earth's, and extremes in temperature and humidity. Even DV tapes, which record their data as binary code, record that data on a magnetic oxide. Keep all of

> **CAUTION**
>
> **Reel Trouble**
>
> 16mm and 35mm film-stocks deteriorate fastest between being exposed and being developed, so it's always a good idea to process your film as quickly as possible. You can keep unexposed filmstock in the freezer, though be sure to let it warm up to room temperature before opening it in order to prevent condensation on the film.

these materials, particularly if they're your camera original, away from sunlight, heat, and high humidity. With video and DV, you have the added worry of electromagnetic force, so you want to keep them away from motors (which have magnets) and high-voltage equipment.

## The Least You Need to Know

◆ Choosing your release format is ideally one of the first decisions you'll make when starting a film.

◆ The format of your final sound mix will depend on your release format.

◆ Either through conforming or an on-line edit, you will create a high-resolution final version of your film.

◆ Always keep a master copy of your edited film safely archived.

# Part 5

# And the Winner Is ... Exhibition & Distribution

It's time to take your tux to the cleaners or buy that designer gown—your premiere is just around the corner. You'll be ready for all the attention because you'll learn how to create a press kit, talk to the media, and find a venue for showing your movie.

Whether you find a distributor, show your film at a festival, or rent a theater and do-it-yourself, it's time for the world to see your idea come to life on the screen.

The red carpet awaits!

# Chapter 27

# Living in Oblivion: Press Kits and Publicity

## In This Chapter

◆ What a press kit is for

◆ Three types of photos to include in your kit

◆ How to decide what makes an effective giveaway

◆ What else you should include in your press kit

You told your family you didn't want to work in sales, but here you are, trying to sell yourself and your film as the next big thing. For some people this is hard to do even under the best of circumstances, but you're probably so exhausted from making your film that the thought of going out to sell your film is in fierce competition with the desire for a long nap. You might ask, can't someone else do it?

Well, yes. Press kits are all about giving other people the raw materials they need to publicize your film. You pull together the material, then you can sit back and let them do the work! The ideal press kit provides basic information about your film as well as materials that newspapers, magazines, websites, television shows, and film festivals can publish or use. Let's look a bit more closely at what a press kit is and what kind of publicity materials should be included.

# Spreading the Word: Press Kits

Press kits are a collection of photos and written information about you and your film that can be given to potential distributors, film festivals, and publications. Traditionally, these are collected loose in a folder or might be bound as a booklet. Because traditional press kits can be expensive to prepare and mail, more filmmakers these days are creating electronic press kits (EPK).

### Staying in Focus

Keep in mind that while JPEG quality might be fine for a website, it might not be good enough for magazine publication. For an electronic press kit, I usually save every photograph in two different formats, one that is low resolution such as JPEG and another in a higher-resolution format for publication.

Even if you are submitting an electronic press kit, you'll usually include some hard copy information, such as a synopsis of the film, an index to what materials are on the CD-ROM or DVD, and your contact information. Because your EPK can get separated from your hard copy info, be sure to label the CD-ROM or DVD clearly as an electronic press kit for [your film's title] and include your name, phone number, and e-mail address in case someone needs to reach you. If you have a website for the film, include that URL on the label as well.

If you can afford it, consider hiring a publicist, someone who makes his or her living developing press kits and publicity materials. If you're short on funds, see if your friends can help. You don't need one person to do it all: A friend who's good at graphic design can prepare the layout, a friend who's good with grammar and spelling can proofread, and so on.

In recent years, websites have become a primary method of creating publicity for films before their release. *The Blair Witch Project* is probably the most notorious, and it's well known because it was so effective. Depending on your server, you may be able to run streaming video clips of your movie as well as downloadable photos.

A good press kit provides just enough information that the reviewer or editor has everything necessary to write about your film, but not so much that going through your materials will overwhelm them. What should you include? I'm glad you asked.

# Snapping It Up: Photos

Newspapers, magazines, and websites love to include a photo with film reviews. Film festivals usually publish a program and are also eager to include photos of the films selected. This is great for you, because potential audience members are more likely to stop and read about your film if there's a photo.

---

**Ditty Bag**

Newspapers generally publish black-and-white photos; magazines may print color or a combination of color and black and white. Websites are generally color. When in doubt, include both color and black-and-white prints if your press kit is all in hard copy. If you can't afford both, go for color. The exception is with electronic press kits: Because a publisher can easily convert digital color photographs to black and white, the only time you'd submit black-and-white pictures in an EPK is if your movie is black and white.

---

As for what kind of photos to include, there are three basic types to consider, and I'll discuss them in order of importance. If you can afford it, include several photos from each type.

## Frame Enlargements

Most of the images we see in film festival programs or print film reviews look as if they came right out of the film. These are sometimes referred to as frame enlargements, implying that a single frame of the film has been treated like a still photograph and blown up for publication.

However, enlarging a frame of your film or doing a screen capture of a video frame rarely provides a still image that's good enough quality for publication. The possible exception is capturing a frame from digital video. These publicity images are in fact not frame enlargements at all but rather staged photographs taken on the set to emulate the film camera's perspective.

This requires a photographer on set who will between shots try to quickly and unobtrusively recreate the film camera's general composition with a still camera. The goal is to find those particular moments to photograph where the characters' interactions or behaviors are expressive and compelling, evoking the mood of your film and hinting at the nature of its story. Not every single moment will make a good publicity shot, so hire a photographer only for those days when there is an image you might want for your press kit.

Ideally, the still photographer would snap these pictures after you've gotten the film shot you need. This helps assure that the actors aren't distracted before their performance.

## Production Stills

Production stills, or behind-the-scenes photos from the set, show you and your crew at work. For these, you want photos that are visually interesting and distinct to filmmaking.

For example, showing your crew sitting on the curb eating lunch doesn't really say "filmmaking." But if we see the dolly grip doing a complex camera movement around the actors or we see the actors in character but surrounded by the camera, the boom mic, and the crew, then we feel like we've gotten a glimpse into what it was like to make your film.

Unfortunately, if your film is done and you're just now thinking of production stills, you're too late. This is why it's important to have a photographer on your set. He doesn't have to be there every day, but he needs to be there more than once.

## Portraits

Portraits of your lead actors and even yourself as the filmmaker are a good addition to your press kit. These could be your actors' headshots, though it's usually nice if there's a certain consistency in tone and feel among all the actors' shots.

If you're having portraits taken specifically for your press kit, you'll want to consider whether or not the actors should appear in costume as the characters they play or in everyday clothes as they really look. Or both. Your decision might be different depending upon the specific film.

If you decide to include a portrait of yourself in the press kit, you could simply have a close-up of you at work rather than a formal portrait. The main goal with these portraits is to provide an image of each key person that emphasizes his or her face. And these portrait photographs are often in black and white.

Providing a variety of photographs allows the publisher to choose what they feel will be most effective. They know their readers best and therefore have a better idea as to which particular photo might make the reader stop and pay attention to the information about your film.

### Reel Trouble

Writing in pen on the back of photographs can damage the picture on the other side. If the image is damaged, the publisher can't use it, and you've just wasted money. Some people suggest writing lightly in pencil on the back, but this can also be a problem if you press down too hard. The best (and most professional-looking) option is to print or write out a small self-sticking label that can be placed on the back of the photo.

Be sure to label the back of each photograph with key identifying information. This includes the name of the person(s) in the photograph; if it's an actor in costume, you may want to also include the name of the character, making it clear which is the actor's name and which is the character's name. You'll also want to include the title of the film and a "photo by" credit for your photographer. If there's room, you may also want to include your name and basic contact info in case the picture gets separated from the rest of the press kit.

If you have a friend who is a good photographer, ask him to come to the set for several strategically selected days. Or if you're running a minimal crew where everyone is doing double-duty, your cinematographer may want to take the photos herself. Just keep in mind that while your cinematographer is taking the photos, she's not able to set up the next film shot.

# Say It with Words: Synopses and Names

The other critical component to your press kit is a written synopsis that summarizes the action of the film. The synopsis ideally stops short of revealing the conclusion of the film, but rather sets up the main characters and conflict, creating curiosity about what will happen next. (See Chapter 7 for more information about writing synopses.)

Besides a one-page synopsis, you'll want to include a brief one-paragraph summary of your film. This shorter synopsis will be particularly helpful for film festivals that publish brief summaries of each film in their festival programs and on their websites.

In addition, you will want to include a list of your key cast and crew. This assures that publication editors have the correct spellings of everyone's name as well as a clear indicator of each person's role on the film.

If you're feeling really ambitious, you can include a behind-the-scenes summary of what it was like making the film. This could include challenges as well as celebrations, and you might include quotes from your actors or key participants of the production. This can give a personal touch to the film, and some editors and reviewers love to be able to give a view of the film other than just what appears on the screen. In a way, this kind of document is the equivalent of a behind-the-scenes documentary, but instead of watching it, we read it.

Finally, many film festivals and potential distributors will ask you to include a transcript of the film's dialogue. This can be particularly important if you're sending materials to publications or festivals that primarily present their material in a different language than your film. Your transcript allows them to more easily translate the dialogue, either for written reviews and translations for the audience or to prepare the film for subtitling or dubbing.

# Most Wanted: Posters

Posters are another important publicity tool for films. While you may not include a full-sized one in your press kit, it's not a bad idea to include a scaled-down version of the poster that could be printed much like traditional movie ads that appear in newspapers.

Selecting the right poster for your film is harder than it may at first seem. In effect, for independent filmmakers who do not have the budget to place trailers on TV or in movie theaters before other films, the poster is basically the only thing potential audience members see before deciding whether or not to spend money to watch your film.

Your poster shouldn't promise more than your film can deliver, but you do want to create "love at first sight" with your poster. You want to make such a strong first impression that the potential viewer cannot help but want to see more, to see your film.

# Are Giveaways Worth It?

Everyone likes to get something for free, especially if it's useful. But as a marketing tool, it also has to be memorable. Giveaways are most memorable if they somehow relate to your film. For example, if your film is about a retired drag car racer, a key ring might be the perfect giveaway whereas a coffee mug would not. If you're going to use giveaways, put some thought into what would be unique and appropriate to your particular film.

The standard giveaways, of course, are ball caps and t-shirts. These might include a catchy logo, if your film has one, or simply the movie's title lettered in the same style as your poster. Because they provide more room for writing, t-shirts could include info on both the front and back. Besides the name of your film, you might include a *tagline* or catchy phrase. Some examples include "in space, no one can hear you scream" (*Alien*), "innocence is a dangerous friend" (*Lawn Dogs*), "passion fades but murder is forever" (*The Paint Job*), "it's not the end of the world … there's still six hours left" (*Last Night*), and "it's 4 A.M.—do you know where your car is?" (*Repo Man*). Most movie posters these days include a tagline. The next time you're at the movies, look at the posters and notice how the poster's image and tagline work together to make the film seem more appealing.

**Defining Moments**

Your film's **tagline** is different from the log line we talked about in Chapter 6. The tagline is a marketing tool, a phrase designed to hook the audience, to make them curious about your film.

Besides being bulky to mail, t-shirts are risky because you have no idea what size the recipient wears. Ball caps may seem the safer choice, but if everyone is sending ball caps, what makes yours stand out from all the rest? How about a coffee mug? A small key chain flashlight? A key ring? A ruler? A pen? Get creative!

Another popular giveaway can be a CD of music from the film, especially if you've used a local up-and-coming band or a brilliant local composer. Just be sure you have the legal rights to reproduce the music and distribute it.

Giveaways cost money, but there are a number of companies that provide cheap items that can be stenciled with your name. You might also look at the businesses in your local community and see if someone would be willing to donate items.

## Just the Facts: Press Releases

Your press kit could also include a pre-written press release that the publication could use. Press releases should never be more than one page long, typed and double-spaced. In a way, a press release is like an announcement. Therefore, there is very specific information that needs to be included.

Press releases usually begin with the words FOR IMMEDIATE RELEASE in capital letters. What follows is the kind of information journalists are always taught to include in their articles: who, what, where, when, why. These press releases, along with the other information in your press kit, can help the local newspapers alert people that you're coming to town to show your film.

Of course, you can also send out press releases without a press kit. Many newspapers will publish press releases if space allows, and this can be a great way to get the word out that you're making a film as well as when you're going to be showing it.

## Getting to Know You

Another item you may want to include in your press kit is a director's statement or brief biography about yourself as the filmmaker. This can help the press understand a bit more about why you wanted to make this film and where it fits in with your other creative work. If your biography is single-spaced with a double space between paragraphs, it shouldn't run any longer than one page. If you double-space with indented paragraphs, figure no more than two pages maximum.

I usually include two biographies. The first is a short one-paragraph bio that covers the basic pertinent information. The second is slightly longer and fills in more detail. I try to avoid a simple listing of facts (date of birth, where I was born) unless that information is relevant in some way to the project.

Biographies are where you present personal information about yourself as a way to encourage people to see your film. There is no one way to do a biography. The successful ones let the reader feel like they have gotten a glimpse of you as a person, not just a name on the screen or poster. What makes you sound interesting? What makes you sound like you have something to say? What makes it seem that you're the perfect person to make this film? Depending on the film, then, the info you include in your biography may vary. You can't say everything about yourself and your life, so what are the most relevant facts an audience of this film would like to know about you?

If you've made several films that all explore similar themes, this might be worth noting in your biography. If you've won awards, that may be good to include, because it indicates other people have thought your films were good and worth watching. If this is your first film, you may want to acknowledge that fact as long as being a novice works for you rather than against you, presented as a strength (fresh eyes on the world) rather than a weakness (inexperience).

You may also want to include brief biographies of your key cast members and crew, especially if they are well known, local celebrities, or have experience in film. Their backgrounds and interests can lend your production more credibility. Anytime you are sending a press kit to the hometown of any of your crew or cast, be sure to include a biography of that person, or at the very least note that this person is from that town. The local papers and television stations are much more likely to cover your film if there's a local connection.

# Everyone's Talking: Reviews

Once your film garners some reviews, you may want to include these as part of your press kit. Good reviews in your press kit are a gentle statement that other people have seen your film and liked it.

### Staying in Focus

Don't let good reviews go to your head or bad reviews break your heart. Reviews are simply one person's opinion. Try not to take reviews personally—they're about your film, not you, even if the comments seem directed to you because you're the filmmaker.

If you decide to include reviews, use only the good ones. If the reviews are long, you may want to use an excerpt. And if the review includes a mix of good and bad, you might consider excerpting just the positive comments, using ellipses (…) to indicate that there is missing information.

Any reviews in your press kit should include the reviewer's name, the name of the publication, and the date. Though published reviews are part of a copyrighted publication, most publishers assume that filmmakers are going to quote excerpts or include full reviews as part of their press kits. If you're in doubt, contact the publishers for formal permission.

You could also include any published news articles or interviews about your film. Anything that reveals insightful or interesting supplemental information.

# Preview Copies and Screeners

Another option is to include a preview copy (or screener) of the film, or if not the entire film, maybe several scenes or the trailer. A screener is usually a specially made dub or copy of your film that periodically inserts a subtitle at the bottom of the image stating that this film belongs to you (or the production company) and is for previewing purposes only. This helps deter pirating and illegal duplication of films but doesn't stop it altogether. Screeners allow critics to look at the film on their own time. The danger, of course, is that watching a video or DVD is very different than sitting in a theater; some films work best with an audience.

If you are going to provide a preview copy of the entire film, make sure the film is finished. Do not submit a work in progress or a version that doesn't have the final sound mix. The same goes for any clips you might include. No matter how much you say that it's a work in progress, if the film is not finished, it's impossible for reviewers to really say what the film's going to be like when it's done. Don't waste their time or yours.

Finally, a word about trailers. Before you try to make one, go and watch a lot of them. And I mean a lot. There is an entire film industry in Hollywood that is just about making trailers. They are an art, not simply a random series of excerpts from your film. A good trailer makes people enthusiastic to see the film; a bad trailer makes them spend their money on someone else's film.

Trailers are best when they don't try to tell the entire film but rather evoke the film's mood and hint at the story. If you make a trailer, keep it short. The old adage "leave them wanting more" is the cornerstone of good trailers; in fact, it's the hallmark of good publicity, period.

## The Least You Need to Know

- Press kits are a great way to help other people publicize your film.

- A good press kit always includes photographs.

- A well-chosen giveaway can make your press kit memorable.

- Everything in the press kit has a single purpose: to make people want to see your film.

# 28

# *The Conversation: Interviews*

## In This Chapter

- ◆ A look at the various types of interviews expected of a filmmaker
- ◆ Soliciting interviews
- ◆ How to turn down an interview
- ◆ Tips for getting ready for an interview

"Word of mouth" begins with you. Let people know you have a film. And show it. If the film is good, other people will start talking as well, telling their friends "You've got to see this movie!" As filmmakers that's our dream, our goal.

There are times when a press kit isn't enough, when reporters or reviewers will want to talk with you in person. If that makes you nervous, just remember that when it comes to your film, you are the expert. No one knows better than you the story and the work it took to bring your film to the screen. With all of the films and media competing for the audience's attention, personally talking about your film can help you get the word out so that your audience—the audience that will most enjoy your film—can find you.

# Print, Radio, TV, and Chatroom Interviews

Interviews can be printed like in a newspaper, or they can be broadcast on radio, television, or over the Internet. Print interviews usually allow the journalist a bit more latitude to rephrase and summarize your comments. Broadcast interviews may condense your comments through editing, but smoothly rephrasing your comments is virtually impossible. Neither type of interview is better than the other. Some of it will depend on your own comfort and personality.

A benefit of print interviews is that they're usually one on one, either in person or over the phone. As a result, they can be more comfortable for a filmmaker who is shy. These kinds of interviews also allow you to compose your answers and rephrase them without the scrutiny of an audience.

> ### Staying in Focus
>
> Before you cry out that you've been misquoted, remember that publications will rarely print your answers verbatim. Some interviewers will ask to tape record the interview, and this can certainly help them be as accurate as possible in writing up your answers. But even then, your printed words may not seem to be the same ones you remember saying. Are you not clearly remembering what you said? Very possibly. Did the interviewer lie? Not likely. So when you're reading the interview, rather than scrutinize every phrase and word choice, pay attention to whether the underlying meaning of your answer comes through.

Broadcast interviews, even when edited and not "live," pretty much show you in real time answering the questions in a highly artificial environment—on a set under bright lights. Also, broadcast interviews are conducted in front of other people besides the interviewer, even if it's just a crew person or two. If you're not one of those spontaneous people who can think quickly under pressure, this can be disconcerting. The advantage to a broadcast interview is that the audience can put a face (or voice or a personality) to your name and feel like they get to know you a little bit, making the idea of seeing your film more personal.

If you're doing a chatroom interview, a moderator is your best friend, even if you're alone typing on your computer at home. The moderator can help keep the conversation focused and also deal with inappropriate questions or comments. Let your moderator be the bad guy, setting ground rules and guiding questions your way. Doing your own chatroom discussion without a moderator can be fun and easy until someone obnoxious begins taking over. Then you'll really wish you had a moderator to help you out.

No matter which interview format you're participating in, try to answer the questions succinctly but thoroughly. You don't want to drone on and on so that the interviewer can't ask another—perhaps more important—question. At the same time, your answers can't be so short that you haven't really said anything. The answers that an interviewer hates most are "yes" or "no," because you've not given any new information for the interviewer to respond to or draw out. Firsthand examples and stories from the production can personalize the material, but again, keep them short and meaningful. Pay attention to your interviewer for cues as to whether you should say more or less.

The first couple of times I did broadcast interviews, I was completely thrown when the interviewer would ask me a question and then immediately look away to check the time or communicate with the crew. Of course, an audience at home couldn't see this because the camera was on me. Interviewers have to make sure the program isn't running over time and that everything is going smoothly, so they become very good at splitting their focus. Even if the interviewer doesn't seem to be paying attention to you, keep talking. Keep looking at the interviewer or if there's a live audience and it seems appropriate, feel free to look around to the crowd periodically as well.

For an unknown filmmaker and film, rightly or wrongly, the audience will associate your personality with the tone of the film. For example, if your film is a comedy but in the interviews you demonstrate no sense of humor, a viewer may have trouble believing you could make a funny film. That's not to say that you should treat the interview like a stand-up comedy club; you just need to be aware that during this interview, you are the closest thing the audience has for understanding what your film is like.

TV interviews can be nerve-wracking, so I try to remember that regardless of how many people might be listening in, I'm really there to talk to one person, the interviewer. And the goals are to talk a little bit about something I love, my film, and to enjoy the conversation.

Besides yourself, other members of your cast or crew might be great interview subjects about your film, either alone or with you. As you well know, Hollywood studios often have their actors do press junkets and interviews about their new films. You can do something similar, though this will be most effective if either the actor is someone well known or someone who has a personal connection or reason to be interviewed, such as being raised in the town where the interview is taking place.

### Staying in Focus

If crew or cast members arrange for interviews on their own, I ask that if possible they let me know ahead of time and provide me a copy of the interview afterwards. This keeps my publicity files current and helps me ensure any publicity about the film is consistent. I try to make sure certain aspects of the film, such as its synopsis, are consistent from interview to interview.

If there's a potential connection between a crewmember and a particular interview, don't hesitate to ask your crew to help out with the publicity if they're willing. They may enjoy the recognition for their hard work as well as reach potential audiences you couldn't have reached otherwise. For example, if a local photography magazine wants to interview your cinematographer about shooting your movie, this is great additional publicity for your film.

If you're being interviewed on television, bring a copy of your trailer or several brief edited clips from your film. Check beforehand to see which format they'd prefer. The program may be able to show an excerpt while you're being interviewed, and just like photos in your press kit, a good clip from your film can help get you an audience. Don't bring your whole film, because they may feel it's too much trouble to hunt for (or cue) a particular scene. If you've already done their work for them, creating self-contained clips that are easy to cue, they're more likely to show it.

For radio interviews, consider bringing a CD of some interesting dialogue that's been edited from the film with appropriate sound effects. Because any silences in audio leave the listener wondering what's going on, you may need to edit the dialogue closer together than it actually appears in the final film, especially if there are no sound effects or music under it. The goal again is to break up the interview with a snippet of the film that might catch the audience's imagination.

# Never Too Proud to Beg: Soliciting Interviews

Of course, after all this talk about interviews, it sounds like people will be pounding on your door and hounding you to talk about your film. But for most of us when we first start, that's hardly the case.

Instead, we sometimes have to let interviewers know we're here and available. This is where press releases can help. Whenever you send out a press release, especially after the film is finished and you're announcing screenings, always include the offer that you (or relevant cast or crew if appropriate) are available for interviews along with a way to reach you. You can say that in your press kit letter as well. When sending out kits to towns where your film will be showing, let them know if you'll be there in person, and if so, offer to meet. (See Chapter 27 for more on press releases and press kits.)

In effect, these are coded ways in which we ask to be interviewed. But if you really want to do an interview for a particular publication or show, then don't be too proud to go and ask. Simply send them a press kit along with a personal letter that says how much you'd love to be interviewed for their program or publication. Ask who you should contact to discuss the possibility further.

# Turning Down Interviews

At first, we're like little puppy dogs. Anyone who shows us a little attention, we're all over them. Someone wants to interview you about your film, no question, the answer is an almost automatic yes. But sometimes you may not feel comfortable with a particular interviewer or the philosophy of a particular publication or show. Or you may just be too busy to accept every interview offer that comes your way.

No matter what your reason for declining an interview, try to adhere to the adage of never burning your bridges. Who knows how you'll feel several years from now when you've got a new film to promote? So a little care and respect now can keep doors open that you may later want to go through.

Whenever you turn down an interview, be as courteous as possible. Thank them for the opportunity but state that unfortunately you're not available and briefly explain why if appropriate. If you're declining for philosophical reasons, you may want to make your refusal more general rather than enter an argument or debate about the merits of the publication, show, or interviewer. Either way, always conduct yourself in a professional manner. Ultimately, the filmmaking world is a very small one.

If you're declining simply because of scheduling conflicts and would really like to do the interview, ask if you can reschedule for another time. But do not use this as a ploy to put off an interview you have no intention of giving.

# Prepping for Interviews

When setting up an interview, there are a few things that might be good for you to know in order to better prepare. After the when and where have been sorted out, my first question is, "Who's the audience?" Who's going to see the interview? What are their interests? The answers to these questions help me figure out what aspects of the film or the production might hook the audience, make them more personally interested in the film. Finding some sort of personal connection between the film and the audience can be extremely helpful. This connection could be someone who starred in the film or the story's relevance to this audience.

Likewise, I usually ask what the general direction of the interview will be. Do they want to know about me as a filmmaker or the movie's story or the process of making the film? Any interview is probably a little of all three, but some interviewers may be primarily interested in exploring or revealing one particular aspect. This is helpful for me to know ahead of time.

While it's okay to ask for a list of questions, I don't hold my breath. Providing you this list is a courtesy, not a requirement, so I'm not offended if they interviewer says no. But even a basic range of question areas can be helpful.

Giving good media interviews is kind of like applying for a job. You're trying to make a good impression. In fact, job counselors often recommend that people practice being interviewed and go to every interview they can, even interviews for jobs they're not interested in. Because each time you do it, the better you get. The same goes for media interviews. With each one, you'll become more comfortable answering questions and hone your answers so that they feel conversational and yet say the most with the fewest words. An added benefit to interviews is that they're a great way to better understand your film.

> **CAUTION**
>
> ### Reel Trouble
>
> In my experience, few people set out to sound pretentious in interviews; it just sort of happens. If I had a magic remedy, believe me, I'd include it with this book. Here's the next best thing, a few things I try to keep in mind during interviews: Be yourself and relax. Don't try to interpret the film; that's the audience's job. Keep the conversation personal and friendly. Treat the interview as a two-way, not a one-way, conversation. Listen almost as much as you talk. There's a difference between talking about your film and bragging. Give credit where credit is due, and acknowledge the other people who worked long and hard on your film. A little humility goes a long way.

If you decide to practice for an upcoming interview, consider that these kinds of rehearsals are not about memorizing or pre-writing answers. They are to help you get better at answering unexpected questions on the fly. Have whoever is helping you never ask the same question twice. And try not to fall so in love with certain questions while prepping that you can't respond to different questions during the actual interview.

It all goes back to that idea that an interview is a type of conversation and to connecting with one other person about your film.

## The Least You Need to Know

◆ Interviews are a great way to generate interest in your film.

◆ It's okay to let a publication know that you're willing to be interviewed.

◆ Sometimes you may decide to turn down an interview.

◆ Practicing for an interview can help you be better prepared.

# Chapter 29

# *The Last Picture Show:* Finding an Audience

## In This Chapter

- ◆ Choosing a venue
- ◆ Film festivals
- ◆ The benefits of having a distributor
- ◆ How persistence can pay off

As you're finishing your film, you'll be eager to show it to audiences. At first this might be your family and friends, but at some point, they won't be enough. You'll want to see your movie on the big screen with an audience primarily made up of people who don't know you and who will be honest and spontaneous in their reactions.

Though finding a distributor is often the ultimate goal, most filmmakers try to build audience through "word of mouth" and generate interest in their films by showing the film on their own. In other words, it's time to make the popcorn!

# Getting Your Film on the Screen

Most major theater and multiplex chains negotiate package deals with distributors. This means that your local theater, if they're part of a larger name chain, has very little room or opportunity to screen films other than what the chain's headquarters dictates.

Just like you made your film independently, your first screenings of the film will need to be done independently as well. If you want to see your film in a large theater, your best bet is to approach an independent cinema house, such as an art movie house or a second-run movie theater. (First-run movie theaters generally show films at full ticket price for the first four to six weeks after release, generating the film's primary box office revenue. When the movie starts bringing in less money and to make room for new movies, the film is then moved to a second-run theater, which can discount the ticket price because they pay less for the right to show the film.) Because they are not part of a large chain, second-run theaters tend to have a lot more control over what goes on their screens. Keep in mind though that movie schedules are prepared months in advance, so you're more likely to get a screening when you want it if you've contacted the owner at least three or four months beforehand.

Though the actual terms may vary from theater to theater, a common technique with independent theaters is to do what is called *four walling*. This means you rent the theater space (the four walls) and split the profits with them. They'll usually provide the projectionist.

Depending on the subject matter or style of your film, art galleries may be a viable alternative to movie theaters. Many art galleries are equipped to project videos and DVDs, and some may even have 16mm or 35mm projection spaces. But because the main focus of galleries is not film, they're probably only able to accommodate fairly small audiences. This isn't necessarily a bad thing; it's always more impressive to fill up a small theater than sit in a large theater that seems nearly empty. Check with your local museums to see if they have screening rooms or film/video exhibition spaces.

Likewise, some large corporations or businesses have theater spaces. In the Chicago area, one of the banks has a great theater space that is available to independent film-makers for rent. Besides businesses, some community and recreational centers include screening rooms. In other words, if there's no theater in your community that will show your film, don't give up. There are plenty of other options.

**Staying in Focus** _____

Simply securing a screening space is only half the battle. If you don't want to be sitting in an empty movie theater or watching your movie with just your friends and family again, you're going to need to advertise, which costs money. Other than press releases, which are usually published for free, any other announcement of your film is going to cost something. Newspaper and magazine ads are expensive, so you may need to be creative in how to let people know that your film will be screening. Post fliers around town, wear a sandwich board, or introduce yourself to people on the street and tell them about your screening. Whatever it takes to get the word out.

Another exhibition venue is the Internet, though this does provide a different kind of viewing experience for your audience than sitting in a darkened theater. There are a number of websites that distribute short films by making them downloadable or viewable as streaming video. Because videos and films can require a great deal of memory or compression in order to be successfully exhibited this way, feature film exhibition on the web is still a ways away from being a strong alternative. However, if you are able to run streaming video from your website, you might consider putting up your trailer or a scene or two from the film as a way to generate interest in your film.

# Let the Festivities Begin: Film Festivals

For most independent filmmakers, the place where we really can build an audience and interest or *buzz* about our film is at film festivals. There are thousands of film festivals in the world, and sorting through which ones offer the best chance of showing your film can be daunting.

Each film festival has its own personality, focus, and bias. Reading about the festivals can help you better decide which ones might be right for your film. If festivals were free, it might be worth sending your film out as many places as you could. But they're not free. Most festivals have processing or entry fees. Depending upon the festival, these can range from $10 to over $100 per entry. Therefore, you need to do a little bit of research.

Before paying your entry fee and sending your film, find out as much about the film festival as possible. Check out the festival website if there is one. Review the entry form and details of each festival very carefully. If possible, try to see some of the films that have won at the festival in previous years; if you can't see them, at least try to find a synopsis or brief summary of previous winning films.

All of these efforts help in making sure that your film is an appropriate fit and that you are eligible. For example, some film festivals are only for documentary films, others are only for underground experimental films. If you've got a feature-length Hollywood-type narrative, you're wasting your money entering either of these festivals.

In addition, many of the best-known film festivals are extremely expensive, and they do not refund the entry fee if you're not selected. For the price of one entry fee at a better-known film festival, I can enter my film at three or four smaller film festivals. If my film gets selected by a film jury for screening (which I'll discuss in a few pages) and/or wins an award, then I might feel that it is worth submitting the film to a festival that has a higher entry fee. Therefore, I usually wait till I've seen how my film has done at some of the smaller (and less expensive) festivals before deciding to pay a hefty entry fee. On the other hand, if you win at a well-known festival, that can give your film more prestige, and if you only have a limited amount of money for entry fees, you may decide it's better to aim high on your first go-round.

## Preparing Your Entry for Submission

All festivals will require you to submit a copy of your film before deciding whether to show it at the festival. In the days when many films were shot on 16mm filmstock, and therefore bulky, heavy, and costly to send, many festivals would ask for a preview tape (such as VHS) with the entry instead. Only if you were selected would they ask you to send a print of the film.

**CAUTION**

### Reel Trouble

Not all film festivals return preview tapes or screeners. Be sure to read the fine print on the entry form to see whether the festival returns entries, and if so, whether they require you to include return postage in your entry form. Also be sure that your tapes, DVDs, or films are clearly labeled with the title of your film, your name, and your contact info.

If your release format is DVD, then there's not much reason to send a preview tape—just send the DVD. But if your release format is 16mm film, then you may want to check and see if they accept screeners for initial review and only send the print if your film is accepted. If they do accept screeners, be sure to find out which format they prefer for previewing.

When preparing your entry, be sure to review the festival's acceptable formats: video, film, DV, HDTV, and so on. Some festivals and awards will only consider film prints. For example, DV and videos are ineligible for the Student and regular Academy Awards; to be considered there, your film has to be in 16mm, 35mm, or 70mm film. But there are other festivals that only accept DV or video. And some will accept all formats.

Also, some festivals may differentiate between origination format (what you shot your film on originally) and release format (how your film has been completed and is meant to be shown). Purist festivals will want the release and origination formats to be the same; for example, a purist film festival will only want films that were shot and released on 16mm or 35mm film; purist video festivals will want the programs that originated and are released on video. However, as media has become more accessible and interchangeable, many festivals accept material originated and released in a variety of formats.

Many festival entry forms will ask you to categorize your film or designate it as fitting into one (or sometimes two) of their pre-defined categories. Some of these categories, such as *feature-length* or *short film*, will be self-explanatory. Others may be more difficult for you to decide between, such as *amateur* or *professional*. If you're just starting out, you're an amateur in that you're relatively inexperienced and do not make your living from making films. The amateur category keeps your film from competing with films made by experienced working filmmakers who might have larger budgets. Other categories might include *narrative*, *documentary*, or *experimental*. At first glance this may seem obvious. But for many of my own films, this can be a difficult call. For example, *Borders* has a narrative, but the film images are out of sequence, making it more experimental. Some documentaries may include narrative or experimental aspects. As a result, choosing the most appropriate category can be tricky. Some festivals have tried to address this by creating additional categories such as *experimental narrative* or *experimental documentary*.

Ultimately, it's your decision which category or categories you place your film in. But make an informed choice by reading that specific festival's definitions for each category, because you may find slight variations in category guidelines from festival to festival.

If you decide to enter your film in more than one category, make sure that's allowed in the festival's rules and also check whether you need to submit a second entry form (and/or fee and/or copy of the film) to be considered for a second category.

Likewise, if you're really prolific and are submitting more than one film to a single festival in the same year, you'll need to submit two separate entry packages (form, fees, film). To avoid confusion at the festival, do not send the two entries in one envelope. Pay the postage for two.

> **Staying in Focus**
>
> Include a press kit with your entry if possible. Even if you don't have a press kit to include, try to send at least a couple of photos from your film that the festival can use in their program or website. See Chapter 27 for more details about the kinds of photos to consider.

# The Art of Negotiation

As a novice filmmaker, it's unlikely that a film festival will want to negotiate for your premiere, but sometimes for filmmakers who have a couple of successful films behind them, this can be an important issue. Basically, in this case a film festival is saying that they'll only accept your film if you agree not to show it at any other festivals (or sometimes any exhibition) before they show it. At one level, this often gives your film a lot more hype at their festival (it's a premiere, after all), but the timing may keep you from getting your film seen at other festivals that you feel would be helpful or important for your film. It's a tough call, but one you probably don't have to worry about for a while.

If your film gets accepted at a festival, see if the festival provides any funds or travel money to help you attend. Not all do, but it's worth asking. Many festivals have a small budget that allows them to bring in some of the filmmakers, because having the filmmakers there enhances the festival and can bring in larger audiences. Everyone wants to meet a filmmaker, especially if they're watching that person's work on the screen.

In exchange, the festival might ask you to speak briefly at the beginning or end of your film. Or they might ask you to sit on a panel of filmmakers. Or present a small workshop to aspiring filmmakers.

Regardless, film festivals are great places to network and meet other filmmakers, and to meet potential producers and distributors. If you do go see your film at a festival, enjoy the spotlight a bit and be sure to talk with some of the other filmmakers who are there. The film business is all about networking, and here's your chance.

# Inside a Film Jury

I've been on a number of film juries over the years, both for film festivals and for granting organizations. Grant review boards usually involve a reasonable number of applications to consider, but film festival juries can sometimes be overwhelmed by the sheer volume of entries that have to be considered. As a result, there are often separate juries for each category (or sometimes even subcategories) of submitted films.

How members are chosen and the inner workings of each jury will vary annually and from festival to festival, but usually each jury is made up of filmmakers and artists who work in moving images. Some festivals may include media students on their juries as well. Juries ensure that more than one person looks at each film, and as a group, they decide which films should be shown at the festival and which of those should receive awards.

The screening process can be more than one step. Sometimes an initial person or jury will simply review every entry to make sure it's eligible for consideration, whether all the requested materials were submitted, and whether the entry was postmarked before the deadline. If it's not, the film won't be reviewed. Other times the jury that decides which films will be shown at a festival is not the same jury that will determine the awards. Each festival is different, but all of them have to arrive at a way to review qualifying entrants.

I've been on juries where I pick up a stack of screeners to watch at home, while my fellow jurors are doing the same thing. After we've all reviewed the films in our categories, we then meet to discuss which ones we feel deserve a screening or award. I've been on other juries that lock us in a room and watch the films one after the other until they're all done. On one jury, this involved sitting in a room for four days nonstop, ordering in pizza and taking brief catnaps while films were being threaded into the projector. Needless to say, that was one of the most surreal experiences of my life. Less taxing are juries I've been on that meet for several three- or four-hour blocks of time spread out over several days.

Regardless of the process, the sheer number of films that have to be reviewed requires most juries to devise a system for quickly making decisions. Many juries that I've been on only watch the first two to three minutes of a short film and maybe the first ten minutes or so of a feature. If at that point it's clear that this is an excellent film and should be shown, we move on. We'll watch it in its entirety later to determine whether it deserves an award. If in these first few minutes it's clear that the film is not the type or quality we want for our festival, we'll put it aside. Sometimes the first few minutes of a film may not seem that good, but we need to see more to be sure. In this case we might scan ahead to the middle or the end to see how the film develops before making a final decision.

> **CAUTION**
>
> **Reel Trouble**
>
> Film jury members have seen hundreds if not thousands of films over their lifetimes, and they've had to sit through more suicide films, slasher films, mock documentaries, and Tarantino rip-offs than you can imagine. Most festivals are looking for the next new thing, not another old thing. Your film won't have a chance if it is filled with clichés.

The way in which many juries determine when to stop screening an entry is to use a counting method. The first person who has seen enough to make a decision calls out "one." When a second person has seen enough, she'll call out "two." The third person calls out "three." Once all the jurors have called out a number, the film is turned off and they talk briefly about the film and whether to include it in the festival.

The bottom line is that many festivals do not watch your entire film during the first round. I tell you this because your film has to start strong. Just like scripts have to grab the reader in the first 5 to 10 pages, your film has to grab the audience in the first few minutes.

# Your New Best Friends: Distributors

With fourwalling and film festivals, you are responsible for all the costs involved in providing a copy of the film to be shown as well as all the advertising costs. If your film is starting to appear in multiple venues at about the same time, having enough copies can become increasingly expensive. Besides getting your film seen by as many people as possible, another major benefit to a distribution deal is that they pay for the prints and advertising.

Most independent filmmakers dream of theatrical distribution, but there are other types as well, including cable and home video. Theatrical distributors will only be interested in your film if they feel they can make back the money it will cost them to print multiple copies of your film and advertise it. A name actor (even someone who is only somewhat famous) increases your likelihood of getting a theatrical distribution deal because the actor's name recognition may help bring in an audience.

Many distributors actually send buyers or representatives to key film festivals, keeping an eye out for films that get a great audience reception. Producer reps attend film festivals as well and have contacts with distributors, so either way festivals are a great place to open the distribution door.

> **Staying in Focus**
>
> You may want to have copies of your film, either on DVD or VHS, that potential buyers can take away with them. Make sure that any materials you hand out look professional and attractive—this goes for your DVD or VHS covers as well. Go the extra mile and have artwork done. Again, the ideal is for your posters, press kit, and film labels to have a consistent style.

But there are other ways to hunt the wild distributor. Besides film festivals, there are other types of showcases called film markets. These are specifically for filmmakers to publicize and (hopefully) show their films to distributors. If you're going to a film market, your chances are best if you have a finished film ready to go as well as a press kit.

Although you ideally go for theatrical distribution first, if you're unable to get a deal, at some point you may want to go ahead and sell your film for cable and/or home video (and DVD) distribution. Many independent films that are not released in theaters go "direct to video."

Whether for theatrical, cable, or home video release, a distribution deal is a legal agreement; be sure to have an experienced entertainment attorney review any document before you sign it.

# Persistence Pays Off

So what happens if your distribution deal falls through (or never happens in the first place) and you haven't gotten into any film festivals? You keep trying.

Just because one distributor has rejected your film doesn't mean they all will. So try again. Certainly, you don't want to wear out your welcome at any one distribution company. If they say no, don't be a pest and keep asking them to reconsider. Be gracious and appreciative of the time spent considering your film, and move on. Who knows, they might distribute your next film, and be much more willing to consider it if you leave them with a good impression this time.

Film festivals are a different kind of situation. As long as your film was finished in the time period the festival rules require, you can reapply. Most festivals do not restrict entries to only those made in the last 12 months. Many allow for a wider window. In those cases, this means that if you didn't get in the first time, you can reapply next year. Of course, there's nothing to say that you won't get rejected again, so it's a gamble. But at most festivals, each year brings a new jury, with different tastes, likes, and dislikes.

The first year I submitted my film *Borders*, every film festival turned it down. I was extremely discouraged. But the next year, I noticed that *Borders* was still eligible in many of those same festivals. I decided to resubmit the film to several festivals that had rejected it the first time—this time, not only did the film get in, it won awards.

## Ditty Bag

Festivals in different parts of the world or even within the United States will consider the same film differently. I've had films rejected by American festivals but accepted at festivals in Europe. Even in the United States, there are regional differences; my films have been eagerly screened in New York but have yet to be accepted at a festival in California. For these reasons you should submit your film to a variety of festivals, and don't get discouraged if one festival turns you down.

Yes, there is a time to move on to a new project and leave the current one behind. Continuing to pay entry fees to the same festival that keeps rejecting the same film is at some point foolish. But be sure you've given your film every opportunity you can by not assuming that one "no" means the answer will always be "no."

## The Least You Need to Know

◆ The final goal of filmmaking is to get your film seen by an audience.

◆ Film festivals offer a great opportunity to show your film and meet other filmmakers as well as distributors.

◆ Besides theatrical distribution companies, there are cable and home market distributors—all are looking for good films.

◆ Persistence is an essential trait of independent filmmakers; don't get discouraged if one festival turns you down. Keep trying!

# Chapter 30

# *The Graduate:* You're a Filmmaker Now

## In This Chapter

◆ Taking a look back at what you've learned

◆ Better technology doesn't necessarily mean better films

◆ How will you measure your success?

◆ Now is the time to get started!

Does it sound odd? You, a filmmaker? But you are! You've made a film, hopefully the first of many successful ones. Take a look around you and thank all the people who have helped. Your crew. Your cast. The people who helped pay for your film by donating either money or services or goods or advice or time. Thank the people who love you and who have supported you.

And go celebrate!

After the party, come back here and we'll take one last look at this wild and wonderful process you've just been through: making a film.

# That's a Wrap!

Right now, you may be feeling like there's so much more you want to know, to learn. But books can only take you so far. The best teacher is often experience, and the only way to get experience as a filmmaker is to make more films.

Throughout the course of this book, you've been introduced to some of the basic concepts behind making independent films, and hopefully these ideas and techniques will give you the desire and confidence to keep learning and make more films.

But my guess is that you've not only learned about filmmaking, but you've learned about yourself as well. If nothing else, you've learned a bit more about how you operate, how you like to work, the qualities you prefer in the people helping you, how much you can slack off and still get the job done, how passionate you are about making films, and the kinds of films you want to make. That's the amazing side effect of any creative endeavor; we learn as much about ourselves as we do about the medium. Filmmaking is no different, and in some ways, it may demand even more of this self-discovery in order to create movies that stand apart from the thousands upon thousands around us at any given moment.

You've learned, too, that filmmaking can be fun, exhilarating, exhausting, frustrating, amazing … and lots of hard work. There are basically two approaches to making a film. One follows the idea that you just go out there and shoot everything in sight, and you'll figure out your film in the editing room. People who operate from this approach deliberately shoot more than they know they will ever need. Such an approach certainly makes pre-production very simple and may at first seem faster than having a lot of pre-production planning. Unfortunately this method can run you way over budget on set because you're shooting more than you need, using up your resources, and taking more time to shoot than you really need. But the real time-consuming work begins in the editing room. You will spend months sorting out what images you have before you can even begin editing. If you love editing, this can be a dream; if you hate editing, it'll be a nightmare.

The second production approach is to thoroughly plan the film and each shooting day before turning on the camera. This means that you spend more time before each shoot, but you save time and resources on the set and ultimately save a lot of time in the editing room. Planning ahead can help assure that all the crewmembers know their job responsibilities and are properly trained on any equipment they'll be using. That you come to the set prepared, with a shot outline, storyboard, or plan for that day's shoot. And that you know and can maximize your resources; how much film-stock or videotape can you safely shoot today and not jeopardize future shots or days of shooting because you no longer have enough? For some filmmakers, this can take some of the joy out of shooting and editing, because it seems like all the creative decisions have already been made. But even the best-prepared plans cannot anticipate everything that might happen in production.

So maybe there is a third approach, a combination of the two that makes use of all the planning but also taps into the spontaneity of thinking on your feet and experimenting on the set. As I noted early in this book, a guiding vision will help you know what your film should look like and recognize it when you're close. Better yet, a guiding vision gives you the freedom to consider other ideas and approaches without losing sight of what will work best for your movie.

My belief about making films is that you have to do the work somewhere. Where you choose to do it is up to you, but the work has to get done or you won't have a film.

So … what did you learn? Stop for a moment and really answer that question as thoroughly as you can. Before you lose these insights, write them down. I know that keeping a journal can sound like homework, but keeping a record of what you learned during this process—what worked well, what you wish you had done differently—will give you a head start on your next film.

# Brave New World of Independent Filmmaking

Despite what a lot of people might think, the future of independent filmmaking is not about the latest software or newest camera. Sure, HDTV (High Definition Television) is on the horizon, and yes, it manages to live up to most of its hype. Yes, it looks like digital sound will be adopted in more and more movie theaters in the coming years. Yes, there will be advances in computer technology that will make shooting and cutting on 16mm and 35mm film seem obsolete. File-sharing and the Internet may create new opportunities for self-distribution. But my guess is there will still be people for a long time who will shoot some of their work on filmstock or release their movie as a 35mm film. Digital theaters may be the wave of the future, but it's a slow-moving wave. And sitting in front of a computer screen isn't the same as watching a movie on a huge screen in a darkened theater.

> **Staying in Focus**
>
> Before you rush out and buy equipment, whether cameras or editing systems, take the time to do some research. Spend your money wisely—especially when it comes to technology, which can become outdated so quickly.

Technology changes all the time. It always has. Will these advances make films easier to make?

Probably. Will these advances make films less expensive to make? Possibly. Will these advances make films better? No.

The actual promise of emerging technologies and advancements in film, video, and computer imaging is that the mechanisms for making films will become more and more accessible. But remember that there is no one way to do anything in film. It's all about being creative, working with what you have, finding a way to make your film with the resources you have and with what you can afford. Sadie Benning made a series of well-known and critically acclaimed films with a toy camera; Jonathan Caouette made an acclaimed feature-length documentary about his life on an old iMac. Having the latest technology or the most expensive camera doesn't assure you'll have a good film.

Cameras don't shoot films. People do. The future of independent filmmaking really rests with the filmmakers, the people like you who have an interest in movies and want to learn how to make them. And then go make one.

Quite simply, the future of independent filmmaking is *you*.

# The World—or at Least Your Next Film—Awaits

In terms of filmmaking, like most things, there will come a point when we'll be faced with the question, What's my measure of success? For some, the answer is fame and recognition. For others, fortune. For still others it's simply the satisfaction of having made another film, no matter who sees it.

Maybe another way of thinking about the question is, Why do I want to make films? Am I making films in the hope that someone in Hollywood will take notice and offer me the chance to make films there? Or do I want to make films in my own home-town?

And what kinds of films do I want to make? Do I want to make features or short films? Narratives or documentaries or experimental films? What kinds of stories do I want to tell? What do I want to reveal?

How do I want to make my films? With friends on the weekends or as a full-time job? The answers to these questions can point the way to what's next for us or at least what we want to be "next."

As you embark on that journey, I'd like to remind you of the kitten experiment I told you about way back in Chapter 1. Many of us make assumptions about our world all the time based on relatively limited information. Filmmaking can be a way in which you look more closely at the world around you, see it in new ways, and then share those observations with the rest of us. Whether you're making character-driven dramatic films or slapstick comedies or action adventures or any genre I could name, you have the opportunity to tell us the story only you can tell. In some ways, filmmaking is simply the act of saying to an audience, "Hey, look over here, pay attention to this."

# Night Is Falling and the Time Is Now

Whether you make a film or not, today will become tomorrow, and tomorrow will become the next day, and so forth. There are always a million reasons to start your film tomorrow, to work on it next weekend, to save up a little more money before you start.

Why not start today? Just for a few moments. Maybe half an hour. As soon as you set this book down … in fact, before you set it down, carry it with you to your computer or to a pad of paper and pencil. When you close the book, promise yourself you'll spend the next half hour writing about your new film. Maybe it'll just be an idea. Or a character description. Or an image. Or a sound. Or a memory. Or a list of people who would be willing to help you make a film.

Tomorrow, add to it. And the next day. And the next.

## The Least You Need to Know

- Making films takes a lot of work, and you have to do the work somewhere, whether that's in development & pre-production, production, or post-production.

- It's important to keep track of what you learned in making each film so that your next film will go even better.

- Filmmaking is less about new technology than the people involved.

- Knowing your goals, why you want to make films, will influence the films you make and the life you live.

- Now is the time to start working on your film.

# Glossary

**ambience (**or **ambient sound)**   The naturally occurring sounds of an environment.

**blocking**   The dynamic and sometimes changing arrangement and relationship of actors and camera to the environment and each other during a scene.

**boom**   The long pole that ends in a microphone and allows for microphone placement close to the action without being visible in the frame. The word also applies to the person who holds this pole, though when this is the case, "boom" is short for "boom operator."

**camera original**   Filmstock or videotape that has actually run through the camera. If you're shooting negative film, your negative would be the camera original. If you're shooting videotape and then putting it in your VCR to watch, you're watching the camera original.

**close-up (CU)**   A shot that emphasizes facial expression or the details of a gesture or a significant object; a shot that frames a person from the neck up.

**continuity**   A set of editing techniques developed in Hollywood that emphasize storytelling through a logical succession of events that continually orients the viewer in time and space.

**cut**   The most immediate transition from shot to shot created simply by inserting the second shot at the exact point that the first shot ends.

**cutaway**    A close-up shot of an object, a gesture, or an element of the environment that is in some way connected with the overall scene or event.

**deep focus**    A focus in which all objects from close foreground to distant background are seen in sharp definition.

**depth of field**    The space in which all objects, at different distances from the camera, appear to be in focus; affected by the focal length of the lens, the distance between camera and subject, and the f-stop.

**development**    The first phase in making a film wherein you develop an initial idea and script it; this is also the time when you begin identifying financial resources and raising money to make your movie.

**dissolve (or mix)**    Where the end of one shot merges slowly into the next; as the second shot becomes distinct, the first slowly disappears.

**distribution**    The process of making your film available to theaters, cable, network television, or home video rental/purchase.

**editing**    The system by which one shot is connected to another; may be employed to create graphic, rhythmic, spatial, and temporal relationships among shots.

**establishing shot**    A shot that provides orientation to the overall environment or location of the action. An example would be a wide angle shot that takes in an entire football field.

**exhibition & distribution**    The final phase in making a film, which includes premiering the film as well as making it available to theaters (theatrical release), cable, network television, or the home video market.

**extreme close-up (ECU)**    A shot that singles out a portion of the face, such as the eyes or lips, or isolates a detail, magnifying the minutiae.

**extreme long shot (ELS)**    A shot wherein human figures are barely visible and are visually overwhelmed by their environment; frequently an establishing shot of landscapes, cities, or other extensive environments where, if present, individual people are a part of the landscape.

**fade in**    A shot that begins in darkness and gradually assumes full brightness.

**fade out**    A shot that gradually grows dim until it is completely dark.

**flats**    Pre-built wall segments that can be used in various combinations to create sets; some flats can have windows or doors to complete the illusion of a real room when put together.

**foreground**   The part of the scene that is nearest to and in front of the audience/camera.

**frame**   1) The boundaries of the image that are created by the sides, top, and bottom of the camera and the screen; 2) a single still image from the sequence of frames which, seen rapidly together, create the illusion of movement; 30 frames per second are recorded and projected in video in order to create the illusion of moving images, 24 fps in film.

**genres**   Types of films classified by their recurring use of specific conventions and elements.

**Golden Mean**   An ancient theory using mathematical relationships to balance compositional elements, particularly proportion and placement, within an image. This theory is sometimes linked with the more modern "rule of thirds," in which the frame is divided into a grid that looks something like a tic-tac-toe board, wherein the intersections of each line become optimal points for placing compositionally significant elements.

**independent filmmaking**   The process of making films without the support of studios, production companies, or other institutions known for producing multiple films by a variety of different filmmakers.

**indie films**   A popular slang term for movies that have been made independently or outside major filmmaking institutions.

**jump cut**   A break or jump in a shot's continuity of time, caused by removing a section of a shot or cutting between shots that are identical in subject, but differ slightly in screen location; when a jump cut occurs, the result is often abrupt and jerky; the subject appears to jump from one location to another for no apparent reason.

**location sound**   Any audio that you record or collect while on the set or location.

**long shot (LS)**   A shot wherein the human figures are more prominent than in an extreme long shot but are still dominated by the environment or background; often considered an establishing shot of interiors.

**matching action (match-on-action or match cut)**   A transition that involves a direct cut from one shot to another that matches it in action or subject matter, oftentimes with the shot scale and camera location having changed.

**medium long shot (MS)**   When photographing a person, a shot that frames the human body from the knees up.

**medium shot (MS)**   A shot wherein the human body is framed from the waist up.

**metaphor**   The comparison of one thing to another.

**MOS**   Stands for "mit out sound" (a corruption of the phrase "without sound") and is used to designate shots that are filmed without audio.

**omnidirectional**   A type of microphone that picks up sounds from all directions.

**over-the-shoulder shot (OSS)**   Used for scenes where two people are talking to each other, a shot of one person's face shot over the shoulder of the other person; oftentimes a part of the shot/reverse shot strategy of editing; usually a little of the second person's shoulder and the back of his head are visible in the frame.

**pan (or panorama shot)**   Rotating the camera from a fixed position along a horizontal plane.

**paper edit**   A written description of the sequence of selected footage to include in the master edit.

**point of view**   1) your perspective on the story that you're telling, which will influence how you tell the story; 2) a type of shot wherein the audience sees what the character sees; 3) the perspective from which the story is presented, as in "point of view character."

**post-production**   The editing and sound-mixing phase of filmmaking, culminating in the creation of a composite print or copy of the film that combines image and sound and is ready for viewing by an audience.

**pre-production**   The phase of filmmaking where you plan how you will actually shoot your film; this phase includes a variety of tasks related to pre-visualization (breaking down the script, production design, storyboards, and so forth), hiring cast and crew, budgeting finances, and scheduling the dates for production.

**presence**   Tracks of sound effects created and mixed in post-production that simulate the sounds we would expect to hear in a given scene's environment. While these might use some of the ambient sounds (or ambience) collected on the set, *presence* is a deliberate construction of soundtracks as a part of the overall sound design.

**prime lens (or normal lens)**   A medium-focal length lens that comes closest to approximating the perspective of the human eye.

**production**   The phase of filmmaking when dramatic performances are recorded by camera and sound.

**rack focus (**or **follow focus)** Moving the focus control of the camera in one continuous motion so that one object goes out of focus as a closer or farther object comes into focus.

**reaction shot** A shot that emphasizes the facial reaction to an event, statement, or activity.

**rear projection** A special effects technique wherein a backdrop is projected on a screen from behind the actors.

**reverse shot** Sometimes a reaction shot, a shot often used during scenes where two people are talking and the editor cuts back and forth between close-ups of each of them.

**rushes** Film, video, or digital copies of your unedited footage so that you can review what you've shot without damaging the camera original.

**scene** The basic building block of drama; a small segment of a film's story, usually containing a single event, moment, or interaction that exists in continuous time and space and helps to move the story forward.

**scratch track** A track of sound that is never intended for inclusion in the final mixed soundtrack of the film, but rather serves as a guide to help in syncing up replacement sounds.

**screen, green or blue** A type of backdrop that actors can perform in front of; later in post-production, the solid color of the backdrop can be replaced by computer with a superimposed image or setting, making it appear as if the actors are in a world too expensive or fantastic to create in reality.

**script** A scene-by-scene or shot-by-shot description of the dramatic action of your story written in a very specific standardized format.

**sequence** A succession of related shots or scenes that develops a section of the narrative.

**shot** A single sequence shot by one camera without interruption.

**shot/reverse shot** A method of editing often used for conversations between two people wherein the editor cuts back and forth between close-ups of the two people.

**sides** A scene or several pages of dialogue from your script used in auditioning actors.

**SMPTE**   Pronounced "simpty," stands for Society of Motion Picture Technicians and Engineers.

**soft focus**   The slightly blurred or hazy effect achieved by shooting slightly out of focus or through gauze or by similar methods.

**storyboard**   A series of sketches that are developed during pre-production to help visualize the key points of a scene, sometimes accompanied by notes of the corresponding audio information.

**straight cut**   See *cut*.

**symbol**   An object or name that stands for something else, especially a material thing that stands for something that is not material.

**telephoto**   A telephoto lens allows a subject that is relatively far away from the camera to appear to be closer.

**theme**   A subtext that the filmmaker has deliberately chosen and developed within the story; a central truth or the hidden meaning of the story.

**tilt**   From a fixed position, moving the camera up or down along a vertical plane.

**timecode**   A reference signal that allows you to quickly locate a specific individual frame of film or video and/or its corresponding sound.

**tracking shot (or dolly shot)**   When the camera as a whole changes position, traveling in any direction along the ground.

**unidirectional**   The type of microphone pickup pattern in which sounds are picked up from one direction only.

**video**   The picture, or visual, portion of a video signal.

**voice-over**   The use of an unseen narrator heard in a television program, or the voice of a visible character indicating thoughts but without motion of lips. Also, the use of narration over related cover footage.

**walla walla**   A technical term for collecting the sound of human voices without recording specific words.

**wide angle**   A lens that gives a wide field of view and creates a great depth of field.

**wild sounds**   Recordings made of sound without a corresponding sync image.

# Appendix B

# Resources

Help for making your films is all around you. Here are some films, books, websites, and software that can help you to either gain more insight into independent films and how to make them, or give you practical information to make your job easier.

## Films

The following films are about the business and process of making movies. Some are funny, some are tragic, but all are an interesting "inside" look at the world of film:

*8¹/₂* (1963, Federico Fellini): narrative

*American Movie: The Making of Northwestern* (1999, Chris Smith): documentary

*Baadasssss!* (2003, Mario Van Peebles): narrative

*Big Picture, The* (1989, Christopher Guest): narrative

*Bollywood Bound* (2001, Nisha Pahuja): documentary

*Hearts of Darkness: A Filmmaker's Apocalypse* (1991, Fax Bahr, George Hickenlooper, Eleanor Coppola): documentary

*Living in Oblivion* (1995, Tom DiCillo): narrative

*Lost in La Mancha* (2002, Keith Fulton, Louis Pepe): documentary

*Overnight* (2003, Tony Montana, Mark Brian Smith): documentary

*Player, The* (1992, Robert Altman): narrative

*Project Greenlight Seasons 1 and 2:* documentary

*Singin' in the Rain* (1952, Stanley Donen, Gene Kelly): musical

The following are several independent films that got made as a result of the film-makers' passion and belief in their vision; some of these directors have gone on to make Hollywood films:

*All the Real Girls* (2003, David Gordon Green): narrative

*The Blair Witch Project* (1999, Daniel Myrick, Eduardo Sanchez): narrative

*Blood Simple* (1984, the Coen Brothers): narrative

*Boys Don't Cry* (1999, Kimberly Pierce): narrative

*Boyz n the Hood* (1991, John Singleton): narrative

*Clerks* (1994, Kevin Smith): narrative

*Daughters of the Dust* (1991, Julie Dash): narrative

*The Evil Dead* (1981, Sam Raimi): narrative

*Go Fish* (1994, Rose Troche): narrative

*Maria Full of Grace* (2004, Joshua Marston): narrative

*One False Move* (1992, Carl Franklin): narrative

*Open Water* (2003, Chris Kentis): narrative

*Roger & Me* (1989, Michael Moore): documentary

*sex, lies and videotape* (1989, Steven Soderbergh): narrative

*Smoke Signals* (1998, Chris Eyre): narrative

*Stranger than Paradise* (1983, Jim Jarmusch): narrative

*Tarnation* (2003, Jonathan Caouette): documentary

*The Wedding Banquet* (1993, Ang Lee): narrative

The following are just a few of the films that have been made outside the Hollywood system:

*Atanariuat* (2001, Zacharias Kunuk): narrative

*Cleo from 5 to 7* (1961, Agnes Varda): narrative

*Crying Game, The* (1992, Neil Jordan): narrative

*Decalogue* (AKA *Dekalog*, 1989, Krzysztof Kieslowski): narrative

*eXistenZ* (1999, David Cronenberg): narrative

*Heavenly Creatures* (1994, Peter Jackson): narrative

*Jesus de Montreal* (1989, Denys Arcand): narrative

*Kes* (1969, Kenneth Loach): narrative

*Last Night* (1998, Don McKellar): narrative

*Mon oncle Antoine* (1971, Claude Jutra): narrative

*Muriel's Wedding* (1994, P. J. Hogan): narrative

*Proof* (1991, Jocelyn Moorhouse): narrative

*Sweet Hereafter, The* (1997, Atom Egoyan): narrative

*Sweetie* (1989, Jane Campion): narrative

*Trainspotting* (1996, Danny Boyle): narrative

*Trust* (1990, Hal Hartley): narrative

*Vera Drake* (2004, Mike Leigh): narrative

*Wings of Desire* (1987, Wim Wenders): narrative

Filmmakers watch and talk about movies, and like most magazines and film critics, have a list of "must-see" films. The following is a brief list of classic films that often serve as a common language or heritage for filmmakers:

*Breathless* (1960, Jean-Luc Godard): narrative

*Cabinet of Dr. Caligari, The* (1920, Robert Wiene): narrative

*Citizen Kane* (1941, Orson Welles): narrative

*Do the Right Thing* (1989, Spike Lee): narrative

*Double Indemnity* (1944, Billy Wilder): narrative

*ET: the Extra-Terrestrial* (1982, Steven Spielberg): narrative

*Godfather, The* (1972, Francis Ford Coppola): narrative

*Graduate, The* (1967, Mike Nichols): narrative

*Hiroshima Mon Amour* (1959, Alain Resnais): narrative

*M* (1931, Fritz Lang): narrative

*Meshes of the Afternoon* (1943, Maya Deren, Alexander Hammid): experimental

*Pulp Fiction* (1994, Quentin Tarantino): narrative

*Raging Bull* (1980, Martin Scorsese): narrative

*Raise the Red Lantern* (1991, Yimou Zhang): narrative

*Rashomon* (1950, Akira Kurosawa): narrative

*Rules of the Game* (1939, Jean Renoir): narrative

*Searchers, The* (1956, John Ford): narrative

*Seventh Seal, The* (1957, Ingmar Bergman): narrative

# Books

Avrich, Barry. *Selling the Sizzle: The Magic and Logic of Entertainment Marketing.* Maxworks Publishing Group, 2002.

Berger, John. *Ways of Seeing.* Penguin Books, 1995.

Biskind, Peter. *Down and Dirty Pictures: Miramax, Sundance, and the Rise of Independent Film.* Simon & Schuster, 2004.

Bordwell, David, and Kristin Thompson. *Film Art: An Introduction.* McGraw-Hill, 2003.

Bosko, Mark Steven. *The Complete Independent Movie Marketing Handbook.* Michael Wiese Productions, 2003.

Egri, Lajos. *Art of Dramatic Writing: Its Basis in the Creative Interpretation of Human Motives.* Touchstone, 1972.

Fitzsimmons, April. *Breaking & Entering: Land Your First Job in Film Production.* Lone Eagle Publishing Company, 1997.

Greenspan, Jaq. *Careers for Film Buffs & Other Hollywood Types.* McGraw-Hill, 2003.

Katahn, T. L. *Reading for a Living: How to Be a Professional Story Analyst for Film and Television.* Blue Arrow Books, 1990.

Katz, Stephen. *Film Directing Shot by Shot: Visualizing from Concept to Screen.* Michael Wiese Productions, 1991.

Kaufman, Lloyd, with Adam Jahnke and Trent Haaga. *Make Your Own Damn Movie: Secrets of a Renegade Director.* St. Martin's Griffin, 2003.

Levy, Frederick. *The Hollywood Way: A Young Movie Mogul's Savvy Business Tips for Success in Any Career.* St. Martin's Griffin, 2002.

Litwak, Mark. *Contracts for the Film & Television Industry, 2nd Edition.* Silman-James Press, 1998.

Lobrutto, Vincent. *The Filmmaker's Guide to Production Design.* Allworth Press, 2002.

Mascelli, Joseph V. *The Five C's of Cinematography: Motion Picture Filming Techniques.* Silman-James Press, 1998.

Merritt, Greg. Film Production: *The Complete Uncensored Guide to Filmmaking.* Lone Eagle Publishing Company, 1998.

Murch, Walter. *In the Blink of an Eye.* Silman-James Press, 2001.

Obst, Lynda. *Hello, He Lied.* Broadway Books, 1997.

Reisz, Karel, and Gavin Millar. *Technique of Film Editing.* Focal Press, 1995.

Press, Skip. *The Complete Idiot's Guide to Screenwriting.* Alpha Books, 2001.

Rabiger, Michael. *Directing: Film Techniques and Aesthetics.* Focal Press, 1996.

Robinson, Bill, and Ceridwen Morris. *It's All Your Fault: How to Make It as a Hollywood Assistant.* Fireside, 2001.

Sonnenschein, David. *Sound Design: The Expressive Power of Music, Voice and Sound Effects in Cinema.* Michael Wiese Productions, 2001.

Vachon, Christine, and David Edelstein. *Shooting to Kill.* Perennial Currents, 1998.

Witcomb, Cynthia. *The Writer's Guide to Writing Your Screenplay: How to Write Great Screenplays and Movies for Television.* Watson-Guptill Publications, 2002.

# Websites

Here are some of the websites you can find with a little searching of the Internet. This list is by no means comprehensive, but serves as an overview of the kinds of resources available on the web.

## Actors' Unions

ACTRA (Alliance of Canadian Cinema, Television and Radio Artists): www.actra.ca

AFTRA (American Federation of Television & Radio Artists): www.aftra.com

SAG (Screen Actors Guild): www.sag.org

## Copyright Registration

The Library of Congress issues copyrights; you can find the forms at www.copyright.gov/forms.

The Writers Guild of America (www.wga.org) offers a script registration service, but this is not the same level of protection as a copyright and is primarily used by writers hoping to sell their scripts in Hollywood.

## Film Festivals

FilmFestivals.Com (www.filmfestivals.com) provides a wide range of film festival info.

WithoutABox (www.withoutabox.com) is a one-stop resource for film festival information and applications, providing a service that helps filmmakers easily submit their films.

## Filmstock, DV, and Videotape

Fujifilm (www.fuji.com) sells film and DV tapes (click on professional products, motion picture).

Kodak (www.kodak.com) offers motion picture film and digital cinema post resources (click on the "cinematography" link).

## General Resources

DVshop.ca offers a variety of resources; in particular, check out the Canadian filmmaking resources with links at www.dvshop.ca/dvcafe/canada/canfilm.html and the U.K. filmmaking resources with links at www.dvshop.ca/dvcafe/film/uk.html.

The Film Centre (www.filmcentre.co.uk) offers links and info for filmmakers in the U.K.

Film Finders' Film Market website (www.filmfinders.com) is a great way to get the word out to potential distributors that you are making a film.

filmmaking.net (www.filmmaking.net) provides resources for new and independent filmmakers around the world.

indieWIRE (www.indiewire.com) shares industry news for independent filmmakers and enthusiasts; can use the site as a guest or register as a member for free to access additional materials.

Internet Movie Data Base (www.imdb.com) is a great resource for checking basic information on thousands of movies.

Irish Film and Television Network (www.iftn.ie) provides links to filmmaking resources on their website for free (check out www.iftn.ie/directory/index1.htm).

## Independent Filmmaking Organizations

AIVF (Association of Independent Video and Filmmakers): www.aivf.org

IFP (Independent Film Project): www.ifp.org

## Labs

Alpha Cine Labs (Seattle): www.alphacine.com

DuArt Post Production (New York City): www.duart.com

FotoKem Film and Video (Burbank/Los Angeles): www.fotokem.com

## Music Rights and Legal Services

ASCAP (American Society of Composers, Authors and Publishers): www.ascap.com (click the link for licensing info)

BMI: www.bmi.com (click the link for licensing info)

Volunteer Lawyers for the Arts: www.vlany.org/res_dir.html

## Stock Footage

BBC Motion Gallery: www.bbcmotiongallery.com (there is a charge)

Creative Commons: http://creativecommons.org (an image exchange where filmmakers can post the restrictions on using their images in your own film)

F.I.L.M. Archives Inc.: www.filmarchivesonline.com (charge)

Historic Films: www.historicfilms.com (charge)

# Software

Every day, new software programs come on the market that make filmmaking easier. Here are just a few to give you an idea of what's out there. With the software name, I'm listing the company's website, but once there, you may need to click the site's link for "products" in order to find the software description.

## Animation

Alias/Wavefront (Maya): www.alias.com

LightWave 3D: www.newtek.com

SoftImage: www.softimage.com

## Editing

Avid Xpress DV and Avid Xpress Pro: www.avid.com

Final Cut Pro: www.apple.com/finalcutpro

## Producing

Cinergy made by Mindstar Productions: www.mindstarprods.com

Filmmakersoftware: www.filmmakersoftware.com

Gorilla Film Production Software: www.junglesoftware.com

Movie Magic: www.entertainmentpartners.com

## Screenwriting

Final Draft: www.finaldraft.com

## Sound

Pro Tools (Digidesign): www.protools.com

## Storyboard

FrameForge 3D Studio: www.frameforge3d.com

Storyboard Artist: www.powerproduction.com

Storyboard Lite: www.zebradevelopment.com

# Index

## Numbers

16mm film, 191
   daylight spools, 196
180-degree rule, 217-218, 251
*1984*, 40
*25th Hour, The*, 280
30-degree rule, 218, 251
35mm film, 191
*8 Mile*, 42

## A

A/B rolling, 293
above-the-line expenses, 166-169
AC (assistant camera), 117
actors
   auditioning process, 128-133
      advertising, 128-130
      callbacks, 132
      monologues, 130
      open calls, 128
      scheduled appoint-ments, 128
      videotaping, 132
   casting, release forms, 133-134
   directing, 180-183
   unions, 127-128
   work styles, 180

ACTRA (Alliance of Canadian Cinema, Television & Radio Artists), 127
ADR (automated dialogue replacement), 229, 259
AD (assistant director), 116, 185-186
advertising auditions, 128-130
aesthetic treatments, 73-76
AFTRA (American Federation of Television and Radio Artists), 127
agreements, crewmembers, 123-124
*Alien*, 306
*Aliens*, 38
Alliance of Canadian Cinema, Television & Radio Artists (ACTRA), 127
*Almost Famous*, 279
ambient sounds, recording, 230-231
*Amelie*, 40
*American Beauty*, 7
American Federation of Television and Radio Artists (AFTRA), 127
American shots, 102
amplitude (sound), 258
analog recordings (audio), 225

analog videotape, 191
   component video, 199
   control tracks, 197
   magnetic fields, 197-199
animals, casting, 128
animation
   computer animation, 272
   short animation, 6
   stop action, 272
answer prints, 294
antagonists, 38
anti-halation layer, filmstock, 194
appreciation for crew, expressing, 238
apprenticeship system (Hollywood), 22
archiving film, 297-298
Art Councils, 86
art director, 118
arts grantors, 85-86
aspect ratios, 214-217
   cinemascope ratios, 214
   television screens, 215
   widescreen aspect ratios, 214-215
assembly edits, 249
assistant camera (AC), 117
assistant director (AD), 116, 185-186
Association of Independent Video and Filmmakers, 85
assumptions, scripts, 91-92
asymmetry, frames, 285

attachments, 88
attention spans, audiences, 15
attenuated filters, 276
audiences
    attention spans, 15
    identifying, proposals,
        67-68
    participation, 18-19
    suspension of disbelief,
        sustaining, 19
audio design, 221
    ambient sounds, 230-231
    analog recordings, 225
    digital recordings, 226-227
    location sound, 222
    microphone placement,
        227-229
    mixing, 265-266
    musical scores, 263-264
    post-production, 226
    presence tracks, 231
    silence, 259-260
    sound mixing, 258-259
    sound relationships, 260
    sound synchronization,
        223-225
auditioning cast members,
    128-133
    advertising, 128-130
    callbacks, 132
    monologues, 130
    open calls, 128
    scheduled appointments,
        128
    videotaping, 132
automated dialogue replace-
    ment (ADR), 229, 259
auxiliary mic (microphone)
    ports, cameras, 223
auxiliary viewfinders,
    cameras, 202
avant garde films, 15

# B

backstory, 92
*Bambi Meets Godzilla*, 281
*Batman*, 41
beats, scenes, 96
*Beautiful Girls*, 114
below-the-line expenses,
    166-169
best boy, 117
Beta SP videotape, 199
*Big Chill, The*, 263
biographical documentaries,
    14
biographies, creating charac-
    ters', 39
*Blair Witch Project, The*, 302
blocking scenes, 182
*Blood Simple*, 270, 280
*Blue*, 113
body microphones, 228
boom operator, 117, 228
boom shots, 108
booms, 25
*Borders*, 63, 282
Bordwell, David, 75
bouncing, lighting, 210
*Boys on the Side*, 280
budgets
    above-the-line expenses,
        166-169
    below-the-line expenses,
        166-169
    big-ticket items, 170-172
    creating, 169-170
    funding, securing, 174-176
    petty-cash expenses, 172
    preliminary budgets,
        creating, 166-169
    records, keeping, 172-174
    shooting budgets, 175-176

# C

C-corporations, 81
cable synchronization, 223
call sheets, posting, 163-164
callbacks, auditions, 132
camcorders
    analog videotape, magnetic
        fields, 197-199
    digital videotape, 199-200
    head rolls, 198
    lenses, 200-203
camera operator, 117
camera original filmstock, 194
cameras, 192
    analog videotape, magnetic
        fields, 197-199
    auxiliary mic (microphone)
        port, 223
    digital videotape, 199-200
    film, 192-194
        camera original, 194
        film speed, 195-196
        layers, 193-194
        perforations, 193
        reversal film, 194
    head rolls, 198
    intermittent motion, 196
    internal microphones, 223
    lenses, 200-203
        auxiliary viewfinders,
            202
        depth of field, 201
        focal length, 200
        handling, 219
        macro lenses, 201
        prime lenses, 200
        telephoto lenses, 200
        wide angle length
            lenses, 200
        zoom lenses, 200

pull down claws, 196
purchasing, 329-330
renting, 192
variations, 192
Campion, Jane, 6
cardioid microphones, 227
cast members
    appreciation for, expressing, 238
    auditioning process, 128-133
        advertising, 128-130
        callbacks, 132
        monologues, 130
        open calls, 128
        scheduled appointments, 128
        videotaping, 132
    crediting, 282
    firing, 239-240
    publicity interviews, protocol, 313
casting
    animals, 128
    children, 128
    family, 126-127
    friends, 126-127
    non-actors, 126
    release forms, 133-134
    union actors, 127-128
casting director, 116, 125
cellulose acetate, filmstock, 193
changing bags, 195
characters, 38-40
*Charlie's Angels*, 271
*Chicken Run*, 272
children, casting, 128
characters
    conduct, 40-41
    creating biographies, 39

passive characters, 41
primary characters, 38
secondary characters, 38
cinema houses, obtaining screening space, 318-319
cinemascope aspect ratios, 214
cinematographer (DP), 117
cinematography, 205-206, 218-219
    180-degree rule, 217-218
    30-degree rule, 218
    aspect ratios, 214-217
    fuses, maintaining, 218
    lighting, 206-207
        continuity, 207
        motivated lighting, 207
        qualities, 207-212
        three-point lighting, 212-214
    shadowing, 206-207
*Citizen Kane*, 43
clapperboards, 224
climaxes, 46
close-up (CU), 103
closed sets, calling for, 234
*Closer*, 255
closing credits, 281
Coen, Ethan, 116
Coen, Joel, 116
Coken, Ric, 259
collaboration
    editing, 250
    importance of, 234-235
*Collateral*, 40
color temperature, lighting, 211
component video, 199
computer animation, 272
concepts, stories, 45

conditions, stories, 41-42
conduct, characters, 40-41
configurations, stories, 43-47
conflict, characters, 39-40
conforming, negative cutting, 293-294
context, stories, 42-43
contingency plans, creating, 163-164
continuity
    continuity editing, 251-254
    lighting, 207, 219
continuity person, 117
contracts, actors, 133-134
contrast ratios, lighting, 207-208
control tracks, analog videotape, 197
copyrighted music, using, 264
copyrights, 65
choreographing scenes, 182
corporations, 81
costs (budgets)
    above-the-line expenses, 166-169
    below-the-line expenses, 166-169
    big-ticket items, 170-172
    creating, 169-170
    full funding, 174-176
    petty-cash costs, 172
    record keeping, 172-174
    shooting budgets, 175-176
costumes, 150-151
coverage, shots, 251
craft service areas, locations, 139
craft services, 235-237
crane shots, 108
crawling titles, 280
creative producers, 116

credit cards, funding films with, 84-85
credits, 280-282
    closing credits, 281
    fonts, choosing, 282-284
    main title sequence, 280-281
    placement, 284-286
    point size, choosing, 282-284
    possessory credits, 281
    scrolling, 280
    timing, 286-287
crewmembers, 117
    appreciation for, expressing, 238
    art director, 118
    assistant camera (AC), 117
    assistant director (AD), 116, 185-186
    best boy, 117
    boom operator, 117, 228
    camera operator, 117
    casting director, 116, 125
    cinematographer (DP), 117
    collaboration, importance of, 234-235
    craft services, 235-237
    creative producer, 116
    crediting, 282
    directing, 183-186
    director, 116
    dolly grip, 117
    electrician, 117
    firing, 239-240
    friends, 120
    gaffer, 117
    hiring, 120-122

letters of agreement, 123-124
line producer, 116
    locating, 119-120
    location scout, 116
    makeup artist, 118
    multitasking, 119
    music supervisor, 118
    picture editor, 119
    post-production supervisor, 118
    producer, 116
    production assistant (PA), 119
    production designer, 117, 145
    production manager (PM), 116
    production meeting, importance of, 186-187
    prop person, 118
    publicity interview, protocol, 313
    recruiting, 120-122
    script supervisor, 117
    skeleton crew, 124
    sound designer, 117
    sound editor, 119
    sound mixer, 117, 222, 258
    still photographer, 118
    stunt coordinator, 118
    stylist, 118
    transportation captain, 118
    union crew, 122-123
    wardrobe person, 118
    wrangler, 118
critical reviews, including in press kits, 308-309
Cronenberg, David, 6

crossfades, 263
crutches, stories, 43
crystal synchronization, 223
CU (close-up), 103
cutaway shots, 252

## D

dailies, 148
day-for-night shooting, 276
daylight spools, 16mm film, 196
dBs (decibels), 258
deal memos, actors, 133-134
*Deceived*, 285
decibels (dBs), 258
*Decline of the American Empire, The*, 280
deep focus, 216
depth of field, camera lenses, 201
Deren, Maya, 6
*Desert Hearts*, 270
development phase (filmmaking), 26
diary documentaries, 14
diffusion, lighting, 210
digital recordings (audio), 226-227
digital tracks, 295-296
digital video, 191
digital videotape, 199-200
diopters, video cameras, 203
dipped mix, 259
directing
    actors, 180-183
    crewmembers, 183-187
    shots, 187-190
    skill assessments, 179

director's statements, press kits, 307-308

director, 4, 116
    producer, compared, 4

director of photography (DP), 117

*Dirty Work*, 279

dissolves, 269

distribution
    negotiations, 324-325
    screening space, obtaining, 318-319

distribution phase (film-making), 27

*DOA*, 43

documentaries, 14

documentation, fundraising, 87-88

dolly grip, 117

dolly shots, 108

double-perf filmstock, 193

double-system sync sound recording, 223

dramatic arcs (plots), 46-47

drop frame (DF) timecodes, 295

duration, films, 15

## E

ECU (extreme close-up), 104

edit decision lists (EDLs), 295

editing, 243-244
    assembly edits, 249
    conforming, 293-294
    continuity, 251-254
    edit decision lists (EDLs), 295
    editing software, 245
    feedback, 250

film lab, 246-247

final cuts, 250

footage, logging, 247-248

insert edits, 252

jump cuts, 252

linear editing, 244-245

non-linear editing, 244-245

on-line editing, 294-295

paper edits, 248

rough cuts, 249

rushes, synchronizing, 247

scenes, 96-97

shots, 107
    pulling, 248

spatial distortions, 254-255

temporal distortions, 254-255

editing in camera, 244

editors, 119

educational films, 14

effects, 275-276
    computer animation, 272
    dissolves, 269
    fades, 268-269
    fast motion, 277
    filters, 276-277
    freeze frames, 270
    makeup effects, 272-275
    optical effects, 268
    reverse imaging, 277-278
    slow motion, 277
    straight cuts, 267
    superimpositions, 270
    virtual sets, 271-272
    wipes, 269-270

Egoyan, Atom, 6

EINs (Employee Identification Numbers), 81

electrician, 117

electricity accessibility, locations, 138-139

electronic press kits (EPKs), 302

electronic slates, 224

ELS (extreme long shots), 100

Employee Identification Numbers (EINs), 81

emulsion, filmstock, 193

*Enduring Love*, 104

equipment
    booms, 25
    budgeting, 170
    cameras, 192
        film, 192-196
        head rolls, 198
        lenses, 200-203
        pull down claws, 196
        renting, 192
        variations, 192
    microphones, placement, 227-229
    purchasing, 329-330

errors and omissions (E&O) insurance, 171

ES (establishing shot), 100, 105

essay documentaries, 14

establishment-breakdown-reestablishment (shooting), 105

*ET*, 113

*Evil Dead, The*, 280

exhibition
    film festivals, 319-320
        entering, 320-321
        film juries, 322-324
        negotiations, 322
    screening space, obtaining, 318-319

exhibition and distribution
phase (filmmaking), 27
*Exorcist, The*, 40, 273
expenses
    above-the-line expenses,
        166-169
    below-the-line expenses,
        166-169
    budgets
        big-ticket items,
            170-172
        creating, 169-170
        full funding, 174-176
        petty-cash expenses, 172
        record keeping, 172-174
    shooting budgets, 175-176
experimental films, 6, 15
exposition, 46
extreme close-up (ECU), 104
extreme long shots (ELS),
    100

# F

fabric noise, 262
fades, 268-269
*Fahrenheit 9/11*, 14
falling action, 46
family, casting, 126-127
fast motion, 277
feature films, stories,
    constructing, 17-18
feedback, edits, 250
film, 191-194
    archiving, 297-298
    camera original, 194
    emulsion, 193
    film speed, 195-196
    image quality, 192-193

intermittent motion, 196
layers, 193-194
loads, 192
ordering, 193
perforations, 193
release formats, choosing,
    290-291
reversal film, 194
short ends, 193
*Film Art*, 75
film festivals
    entering, 319-321
    film juries, 322-324
    negotiations, 322
film juries, film festivals,
    322-324
film labs, 246-247
film schools, 23
film speed, 195-196
filmmaking, 13
    avant garde films, 15
    documentaries, 14
    independent filmmaking,
        24-25
    institutional filmmaking,
        22-23
    narratives, 14
    phases, 26-27
films
    budgets
        above-the-line expenses,
            166-169
        below-the-line expenses,
            166-169
        big-ticket items,
            170-172
        creating, 169-170
        full funding, 174-176
        petty-cash expenses, 172

record keeping, 172-174
    shooting budgets,
        175-176
duration, 15
frames, 12-13
genres, 18
photographic medium, 12
scheduling, 155-158
    call sheets, 163-164
    contingency plans,
        163-164
    shooting schedules,
        161-163
    workdays, 159-160
titling, 279-280
filmstock, 191
filters
    effects filters, 276-277
    handling, 219
    lighting, 211-212
final cuts, 250
Final Draft screenplay
    formatting software, 51
*Finding Nemo*, 38
firing cast/crewmembers,
    239-240
flats, creating, 148-149
focal length, camera lenses,
    200
footage, logging, 247-248
*Forces of Nature*, 113
formats, release formats,
    choosing, 290-291
foundations
    proposals, writing for,
        62-68
    synopses, writing for,
        68-70
    treatments, writing for,
        68-76

four walling, 318
fps (frames per second), 12-13
frame enlargements, press
  kits, 303
frames (motion pictures), 12
  asymmetry, 285
  fps (frames per second),
    12-13
  freeze frames, 270
  mise-en-scene, 75
  reframing, 107-109
freelance filmmaking, 24
freeze frames, 270
frequencies, sound waves, 258
friends, casting, 126-127
funding
  credit cards, 84-85
  grantors, 85-86
  in-kind services, 86-87
  investors
    corporations, 81
    finding, 80
    general partnerships,
      81-82
    limited partnerships, 82
    LLCs (limited liability
      companies), 82
    sole proprietorships, 80
  loans, 84-85
  securing, 174-176
fundraising, 83-84, 165
  documentation, 87-88
fuses, maintaining, 218

**G**

gaffer, 117
Garabedian, Robert, 245
*Garden State*, 45
general partnerships, 81-82

generation loss, videotape,
  198
genres, 18
giveaways (promotional),
  306-307
goal statements, proposals, 66
Golden Mean, 284
grain, prints, 194
grantors, 85-86
  film juries, 322-324
  proposals, writing for,
    62-68
  synopses, writing for,
    68-70
  treatments, writing for,
    68-76
green rooms, locations, 139
green screens, 137
grips, 117
guerrilla filmmaking, 24

**H**

handheld shots, 108
hard lighting, 210
harmonics, 258
*Harry Potter and the Prisoner
  of Azkaban*, 19
Haynes, Todd, 6
HDTV (High Definition
  Television), 329
head rolls, cameras, 198
headshots, 129
hertz (Hz), 258
High Definition Television
  (HDTV), 329
high key lighting, 207-208
hiring crewmembers, 120-122
historical documentaries, 14
Hitchcock, Alfred, 6

Hollywood, apprenticeship
  system, 22
*Home for the Holidays*, 44
*House of Flying Daggers*, 163
*House of Sand and Fog, The*, 93
Hz (hertz), 258

**I-J**

*I've Heard the Mermaids
  Singing*, 280
ideas
  choosing, 31-33
  copying, 30
  pitching, 58-60
  writing, 30
IFP, 85
image quality, filmstock,
  192-193
images, fps (frames per
  second), 12-13
improvisation, character
  interactions, 181
in-kind services, 86-87
independent filmmaking, 4,
  11, 24-25
  freelance filmmaking, 24
  guerrilla filmmaking, 24
  institutional filmmaking,
    compared, 23
indie films, 22
industrial filmmaking, 23
innertitles, 282
insert edits, 252
institutional filmmaking,
  22-23
intended audience, identifying, proposals, 67-68
inter-negative, creating, 294
inter-positives (IPs), creating,
  294

internal microphones, cameras, 223
interviewing potential crewmembers, 121-122
interviews
  declining, 315
  giving, 312-314
  preparing for, 315-316
  soliciting, 314
investors
  corporations, 81
  finding, 80
  general partnerships, 81-82
  limited partnerships, 82
  LLCs (limited liability companies), 82
  proposals, writing for, 62-68
  sole proprietorships, 80
  synopses, writing for, 68-70
  treatments, writing for, 68-76
issue-oriented documentaries, 14
Ivory, James, 116

*Jaws*, 40, 113, 275
Jeunet, Jean-Pierre, 6
jump cuts, 252
juries, film festivals, 322-324

## K–L

Kentis, Chris, 116
key/fill ratios, lighting, 208
kHz (kilohertz), 258

*Last Night*, 42, 306
Lau, Laura, 116

lavaliere microphones, 228
*Lawn Dogs*, 306
layers, filmstock, 193-194
Lee, Spike, 6
lenses, 200-203
  auxiliary viewfinders, 202
  depth of field, 201
  focal length, 200
  handling, 219
  macro, 201
  prime, 200
  telephoto, 200
  wide angle length, 200
  zoom, 200
letters of agreement, crewmembers, 123-124
life experience, importance of, 7-9
life models, 35-36
lighting, 206-207
  bouncing, 210
  continuity, 207, 219
  filters, 211-212
  heat, 218
  motivated lighting, 207
  qualities
    contrast ratios, 207-208
    hard lighting, 210
    high key lighting, 207-208
    low key lighting, 207-208
    scrims, 208
    side lighting, 209
    soft lighting, 210
    temperature, 211
    top lighting, 209
    under lighting, 209-210
  qualities, 207-212
  three-point lighting, 212-214

limited partnerships, 82
line producer, 116
linear editing, 244-245
listing
  settings, 136
  shots, paper edits, 248
lists (shots), 110
literary phase (filmmaking), 26
LLCs (limited liability companies), 82
loads, films, 192
loans, obtaining, 84-85
location mixer, 222
location scout, 116
locations
  craft service areas, 139
  electricity accessibility, 138-139
  finding, 136-137
  green rooms, 139
  permits, 139-141
  release forms, 139-141
  restrooms, 139
  settings, compared, 135
  sound considerations, 137-138
  sound design, 222
  space issues, 137
  utilizing, 141-143
  virtual sets, 271-272
*Lock, Stock and Two Smoking Barrels*, 270
log sheets, music mixing, 266
logging footage, 247-248
loglines, scripts, 57
long focal length lenses, 200
long shot (LS), 101
long takes, 107
loop groups, 259

low key lighting, 207-208
LS (long shot), 101
lulls, 260

# M

M&E (music and effects), 292
macro lenses, 201
main title sequences, 280-281
    fonts, choosing, 282-284
    placement, 284-286
    point size, choosing,
        282-284
    timing, 286-287
makeup artist, 118
makeup effects, 272-275
manuals, cameras, referring
    to, 192
marketing
    giveaways, 306-307
    interviews
        declining, 315
        giving, 312-314
        preparing for, 315-316
        soliciting, 314
    posters, 306
    press kits, 301-302
        director's statements,
            307-308
        photographs, 302-305
        press releases, 307
        preview copies, 309
        reviews, 308-309
        synopses, 305
    publicists, hiring, 302
    websites, 302
Maslow, Abraham, 96
master scene format (scripts),
    51-55

master shots, 105
matching action shots, 251
MCU (medium close-up),
    103
media grantors, 85-86
medium long shot (MLS),
    102
medium shot (MS), 102
Merchant, Ismail, 116
metaphors, use of, 113-114
microphones
    auxiliary mic ports,
        cameras, 223
    body, 228
    internal (cameras), 223
    omnidirectional, 227
    placing, 227-229
    shotgun, 228
    unidirectional, 227
MiniDVs, 199
mise-en-scene, 75
mixing audio, 258-259,
    265-266, 292
MLS (medium long shot),
    102
monologues, auditions, 130
Moore, Michael, 6
motivated lighting, 207
MS (medium shot), 102
music supervisor, 118
musical scores, 263-264
*My Best Friend's Wedding*, 45

# N

Nair, Mira, 6
*Narc*, 174
narrative films, 14
narrative treatments, 71-72

negative cutting, 293-294
*New York, New York*, 285
noise floors, 225
non-actors, casting, 126
non-linear editing, 244-245
non-union crews, hiring,
    122-123
normal lenses, 200

# O

off-screen spaces, 263
omnidirectional microphones,
    227
on-line editing, 294-295
open calls (auditions), 128
opening credits, 280
*Opposite of Sex, The*, 280
optical effects, 268
optical tracks, 295-296
optimal recordings, analog
    recordings, 225
ordering film, 193
outlines
    shot outlines, 110
    writing, 48
overexposed images, 207
overlapping action shots, 252

# P

pacing, 255
    scenes, 96
*Paint Job, The*, 306
pan shots, 108
paper edits, 248
parallax view, cameras, 202
parentheticals, scripts, 53
partnerships, 81-82

PA (production assistant), 119
passive characters, 41
Perez, Manuel Peña, 147
perforations, filmstock, 193
permits, obtaining for
   locations, 139-141
perspectives (sound), 260-262
phases, filmmaking, 26-27
photographic mediums, 12
photographs
   press kits, synopses, 305
   publicity photographs,
      302-305
pickup days, 163
picture editor, 119
picture locks, 250
pitch (sound), 258
pitching ideas, 58-60
placing microphones,
   227-229
*Pleasantville*, 44
plots, 43-45
   climaxes, 46
   concepts, 45
   dramatic arcs, 46-47
   exposition, 46
   falling action, 46
   resolutions, 46
   rising action, 46
PM (production manager),
   116
point of view (POV), finding,
   30-31
Polish, Mark, 116
Polish, Michael, 116
portraits, press kits, 304-305
*Poseidon Adventure, The*, 21
possessory credits, 281

post houses, 295
post office boxes, renting, 121
post-production, sound
   design, 226
post-production (editing), 27,
   243-244
   assembly edits, 249
   continuity, 251-254
   editing software, 245
   feedback, 250
   film lab, 246-247
   final cuts, 250
   footage logging, 247-248
   linear editing, 244-245
   non-linear editing,
      244-245
   paper edits, 248
   rough cuts, 249
   rush synchronization, 247
   shot pulls, 248
   spatial distortions, 254-255
   temporal distortions,
      254-255
post-production supervisor,
   118
posters, 306
POV (point of view),
   finding, 30-31
practicals, lighting, 212
pre-production phase
   (filmmaking), 26-27
premises, developing, 31-33
premixes, audio, 266
presence tracks, 231
press kits, 301-302
   electronic press kits (EPK),
      302
   preview copies, 309
   production stills, 303
   synopses, 305

press releases, 307
preview copies, press kits,
   including in, 309
primary characters, 38
prime lenses, 200
principal photography, 27
prints
   answer prints, 294
   grain, 194
   marrying, 293
      negative cutting,
         293-294
      on-line editing, 294-295
   release formats, choosing,
      290-291
   release prints, creating, 297
preliminary budgets, creating,
   166-169
producer, 4, 116
   director, compared, 4
product placements, 86
production assistant (PA), 119
production design, 145-147
   costumes, 150-151
   props, 149-150
   sets
      creating, 147-148
      flats, 148-149
      virtual sets, 149
production designer, 117, 145
production manager (PM),
   116
production meetings, importance of, 186-187
production phase (film-
   making), 27
production stills, press kits,
   303
promotional giveaways,
   306-307

prop person, 118
proposals, writing, 62-65
    goal statements, 66
    target audience, 67-68
    themes, 65-66
props, 149-150
    stories, 43
protagonists, 38
publicists, hiring, 302
publicity
    film festivals, 319-320
        entering, 320-321
        film juries, 322-324
        negotiations, 322
    giveaways, 306-307
    interviews
        declining, 315
        giving, 312-314
        preparing for, 315-316
        soliciting, 314
    posters, 306
    press kits, 301-302
        director's statements, 307-308
        photographs, 302-305
        press releases, 307
        preview copies, 309
        reviews, 308-309
        synopses, 305
    publicists, hiring, 302
    websites, 302
pull down claws, cameras, 196
pulling shots, 248

Q

qualities, lighting, 207-212
    contrast ratios, 207-208
    filters, 211-212
    hard lighting, 210
    high key lighting, 207-208
    low key lighting, 207-208
    scrims, 208
    side lighting, 209
    soft lighting, 210
    temperature, 211
    top lighting, 209
    under lighting, 209-210
quartz bulbs, replacing, 219
query letters, sending, 57-58

R

rack focus, 216
Raging Bull, 40
re-recordists, 258
reaction shots, 253
record keeping, budgets, 172-174
Red, 113
reels, potential crewmembers, viewing, 120-121
reframing shots, 107-109
rehearsals, importance of, 180-181
relationships (sound), 260
release formats, choosing, 290-291
release forms
    casting, 133-134
    locations, obtaining, 139-141
release prints, 294
    creating, 297
rem-jet coating, filmstock, 194
renting cameras, 192
Repo Man, 306
Resident Evil, 280
resolution, images, 46, 215
restrooms, locations, 139
resumés, reading potential crewmembers', 120-121
reversal film, 194
reverse imaging, 277-278
reverse shots, 217, 253-254
reviews, press kits, including in, 308-309
rising action, 46
Roberts, Julia, 280
Rope, 107, 270
rough cuts, 249
Rozema, Patricia, 122
Rudolph the Red-Nosed Reindeer, 272
rushes, 147-148
    synchronizing, 247

S

S-corporations, 81
SAG (Screen Actors Guild), 127
salaries, budgeting, 166, 170
saturation, images, 216
scenes
    adding, 96-97
    average length, 55
    beats, 96
    blocking, 182
    breaking down, 94-96
    creating, 47
    describing, 52
    dividing, 105-110
    editing, 96-97
    pacing, 96
    shooting, 105-110
        establishment-breakdown-reestablishment, 105

shots, 100, 104-105
 close-up (CU), 103
 editing, 107
 establishing shot (ES),
  100
 extreme close-up
  (ECU), 104
 extreme long shot
  (ELS), 100
 long shot (LS), 101
 long takes, 107
 master shots, 105
 medium close-up
  (MCU), 103
 medium long shot
  (MLS), 102
 medium shot (MS), 102
 reframing, 107-109
 shooting scripts,
  110-111
 shot lists, 110
 shot outlines, 110
 storyboards, 112
 two shot, 104
 wide shot (WS), 100
scheduled appointments
 (auditions), 128
scheduling
 expense budgeting, 166
 films, 155-158
  call sheets, 163-164
  contingency plans,
   163-164
  shooting schedules,
   161-163
  workdays, 159-160
Schultz, Gary, 273
Scorsese, Martin, 6
scratch tracks, 227-228

Screen Actors Guild (SAG),
 127
screeners, including in press
 kits, 309
screening space, obtaining,
 318-319
screenplay formatting
 software, 51
screenplays
 assumptions, 91-92
 scenes
  adding, 96-97
  breaking down, 94-96
  editing, 96-97
 scheduling, 155-158
 stage readings, 90
 subtext, 92-94
 text, 92-94
 text analysis, 90-91
 themes, 92-94
 timing, 154-155
scrims, lighting, adding to,
 208
script supervisor, 117
scripts, 50
 assumptions, 91-92
 average length, 53
 loglines, 57
 parentheticals, 53
 proposals, writing, 62-68
 query letters, sending,
  57-58
 scenes
  adding, 96-97
  breaking down, 94-96
  describing, 52
  editing, 96-97
 scheduling, 155-158

screenplay formatting
 software, 51
shooting scripts, 110-111
staged readings, 90
subtext, 92-94
synopses, writing, 68-70
text, 92-94
text analysis, 90-91
themes, 92-94
timing, 154-155
title pages, 53
treatments, writing, 68-69,
 71-76
writing, 50
 master scene format,
  51-55
 split script format,
  55-56
scrolling titles, 280
*Se7en*, 42, 281
secondary characters, 38
sensitometry, filmstocks, 195
set courtesy, 187
set dressers, 118
sets, 147
 creating, 147-148
 flats, 148-149
 set dressing, 149-150
 shots, coverage, 251
 virtual sets, 149, 271-272
settings
 listing, 136
 locations, compared, 135
 stories, 41-42
*sex, lies and videotape*, 280
shadowing, 206-207
shadows, diminishing, 210
sharpness, images, 215
*She's Gotta Have It*, 280
shooting budgets, 175-176

shooting scenes, 105-110
shooting schedules, 161-163
shooting scripts, 110-111
short animation, 6
short ends, 193
short films, stories, constructing, 16-17
short focal length lenses, 200
shotgun microphones, 228
shots, 100, 104-105
  boom shots, 108
  close-up (CU), 103
  continuity editing, 251-254
  coverage, 251
  crane shots, 108
  cutaway shots, 252
  directing, 187-190
  dolly shots, 108
  editing, 107
  establishing shot (ES), 100
    television, 105
  establishment-breakdown-
    reestablishment, 105
  extreme close-up (ECU),
    104
  extreme long shot (ELS),
    100
  handheld shots, 108
  listing, paper edits, 248
  lists, 110
  long shot (LS), 101
  long takes, 107
  master shots, 105
  matching action shots, 251
  medium close-up (MCU),
    103
  medium long shot (MLS),
    102
  medium shot (MS), 102

outlines, 110
pan shots, 108
pulling, 248
reaction shots, 253
reframing, 107-109
reusing, 252
reverse shots, 217, 253-254
rough cuts, 249
shooting scripts, 110-111
slating, 223-225
steadycam shots, 108
storyboards, 112
tilt shots, 108
tracking shots, 108
transitions, 253, 267
  dissolves, 269
  fades, 268-269
  freeze frames, 270
  straight cuts, 267
  superimpositions, 270
  wipes, 269-270
trucking shots, 108
two shot, 104
wide shot (WS), 100
zoom shots, 108
side lighting, 209
*Sideways*, 19
*Silence of the Lambs*, 41
single-perf filmstock, 193
six track master mix (STMS),
  292
skeleton crew, 124
*Sky Captain and the World of
  Tomorrow*, 149, 271
slates, 223-224
*Sleeping with the Enemy*, 44
slow filmstocks, 195
slow motion, 277
soft lighting, 210

software
  editing software, 245
  screenplay formatting
    software, 51
sole proprietorships, 80
*Sophie's Choice*, 45
sound cues, 112
sound design, 221, 257
  ambient sounds, 230-231
  analog recordings, 225
  digital recordings, 226-227
  location sound, 222
  locations, 137-138
  microphone placement,
    227-229
  mixing, 265-266
  musical scores, 263-264
  post-production, 226
  presence tracks, 231
  silence, 259-260
  sound mixing, 258-259
  sound relationships, 260
  sound synchronization,
    223-225
sound designer, 117
sound editor, 119
sound effects, 267
sound mixer, 117, 222, 258
sound mixing, 292
sound waves, 258
soundtracks, 263-264,
  295-296
space, locations, 137
spatial distortions, 254-255
special effects, 267, 275-276
  computer animation, 272
  dissolves, 269
  fades, 268-269
  fast motion, 277

filters, 276-277
freeze frames, 270
makeup effects, 272-275
optical effects, 268
reverse imaging, 277-278
slow motion, 277
straight cuts, 267
superimpositions, 270
virtual sets, 271-272
wipes, 269-270
*Speed*, 43
split script format, 55-56
sprocket holes, filmstock, 193
squib, 275
staged readings, scripts, 90
*Star Wars*, 263, 269
steadycam shots, 108
still photographer, 118
still photographs, press kits, 302-305
STMS (six track master mix), 292
stop action, animation, 272
stories
concepts, 45
constructing, 16
feature films, 17-18
short films, 16-17
elements
characters, 38-39
conditions, 41-42
conduct, 40-41
configurations, 43-47
conflict, 39-40
context, 42-43
crutches, 43
outlines, 48
scenes, creating, 47
story expenses, budgeting, 166

storyboards, 112
straight cuts, 267
*Straight Out of Brooklyn*, 107
*Stranger Than Paradise*, 110
structures, stories, 43-47
studio system (Hollywood), 22
stunt coordinator, 118
stylists, 118
subtext, scripts, 92-94
subtitles, 282
Super8 film, 191
superimpositions, 270
suspension of disbelief, sustaining, 19
Swider, Chris, 40
symbols, use of, 113-114
synchronization
rushes, 247
sound, 223-225
synopses
press kits, 305
treatments, compared, 68
writing, 68-70

**T**

table reads, 181
taglines, 306
tail roll, cameras, 198
takes, assembly edits, 249
Tarantino, Quentin, 6, 280
target audience, identifying, proposals, 67-68
Teitel, Robert, 116
telephoto lenses, 200
television, establishing shots, 105
television production, 23

television screens, aspect ratios, 215
temperature, lighting, 211
temporal distortions, 254-255
terminating cast/crew members, 239-240
*Terminator, The*, 40
*Testament*, 14
text analysis, scripts, 90-94
theaters, obtaining screening space, 318-319
*Thelma & Louise*, 92
themes
developing, 31-33
proposals, 65-66
scripts, 92-94
*There's Something About Mary*, 275
Thompson, Kristen, 75
three-point lighting, 212-214
Tillman, George, 116
tilt shots, 108
timbre, 258
timecode slates, 223-224
timecodes, drop frame (DF), 295
timing, scripts, 154-155
title pages, scripts, 53
titles (text), 280-282
closing credits, 281
fonts, choosing, 282-284
main title sequence, 280-281
placement, 284-286
point size, choosing, 282-284
possessory credits, 281
scrolling, 280
timing, 286-287
titling films, 279-280

*Tomb Raider*, 280
tonal range, 258
top lighting, 209
tracking shots, 108
transitions, shots, 253, 267
   dissolves, 269
   fades, 268-269
   freeze frames, 270
   straight cuts, 267
   superimpositions, 270
   wipes, 269-270
transportation captain, 118
treatments
   aesthetic treatments, 73-76
   narrative treatments, 71-72
   synopses, compared, 68
   writing, 68-69, 71-76
*Tron*, 272
trucking shots, 108
two shot, 104

## U–V

under lighting, 209-210
underexposed images, 207
unidirectional microphones, 227
union crews, hiring, 122-123, 127-128
UPM (unit production manager), 116

variable areas (optical tracks), 295
video cameras, 200-203
videotape, 191
   emulsion, 193
   generation loss, 198
   layers, 193-194
   release formats, choosing, 290-291

videotape
   analog videotape
      component video, 199
      magnetic fields, 197-199
   auditions, 132
   digital videotape, 199-200
viewfinders, cameras, 202
virtual sets, 271-272
   creating, 149

## W–X–Y–Z

walla walla, 259-260
wardrobe, 150-151
wardrobe person, 118
*WarGames*, 14
*Watership Down*, 38
websites, creating publicity websites, 302
*When Night Is Falling*, 114
*White*, 113
white balance, lighting, 212
wide angle length lenses, 200
wide shot (WS), 100
widescreen aspect ratios, 214-215
wild sounds, recording, 230-231
Williams, John, 263
window dubs, 246
wipes, 269-270
*Wizard of Oz, The*, 93
workdays, scheduling, 159-160
wrangler, 118
writing
   characters, 38-39
   conception phase, 33-34
   embellishments, 34
   ideas, 30
   imagery, 35

   life models, 35-36
   outlines, 48
   scripts, 50
      master scene format, 51-55
      split script format, 55-56
written permissions for casting, 133-134
WS (wide shot), 100

Xpress Pro, 245

zoom lenses, 200
zoom shots, 108

1997 - Winter clothes.

2007 - Fall type - clothes.

Call 4.45 - 5.15 pm.

Pineapple Juice
Soya Sauce
Sesame Seed oil
onions
Oyster Sauce
Salt
pepper
Olive oil
ground beef

Black Sweet Sauce
Bacon (Smoked)
Crushed garlic
onions
Salt
pepper
Olive oil
Chives
ground beef.